publication supported by a grant from
The Community Foundation for Greater New Haven
as part of the *Urban Haven Project*

# THE FIRST
# ATOMIC
# BOMB

# THE FIRST ATOMIC BOMB

The Trinity Site in New Mexico

*Janet Farrell Brodie*

University of Nebraska Press | LINCOLN

The University of Nebraska Press is part of a land-
grant institution with campuses and programs on the
past, present, and future homelands of the Pawnee,
Ponca, Otoe-Missouria, Omaha, Dakota, Lakota, Kaw,
Cheyenne, and Arapaho Peoples, as well as those of the
relocated Ho-Chunk, Sac and Fox, and Iowa Peoples.

Library of Congress Control Number: 2022045027

Set in Minion Pro by A. Shahan.

With love to:
Joaquin Raven
Fiona Wren
Niko Peregrine
Wilder Swift

# CONTENTS

List of Illustrations     xi

Preface     xiii

Acknowledgments     xv

Introduction     1

ONE   The Trinity Test     5

TWO   Dispossessions     41

THREE   Building the Test Site     67

FOUR   Post-Test Events at the
Trinity Site, 1946–67     103

FIVE   The Army, the Air Force,
the Navy, the Atomic
Energy Commission,
and the Trinity Site     123

SIX   The Trinity Radiation
and Its Afterlives     149

SEVEN   Historical Preservation
of the Trinity Site     175

Notes     203

Bibliography     247

Index     261

# ILLUSTRATIONS

*Following page 122*

1. Trinity area landscape, 1945
2. Windmill, water pump, and water storage tank on platform
3. Transporting old ranch water tank to Trinity Base Camp
4. Trinity Base Camp
5. Men at Base Camp in line for food
6. Transporting Jumbo from the railroad siding to Trinity site
7. Jumbo en route
8. Jumbo, unscathed after the Trinity test
9. Stacking explosives for the 100-Ton test
10. Constructing the 100-Ton test
11. Posing before the 100-Ton test
12. Desert landscape and trucks near the Trinity site
13. Hoisting "the gadget" up into the tower
14. The bomb being hoisted up into the tower
15. Unidentified soldier setting up experiments before the Trinity test
16. The Trinity explosion at sixteen seconds
17. Debris in the desert after the test
18. Debris and decaying bunker after the Trinity test
19. Ruined bunker
20. Open House 1965
21. Crowd at Open House 1965
22. Open House 1968 parking lot and "Keep Out" sign
23. Cars at Open House 1968
24. Downwinder protest at entrance to Trinity site, Open House 2016
25. Ring created for the mounted military police detachment at Trinity
26. Robert J. S. Brown's bolo tie made of trinitite
27. Nagasaki, September 1945

# PREFACE

On her first trip to America in 1999, Kyoko Hayashi, an award-winning Japanese novelist and memoirist, made a personal pilgrimage to the Trinity site, hoping to better understand the atomic bomb that had killed so many of her family, her neighbors, and her fellow citizens in Nagasaki, Japan. She reported later that—in looking out at the desert from the Trinity site— she had been transformed. Fourteen years old the day of the bomb, she suffered physically from the bomb's effects for the rest of her life, but she also suffered from the inescapable identity of being a hibakusha ("A-bomb victim"). The hibakusha have been regarded in Japan for decades with both shame and pride, respected yet also reviled, honored yet rendered invisible, shunned because their very existence brought painful national reminders of the war, the losses, and the defeat, which many Japanese believed was caused by the atomic bomb. Hayashi had spent long years, as she later explained, on a spiritual journey trying to understand the meaning of the death of her friends in Nagasaki and living with constant fear of her own death from the radiation.[1]

Standing at the Trinity site she came to a profound new realization: "I shuddered as the silent waves were approaching from the bottom of the land, far off mountains with the red surface and brown-colored wilderness. Oh, how hot it would have been—. Until I stood here at 'Trinity site,' I had thought that the first victims of the atomic bomb on earth were us—the humans. I was wrong. The first victims were here. They were here without crying or screaming. Tears welled in my eyes." She came to a new and deeper awareness: "Standing in front of the obelisk, I was truly bombed for the first time."

The Japanese documentary filmmaker Yoshihiko Muraki also found a new way of thinking about the 1945 atomic bombs based on a visit to the

Trinity site. He came to America to make a documentary for Japanese television, "Memories of the Trinity Bomb." He explained the new perspectives he came to have about the atomic bombings in Japan after being at the Trinity site: "I came to realize that by looking at the atomic bomb from July 16 instead of August 6, we may be able to grasp the complexities of the bomb from a different angle." To Muraki, the Trinity site—the atomic bomb in the New Mexico desert—was the first transformation of the world. The second transformation occurred at Hiroshima, and the third at Nagasaki. The bomb dropped in the New Mexico desert and the two dropped on Japanese cities thus created a new kind of Trinity.[2]

These observations helped shape my book: the many and often little-recognized effects of the atomic bomb, the surrounding desert, the sensations evoked by being a tourist at the site, the understanding that what exploded at Trinity was the first atomic bomb. Hayashi's response is unusual for taking in the entirety of the site: its seeming barren vastness, but also the plants and animals, all of which she identifies as having been bombed, as she herself was by the second plutonium bomb. The land of the Trinity site may appear to some viewers to be barren and desolate, but it has been home to many plants, insects, reptiles, birds, and mammals and has been traversed, lived on, and fought over by humans for centuries. It holds many meanings.

# ACKNOWLEDGMENTS

Many people helped me with this book, providing advice, information, and access to materials. I am very much in their debt. Thanks again to Rebecca Collinsworth, archivist at the Los Alamos Historical Society Archives, who responded to numerous inquiries, kindly sent copies of interviews conducted by the historical society, and also granted me permission to quote from those interviews. Alan Brady Carr, historian at Los Alamos National Laboratory (LANL), provided copies of documents, an early read of one of his own forthcoming articles, and thoughtful advice. The Atomic Heritage Foundation granted me permission to quote from several of its online interviews with Los Alamos men and women. Archivist Cody White provided help in the National Archives and Records Administration (NARA) Denver archives, and Sherri Sheu, at that time a history doctoral student at the University of Colorado at Boulder, provided superb photographic records of the contents of several boxes of those Park Service materials. Monica Dorame, government information specialist at the University of New Mexico Library in Albuquerque, worked hard to track down the trove of important materials the Los Alamos Historical Document Retrieval and Assessment (LAHDRA) group donated to Zimmerman. For many years archivists and librarians in the Claremont College system provided help and advice about my research, and I am grateful for their professional aid and friendship, especially that of Adam Rosenkranz and Lisa Crane.

Several authors of books and other studies about the Trinity site took time to answer my questions and to offer research advice. Thomas W. Merlan responded to questions; his richly detailed commissioned study of life at the Trinity Base Camp is an exceptional source that deserves to be more readily available. David T. Kirkpatrick and Deborah M. Dennis at Human Systems Research Inc. gave me helpful advice about tracking down sources. Joseph Shonka, whose work for the LAHDRA project deserves much commendation, answered many questions. Several people at the White Sands Missile Range provided advice and materials. Gerold Veara was extraordinarily generous in providing access to archival materials and photographs. Bill Godby, archaeologist at the White Sands Missile Range, provided detailed answers to questions about the history of preservation work at the Trinity site and sent very useful materials. I also thank Darren Court, director of the White Sands Missile Range Museum, and Jim Eckles for their help. For photographs, many thanks to Debra Lewandowski and the staff at the Tularosa Basin Historical Society; John Tyler Moore, the image archivist at the Los Alamos National Laboratory; and Gerry Veara (noted above). For help processing photographs to meet the standards of the University of Nebraska Press I am grateful to Mark Buchholz, in Digital Productions at the Honnold-Mudd Library of the Claremont Colleges. Olga Helmy provided superb photographic assistance and advice.

A few of the talented history graduate students at my university (Claremont Graduate University) worked as my research assistants, and I thank them once again, deeply, for their imaginative and resourceful hard work on this book. In alphabetical order they are Kerri Dean, Katrina Denman, Michelle Hahn, Jonathan Hanna, Myles Mikulic, and Clark Noone. Although they were not all directly involved in this book project, for many discussions of history, teaching, and writing over the years I am especially grateful to colleagues Hal Barron, Vivien Hamilton, Helena Wall, Jean Schroedel, Lisa Cody, Robert Dawidoff, and Terri Snyder. For over twenty years I've been part of a group of women historians that meets monthly to read and discuss our writing projects. I am indebted for immeasurably helpful readings of many drafts of these chapters to Emily Abel, Carla Bittel, Sharla Fett, Alice Wexler, and new member Charlotte Borst.

Three outside readers gave helpful advice that greatly added to my manuscript. I am especially grateful to University of Nebraska Press editors Bridget Barry and Sara Springsteen, who responded promptly and helpfully to questions and concerns, and to Kerin Tate for copyediting beyond all of my expectations.

A very special and heartfelt thanks to Char Miller for friendship and collegiality over the years in the Claremont Colleges. Char invited me to write this book as part of his series America's Public Lands, and honored and intrigued, I loved the idea. He writes superbly and quickly, so I am grateful for his exemplary patience given how long I've taken. He never raised an eyebrow when I found yet more archives to visit or new materials to pursue. Therefore, my gratitude, Char, and here's to hopes of post-pandemic returns to coffee in Claremont.

Finally, my deepest thanks to Bruce. A superb psychologist and writer, he knows when and how to offer support and comfort and when to tactfully disappear until a chapter gets sorted. He has given thoughtful editorial advice at every stage and has read more drafts than any human should have to endure. For such goodness and help I can only marvel, with gratitude and love.

Permission to quote from numerous interviews was provided courtesy of the Atomic Heritage Foundation and the National Museum of Nuclear Science and History, all rights reserved. The Warren Nyer interview is quoted courtesy of S. L. Sanger, the Atomic Heritage Foundation, and the National Museum of Nuclear Science and History. The David P. Rudolph interview is from the Stephane Groueff Collection, Howard Gotlieb Archival Research Center at Boston University, courtesy of the Atomic Heritage Foundation and the National Museum of Nuclear Science and History.

Portions of chapter 6 previously appeared in "Contested Knowledge: The Trinity Test Radiation Studies," in *Inevitably Toxic: Historical Perspectives on Contamination, Exposure, and Expertise*, edited by Brinda Sarathy, Vivien Hamilton, and Janet Farrell Brodie (Pittsburgh PA: University of Pittsburgh Press, 2018).

# THE FIRST
# ATOMIC
# BOMB

# Introduction

The title of this book comes from a growing belief that the test of the atomic device in the New Mexico desert three weeks before the atomic bombing of Hiroshima was more than the test of the "gadget," as the scientists dubbed it. It was, more accurately, the world's first atomic bomb. Immensely more powerful than any weapon the world had seen, its effects on the surrounding and "downwind" communities have lasted for decades and, indeed, are still present. The place where that first explosion took place is today an officially designated National Historic Landmark. The Trinity test site is one of the strangest of all such designated historical areas. The official site, whose boundaries remain debated, contains one twelve-foot stone obelisk with two messages. The first reads (with missing punctuation), "Where the world's first Nuclear Device was exploded July 16, 1945 Erected 1965 White Sands Missile Range J. Frederick Thorlin, Major General, U.S., Army, Commanding." The second, added a decade later below the first, says enigmatically: "The site possesses national significance in commemorating the history of the U.S.A."

The sealed-off site is open to the public only one day a year. (For a few years it was open two times annually, but in 2018 the army reverted to once a year. It appears to be back to twice a year as of 2022.) It is surrounded by the White Sands Missile Range, where since its creation in 1942, military missiles and other weapons have been tested. Near the Trinity site also lies one of the newest U.S. National Parks, the former White Sands National Monument, created in 1933 to protect the stunning beauty of its gypsum dunes, brilliantly white, even blinding in the sun, and dazzling in the moonlight. Although several thousand visitors annually make the

1

long drive to the White Sands, it closes to tourists on occasion when the military conducts missile tests overhead.

This book, then, is about a site in the New Mexico desert, a spot where scientists, technicians, and the U.S. Army exploded the first atomic bomb at dawn on a July morning, helping to end a world war two months later. This is a history about that site: its selection, its construction and deconstruction, and the many attempts to preserve it. I pay less attention to the famous scientists who invented the bomb than to the construction workers, the technicians, the enlisted men and women whose work made the test possible, those who guarded the site, those who helped with the many experiments before and after, and those who obeyed orders from above and accommodated to the war in a hot, dry, desolate area of the nation. The scientists appear, of course, but they do not take center stage. Nor even, for that matter, does the atomic bomb itself. This is much more a book about a place, an environment that carries special historical weight in American memory. It is a landscape with a history of dissonant encounters and contestations among many different groups. In 1880 the land that later became the Trinity site lay near the Battle of Hembrillo, one of the last battles between the nearly defeated Apaches and the U.S. Army. Thus, as archaeologists Morgan Rieder and Michael Lawson point out, "only 63 years separate the bow-and-arrow era from the nuclear age."[1]

After World War II, the area surrounding the Trinity site area became an even larger militarized landscape for testing the new weapons of the postwar United States. It continues to be an area that some critics view as a vast "sacrifice zone" in the "tainted desert" of the American West.[2] Historian Ryan Edgington notes insightfully that the Trinity site reveals "new values extracted from purportedly ruined landscapes." At Trinity an "international site of remembrance emerged from the contaminated desert."[3] To some critics, the Trinity site represents a national guilt symbol "similar to a German concentration camp."[4] To local "downwinders" who seek restitution for the effects of their families' exposure to radiation from the test, the Trinity site has become a place where they can express their anger and sense of bereavement and national betrayal. To many others, the site signifies American scientific know-how, national prestige, and military might: the place where the bomb that ended World War II—the weapon that changed the nature of warfare—exploded so powerfully. Increasingly, too, it signifies the time and place where America unleashed the world's first atomic bomb—on itself.

## Overview

The book begins with the test itself on a stormy mid-July dawn as official and unofficial men and women watched from afar and monitors throughout the state tracked the test's results. Chapter 2 explores the long history of groups traveling through and contesting possession of New Mexico's Tularosa Basin: Native Americans, Mexican and then Mexican Americans, and Anglos from around the nation and the world. It looks at multiple kinds of dispossession. Chapters 3 and 4 focus on construction of the test area and then what occurred on the site in the postwar decades. Chapter 5 explores the militarization of the Trinity area desert as the army, air force, and navy took possession of the land and air during and after World War II. Chapter 6 looks in detail at the radiation from the test. That issue has become more controversial over the decades and remains, arguably, a crucial issue for many people, especially New Mexicans. The book concludes with chapter 7, examining the relationships between tourism and the Trinity site. For decades different groups worked to preserve the area because of its historical significance, but even with the growing popularity of nuclear tourism worldwide, the Trinity site has remained shut off from access except for once or twice a year.

A note about terminology: the name of the military area surrounding the Trinity site changed over the years, as did the military's boundaries. Designated the Alamogordo Bombing and Gunnery Range in 1941, the name changed in 1945 to the White Sands Proving Ground. In 1947 the name became the New Mexico Joint Guided Missile Test Range, and in 1957 it was renamed the White Sands Missile Range. In this book I have used the latter name almost exclusively for the sake of clarity, but in a few places where it seemed important for the historical chronology I call it the White Sands Proving Ground.

## Sources

Many historical materials document the Trinity test in books, articles, online sites, and manuscript collections in diverse places. Its technical aspects have been well studied by historians. I have profited from reading them and I cite many in the bibliography. Archival materials are rich and abundant; I delved deeply into National Park Service records, the Leslie Groves materials, and other collections in the National Archives repositories in Denver, Colorado, and in College Park, Maryland. The Ferenc Szasz papers at the Zimmerman Library at the University of New Mexico proved exceptionally rich. Szasz's own 1984 history of the Trinity test remains highly respected and engagingly readable; his research files and copies of documents (some no longer available elsewhere) are truly invaluable. The Zimmerman Library is an exceptionally wonderful place to do research, with helpful staff and free scanning machines. The White Sands Missile Range in New Mexico has important materials, but they are hard to use because there is no established archival access for outsiders. Some of my earlier work in archives proved useful at times for these chapters, particularly the two Stafford Warren collections at UCLA, the radiological warfare collection at the National Security Archive in Washington DC, and the Advisory Committee on Human Radiation Experimentation Collection at the National Archives in Maryland.

The interviews with a wide array of people connected to the Trinity test are rich and remarkable. Most are available online through the Atomic Heritage Foundation's "Voices of the Manhattan Project." I thank them here, formally, for permission to quote from specific interviews. The Los Alamos Historical Society also conducted interviews, and I am deeply grateful to their archivist, Rebecca Collinsworth, for sending me transcripts of several. In addition, oral histories and interviews from people connected to the Nevada Test Site, housed at the University of Nevada or available online, have deep importance for studies of America's nuclear testing, although only a few pertain directly to the actual Trinity test.

Online sources, websites, and blogs provide increasingly numerous materials for researchers working in the history of nuclear testing and for the Trinity test itself. The Nuclear Test Archive in Las Vegas holds treasures, many of which are available online, and the staff efficiently provides copies (although many documents have been redacted and others, even if listed, appear to be no longer available). Alex Wellerstein's blogs and writings are always stimulating and deeply researched; Carey Sublette's Nuclear Weapons Archive website has also been invaluable.

# ONE

## The Trinity Test

At 5:00 a.m., July 16, 1945, after hours of thunder, lightning, and rain, a lull occurred in the weather, and the Manhattan Project scientists and technicians, on tenterhooks all night long, after two delays received final approval to begin last-minute preparations to detonate the world's first atomic bomb. Half an hour later, the bomb, sitting in a one-hundred-foot steel tower in a secret test site in the south-central New Mexico desert, exploded, changing the world. The 18.6 kiloton explosion was four times more powerful than predicted, and watchers saw roiling black clouds, a blinding flash of light, and then a ball of fire rising from the earth. They also observed the slowly developing stem of the now iconic image of the nuclear era: the mushroom cloud.[1] The photographs and movies of the event do not convey the sound, but the extraordinarily loud boom of the explosion reverberated, bouncing back and forth between the surrounding mountain ranges. One observer remembered the "sense of this ominous cloud hanging over us. It was so brilliant purple, with all the radioactive glowing. And it just seemed to hang there forever." The thunder from the blast "bounced on the rocks, and then it went—I don't know where else it bounced. But it never seemed to stop. . . . It just kept echoing back and forth in that Jornada del Muerto. It was a very scary time when it went off."[2]

Joe Lehman, a master sergeant with the Special Engineer Detachment (SED) at Los Alamos, who had been reassigned for several months of work at the Trinity site, still had vivid reactions decades later. Assigned to a hill a few miles from the test tower, his first reaction was shock: "Those of us who had been in the military and been on the firing ranges and bombing ranges know that you see an explosion and poof it's over with." The atomic explosion was very different: "This thing seemed to have a life of its own, it just kept going, roiling, climbing, doing things, changing color, changing shape and where was it going to stop. . . . It was different from anything we had ever seen." Everything just seemed to keep expanding and moving and "the cloud didn't want to stop." He added, "The combination of the flash, the blast of air, the fantastic noise, and then the sight of this column climbing and climbing and just broiling and climbing. Now within minutes we began to see the sun reflecting off the dust particles and the colors were fantastic. There was nothing one could do except sit there in amazement of what had just happened."[3]

Many accounts of the Trinity test exist. Unlike those involved in other events of World War II, after which participants in battles returned home and often remained silent about their experiences sometimes for decades, those who were officially involved with the Trinity test wrote about it or talked about it. Robert Oppenheimer, head of the Los Alamos project to design and build the bomb, is often quoted: "We waited until the blast had passed, walked out of the shelter, and then it was extremely solemn. We knew the world would not be the same. A few people laughed, a few people cried. Most people were silent. I remembered the line from the Hindu scripture, the Bhagavad Gita: Vishnu is trying to persuade the prince that he should do his duty, and to impress him he takes the multiarmed form and says, 'Now I have become Death, the destroyer of worlds.' I suppose we all thought that, one way or another."[4] His brother, Frank, also a physicist working on the project, could not remember his brother's words but thought that they both said simply, "It worked."[5] Kenneth Bainbridge, in overall charge of the test, said, "No one who saw it could forget it, a foul and awesome display." He congratulated the other leaders at the main control bunker on the site, and then finished by saying to Oppenheimer, "Now we are all sons of bitches." Oppenheimer later told Bainbridge that it was the "best thing anyone said after the test."[6]

Brigadier General Thomas Farrell, also at the control bunker, had different, far more celebratory memories: "The countdown was very dramatic. I've had a lot of countdowns since but this one was different." Everyone, Farrell recalled, just stood staring straight ahead, not breathing in the darkness filled with thunder and lightning. Then came the loudspeaker and the automatic countdown: 5-4-3-2-1 "and then zero, and then the thing went off. All the darkness changed to this great light that flooded the whole sky in the black desert. Then the tension was ended, and we all started cheering." Everybody went outside to take a look at the "great lighting effects. . . . After a few minutes everybody was congratulating each other."[7]

The story of the Trinity test has been told in fiction, graphic novels, participants' firsthand accounts, and even in an opera—Peter Sellers's 2005 *Dr. Atomic*. Historians have written numerous rich and detailed accounts of the scientific facts about the test, the experiments, and the results. We know much less about those who built the site, oversaw the equipment measuring the test results, took photographs, or stood by in case of medical emergencies. The men and women who traveled to nearby hills and saw the test unofficially are also a significant but often overlooked part of this history.

## The Manhattan Project: An Overview

Many aspects of the development of the atomic bomb still astound. In just thirty-five months in the middle of orchestrating, funding, and fighting a two-front world war, the United States created a huge scientific and industrial enterprise code-named the Manhattan Engineer District (later simplified to the Manhattan Project), under which scientists, engineers, technicians, and other workers of all kinds succeeded in theorizing, designing, manufacturing, and testing an atomic bomb. Then, in an additional twenty-four days, from July 16 to August 9, 1945, the United States brought the materials to a remote Pacific island, assembled the bombs, and dropped them on two Japanese cities, ending the war. The atomic bomb project, a world-changing scientific and military accomplishment, remains lauded, lamented, and argued about to this day. The U.S. government had never before attempted anything so large, involving so many sites and people and costs, and it did so while maintaining extraordinary and unprecedented secrecy.[8]

Most histories of the Manhattan Project's atomic bombs focus on the roles and work of the scientists, which, although fundamental to the invention of the bomb, nevertheless slight the enormity of other contributions. The Manhattan Project included scientific laboratories that invented, produced, and tested new weapons of mass destruction, but it was also, in the words of biographer and historian Robert S. Norris, "a gigantic industrial and engineering construction effort, run by the military under great secrecy." To produce materials for atomic bombs the United States took over tens of thousands of acres of privately owned and state-owned land in many locales. It required building housing, schools, hospitals, and other facilities for a workforce that eventually numbered in the tens of thousands, very few of them actually knowing with any certainty what they were working to produce. (This is discussed more fully in chapter 3.)

The time frame from physicists' first serious theorizing about nuclear fission until the invention and testing of an atomic bomb was shockingly short. Accounts of the discovery of nuclear fission give varying degrees of credit to different scientists, but all accounts focus on 1937 and 1938 with physicists in several countries studying the process of bombarding atomic elements with neutrons. Italian physicist Enrico Fermi and coworkers experimented in Rome; Otto Hahn and Lise Meitner, joined by Fritz Strassman, did the same at the Kaiser Wilhelm Institute in Berlin; Irene Curie experimented in Paris; Philip Abelson experimented in the radiation laboratory at the University of California, Berkeley; and Norman Feather and Egon Bretscher experimented at Cambridge University.[9] It took some nine months for the phenomenon of a nuclear chain reaction to be understood, if imperfectly.[10] Scientists around the world reacted with intellectual fascination to the nascent understanding of fission, but also with dawning horror, because in an expanding war around the world with Nazi Germany and Japan, some recognized that fission might provide the basis for a new kind of powerful military weapon—an atomic bomb. German physicists and scientific laboratories were among the best in the world even if many of the most brilliant faculty had fled, or been forced to flee, to other countries. Fear ran deep that the Nazis might produce atomic weapons.

In the United States, émigré scientists voiced early and prescient worries about the weapon potential of fission. Leo Szilard, the Hungarian physicist working in Berlin who came to the United States when Hitler rose to power in Germany, took an early active role in trying to convince U.S. authorities of the military potential of atomic energy.[11] Szilard left his professorship at the University of Berlin in 1933, fleeing to the United States, where he worked for a while at Columbia University and then took a research position at the U.S. government–sponsored "Metallurgical Lab" at the University of Chicago. In their alarm about the potential weapon in nuclear fission, Szilard and his physics colleague, Eugene Wigner, called on

Albert Einstein for help; Einstein composed a letter to President Roosevelt describing atomic fission and the possibility that a powerful new weapon—an atomic bomb—could be created from the process. For weeks the scientists mulled over finding the right person to deliver the letter in person to FDR, finally persuading the president's longtime friend, the economist Alexander Sachs, to arrange a face-to-face meeting during which Sachs delivered the letter and summarized in his own words the story of fission and its devastating military potential.[12]

Laura Fermi, wife of the famed physicist Enrico Fermi, explained later why it was the exiled European scientists who alerted the U.S. president rather than their American colleagues. European universities had for a long time been closely allied with governments and political leaders, and faculty recognized that they could participate in issues beyond their immediate departments or disciplines. At that time in the United States, universities were only beginning to have such close ties, and the American scientists rarely thought of using their academic positions to affect politics and political actions.[13] After receiving Einstein's letter, FDR created the Uranium Committee in autumn 1939, which at first worked rather generally to coordinate research into the properties of uranium. In June 1940, when news reached U.S. officials of Germany's expanded uranium research, FDR created a larger committee, the National Defense Research Council (NDRC), to begin serious investigation into methods for separating uranium isotopes. The following year, in June 1941, four months after scientists at UC Berkeley discovered plutonium, FDR created the Office of Scientific Research and Development (OSRD) to work on ways to separate uranium isotopes and to produce plutonium.[14]

Officials at the NDRC and OSRD recognized the enormous challenges. To make an atomic bomb would require large amounts of the rare uranium U-235 and the newly discovered element plutonium for the core of the bombs, a process that Nobel laureate physicist Neils Bohr warned would turn the United States into "one huge factory."[15] This indeed is close to what actually happened as around the nation, huge secret factories began to function to produce uranium and plutonium and other crucial materials for atomic bombs.

The autumn and winter of 1942 saw a transfer of authority over the bomb project from the OSRD to the newly established, code-named "Manhattan Engineer District" (the MED or the Manhattan Project), and vast new authority and funding was granted to the bomb project. The MED began to oversee and coordinate construction of the massive plants necessary to produce bomb-quality uranium and plutonium; it became the most massive building project up to that time in U.S. history. In the next few months, the Manhattan Project gained charge over the entire atomic bomb project.[16]

*Groves*

Secretary of War Henry Stimson appointed General Leslie R. Groves to head the Manhattan Project in September 1942.[17] His earlier work overseeing large and complicated construction projects gave Groves the crucial experience to handle the immensity of the Manhattan Project, although reminiscing later he recalled that in first accepting the Manhattan Project position his understanding of the job was very narrow. Groves expected that his responsibilities "would be limited to the single task of building and operating the production plants and, as a side issue, assisting the various laboratories in securing equipment and supplies." This, he quickly learned, "was a most optimistic outlook and I was soon disillusioned."[18]

It became clear very quickly that vast industrial resources would be needed to produce enough of the fissionable materials required for even a few atomic bombs. It would require building gigantic plants in several locations; roads, transportation, and housing would have to be created for the tens of thousands of workers needed. Workers and their families would need schools, hospitals, stores, and churches. Here the wealth of the United States becomes apparent. The oversight committees chose to go ahead with three simultaneous methods for producing the necessary uranium and plutonium. All required unprecedented amounts of money, land, materials, and workers. At Oak Ridge, Tennessee, the Army Corps of Engineers built two full-scale experimental plants to process uranium; at Hanford, Washington, Manhattan Project officials built another vast complex of nuclear reactors and chemical separation plants to produce plutonium; and a third set of secret laboratories was built high in the mountains of New Mexico to design and produce the bombs.[19]

The atomic bomb project also required the creation of scores of other plants and labs around the country, including offices in Chicago, Berkeley, and Columbia University, which were located close to each district's university laboratories. Across the country companies came under secret contracts to produce other kinds of materials necessary for the atomic project. In some cases town residents did not learn until decades after the war about those contributions to atomic warfare.[20]

Manhattan Project officials chose not to waste time or energy on pilot projects. Groves noted in 1942 that "a wrong decision that brought quick results was better than no decision at all. If there were a choice between two methods, one of which was good and the other promising, build both. Time was more important than money."[21] Thus, the Manhattan Project went ahead with building simultaneously the three huge and costly facilities to produce sufficient quantities of plutonium and uranium. In the same months, Groves, working with trusted colleagues in the Army Corps of Engineers, began obtaining the hundreds of men who would build and maintain those facilities; he orchestrated the hiring of eminent scientists from around the country, men (and a few women) who were persuaded to leave their quiet academic environs for an unknown part of the desert to work on an unspecified top-secret project.

In the opinion of historian James Carroll, Groves's extraordinary power "was without American precedent before or since."[22] During the Pentagon project, Groves gained a solid reputation for efficiency, hard-headed decision-making, and calmness under intense pressure. On the atomic bomb project, he honed those and other qualities. Proving himself more than an efficient and tireless organizer, Groves demonstrated considerable scientific know-how and real brilliance in selecting leaders of the atomic bomb project. Physicist I. I. Rabi called him an "eccentric administrative genius."[23] Groves also received severe criticism in the months and years after the war, and his reputation remains clouded today. Some of the animosity comes directly from his linkage to the creation of atomic weapons; some comes from memories of his bizarre statement before Congress shortly after the war that claims of radiation in Japan were exaggerated and that radiation sickness was "a very pleasant way to die."[24] Groves also made enemies in Congress and the Truman administration by his fierce resistance to the creation of the Atomic Energy Commission (AEC) and to its first leader, David Lilienthal. Groves remained fiercely critical of the very idea of civilian control over the nuclear weapons that he had helped birth.

During and after the war, however, Groves also had staunch supporters. Physicist Harold Agnew, who worked at the Met Lab in Chicago for a year before going to Los Alamos in 1943 to work in the Experimental Physics Division and then took over as director at Los Alamos after the war when Bradbury retired, praised Groves as "one of the heroes of the whole project." Groves, said Agnew, "picked the people, Groves made the decisions." Furthermore, Groves allowed Oppenheimer to run Los Alamos in a nonmilitary way. Agnew added that, unlike the always dapper Oppenheimer, Groves was "rumpled looking." At times "he looked a little disheveled." But for pure management genius, and for sticking his neck out and getting the funds and picking the right people and knowing when to do what, he put it all together.[25]

Groves, renowned for his obsession with secrecy, could at times be startlingly forthright. He once told the army officers stationed in Los Alamos, "At great expense we have gathered on this mesa the largest collection of crackpots ever seen."[26] Another time he described his role in the Manhattan Project as that of an impresario in "a two-billion-dollar grand opera with thousands of temperamental stars in all walks of life."[27] Immediately after the success of the Trinity shot, Groves recalled the past few years as similar to the precarious feat of Charles Blondin, who walked on a tightrope across Niagara Falls.

Groves's relationship with Oppenheimer startled many people then and now. Groves shared some of the ubiquitous American anti-Semitism, but he nevertheless recognized organizational genius and leadership qualities in Oppenheimer, who seemed to many people to be a brilliant young scientist but too otherworldly and overly intellectual to ever run one of the most complex scientific projects in history. Groves selected Oppenheimer to oversee Los Alamos and generally listened and acquiesced to what the scientist said about the lab's needs. Groves appeared at and spoke in defense of Oppenheimer at the infamous Atomic Energy Commission hearing in 1954 that stripped Oppenheimer of his security clearance and insinuated that he had been disloyal—a spy.[28]

*Oppenheimer*

Along with Groves, the individual most responsible for the overall success of the Manhattan Project was J. Robert Oppenheimer, the thirty-nine-year-old physicist from UC Berkeley who oversaw the work at Los Alamos to develop and design the atomic bombs. Groves first met Oppenheimer on a visit to the University of California campus on October 8, 1942, to meet the scientists most deeply involved in atomic energy. Impressed by the young physicist's charm and scientific knowledge, Groves was also apparently taken with his seeming malleability. Groves had a precise sense of the kinds of personalities he could and could not work with, and that ruled out several of the more renowned senior scientists working in nuclear energy, particularly Ernest Lawrence. Groves's reputation grew during the Manhattan Project years in many ways, one of which was as a shrewd judge of leaders. The academic world respected Oppenheimer for multifaceted brilliance (he knew several languages and was thoroughly comfortable among humanists as well as scientists), but he had no experience running any kind of scientific laboratory and no experience as an administrator. Groves overlooked this and apparently liked Oppenheimer's modesty: "He told the general that no one knew much and that they would have to make it up as they went along."[29]

As historian and physicist Jeremy Bernstein notes, "Viewed from the outside, Oppenheimer was the most unlikely choice imaginable. He had never managed anything. He was a theorist whose attempts at experimental physics had been disastrous. He was an aesthete who read poetry in several languages, and he had a ton of left-wing baggage." And yet, it was as if all of Oppenheimer's gifts "had been hoarded" for the Los Alamos experience. He had an "instantaneous ability to comprehend and synthesize scientific ideas." Hans Bethe told Bernstein that Oppenheimer understood every aspect of the program at Los Alamos "from physics to the shop and he could keep it all in his head."[30] At Los Alamos, Oppenheimer rose in every way to the demands of the job, excelling in the scientific questions as well as the more mundane managerial demands of what grew to be a town of three thousand people by the end of the war. The reprisals from the bitter enemies Oppenheimer created, in particular Edward Teller, came later.[31]

### Monetary Costs of the Manhattan Project

Creating an atomic bomb cost the United States more money than any other activity in the nation's history, although even the most rigorous attempts to calculate with precision how much money the United States spent on nuclear weapons during and immediately after World War II daunts scholars. From the 1940s to the early 1960s, no one kept detailed budgetary data about the costs of nuclear weapons. When David Lilienthal, the first chairman of the Atomic Energy Commission, presented the AEC's first budget to Congress in 1947, he stated that the commission had no traditional way to justify the requests because they had no set of books showing any costs "since the Army's Manhattan District didn't have or keep any."[32] An air force history of the early atomic era noted in 1951 that there was "no itemized record of the military expenditures, either direct or indirect, for the atomic energy program."[33] Nor have researchers been able to reconstruct the costs incurred at separate nuclear weapons facilities because of "the lack of rigorous accounting procedures, and poor historical records" and because so much secrecy surrounded many of the activities.[34] The most reputable estimate of actual expenditures for the Manhattan Project through the end of 1945 is $1.9 billion (in 1945 dollars; $21.6 billion in 1996 dollars).[35]

## The May Test (the 100-Ton Test)

On May 7, two months before the official test of the plutonium device, a rehearsal test took place at the Trinity site. Oppenheimer persuaded Groves of the crucial need for a preliminary experimental test, and Groves reluctantly agreed. The "May test" or the "100-Ton" test or "the shakedown test," intended as a full dress rehearsal for the major event scheduled for mid-July, proved to be the largest single explosive event up to that time in history.[36]

Although the confluence of events aroused little comment at the time, the May rehearsal also turned out to be the day that Germany surrendered to the Allies in Europe. The May test has received scant attention in most histories of the Trinity bomb, but some of its details merit close scrutiny.[37]

Scientists wanted a full dress rehearsal before the actual test for various reasons: to calibrate equipment, to practice where everyone would be during the actual test, and to check the communication systems. A few also wanted to know more about the ways the radioactive materials would disperse. A twenty-foot-tall wooden platform (in some accounts, a "tower") was built eight hundred yards southeast of where the Trinity bomb would later be detonated from its own steel tower. Army men stacked wooden crates filled with one hundred tons of high explosives.[38] Richard Tolman, a theoretical physicist from Cal Tech who was brought to New Mexico temporarily to provide scientific advice, sent a detailed report to Groves a few days after the test, stating that the "detonation was evidently high order" because it produced a "highly luminous sphere" and then "the ascent of the expected hot column . . . mushroomed out at a height of some 15,000 feet, at a level where atmospheric instability was indicated by meteorological observation."[39]

In the words of an early Los Alamos history, one of the major lessons from the May test was that "men who had worked in well-equipped laboratories became familiar with the difficulties of field work."[40] This included most of the scientists and also the young Special Engineer Detachment draftees. Tolman told Groves that the responsibilities had been heavy, especially for the inexperienced "SED boys," and he believed it had been "a good shakedown preparatory to the final test." Tolman took note of some specific errors: "Two operators, probably SED boys, failed to push buttons at the north and south 10,000 yard stations to actuate cameras." So, for the actual test, officials put the cameras on automatic controls.[41]

Scientists still knew little about the effects of blasts larger than a few tons of high explosives, so the May test was expected to help the Trinity crew create structures for the experimental instruments that would better withstand the effects of the final test.[42]

The scientists learned a lot from the 100-Ton test. The churned-up dirt destroyed some sensitive experimental instruments, so in one immediate response, night crews began to pave some twenty-five miles of roads around the site to better protect both instruments and humans. Following the trial test, scientists recognized the need to elevate or bury the electrical cables so crucial to many experiments. One of the most serious problems revealed by the trial run occurred when an electrical signal from an unknown source set the test off 0.25 seconds early, thereby ruining much data monitoring. The May test also brought home the desperate need for better communication systems both at the Trinity site itself and with Los Alamos (which was done via Albuquerque and Santa Fe, since secrecy required that nothing ever went directly between the Trinity site and Los Alamos). The public address system needed to be more reliable around the whole Trinity site but especially between the bunkers.[43] Radio communication needed especially serious attention, given that the entire test relied on only one frequency with a signal that was weak and subject to interference.[44]

The rehearsal test underscored a dire need for more vehicles. Officials requested an additional fifteen sedans, sixteen weapons carriers, thirty-two "carryalls," eleven jeeps, and thirty cars. It remains unclear how many of those requests were honored. The rehearsal also revealed serious understaffing at the site, especially staff to help with procuring, shipping, and organizing equipment and provisions. Interestingly, the May test also demonstrated the need for additional help in the mess hall so that chefs and kitchen patrol workers did not have such onerous eighteen-hour days. Amid the sophisticated scientific lessons the May test delivered, it is refreshingly down-to-earth that the test leaders acknowledged that the kitchens needed water-softening equipment and a steam bath for dishes.

Finally, the May test brought to light the exceeding difficulty of keeping track of people. Tolman's report must have enraged the always security-obsessed Groves by noting that some people went into the test area "without authorization to distribute mice for biological experiments with consequent damage to electrical connections."[45] Bainbridge's report indicated two kinds of personnel problems. Some people could not be accounted for just before the test, but the more serious problem came from trying to keep control over verification of who was allowed to be where. The "guarding rules" proved to be too rigid, causing some serious delays in the test countdown. Bainbridge therefore proposed new rules to allow anyone having legitimate business outside the base camp to have free access to all parts of the test area: "Free access was feasible as by mutual agreement; each respected the others' problems, troubles, and need for unhampered work in getting the job done." Finally, as in more prosaic workplaces, Bainbridge reminded everyone "not to kibitz at the tower during assembly, hoisting, checking, i.e, any time after assembly started."[46]

Some of the least publicized of the May test results, both at the time and in later decades, related to the radioactivity. In the hope of gaining clearer understanding and data about how the radiation would be dispersed in the big test in July, officials obtained a small amount of plutonium (in a "slug") from Hanford. They dissolved the plutonium through a complicated chemical process and poured it into flexible tubing that they then threaded through the one hundred tons of high explosives being stacked for the experiment.[47] The scientists wanting to understand the bomb's explosive power (its "yield") agreed that measuring the fission products in the soil right after the blast would provide the most accurate measurement of that power.[48]

Many of the radioactive-measuring methods used in the May test and later in the Trinity test came from Herbert Anderson, who as a graduate student in physics at Columbia University began working on nuclear fission with Enrico Fermi as soon as the Italian physicist arrived at the university. Fermi and Anderson conducted early experiments with nuclear chain reactions first at Columbia and then at the University of Chicago, where under the football field their group created the renowned first self-sustaining nuclear chain reaction. Anderson accompanied Fermi to Los Alamos in November 1944, where both worked in the new Fission Studies section of the division (named for and headed by Fermi) that had been formed a month earlier.[49]

Anderson devised ways to measure the efficiency of the blast by studying how much of the radiation was deposited over the area near the detonation site and by taking measures out from there. His method also involved studying what happened to the radioactive particles as some were deposited on the surface of the ground, some were mixed with the rubble on the ground, and some were dispersed into the air. Going into the bomb crater as soon as possible after the blast in newly plated, lead-lined army tanks, men scooped up the soil and debris and returned it to the labs where radiochemists measured the ratio of fissioned to unfissioned material.[50]

The official findings from the May test emphasized that the radioactivity was so low that workers could safely spend several hours in the test area after the detonation.[51] The lab results from the 100-Ton test, however, contained surprises. Sifting the dirt picked up around the crater through a fine mesh, Anderson learned that the finest particles were up to three times more radioactive than the larger ones.[52] This should have raised alarms given the serious windstorms that swept through the New Mexico plains, but apparently did not. Anderson does not appear to have explained the implications of that discovery, at least in writing, although it underscored concerns voiced that spring about the potential dangers from the radioactivity. Joseph Hirschfelder and John Magee wrote in a mid-June memo, "If all of the active material were to condense onto cold sand particles with the same distribution of activity versus particle size that H. L. Anderson found in the 100 ton Trinity shot," a dangerous amount of "active material" might come down on nearby towns.[53] If the finer-grained soil (dust) following a nuclear explosion proved to be especially radioactive, the implications about the spread of radiation far from the test site in wind-blown New Mexico were serious indeed. Such worries, however, remained little publicized—voiced quietly only among a few of the Trinity scientists.

The general reaction to the May test appears to have reassured almost everyone of the low risks of radiation dangers, although almost all interest focused on the test site workers' exposures rather than test fallout over wider areas. Anderson himself wrote that the men involved in threading the plutonium into the high explosives were not exposed to dangerous levels before or after the test; he included names and exposures of eight men who did that work, and who may have driven the tanks into ground zero and gathered the soil samples.[54]

In the Los Alamos colloquium honoring Anderson after his death, his longtime colleague Darragh Nagle reminded listeners that Anderson and his group clad a Sherman tank with radiation protection armor so the driver and technicians could go into the radioactive area to gather earth samples without overexposing those inside to radiation: "It was characteristic of Anderson that he made the first run through the crater himself, shortly after the explosion—an operation fraught with danger because the tanks had a frequent and annoying habit of stalling at embarrassing moments. In fact, a sister tank, which might have served as a rescue vehicle, had stalled that very morning and was out of service for several hours."[55]

American military officials may also have been interested in the ability of such specially armored tanks to protect their crews from radiation. The army expected to send men into areas of Japan to conclude the war and may have wanted information about how best to protect tank crews from radiation remaining after the atomic bombings. Thus, the May test information would have been welcomed. There is another possibility, as well, to explain some of the interest in the radiation from the May and Trinity tests. As I discuss later, American military and civilian officials began to focus on the potential "weaponizing" of radioactive materials dispersed as sprays, aerosols, or dusts in enemy territory. The army may have wanted any information about the radioactivity from the May test to further their deepening interest in radiological warfare.[56]

General Groves, always worried about lawsuits from irate citizens whose homes might have been damaged by the goings-on in the New Mexico desert, expressed great relief that no one complained about the May test. He also wanted to preserve absolute secrecy, so the lack of complaints relieved him on that score as well. Groves had requested that army intelligence personnel be placed around the state before the May test to observe and report on reactions of townspeople and local ranchers. One report, from

Major Claude C. Pierce, noted that light from the blast could be plainly seen at Alamogordo, sixty miles away. The sound could be heard twenty-five miles away at Oscura, and eighteen miles away at Carthage, but only faintly at Alamogordo. No one reported any physical damage.[57]

After May 7 everyone appeared to have more confidence about the quickly approaching actual test as the pace of preparation became faster and more relentless. Truck traffic increased; military vehicles carried large numbers of men back and forth. Local people in Socorro, San Antonio, and Carrizozo became aware of increased activities in the northwest corner of the Alamogordo Bombing Range, but Groves's carefully placed spies reported that the public in general appeared to believe that everything was related to the well-known and older Air Corps installation. Intelligence agents did not believe that any local citizens made a connection between whatever was going on at the very secret Los Alamos site (Site Y) and the equally secret Trinity site.[58]

## The Test Itself

It took two additional months of frenetic work after the May test before the actual test in mid-July. After three years of intense theoretical work and experimentation in a dozen different fields, often day and night, scientists believed it would be possible to conduct an actual test. The same intense work schedules and frantic pace occurred at Oak Ridge, at Hanford, and at scores of small, secret workshops around the country producing equipment and materials for the bomb. The scientists working to create the world's first atomic explosion called it "the gadget" partly to preserve the secret of the project but also because it did not yet exist in traditional bomb format that could be loaded onto a plane and dropped over an enemy target. Perhaps, too, the scientists felt uncomfortable thinking of themselves as inventors of the world's first atomic weapon.

They planned to detonate the gadget in a tower constructed at what was variously called at the time "zero" or "ground zero" or "GZ." (In this book I refer to it as ground zero.) At sites located ten thousand yards (almost six miles) north, west, and south of the tower, workers constructed bunkers below ground and covered them with dirt. The bunkers housed instruments to record and measure light, sound, shock waves, and radiation from the test, as well as to shelter the scientists and enlisted men monitoring that equipment. No bunker was built east of the tower because everyone expected that the prevailing winds would blow in that direction, carrying any dangerous radiation. As I note below, however, officials were determined to hold the test at a time when the wind did not blow east.

Scores of SED men who had been involved in all aspects of the bomb project for years at Los Alamos, along with civilian scientists and engineers, worked feverishly at Trinity to set up the experiments and to oversee the equipment. They strung miles of telephone wires from bunkers to the tower and to recording equipment beyond. They positioned experimental boxes to capture elusive data about light, wind, and earth movement. The highest priority tests focused on measuring blast and ground shock while other measures would calculate the power of the bomb and track how efficiently the detonators worked in the experimental design for the implosion trigger. Carlton Hoogterp set up small wooden boxes around the tower. Seismographs and other devices were set up to measure earth motion. This was done partly in case there were later lawsuits, as Groves feared might happen. So ground shock measurements were made at 800, 1,500, and 10,000 yards and from 50 to 100 miles from ground zero. One measurement system involved stakes set up at measured distances from ground zero. They were remeasured after the explosion. Technicians set up geophones (transforming ground vibrations into electric signals) as well as seismographs at N 9000, Tularosa, Carrizozo, San Antonio, and the base camp.[59]

In his account of the Trinity test, Bainbridge provided heartfelt recommendations about any future tests, particularly about the need for longer planning time and for more people to conduct the tests and calibrations. Scientists J. L. McKibben and W. W. Titterson, he noted, had been "overloaded almost beyond human endurance for the period of two weeks preceding the test." He added that Sergeant Jopp "was called upon day or night whenever any emergencies arose, such as broken wires, or when unauthorized and unreported splicing of wire was done by some irresponsible person in a hurry." To this the usually mild Bainbridge added, "Shooting is much too good for anyone who crosses up the wires."[60]

A later concern rather than an early priority, they set up equipment to measure the radiation from the bomb. As I discuss in chapter 6, retrospective accounts by several Manhattan Project officials emphasize that concern about radiation ranked high on their list of pre-test concerns, but pre-test documents do not bear those claims out.[61]

In addition to instruments to measure the bomb's effects, officials wanted many cameras set up to photograph every second of the explosion: photographs that would record the size of the fireball and the timing of its changing shapes and colors until the radioactive cloud was out of photographic range. Technicians set up some fifty cameras that would take motion pictures in black and white and a few in color, all to be overseen by professional photographers. Fastax cameras would take ten thousand frames per second, spectrographic cameras would record light from the fireball, and pinhole cameras would record gamma rays.[62] In addition, scientists and military personnel stationed around the site received simple handheld cameras. Some of those photographs later proved to be among the best taken, the most frequently reproduced, and the most well known.[63]

During a night of almost unbearable tension, filled with harrowing uncertainties about whether there would even be a detonation or whether everything would "fizzle," a bizarre occurrence deserves brief mention, although, interestingly, it appears in very few formal accounts of the test. Seconds before the explosion, the loudspeaker at the tower suddenly began to blare forth the "Star-Spangled Banner." The radio wavelength from Trinity accidentally crossed with radio station KCBA in Delano, California, where the Office of War Information was sponsoring a Voice of America program aimed at Latin America.[64]

As the appointed hour for the test arrived, each bunker was under the nominal control of a Los Alamos scientist and a medical official while sometimes a dozen other scientists and SEDs conducted last-minute checks of equipment; all were prepared to lie flat on the ground outside the bunker, wearing protective eyeshades, during the detonation.[65] Los Alamos scientist Robert Wilson and medical doctor Henry Barnett served as commanders at the North 10,000 bunker; others stationed there included Warren Nyer, Heinz Barschall, Robert Walker, Berlyn Brixner, and many cameras. Those at the West 10,000 bunker included John Manley and Julian Mack, with John Fuqua stationed in a block house nearby with orders to track the cloud with his flashlight after the explosion. Frank Oppenheimer and physician Louis Hempelmann had charge at South 10,000 (the Command Bunker) along with Samuel Allison (who did the final countdown), Joseph McKibben, Donald Hornig, Kenneth Bainbridge, Robert Oppenheimer, George Kistiakowsky, General T. F. Farrell, and John Williams. General Groves wanted the key scientists and political leaders distanced in case of disaster, so most remained at the base camp, 9.5 miles from ground zero.[66]

At the South 10,000 Command Bunker, test director Kenneth Bainbridge dashed in from last-minute patrolling around the tower and, according to careful plans, with half a minute before detonation, opened the padlocked box that contained all of the arming and timing circuits for the many tests to be conducted right after the detonation. The box open, he moved the firing switch into "ready" position, thus fully arming the bomb.[67] At minus ten seconds Bainbridge rushed out of the bunker and lay on the ground. Sam Allison, who did the final countdown over the PA system, was already outside on the ground with several others.[68]

Val Fitch, an SED at Los Alamos and later a Nobel laureate in physics, was also at the Command Bunker. Just before the explosion he went outside with his welding glass to cover his eyes. Even though he was faced away from the tower, the "enormous flash of light" overcame the protection from the welding glass: "It's the most surprising thing of all, is that fantastic flash of light. Then of course you see the dust cloud and the ball slowly rising off the ground in the famous mushroom cloud." He got to his feet, forgetting momentarily about the expected shockwave, then dove back down on the ground in time to "hear that fierce rumble. First that blast and then the rumble of the sound off the nearby mountains, going off the mountains." Fitch recalled, "It's hard to overstate the impact on the senses of something like that. First the flash of light, that enormous fireball, the mushroom cloud rising thousands of feet in the sky, and then a long time afterwards, the sound. The rumble, thunder in the mountains. Words haven't been invented to describe it in any accurate way." Fitch found, emerging from the main control bunker, a single military police officer at the door. "I saw him with an absolutely ashen face and I simply remarked to him, 'Oh, the war will soon be over.'"[69]

Warren Nyer, stationed at the North 10,000 bunker after spending six weeks in the desert putting out the "piezo gauges" to measure the test's air blast, recalled the mushroom cloud "just going on forever in the sky and how enormous the whole thing was, of brilliant colors. I think the most impressive thing, though was the ionization effects. It looked like a living thing with a blue glow. . . . The mountains stood out like paintings of someone on the moon. Just the contrast between the mountains and the black of the sky was just something I had never seen before."[70]

Obeying earlier orders, Joe Lehman and his fellow military police officers (MPs) lay on the ground moments before the detonation, feet pointed toward the blast site, arms covering eyes. He could hear the countdown from a loudspeaker mounted in his area and he could hear the other MPs nearby: "There were a lot of people praying really seriously. Because no one really knew whether this chain reaction could be stopped or whether it would be stopped. We could be all facing our last minutes on this earth. I thought about that many times. I guess I compared it to what I understand happens in combat, when you know that where you are is probably going to be your last step on this earth. It made quite an impression. Then we realized, hey, we're still here, we're still breathing. We have just witnessed a new era."[71]

The North 10,000 bunker, occupied by photographer Berlyn Brixner and dozens of cameras, also included equipment set up to measure the neutrons, alpha rays, and gamma rays given off by the explosion. The men at that bunker panicked immediately after the test when instruments showed unexpectedly high levels of radioactive debris coming down in their area, and Henry Barnett (the physician in charge at that post) ordered everyone to evacuate. In Warren Nyer's later recalling, the cloud seemed to be coming in their direction. It cut them off from the main road back to the base camp, so they took a back road, "and every time we took a turn on the back road it seemed like the cloud was turning to follow us. So we had our respirators on while we were in the car." The cloud eventually disappeared, but Nyer's lasting memory was that "after the awesome thing we had just seen, everybody was pretty well shaken."[72] Later, it was discovered that the recording instruments had malfunctioned and were transmitting inaccurately high radiation readings. However, in spite of what at the time was regarded as a false alarm, the cloud from the detonation did head north and then west before changing direction to go east, and it was radioactive, just not as lethally radioactive as the faulty equipment led the fleeing men to believe.[73]

Around New Mexico and neighboring states Trinity men had placed equipment earlier so as to measure ground shock and blast effects. Scientists wanted data to deepen their understanding of the bomb, and General Groves wanted data to protect against possible later lawsuits about damage to homes and businesses. Groves was greatly relieved by reports that almost no damage had been reported.[74] At the test site itself, however, some equipment suffered unanticipated damage. When a technician made a quick trip to the North 10,000 bunker two to three days after the test to retrieve film, he was shocked to find the film totally blackened from the radiation.[75] Fitch and another SED named Linton stayed around the test area for two to three days to pack up the equipment to take back to Los Alamos. As they drove about half a mile west of the former tower at ground zero they passed the small bunker where before the test they had strung cables and carefully arranged instruments. Now they saw the cables flung back over the bunker and all the dirt they had piled on top had been blown away. The bunker was "just sitting there, bare."[76]

## Other Observers and Their Reactions

Many people saw the Trinity test from unofficial areas far from the actual test site.

Some scientists and political leaders received special, official invitations to watch the test from Campania Hill, some twenty-two miles northwest of ground zero and ten miles southeast of the town of San Antonio. They arrived at Los Alamos in varying ways—many by car and some by plane to Albuquerque—and at 2 a.m. the night of the test, buses took them to the hill. Once there, they waited through the long, cold, rainy hours as the test was delayed and delayed again. The only thing to be seen was a searchlight to the southeast. To add to their misery, they had no information about when the device would be detonated or even the direction to look to see it.[77] The test authorities had forgotten to set up communication with them, so they had no way to hear what was going on at the test site. Los Alamos scientist Richard Feynman worked for hours, unsuccessfully, trying to get the radio to work.

The distinguished guests on Campania Hill included British scientists Sir James Chadwick, discoverer of the neutron, and Dr. Charles Thomas of the Monsanto Company, which was deeply involved in production of bomb materials. Thomas spoke of it later to Ernest O. Lawrence as "being the greatest single event in the history of mankind." Lawrence himself left his radiation laboratory and cyclotron at the University of California, Berkeley, to attend the test. He left a scrawled handwritten account in his personal papers: "The grand . . . almost cataclysmic proportion of the explosion produced a kind of solemnity in everyone's behavior immediately afterwards: there was restrained applause, but more a hushed murmuring bordering on reverence in manner as the event was commented upon."[78] Lawrence believed that all present shared "a feeling that we have this day crossed a great milestone in human progress."

A number of Los Alamos scientists who had not directly participated in Trinity preparations also traveled to Campania Hill to view the test: Edward Teller, Hans Bethe, Edwin McMillan, and Robert Serber. I. I. Rabi reported that he was overwhelmed by the spectacle of the explosion and that he "got gooseflesh when he realized what it meant for humanity."[79] Charles Critchfield, a member of the Ordnance and Engineering Division at Los Alamos, who worked on designing the bomb's crucial "gun gadget," recalled years later that the night before the test he went with a number of others to what he described later as a site about twenty miles from Trinity to watch the shot. It was probably the Campania Hill site: "My impression of it was, what I think of when I remember the emotion I had, was that when I was a kid I liked to read *Arabian Nights* and this reminded me so much of Aladdin's wonderful lamp. Twenty miles away, a piece of uranium [*sic*] about the size of a golf ball suddenly turned into 20,000 tons of TNT. It's just unbelievable."[80]

Cyril Smith, watching from Base Camp, was not reminded of Aladdin's wonderful lamp. Instead, the experience "produced very definite reflection that this is not a pleasant weapon that we have produced." He then reflected on "the manner of defense against it and the realization that a city is henceforth not the place in which to live."[81]

### Radiation Monitors at the Trinity Test

Men (and one woman) settled into areas around the Trinity site and in the surrounding countryside with monitoring equipment to track and record the radioactivity and fallout right after the test and for hours later. A few continued to monitor and keep records for weeks. (Chapter 6 has more discussion of the monitors and their findings.) Test officials also set up "searchlight stations" to illuminate and trace the position of "the cloud" second by second after the test. Sources are uncharacteristically vague about just where the stations were located and who manned them, but L-2 was at or near West 10,000, L-3 was near North 10,000, and L-7 and L-8 were "east of Bingham."[82] Although some of the radiation monitors expected to help evacuate townspeople and ranchers if dangerous radiation threatened, their main job was to track and record the radiations for better scientific understanding of the strength of the bomb. The Trinity test gave them such valuable experience with the machines that several of the men were sent to Japan a few months later to measure the radiation in Hiroshima and Nagasaki.[83] The day before the test a group of the radiation monitors and men from "Intelligence" (identified as "G-2" men under a Lieutenant D. Daley) met in Santa Fe for final instructions and to receive radiation detection instruments.

During the test itself groups of two men each were stationed in five towns in New Mexico, usually one doing scientific work and one overseeing security. Carl Hornberger, part of Los Alamos's T/5 group (spectography and photography of the bomb), along with Captain R. Tybout and Richard Foley, went to Fort Sumner. Alfred Anderson and Special Agent Julian Bernacci went to Nogal, Joel Greene (Los Alamos T/4, meteorology) and Charles Nelly to Roswell, Robert Leonard (Los Alamos T/3, measurements) and Special Agent William McElwreath to Socorro, and Philip Levine (Los Alamos T/4, meteorology) to Guard Gate 2.[84] The one woman monitor, Elizabeth ("Diz") Graves, a PhD physicist working at Los Alamos on fast-neutron scattering, was seven months pregnant, so she and her husband Al both sat in a rented room in Harry Miller's Tourist Court in Carrizozo. Their baggage included a seismograph, a shortwave radio, a portable electric generator, and a Geiger counter that they positioned in the window pointed toward the Trinity site forty miles west.[85] Another group of some ten Los Alamos scientists and health officials, headed by Joseph G. Hoffman, traveled local roads with monitoring equipment to track the movement of the "cloud" and to measure the radioactivity.[86]

Several of the "searchlight crews" reported mishaps and problems. Arthur Breslow, with the searchlight crew at the L-7 station, took readings of the "falling particles from the cloud which had passed overhead."[87] After five readings his radio failed, so he hopped in the car and drove fast to get to the radio at L-8, leaving behind colleagues R. White and E. Rehn. Speeding to L-8, topping the mountain pass on Highway 380, 10.4 miles east of Bingham, he saw the valley below covered "with a strata of sand-like dust" that formed clouds below the road. Realizing that in his haste he had left his respirator behind, Breslow breathed through a slice of bread until he got to L-8 only to find that "there was danger of an immediate evacuation and the count was rising rapidly." Since he had no other way to communicate with the men back at L-7, Breslow turned around immediately and raced back to warn them. The men evacuated, recording the radiation readings on the Victoreen all the way back to Base Camp. The maximum radiation readings were not alarmingly high (2.0 roentgens per hour at White Store, which was six miles east of Bingham), and after they gave that information to the sergeant in charge of a small convoy at Bingham, someone made the decision not to evacuate the town.[88]

Captain Henry Barnett watched the test from the North 10,000 site. Immediately after the detonation he left to go to the nearby searchlight station, referred to in his later notes simply as "9000." (Barnett's memo included many of his own coded words, probably as a shorthand for himself rather than a fear about unauthorized readers.) When Barnett arrived, the equipment was registering radiation readings of over 10 roentgens per hour (R/hr). A superior officer ordered the "immediate evacuation of *everyone*." Assisting in the evacuation, Barnett rode in the last car out. However, on the way down the "escape road" the instruments began to register no radiation, and the men came to believe that the original reading had been wrong. This sounds very much like the account of what happened at the nearby North 10,000 site right after the test when men fled because of the high radiation readings that turned out to have been malfunctioning instruments; Barnett may have confused the details.[89]

*Evacuation Crews*

Although far from the top-listed concerns of the Trinity test planners, some did think about the need for plans in case any townspeople or ranchers needed emergency evacuation after the test. Brigadier General Thomas F. Farrell (army air force) was one who did make plans. Farrell had worked well with Groves in the Army Corps of Engineers military construction program early in the war and, upon the urging of the secretary of war that Groves appoint a second in command, Groves placed Farrell in that position early in 1945.[90] Groves himself was only able to make three quick visits to Trinity between April and the test in July, so Farrell made several extended visits to the test site and reported regularly to Groves about the preparations.[91] Following the May test, Farrell worked out more formal plans for help from the army in case an emergency evacuation of New Mexico civilians was needed in July. With Major General Richard Donovan, deputy chief of staff for service command, Farrell discussed plans for obtaining assistance if necessary from the 8th Service Command. (An army service command provides service and supplies for military needs.) Farrell did not expect such assistance to be required, although he noted that at the most they might need help in evacuating about 1,500 people.[92] He explained that the army's military police, who were already ensconced in work at Trinity, would provide their own resources "to the extent available" for any evacuation. The emergency planning also included Farrell's consultation with the commanding general of the Second Air Force so that if an evacuation did prove necessary, transportation would be available to the Alamogordo Air Base and to Kirtland Field (in southeast Albuquerque). In such a case the army might require service command assistance in obtaining tents, food, supplies, special vehicles, "and other services." Farrell told the commander that Major Palmer, already deeply enmeshed in Trinity work, would work out further detailed arrangements.[93] The officially appointed radiation monitors were prepared to help evacuate townspeople or ranchers in an emergency, but that was not their primary job and they did not end up being asked to help in such ways.

Beyond that, details are sketchy—even confusing—about the evacuation crews. One document describes a group of ninety-one enlisted men and one officer being sent "on a mission of top secrecy," also described as "temporary duty to Albuquerque." (No one was ever to refer to the Trinity site openly.) They departed on the afternoon of July 14 and returned in the late afternoon three days later. It was all so secret that the official army morning report made no mention of the men's departure, and base officials had to issue a special explanation to cover the men's unused rations. As noted above, the temporary group commander for that exercise was Los Alamos's Major T. O. Palmer. A different source mentions that ninety-four men from a Provisional Engineer Detachment group (PED) that was not part of the PEDs already at Los Alamos were sent to help in case of emergency evacuations.[94]

Some of the military police stationed at Trinity also received temporary assignments to join the evacuation crews. That is how Joe Lehman, quoted earlier as he observed the test, ended up being part of a convoy of thirty-six trucks and jeeps, prepared to evacuate "any of the people" in case of an accident or a shift in the wind or "any kind of a circumstance." In a later interview Lehman recalled that the evacuation crew was about sixty to seventy people, two per vehicle.[95] At a planning session at the

Trinity site, men were assigned to certain areas of about ten square miles on maps. When "the dust from the column of the mushroom began to settle" they were called and directed "to proceed to our area with our Geiger Counters to be sure that there was no one in this particular area." His group found no one in their area, although they stumbled across the remains of an old farmhouse.

In the end, no ranchers or townspeople were evacuated. Some little-known reports contain information about radiation monitors becoming alarmed in midmorning over high gamma radiation readings. One occurred about four miles outside of Bingham. Robert R. Leonard, a sergeant with the SED, and William J. McElwreath, variously identified as a special agent with the Counterintelligence Corps and a member of G-2 (Intelligence), monitored barograph equipment during the test and patrolled Highway 380 "for any loitering cars." Four miles east of Bingham their equipment showed 6.5 roentgens per hour, which they regarded as "dangerously close to the evacuation limit." They went into Bingham and found Hoffman, the chief radiation monitor, who sent them back out onto the highway. The town was not evacuated.[96] The official evacuation detachment soldiers remained in their bivouac area near Guard Post 2, returning to Los Alamos the afternoon of the test. It is telling that the intense relief expressed by one Trinity official did not focus on the fact that there had been no radiation emergencies, but that no security issues had arisen even with so many new men so close to the test area.[97]

In an interview decades later, Los Alamos health physicist Louis Hempelmann recalled how worried he and others had been because they would not have been able to evacuate many people with only twenty or thirty trucks.[98] Roger Rasmussen, an electrical engineer with the Los Alamos SEDs, recalled being part of a last-minute emergency team. He and seven other GIs rode in trucks to the Trinity site, where they learned that their team would provide emergency evacuations of farmers, ranchers, or others "down that way towards the south" if the cloud drifted in that direction. The group was not called to action, but Rasmussen commented later that he still had no idea whether the cloud ever actually drifted toward or near them. They had been issued no equipment: no film badges, no goggles. "We just stood there in the path of this thing. Everybody else was safely behind barricades and lead glass. I don't know if we were exposed or not. Never found out."[99]

In addition to the evacuation crews and the radiation monitors, men from army intelligence units had diverse assignments. Some joined up with the evacuation crews. Others went to towns around the state to observe local reactions, to note any damage to homes or businesses, and if necessary, to reassure citizens that nothing unusual had occurred. Others were posted along roads that passed through thirty-two towns and cities up to one hundred miles away from the test site; six men went to "headquarters" in Albuquerque, four to Trinity itself, and four to Los Alamos.[100] Some carried recording barographs so as to have records of blast and earth-shock, but they were also under orders to be alert to passing traffic. Leonard and McElwreath, noted above, were setting up barograph equipment at 4:45 a.m. when a Dodge truck sped by. They stopped it and questioned Gabriel Montoya of Socorro and two others in the truck, who were going to Carrizozo to get a load of lumber. Leonard and McElwreath later drove into Bingham to query local reactions. R. H. Dean, owner of the Bingham General Store, told them that about 5:45 "he heard an explosion that shook his house and broke two windows." His wife concurred. The two men examined the windows, measured the radiation level as 1.5 roentgens per hour, and drove east to Carrizozo.[101] No reports provide any explanation of what the monitors and MPs told local people, especially about the radiation monitoring. How did they explain the equipment they carried, the measurements they made of air, the soil samples they gathered and, later, the measurements that some took of the thickness of adobe or wooden walls, in attempts to gauge the penetration of radiation.

## Secrecy and the Trinity Test

The atomic bomb project was one of the most well-guarded secrets of World War II, and the Trinity test was a crucial part of that top-secret enterprise. The Manhattan Project as a whole was swathed in secrecy, beginning with the coded name itself, and the pretense that the Manhattan Engineer District was simply another project similar to others run by the Army Corps of Engineers. Congress provided no oversight or approval of the project's budget. The techniques that turned fission into a nuclear weapon and the later techniques that enabled greatly expanded production of such weapons all reinforced what was becoming a widening and deepening culture of secrecy. Senator Daniel Patrick Moynihan argues in his book, *Secrecy*, that the bomb constituted "the most fearsome secret in the history of warfare."[102] So much about the Manhattan Project remained highly classified and secret throughout the war that workers at the plants themselves were not told what they were producing or for what ends. Many workers never figured out what everyone was working on so feverishly at Oak Ridge, at Hanford, and at Los Alamos. Others who learned tidbits of information preferred to compartmentalize and not talk about it with coworkers or friends, even those they worked alongside daily. They certainly did not write home with any details because mail was censored, and anyone revealing too much information would have been removed from the job, possibly charged with criminal acts, or even jailed.

Although obsessed with secrecy, the Manhattan Project officials could not keep all secrets, and in spite of the veils of classification, the secrecy surrounding the Trinity test had considerable permeability. Men and women working at Los Alamos who were not supposed to know about the impending test nevertheless learned about it by various means and made their way quietly up the hills to watch, in the cold dawn, one of the world's most revolutionary events. In one case, hours before the test, wives of several of the scientists and other test officials left Los Alamos and drove a few miles away to an observation point in the mountains.[103] From there they witnessed the bright light of the detonation, the mushroom cloud ascending into the sky, the purple and blue gradually dissolving. Their recorded memories are scant, as are details about their understanding of what they witnessed. Almost all of their memories came from interviews decades after the test.[104]

Lilli Hornig, a Czech émigré, worked originally as a chemist at Los Alamos but was transferred to the explosives division because it was considered safer for her reproductive health. Her scientist husband, Don Hornig, had the high-pressure responsibility of being the final person who could push the button to jettison the test up until seconds before the bomb detonated. Wanting to see the test, she drove her small car up Sandia Mountain, "which had a nice road to the top and a clear view 110 miles down to the Trinity site." One passenger was Betty Thomas, whose husband, Earl, was at the Trinity site, and another was David Anderson, who was part of the X group (detonator group) at Los Alamos. They knew that the shot was scheduled to go off before sunrise, so they sat out on a mountain ridge at ten thousand feet, dozing in their sleeping bags on the ground, and got up at 3 a.m. Not knowing of the weather-related delay, they waited and waited. Finally, near dawn, disappointed, they said to themselves, "Well . . . it's not going to go today." Back in the car, however, just as Hornig reached for the ignition key, "the thing bloomed in front of us." Later she remembered it as "just incredible."[105]

Meta Newson, married to Los Alamos physicist Henry W. Newson, went with two women friends who worked at Los Alamos (although she did not identify them or where they worked). They asked her to drive "because they were afraid of that little, tiny, narrow dirt road going up there." In this recounting, the women were apparently expected, or at any rate they were not turned away when they showed up in the mountains at a radio shack that had been set up to monitor the test. Newson did not name the men monitoring the radios but said, "They told us just exactly where to sit and which direction to look and everything." She added, "It was beautiful because the colors, all, you know, the clouds were all these different colors. . . . We got the sound, I think it was about 13 ½ minutes later."[106] Pat Krikorian, a secretary in the Women's Army Corps (WAC) at Los Alamos, drove up into the Jemez Mountains with a group of friends to watch the test. Krikorian arrived at Los Alamos in August 1943, and told interviewers later that neither she nor her WAC colleagues knew "exactly what was going on" even though she and the other secretaries walked through the shops daily. But they gained knowledge of some things. She recalled later that on the eve of the Trinity test she and several friends "knew that something was going on there" and they drove "up in the Jemez" somewhere "out on the Dome Road."[107]

Most wives of workers at Los Alamos, even those of the most exalted of the scientists, were not supposed to know what their husbands were working on. General Groves's wife, who lived in Washington DC throughout the war, stated later that she had no idea about the purpose of her husband's work at Los Alamos until the city of Hiroshima was bombed. Laura Fermi says that she, along with other wives, did not fully realize that Los Alamos was constructing atomic bombs until Genia Peierls raced into the apartment on the morning of August 7 at about 10:30 and said, "Our stuff was dropped on Japan. Truman made announcement. It was transmitted ten minutes ago in Tech Area. Over paging system."[108] Fermi says that she "might have guessed at least after the Trinity test," but Enrico said nothing about it even after that successful test. She describes a "voluntary system of censorship" and "the lid of secrecy" over nuclear physics such that no word of the bomb project reached her ears for five years, "from the summer of 1940 to that of 1945, when secrecy was partly lifted after an atomic bomb was dropped on Hiroshima."[109]

Adrienne Lowry, married to the head of the Chemistry Division at Los Alamos, knew nothing about what her husband, Joe, worked on at Los Alamos or even that he actually participated in the Trinity test. She recalled later: "A lot of wives found out what was going on, but my being the wife of Joe, he never said anything [laughs]." However, later, she realized that "there was a big secret hoopty-do rowdy-dow going on." A lot of wives "went down and spent the night on . . . [a mountain] outside of Albuquerque. They spent the night up there and they could see the explosion from the mountain." She repeated that although a lot of wives "were told what was going on. . . . I was not. Joe, he could not tell me."[110]

Beckie Diven, one of the women lab technicians at Los Alamos, recalled in a much later interview that she, "along with many other people," got up at dawn "and looked to the East to see if we would see it. I didn't see it when I expected it and went back to bed and missed it. Some people were on the roof of our dorm, I wasn't that dedicated."[111] Similarly, Kay Manley says that some of the wives wanted to see the blast and went up into the Jemez Mountains, but they ended up not seeing a thing. She did not go because she did not want to leave her children alone. Manley told interviewers years later that she never pressed to know the purpose of the project at Los Alamos; she understood enough to know that it was a new kind of weapon, but she did not want to know more.[112]

The week before the test, intelligence officials at Los Alamos learned that "various personnel intended to make unauthorized observations of the final shot from highways near Trinity and from the Sandia Mountains near Albuquerque." General Farrell and Colonel Tyler learned of such plans but didn't want "aggressive actions" taken other than discouraging such unauthorized trips. The military police at all Los Alamos gates were ordered to take mileage readings on all cars that left and returned between 5 p.m. July 15 and noon the following day. Their report included a list of ten men, the time they left Los Alamos, and the time they returned. The mileage on their speedometers suggested that "they might have viewed the shot without authorization."[113] Records don't indicate whether those men were reprimanded or not.

Many—perhaps even most—of the people at Los Alamos slept right through the events at Trinity. Jean Critchfield recalled later that men left Los Alamos, and although her husband did not tell her what exactly was going on, he suggested that she drive up in the Jemez Mountains at 5 a.m. "and just look out at the sky." She had two small children and recalled that she was not about to get up at five o'clock and drive anywhere, so she just slept through everything. She recalled that she had not known what was going on "and I didn't want to know." She knew it was a test of some kind because there had been booms going off all around Los Alamos. Her husband underscored her lack of knowledge of the test: "Jean had no idea what to expect. I never discussed the work at all at home."[114]

Almost none of the interviews with Manhattan Project personnel conducted years later contain negative reflections about the Trinity test or the atomic bomb project. One exception comes from Joan Hinton, one of the few women scientists at Los Alamos. She wanted to see the Trinity test, so she rode on the back of a friend's motorcycle to the top of a mesa from which they saw the explosion and "returned home stunned." She later joined an antibomb group at Los Alamos that sent to every mayor of large U.S. cities a sample of the sand that they dug out at Trinity, with a note that said, "Do you want this to happen to your city?"[115]

Elsie McMillan, wife of Nobel Prize winner Edwin McMillan (a physicist who after the war became head of Los Alamos for the next twenty-five years) and sister-in-law of Nobel Prize winner Ernest Lawrence, came to Los Alamos in 1943 with her husband and baby daughter, Ann. She figured out the purpose of the lab, but when she mentioned to her husband that she understood the goal at Los Alamos was to create an atomic bomb, he was horrified that she knew and warned her that it could get him fired. She recalled later that very few of the wives of the scientists knew what their husbands were working on, and even those women who themselves worked in the labs were ignorant, or so she believed.[116] McMillan noted that of course Kitty Oppenheimer knew all about what was going on, but the wife of Luis Alvarez did not, even though Alvarez had a major role at Los Alamos in developing the lenses for the Trinity bomb. McMillan remembered being grateful that she knew the secret because it helped her understand "when my husband left me, place unknown." Or why her husband "worked all hours of the day and night, when my husband and other husbands looked so drawn, so tired, so worried." She and many other wives did not know why their husbands disappeared periodically in the spring and summer of 1945, "destination to wives unknown." In those months, she recalled later, "we all felt that a crisis was pending. Nerves were on edge. The seasonal thunderstorms had started. Each afternoon, the heavens would open up. Inwardly, I quaked, as darkness descended. Lightning came in great jags down the sky."

McMillan learned somehow (but she did not explain how) that there was to be a test near Alamogordo at White Sands, where she and her husband had visited with "carefree abandon a few years ago." She asked her husband "in all innocence" what would happen. "It seemed an easy question," but it took him a while to answer. Finally, he said, "There will be about fifty of us present, key workers. We ourselves are not absolutely certain what will happen. In spite of calculations, we are going into the unknown." Edwin McMillan told his wife that the scientists believed that there were three possibilities: "One, that we will all be blown to bits if it is more powerful than we expect." The world would be told if that happened, he tried to reassure his wife. "Two, it may be a complete dud. If this happens you will also be told." The third possibility, said McMillan, was "it may as we hope be a success. We pray without loss of any lives. In this case there will be a broadcast to the world with a plausible explanation for the noise and the tremendous flash of light which will appear in the sky."

Ed Rynd, a machinist at Los Alamos, applied for a furlough in July 1945, hoping it would be granted before the Trinity test so that he would be back in Los Alamos when the test took place. He recalled later what he knew about the test and when he knew it: "Well, we only knew that they were going to test. You didn't know the exact date, unless you were involved with Trinity itself. But the rumor was around that they were going to test." Rynd recalled that some of the men knew about the test, and he was aware of them leaving Los Alamos so they could try to watch it. He, however, just went to bed: "Of course, we didn't know whether it was going to be successful or not. Of course, we'd heard the rumor that it might set the atmosphere on fire. And that gave us a little bit of a concern. But [we] hoped for the best."[117] Klaus Fuchs, later identified, tried, and jailed in Britain as one of the spies passing secrets about the work at Los Alamos to the Russians, watched, alone, from a nearby hill.[118]

It is clear from later interviews that many at Los Alamos and the Trinity site understood how to negotiate the secrecy. Hans Courant, SED (and son of a famous German scientist), worked in electronics at Los Alamos. He was at the Trinity site and saw the test. Immediately afterward, as he and a few other men rode back to Los Alamos in the back of a military truck, they were warned against talking to anyone from "the outside" about anything they had worked on and seen. He realized that the test "was still a really big secret. It had not been announced" and for him, back at Los Alamos, "it was really a difficult few days."[119] Roger Rasmussen worked as an electrical engineer with the SEDs at Los Alamos, building electronic items to record the Trinity test. Two nights before the test he and a few other men were told to wear work clothes and to report to an area where he and seven other soldiers piled into a vehicle originally intended to carry troops to battle. Part of a convoy, they drove along an old and winding road past Socorro, eventually stopping in San Antonio, where all the GIs piled out of their vehicles and bought everything the grocery store carried. Back in their vehicles, the convoy went into the White Sands National Monument. Rasmussen remembers that there was nothing anywhere and the vehicle drove and drove. Eventually they stopped east of the Trinity ground zero site looking over directly toward the bomb tower about five or six miles away. He recalled later that they were "eight little tiny beings sitting on the side of a mountain" but that they had "the greatest view" of the test. Although the army had not explained anything about what was going on or why the men were there, Rasmussen knew what was going on, as did the rest of his group. "I did not know any of the other seven GIs I was down there with, but we knew what we were waiting for. You had to know by then. I had been in the laboratory since the start of 1945. I had wised up. Everybody wised up."[120]

For one of his several jobs at Los Alamos, Bob Porton broadcast music and light news over the military's authorized radio station. At about noon on July 16 just as he started the regular broadcast, scientists began pouring into the small control room and studio. Some forty-five men "jammed" in as he and his partner looked at each other and thought, "Hey boy, something big is happening." No direct communications were permitted between Trinity and Los Alamos, so the broadcasters tuned in to an Albuquerque station. They heard the broadcaster report that the commanding officer at the Alamogordo Air Base had announced that a huge ammunition dump had blown up on the base. It was an accident, but there were no injuries. Porton recalled that when they heard that news "all these guys in the studio and everything [their] faces broke out in grins and they hugged each other and that was their first knowledge that it had been successful."[121] Shortly thereafter one of the men in the studio told Porton what had actually happened.

Porton, reminiscing in a much-later interview, talked about secrecy at Los Alamos. He said that he had no prior knowledge about the test, but "let me put it this way, if I had wanted to I could have found out." He was careful not to seem to pry into what he was not supposed to know. He had heard reports of several GIs "who goofed off [and] either went to Santa Fe and had too much of the juice and shot off their mouth or said something and they were shipped out they tell me to some isolated island somewhere." He made up his mind that he would never do anything or say anything that would get him removed from Los Alamos.[122]

As in any culture of secrecy, significant differences existed in the lines of communication, in the networks of who knew what and how they learned information, and in the details known. At Los Alamos the civilian scientists often came from universities which, in those days, had few classified projects and little requisite secrecy. During the war, Americans involved with classified projects had to school themselves in how to live in a relatively new and deepening culture of secrecy. Some dealt with it more lightheartedly than others. Some of the European scientists at Los Alamos took security procedures far less seriously than their American counterparts, or they resisted the secrecy more vigorously. Enrico Fermi recalled later how he transgressed security precautions, and Richard Feynman also delighted in circumventing the security guards. The wife of one scientist, though, recalled how hard it was for her to maintain any kind of friendship with non–Los Alamos people because she feared saying too much about what might have been classified. She had to sort through the legal and the forbidden topics. She also worried about what the security people might think if they saw her talking to non-security-cleared people. The different levels of acculturation in that security culture governed what one could and could not say, what topics should be broached or ignored, and what details could be revealed.

Secrets—and memories about keeping secrets—can have long lives. In the years after the war, especially when pressed by historians and interviewers, ranchers and townspeople who lived in areas of New Mexico surrounding the Trinity site occasionally opened up about their varying degrees of knowledge of the bomb test that had been both a major secret during the war and yet also not such a secret. The night before the Trinity test a young girl sleeping on the porch of her family's small adobe house in the countryside north of the test site watched the extraordinary sight of trucks driving slowly along the dirt road. An overhanging branch from one of the ancient cottonwoods planted by her grandfather stalled the silent convoy. The porch was only about one hundred feet from the road, but the house was hidden by bushes and the tall trees, and she watched as men got out of what she recognized as army trucks and lifted the branch with sticks so the trucks could pass underneath. The trucks were "slow, very slow" and traveled with only parking lights on. They made no noise at all and the family's dogs did not even bark. Ten days later she heard talk about an explosion somewhere, maybe in White Sands. "My sister didn't pay attention, but I did."

When she heard about the Hiroshima bomb a few weeks after that nighttime experience, something clicked: "Wow, that must have been when they were taking that bomb right in front of . . . our house." She never told her parents about it because they would have been annoyed that she was awake. She told interviewers later, "I didn't blab or anything like that." She recalled only that her family and neighbors had paid little attention except to say "Well, they're doing something secret."[123] At the moment of the explosion, a rancher between Alamogordo and the test site woke suddenly because it was as if "somebody turned on a light bulb right in my face." His first thought was that a plane had crashed in the yard.[124] When investigators nosed around local towns to ferret out any rumors about what had happened at Trinity, they heard that some people thought a plane had dropped bombs or that a bomber had exploded and burned in the air.[125] An itinerate sheepherder, Jack Denton, "just a drifter working not over 15 miles from it [the Trinity test]," was knocked off his cot. "Everyone else slept on," but "it scared the hell out of him."[126]

Within hours of the successful Trinity test, the uss *Indianapolis* steamed out of the harbor in San Francisco, under the Golden Gate Bridge, and headed across the Pacific to Tinian Island, where the preparations for the atomic bombings were underway, awaiting only some crucial component parts. The *Indianapolis* made it successfully to Tinian, where its world-changing cargo of the Hiroshima bomb's uranium core was unloaded. On the return trip, as is well known, a Japanese torpedo sank the ship and, through several tragic, flukish failures of communication, Allied ships failed to come to rescue survivors for several days. Sailors who survived the sinking of the ship died from thirst, exposure, and sharks. Meanwhile the ship's secret cargo became the bomb that destroyed Hiroshima. Ten days after the Trinity test, components for the Nagasaki bomb, essentially identical to what was tested at Trinity, arrived on Tinian by Air Transport Command c-54 cargo planes. Five such planes left Kirtland Air Force Base in Albuquerque, New Mexico, July 26, as soon as news arrived that the uss *Indianapolis* had arrived at the island and that its uranium cargo had been safely unloaded. Two of the huge planes carried the plutonium core and the initiator for the Nagasaki bomb; three others carried final components for the Hiroshima bomb. Two nights after that, on July 28, three b-29s left Kirtland, carrying the final parts of the plutonium bomb's high-explosive preassembly.[127] Meanwhile, after unloading the uranium and bomb parts at Tinian, the uss *Indianapolis* headed for Guam, unaccompanied, and its horror began. The horror in Hiroshima and Nagasaki came a few days later.

# TWO

## Dispossessions

Laura and B. O. Burris had owned their small ranch in the Tularosa Basin of New Mexico for three years and had just moved into the newly built ranch house in the fall of 1941 when members of the Army Corps of Engineers came by on December 16 "and told us that the Government must have our ranch for military purposes."[1] They had a four-year-old son and Laura was pregnant as they moved their 450 cattle and horses in February. They rented pasture for their animals, but they themselves moved to towns, first to Truth or Consequences, New Mexico, and then to Las Cruces, New Mexico. They received no money until 1943, when the government sent a check for $3,000. The government allowed the Burrises to return to their ranch in late 1946 for a few months, but then they were "evicted again," probably because of expansion at the new White Sands Proving Ground (WSPG) or possibly because of ongoing experiments at the nearby Trinity site. The timing of their first order to evacuate makes it appear related to the expansion of the Alamogordo Army Base in early 1942, but the couple learned later that their ranch lay about ten miles south of where the Trinity bomb was exploded two and a half years after they first turned it over to the army.

When her husband died in 1950, Laura married Ira McKinley, a local rancher, and persisted in her fight for what she insisted was fair recompense for the Burris ranch. In 1972 when the government tried to purchase the ranch without including the grazing leases in its total worth, she was one of the angry ranchers who refused to sell. As it did with other noncompliant ranchers, the government brought formal condemnation proceedings against her ranch, offering payment of $37 per acre, but she refused to sign the condemnation deed. Laura McKinley presented her case to a special review panel of the U.S. General Accounting Office in January 1983, arguing for fair compensation. The evidence she submitted included estimates of the current market value of her ranch based on studies by New Mexico State University professors whose help she had enlisted. Their figures evaluated the present market value of her ranch as $675,000. The government had paid her $66,494 over the years, so she argued that she was owed $608,506.[2]

Laura McKinley was one of 100 to 120 ranchers in the Tularosa Valley area of New Mexico who were forced to leave their ranches because of America's expanding military needs in World War II and the Cold War. Most of the ranchers left unhappily but, during the war, willingly because they supported the nation's war efforts and believed it to be their patriotic duty to let the military use their land. After the war, however, some became embittered when they were allowed to return to their ranches very briefly before being forced off again when military bases expanded, when they were given conflicting promises about eventual return, and when, in 1970, they were told they had to sell to the government and at a price many regarded as unjust. This chapter examines that history, but it does so by looking first at the long history of land controversies and violence in New Mexico's Tularosa Basin.

## The Long History of Conflicts over Land

The desert area of New Mexico's Tularosa Basin differs from the spectacular grandeur of other deserts nearby. It has none of the awe-inspiring red rock formations or deeply eroded canyons found in Utah, Colorado, or other parts of New Mexico and Arizona; it has no gleaming white dunes such as those protected and revered in nearby White Sands National Park. Instead, the landscape is flat scrubland, sagebrush, and eroded shallow gullies in the sandy soil, with little else for the eyes to focus on apart from the clouds and the sky. The basin, about 150 miles long, covers an area of almost 6,500 square miles, with low mountain ranges on the eastern and western sides. This arid land that appears so uninviting, desolate, unlivable, and barren—a land with seemingly little worth—nevertheless has had a long and often troubled human history. Conflict over the land—the right to travel across areas, the right to gather plants or to hunt, access to water, and legal ownership—was for centuries a key part of human contact.

Native groups from the many tribes in the Southwest traversed the area, and over the centuries diverse groups of those Native Americans, as well as Hispanics from Spain and Mexico and Anglo-Americans, contested access to the land; the area exists as a complex historical mosaic of land use and loss.[3] The history of the American West, as historian Patricia Limerick famously reminded us decades ago, is of conflict and conquest, and the area that became the Trinity site is no exception.

Archaeologists and anthropologists document evidence of human occupation of the Tularosa Basin as long as approximately twelve thousand years ago. They have found tools and brush-dome-type housing over shallow pits dating from the "Chijuahua Archaic" of 6000 BC through 200 AD. By 1000 AD there is evidence of "pithouse villages" in many parts of the basin; some of the villages may have been agricultural.[4] By the early fourteenth century, however, sustained drought had driven humans elsewhere, abandoning their villages. For two hundred years, from around 1350 to 1530, there is little evidence of settled human cultures in the Tularosa Basin and White Sands area, although the Mescalero Apaches apparently passed through on seasonal searches for mescal for their religious ceremonies.[5]

In the mid-sixteenth century, Spanish explorers and "conquistodores," French adventurers, Iberians born in Mexico, as well as servants, including those descended from African slaves, began making the arduous journey north from Mexico to Santa Fe, traveling along what maps began to depict as the "Jornada del Muerto" (journey of death). They came for various reasons: some sought gold, others came to establish Spain's official claim to the territory, and still others, such as the Franciscan friars, came hoping to convert Natives and establish Catholic missions. They encountered Native groups living in what the Spanish termed "pueblos" as well as groups of Athabascan speakers living in the local mountains. Those groups now generally identified as Mescalero Apaches resisted outsiders' attempts to colonize and settle the area, delaying serious European presence in the Tularosa Basin for centuries.

As the numbers coming to the new world increased, Spanish authorities sought to keep control over both the explorations and early settlements in the New World. They tried, in particular, to maintain Spanish law and legal traditions over land allocations, although with decidedly mixed success. Spain attempted to preserve communal traditions within the pueblos by appointing a "Protector of Indians," who from the mid-1600s to 1717 and again from 1810 to 1821 provided legal and material help to the pueblos. The Protector of Indians adjudicated disputes over communal rights to water, timber, and hunting areas.[6]

The Spanish powerfully disrupted and destroyed Native lives, livelihoods, and traditions. In 1680 Pueblo Indians mounted one of the most widespread and successful Native rebellions in the history of the Southwest. The southern New Mexican Puebloans, joined by Hopis and Zunis in the west and the Apaches, Utes, and Navajos also in the west, brought a well-organized offensive against the Europeans, attacking and successfully destroying settlements and towns, records and structures alike, and driving two thousand Spanish settlers south to Mexico. The Pueblo Uprising of 1680 was so widespread and so successful that the Spanish effort to reestablish settlements and political, religious, and legal oversight—the so-named "Spanish Reconquest"—took thirteen years. One of the lesser-known results of the uprising that was to have serious consequences for decades was the destruction of Spanish records, especially land ownership records, many of which had not been copied or archived elsewhere. This compounded the problems faced later by all groups including the Native Americans as the Spanish and then the Mexicans tried to reconstruct historic legal landholdings.[7]

As the Spanish explored and settled, diverse groups of Native Americans fought with each other as well as with Europeans for access to resources and for ease of travel throughout the Southwest. Historian Pekka Hämäläinen notes that Native peoples from the Great Plains to New Mexico's borderlands had by the early eighteenth century experienced "centuries of dispossession" in a "volatile and violent multipolar world" that was "an already colonized landscape."[8] By the early eighteenth century, conflict among tribal groups escalated as the Utes and Comanches moved westward from the Great Plains into areas of what we now know as New Mexico. As they did so, they fought with Apache groups that had already established so strong a presence that the Spanish called the area "Apacheria." The 1720s and 1730s saw deadly and sustained conflict between the Comanches and their allies, the Utes, versus the many different Apache groups—the Palomas, Cuatelejos, Penxayes, Carlanas, Sierra Blancas, Jicarillas, Pelones, and Lipans.[9] The Apaches, weakened by long internal conflicts with other tribal groups, became increasingly vulnerable to Comanche attacks as they shifted from their centuries-old nomadic life to more settled villages where they practiced systematic farming, created irrigation systems, built mud houses, and began to grow maize, beans, squash, watermelons, and pumpkins. By midcentury, the fierce, slave-owning, and sophisticated trading Comanche had "unhinged" the world of the southern plains.[10]

During this period of intense internecine warfare among Native groups, the Spanish continued attempting to make permanent settlements in New Mexico. Authorities granted significant amounts of land to groups in hopes of recreating Spanish-style settlements of fortified villages built around a plaza. Seeking ways to withstand attacks by the Comanches, Utes, and Navajos, the Spanish governor in New Mexico in 1749, Velez Cachupin, established community grants of land to individual Hispanos (Spanish descendants), "Genizaros" (Hispanized Indians, some of whom were nomadic and some of whom lived in the pueblos), and the pueblo communities themselves.[11] The system appears to have worked relatively well in the eighteenth century because the official Protectors of Indians had considerable power to distribute land, and they sought to honor the communal system of the restored pueblos. However, contests over land brought wealthy Hispano families into court and into confrontations with Natives. The historian Malcolm Ebright documents three centuries of fights for control of some of the valuable tracts of irrigable land that had formerly been under control of the pueblos.[12]

Some salutary changes followed Mexican independence from Spain after protracted warfare from 1810 to 1821. The new Republic of Mexico outlawed slavery, abolished the legal caste system, and reinvigorated trade—reforms that affected residents in New Mexico as well as those elsewhere in Mexico. Other changes enhanced injustices. The undermining of land distribution traditions became especially unjust. Historian Roxanne Dunbar-Ortiz notes that more land grants were made in New Mexico during the short Mexican period than in the entire Spanish colonial decades.[13] Although some grants went to communal groups, the landholding power and wealth of a few New Mexican elite families increased, and greater numbers of people grew poorer under Mexican rule. The Perea, Otero, Armijo, Chaves, and Sandoval families came to own vast areas of land and employed hundreds of laborers, maintaining their power and wealth by intermarriage and by becoming government officials. Wealthy Hispano families fought in courts and otherwise for Natives' land, especially for former pueblo communities with their invaluable access to water and irrigable tracts.[14] By the early nineteenth century, class divisions deepened. Wealthy Hispano families now had flocks numbering in the hundreds of thousands and hired poor villagers to watch over the flocks. Sometimes the watchers were allowed to keep 10 to 20 percent of the lambs born each year; thus the poor accrued something of a livelihood and had some access to wool and meat for their families.[15] But at the same time, the small frontier villages peopled by genizaros and impoverished Mexican farmers and sheepherders bore the brunt of not infrequent attacks from the Navajos and Mescalero Apaches.

After the United States started, fought, and won an aggressive war against Mexico between 1846 and 1848, the newly acquired territory of New Mexico became part of the American Union.[16] Congress authorized a legal system and a territorial government in late 1850, but as historian Laura Gomez argues, New Mexico existed for the next sixty-four years "in an ambiguous political relationship with the U.S., part colony and part territory-to-be-annexed."[17] Under the Treaty of Guadalupe Hidalgo at the end of the war in 1848, the 115,000 former citizens of Mexico living in what was now a U.S. territory became federal citizens of the United States but not state citizens. Ironically, being a federal citizen did not grant voting rights, which only came with state citizenship.[18]

During and after the war with Mexico, the U.S. Army fought a second war of conquest in the southwestern borderlands to subdue Native Americans, particularly the Apaches, Yavapais, and Navajos. The U.S. treaty with Mexico in 1848 included what the Mescaleros considered to be their land. The Mescalero Apaches and Navajos fought American settlers moving into the area and fought the U.S. Army as it established forts in Native territory. The 1850s and early 1860s saw escalating violence between tribal groups, white settlers, and the army. In spite of multitribal alliances and some highly successful attacks on Mexican, Hispanic, and American settlements, farms, and ranches and successful battles against American troops, the Native tribes were eventually conquered and punished. The Mescalero Apaches, forced to sign a treaty in July 1853, were pushed onto a reservation near the U.S. Army base at Fort Stanton (near Lincoln), New Mexico. In the early 1860s Kit Carson forced some four hundred Mescalero Apaches to move onto a forty-square-mile tract named Bosque Redondo on the Pecos River in eastern New Mexico, where the U.S. government attempted to turn them into Christian farmers. The U.S. Army called it a reservation, but to the Natives then and today, it was a prison camp where the alkaline water and poor soil brought untold deaths from illness and starvation.[19] The 1870s and 1880s saw renewed violence between the Mescalero Apaches, American Anglos, and Hispanics. As white settlers moved into farm and ranch areas of eastern New Mexico, Apache warriors who had bolted from the Bosque Redondo carried out raids, most famously led by Apache chief Victorio, then by his son-in-law Nana, and then by Geronimo.

The Navajos, too, fought both white settlers and the army invading their traditional lands. Some one thousand Navajo warriors sacked Fort Defiance in Arizona in April 1860, and the army retaliated by destroying Navajo fields, orchards, houses, and livestock. The army's Kit Carson became infamous for his brutal destruction of hundreds of Navajo fruit trees, gardens, and wells in Arizona's Canyon de Chelly and then marching 8,500 men, women, and children 450 miles across New Mexico to the Bosque Redondo "reservation" in the winter of 1863.[20] Remembered as "The Long Walk" in Navajo history, some two hundred died of cold and starvation on the way and more died in the harsh conditions of the camp. In 1868 the Navajos signed a treaty under which the United States restored to them a small area in their original territory.

Although groups fought over many issues in those decades, land was a chief source of disputes, and under U.S. rule, land issues in New Mexico (including pueblo land as well as land owned by individuals) grew ever more complex. American military and civil officials taking over the territory, as historian David Caffey notes, "had no idea what they were getting into with respect to traditions of land tenure and of grants made under Spanish and Mexican administration."[21] U.S. officials faced the problems of incomplete documentation, "ambiguous and overlapping grant boundaries," confusion about the precise nature of ownership rights, and the names and identities of owners and beneficiaries. U.S. official and legal responses to issues involving land consistently proved to be insufficient and dilatory. Some stemmed from U.S. incomprehension of traditions of legal communal land ownership. Even more stemmed from greed as the Homestead Act, a mining frenzy, the coming of the railroad in the late 1870s, and the rapid growth of Anglo towns such as Alamogordo and Carrizozo fueled land speculation.

The U.S. Congress itself attempted to oversee some of the land conflicts in New Mexico, but the number and complexity of the issues proved overwhelming. Spanish and U.S. law differed substantially with respect to land ownership and, so too, the old communal land grants approved under Spanish and then Mexican rule proved especially troublesome. Most of the grants allocated communal grazing and wood-gathering rights; communal water allocation was especially foreign and little understood in American law. Boundaries in many cases were imprecise. In those confusing and perilous years large areas of what had traditionally been common lands and communal water sources now passed into private (usually Anglo) hands.

Congress established the Office of Surveyor-General in 1854 to adjudicate land titles granted under Spanish and Mexican rule, but with so much confusion and discord, with processes so uncertain and slow, Congress created a new entity in 1891: the Court of Private Land Claims. This became one of several specialized judicial bodies created to handle complicated, technical cases.[22] One scholar notes that from its founding until it was dissolved in 1904, that court "struggled through perhaps the most tangled thicket in American law, the confused multitude of hoary Mexican and Spanish land grants in Arizona and New Mexico."[23] Although the official American treaty with Mexico promised to honor property and other rights of former Mexican citizens in the conquered territory, this rarely happened.[24] Within a half century, significant numbers of Hispano and Mexican land owners lost possession of their properties to Anglos. Some cases involved outright land grabs, but even land title cases taken to court faced long legal delays, with many deliberately drawn out to discourage the plaintiffs. With little circulation of actual money in the territory, land became the useful and desirable currency; land, or sometimes sheep, became common currency for cash-poor ranchers.[25]

Through unscrupulous and illegal practices, Anglos who created the notorious "Santa Fe Ring" acquired vast tracts of land in the territory—and then the state—of New Mexico in the 1870s and 1880s. In lawsuits, American judges tended to ignore the long history of communal land grants and gave only individuals rights to common lands with pastures, timber, and game, thus invalidating the claims of other communal owners.[26] Some courts published only in English in newspapers or did not publicize upcoming cases at all. When those involved in a case failed to show up in court, others were declared the owners of the land. Even when Congress created the Court of Private Land Claims, land decisions remained murky and often unjust. In the entire Southwest, the largest number of land problems the court dealt with came from New Mexico.[27] The legal and cultural differences governing land ownership along with the outright chicanery of some U.S. officials have complicated attempts by historians to recreate who owned what and where and the ways by which some lost and others gained landed property. The history of land ownership in New Mexico in the late nineteenth century is full of blanks and wormholes.

In the complex history of those land conflicts, especially in the nineteenth century, one result is clear. Once the U.S. Army captured Apache war chiefs (especially Geronimo) and New Mexico appeared to be safe from Native American raids, white settlers began to move into the territory in great numbers, wanting to take advantage of the Homestead Act and lured by speculators' exaggerated notices of ample water, minerals, and ranching potential. Some would-be ranchers who came to the Tularosa Basin in the late 1860s and 1870s left out of fears about Native American violence but returned in the late 1880s. Miners who had come to southern New Mexico in the period from 1868 to the 1880s prospecting for gold, silver, copper, and turquoise had largely dwindled by the early 1890s, but a new wave of Anglo migration began in earnest. Many, arriving with sparse resources, hired themselves out as ranch laborers or herd tenders or worked at diverse jobs in towns while trying to put together funds to buy farming or ranch land. Some came who had first attempted ranching in Texas but were driven out by the drought there in the late 1880s.

The migrating Anglos encountered Mexican and Hispano settlers with very old ties to the land. Consider, for example, the roots of Priscilla Baca Ortiz, who, with her mother, Barbarita Baca, brought lawsuits against the government for the loss of the family ranch to the White Sands Missile Range. Her grandfather Carpio Chavez, born in New Mexico in 1846, raised stock and farmed, and by 1900 he owned his own house in Socorro County. He spoke Spanish and could also read and write in English. His wife, Beatriz, also a native of New Mexico, aged thirty-four in 1900, had been married seventeen years and had borne nine children, of whom five were living. She, too, could read and write (presumably in Spanish), but she "spoke no English." The census listed the family as "white."[28] Their second child, Barbarita, married Geronimo S. Baca, both listed in the census as speakers of English whose native language was Spanish. (The 1900 census listed Barbarita at age twelve as not speaking English, but the 1920 census taker crossed out Spanish as her native tongue and that of her parents.)

In 1880, when Geronimo Baca was nine, his family lived in San Antonio (Socorro County). The census listed both his mother and father, born in New Mexico, as white. Their neighbors listed on the same census page all had Spanish surnames: Gonsales, Garcia, Chaves, Gallegos, Romero, Lucero, Ortega.[29] By 1920 Geronimo Baca, aged forty-nine, and Barbarita Chavez Baca, thirty years old, had four children, owned their house, and he reported his occupation to the census taker as a retail merchant. In that same 1920 federal census covering Socorro, New Mexico, their immediate neighbors came from Kansas, Missouri, Iowa, Indiana, Illinois, Ohio, Pennsylvania, Texas, Kentucky, California, Canada, Scotland, and Germany.[30]

In the 1930s Barbarita and Geronimo owned a ranch they either inherited or bought from Barbarita's parents. Barbarita and their daughter, Priscilla Baca Ortiz, were among other ranching families protesting the loss of their ranches to the U.S. military during and after World War II. The army's White Sands Missile Range in the early 1980s offered Barbarita $172,587.34 for her land, which she refused to accept. She became one of a handful of the government's pending condemnation cases in 1983.[31]

Details are sparse about how most of the early Anglo ranchers in the Tularosa Basin got their land. Some "patented" government-owned acreage through the Homestead Act, filing claims that they then recorded with the land office of their county. In the written memoirs of their descendants, some early ranchers bought already existing ranches. Sometimes the historical records name the ranch or its former owner, but more frequently the details are scanty. Occasionally a few depositions and legal documents provide glimpses into early patterns of land acquisition. In 1888 the Beasley family and the J. D. Isaacks family migrated together to New Mexico, escaping drought in Texas. Both families lost their land to the army during and after World War II and were among the ranchers fighting for restitution for decades afterward. The two family groups settled at first in Soledad Canyon (to the southwest of today's Trinity site), where they encountered a variety of ways others used to survive financially in the area. A neighbor, Jeff Ake, for example, did not file a claim for a homestead but instead filed mineral claims, which he said offered "the easiest way to hold land there."[32] Henry and T. J. Moody, along with Ake, often worked in a nearby town or hired themselves out to other ranchers. They tended flocks of sheep—some theirs and some belonging to others in the canyon and intermittently prospected for minerals. Eventually the Beasleys and Isaackses pooled their resources and bought out the neighboring Moodys, although there are no details about the financial arrangements. They "patented" some sections of land and registered them with the county deed records.[33] The Soledad Canyon area had plentiful water and, although noted as being "rough country" for cattle, it proved fine for raising sheep and goats.[34]

In 1900 George and Sarah Beasley bought a homestead from the Rickers, who had filed a homestead claim in 1898. A few years later, in 1916, George Beasley bought eighty more acres in Soledad Canyon "from Jesus Martinez, a goatherder for one of the Ascarate daughters."[35] Although regrettably sparse in details, the federal census provides a few tantalizing glimpses about the Ascarate family.[36] Four years after the sale of the Soledad Canyon acreage, three Ascarate daughters, all in their twenties, lived with or near their parents in Las Cruces, one of the larger towns in the area. Their father, Guadalupe Ascarate, aged seventy-three, was listed as head of the household, with no occupation. Born in Mexico, his parents brought him to the United States when he was one year of age, and he became a naturalized citizen in 1885. He could read and write, and he spoke both Spanish and English. His wife, Helen T., aged sixty-five, born in New Mexico (as was her mother, although her father was French), spoke no English. Perhaps, with no son as heir, the daughters received parcels of the family land; one daughter may have sold her share to Jesus Martinez, who worked for the family as a goatherd or sheepherder. In the long history of New Mexican labor, as noted earlier, tending sheep for wealthy landowners was one way for any impoverished individuals among Hispanics, Mexicans, and Mexican Americans to gain a stake and a livelihood.

Among the wealthiest and eventually most politically powerful families in the Tularosa area, the Bursums owned ranches that eventually extended to over two hundred thousand acres north and northwest of what became the Trinity site. Holm Olaf Bursum III recalled later that his grandfather, who had been born in Iowa in 1867, moved to New Mexico and by the 1890s had begun to acquire land "from people who couldn't make a go." In such a desert it took a lot of land to raise enough livestock to make a living: "Because of lack of water you can only get about 7 or 8 cattle per 640 acres and you can't make a living raising 8 or 10 cows."[37] He did not say anything more about who those earlier failed settlers had been, but by purchasing their properties and filing claims through the Homestead Act, the extensive Bursum ranching empire, according to a grandson, "was all put together about 1918." In the early days as they pieced together their ranching livelihood, the Bursums lived in Socorro, where according to the 1910 census Olaf was "an employer" and a "raiser of livestock." His immediate town neighbors were all Hispanic: Florencio Maya, a Baca, a Gomez, and a Bareras, all of whom spoke Spanish natively and who were listed as "herder," "stockraiser," "laborer," "servant," and for several of the women, "laundress."[38] Such neighborhood connections may have been how Bursum learned about available ranches from people struggling financially. The first ranch that he acquired (his term was "put together") was the "Melecio Apodaca place."[39] Later described as being "south of present day Stallion Site," this would have put it right on the Trinity site.

How and why the Apodaca family's land became Bursum land remains unclear, but the Apodacas had long roots in New Mexico and turn up in the federal censuses for over seventy years.[40] Sinfuriana G. Apodaca, a seventy-year-old widow in 1920, lived with her only surviving child, a thirty-one-year-old son variously listed as Patio (in 1910) and Pablo (in 1920). Sinfuriana's parents had both been born in New Mexico and appear in the federal censuses from 1850 to 1920 (living near other Apodacas). Although they could read and write, they did not speak English. Neither did Sinfuriana, her son, or his wife (who was listed as illiterate). Pablo appears as a "landowner" but also a "dewer" who worked at home. (I have not been able to determine what it meant to be a "dewer.") Melecio Apodaca, possibly a brother or cousin, lived nearby in 1920. The census recorded his occupation as "rancher for wages."

In 1922, when he was U.S. senator from New Mexico, Holm Bursum introduced a bill that opened the way for non-Natives who had ten years of residency in the state to take possession of pueblo lands. A coalition of leaders from those pueblos, advocates for Native American rights, and New Mexico citizens fought and defeated the Bursum Bill the following year, but it remains a reminder that the land history of the past is rarely ever past.

## White Sands Ranchers and the U.S. Military

It is difficult to document the ranchers whose property was taken specifically for the Trinity test, but two congressional hearings yield important details about ranches taken in the Tularosa Basin for the expansion of the Alamogordo Army Base in 1941 and for the creation of the White Sands Proving Ground in 1945 and its expansion, which became the White Sands

Missile Range in 1958. In 1983 and again in 1990 senators from New Mexico held hearings in the U.S. Congress to listen to the complaints of ranchers who lost their properties to the military during World War II and ensuing decades. Some ranchers and their descendants testified in person while others submitted documents about their land and losses. Precise numbers are hard to pin down, but according to one army official, when the army began using the New Mexico range lands in 1942, almost all the land came from about fifty large ranching units.[41] Documents submitted for the 1983 congressional hearing list about one hundred names of ranchers from central New Mexico who had been compensated for having been forced off their land for the expanding gunnery and bombing range. (Some names appear more than once on the list.)[42]

Pinpointing ranch locations is complicated in New Mexico, as in other parts of the arid West, because frequently they were not contiguous. An individual or family might own a ranch located in several parts of the county or even in several counties. Sometimes, but not always, one section would be identified as "ranch headquarters" or "the home place," but commonly maps label different places as being the same ranch. As one rancher explained to Congress in 1989, ranchers needed a lot of land in diverse areas because "the sparse grass found in southern New Mexico that is edible by cattle is often unequally and haphazardly distributed across the land. Thus, a significantly large land area is required to spread the risks created by nature's whimsical distribution."[43]

No single good source exists that locates and names the ranchers in the area before the Trinity test. The single best evidence comes from several maps in the Los Alamos Historical Document Retrieval and Assessment Project (LAHDRA) sponsored by the Center for Disease Control in 2010.[44] Preparations for the Trinity site included serious attempts to map the nearby ranches in case of accidents before and during the test (as already noted), but test officials and other Manhattan Project authorities later recognized the inadequacy of those efforts. After the test, officials were shocked to discover the existence of ranches not on their maps. The LAHDRA report's tables mark ranches within three concentric circles of the test's ground zero: within the ten-mile radius, the twenty-mile, and the thirty-mile. The maps do not name the ranches and miss some, but by piecing together a range of sources, a few can be identified. Within the ten-mile radius of "ground zero" were the ranches of A. D. Helm and H.

B. Helm almost directly east; George McDonald's ranch, which became the bomb assembly site; "the old McDonald ranch" to the southeast, which became part of the base camp; and to the west the Charles H. Story ranch, the George H. Foster ranch, and one of the Green ranches.[45] The closest ranch to "ground zero" was probably the Story ranch, only 1.75 miles away.[46] The McKinley (Burris) ranch was southeast of ground zero and probably within the ten-mile radius since Laura McKinley described it as being close to George McDonald's.

Numerous ranches fell between the ten- and twenty-mile radii of Trinity ground zero. To the north and northeast were Bursum, Muncy, Gallegos, F. Thurman, Romero (possibly Lucero Romero or there may have been a separate Lucero ranch), Padilla, Chavez, Nep Chavez, Hills Home ranch, Coker, and Del Curts. More directly east were the ranches of Baca and Ratliff, and slightly southeast of the Ratliffs were the ranches of Kiloore, Gallagher, Nolda, and Barnes. Within the twenty-mile radius (south of Bingham and north of the towns of Adobe and White Store) was the Dean ranch and to the southeast but slightly outside the twenty-mile radius, the Withers ranch. To the southwest were the Beasleys in Soledad Canyon and more directly to the west were the Harriet ranch headquarters, the Bruton ranch, and the Fite ranch. To the north was the Williams ranch. While 90 percent of the ranchers near the Trinity site area in 1945 identified as Anglo, some 10 percent identified as Hispanic. Those with Hispanic surnames identified in the LAHDRA materials had ranches between the ten- and twenty-mile radiuses: Gallegos, Chavez, Romero, Padilla, and Nep Chavez. The Baca ranch was farther away, to the northeast of the test site.[47]

### Ranchers' Disgruntlement and Protests

Some of the Tularosa Basin ranchers claimed later that they had received verbal promises of being allowed to return at the end of the war. Some did return, briefly, although they were then removed in 1949 and 1950 as the missile range expanded. Some recalled promises from the evicting officials that the army would take care of the possessions they left behind and that all could be reclaimed when peace resumed. Court records are full of ranchers' ire at what they considered to be the low compensation the army offered when they found their homes torn up, their windmills destroyed, their fences torn down, and their outbuildings left derelict or vandalized.[48]

There are no records of ranchers refusing to leave when ordered to do so during the war, although some sought delays so as to have more time to find pastures to rent for their animals and housing to rent for themselves. During the war the ranchers apparently believed it their patriotic duty to help the war effort even if it meant a diminished livelihood, which they believed would be temporary. Their bitterness, protests, and lawsuits came after the war. They took pride in being loyal American citizens willing to help the war effort in every way. Some had sons who served in the army and navy overseas. A few complained later about what they experienced as rude and abrupt treatment from some members of the Army Corps of Engineers who delivered the evacuation notices and who oversaw the actual departures. But apart from Tom McDonald (whose case is presented at the end of this chapter), there is little evidence of ranchers resisting the removal orders during the war.

Initial complaints centered on other issues. First, the timing and rushed pace of their eviction: it was winter and they had to move herds of cattle or goats, some of whom gave birth en route. Since so many ranchers from the same area were being forced off of their lands, it was hard to find affordable pasture lands nearby; some were forced to sell their stock at sale prices. All of the families had to find other places to live, which proved complicated given the war. They also had to find other livelihoods, and that was difficult for many who came from generations of ranchers and had few other marketable skills. The military allowed a few families to return to their property after the war—some returned in 1948 and others years later—and many reported finding their equipment damaged (windmills were sometimes ruined by gunshot), their water troughs ruined, and their houses in disrepair from deliberate mistreatment or neglect.

The greatest anger erupted among ranchers after army representatives called a public meeting in Las Cruces on March 27, 1970. Many of the ranching families attended, expecting good news about the return of their properties. Instead, they were shocked to be told that the government wanted continued use of their ranches and ranchlands for an indeterminate number of years, perhaps for decades. In some cases the army offered ranchers new leasing contracts, but in other cases the army simply wanted to take over the properties outright. Then came the second shock: the government's assessment of the worth of the ranches to be bought or to continue to be leased. Government officials informed the ranchers that they had been paid adequately over the preceding thirty years and that the final price for their entire property or for the government's continued rental would be calculated in a new way using a formula that assessed only the worth of the ranchers' privately owned acres, factoring in the fees the ranchers had paid over the years for the annual federal and state grazing permits. It was these announcements that evoked the ranchers' fury. In ranchers' eyes, for the government to assess a ranch's worth based solely on the acres the rancher actually owned violated long-standing tradition and current practice. When ranchers bought and sold their ranches, the grazing leases added substantive total worth and had been factored into evaluations and sales for decades. As several disgruntled ranchers noted in their protests, when the IRS calculated inheritance taxes, the government always factored in the worth of the grazing leases as part of the total worth of the taxable property. Under this new system, ranchers complained of seriously low evaluations of the total worth of their ranches. For some ranchers there was also an added blow. In a few cases, the government declared that the money paid over the past twenty years constituted the sum total the ranchers would receive for their properties.

One final issue added to the Tularosa Basin ranchers' sense of injustice. When they compared their lot to the treatment of ranchers on the McGregor Range across the valley, their anger mounted. The government purchased ranches in the McGregor Range in 1956, paying total prices that included the considerable value added by the federal and state grazing permits. In some cases the government even paid to help ranchers relocate. The differences in treatment appeared and reappeared in ranchers' grievances over the years.[49]

The changes in the way the Tularosa Basin ranch owners were compensated, indeed what they protested as an outright seizure of their properties in peacetime without adequate compensation, appeared to them to be profoundly peremptory and undemocratic.[50] In later congressional hearings seeking compensation for the ranchers, New Mexico senator Pete Domenici emphasized that the ranchers had done their part for the war; they were loyal and patriotic citizens; their protests did not come during the war and were sporadic even in the twenty-year period from 1950 to 1970 when the government continued to lease their lands for use by the White Sands Missile Range. The ranchers sought redress only in 1970, when they learned that they would not be able to return to their properties at all and that payments were far less than what they believed the ranches were worth.

Some ranchers, in spite of their anger, acquiesced to the new policies in 1970. The majority of the White Sands ranchers do not appear in legal or congressional records protesting their treatment; they appear to have accepted the settlements or they have simply disappeared from records, certainly from the later legal and political contentions. Two identified ranches very close to the Trinity site's ground zero—the Story ranch and the Foster ranch—do not appear in later records. It may be that those owners sold the ranches and the new owners were among the ranchers suing the government in later years, but the records are silent on this. Some ranchers apparently agreed to the new lease terms or acquiesced in the sale price offered by the army. Sources are unclear about the numbers and names, but some forty-six families seem to have settled with the authorities. Others refused to sign the "voluntary sale contracts," and the army filed formal "leasehold condemnation cases" against them.[51] Before the land condemnation commission heard their cases, as many as fifty-five ranching families reached agreement with the government, but as of October 1982, cases were still pending for the ranches of Barbarita Baca, Meldene Green Danley, Robert L. Isaacks, Carmine and Dave and James T. McDonald, and Lupita Rodriguez Gallegos.[52] Without extensive research into legal history it remains unclear what happened in those cases, although there is a vague reference to three being settled "after a successful appeal by the government."[53]

Some of the disgruntled ranchers turned to their state political leaders and to congressional representatives for legal redress, and their anger spurred action from their congressional representatives, who held hearings in 1983 and again in 1990 to try to secure payment for the ranchers via Congress. They hoped for such compensation under amendment "Section 315q," Title 43, of the Federal Grazing Act by which Congress (rather than the army or the Department of the Interior) could determine compensatory payment to holders of grazing permits or licenses canceled for war or national defense. Under this act, Congress would determine what was fair and reasonable compensation.[54] Neither congressional hearing, however, brought financial solace to the aggrieved ranchers.

Representative Joe Skeen and Senator Pete Domenici from New Mexico both introduced bills to Congress. The bills sought compensation for the larger group of ranchers displaced by the White Sands Missile Range, but in the printed version of the bill Skeen inserted into the record specific reference to the atomic bomb test: "The productive land these ranchers gave up was ultimately used to develop and detonate the most destructive weapon known to mankind: the atomic bomb."[55] The bills did not make it out of their respective House and Senate committees.[56] Skeen's November 1983 bill was replaced by a resolution to refer the ranchers' cases to a U.S. claims court. The claims court heard the ranchers' cases in January 1988 and issued a decision in late March. The judge ruled that the ranchers did not have a legal or equitable claim against the United States.[57] In a later court case the judge ruled that the grazing permits were not property "for purposes of the just compensation clause." Property rights could not accrue to holders of grazing permits, which had no "compensable value in their own right."[58]

## The Military's Case

Taking over privately owned lands through the legal process known as "eminent domain" had been established procedure since the days of the early American republic. To the army, the process raised no concerns at all. Under the U.S. Constitution and well-established case law, property can be legally acquired even from unwilling individual citizens, businesses, or governmental entities through the process known as "condemnation." Under eminent domain the government can legally take private land if the owner is offered "just compensation" and if the property is taken for public use. The owner's consent is not mandatory. If the owner refuses to sell, the government files a court action involving a condemnation hearing, sometimes called a "taking"—a governmental action that, under the Fifth Amendment, requires "fair and equitable compensation." At the scheduled hearing the government has to show that the money offer is reasonable and that the property is being taken for public use. Either side may then appeal.[59]

This taking of private property by federal authorities in the United States has generated deep and long-lasting controversy and anger. During the New Deal the National Park Service turned to eminent domain to expand land acquisition for national parks, for historic sites, and for natural resource protection. In the views of many people, those actions created invaluable new parks and preserved many of the nation's most glorious natural treasures. In the eyes of others, especially in the American West, the actions constituted a power grab by the federal government that has continued unabated for decades, overriding the rights of individual citizens. During the New Deal, the Tennessee Valley Authority (TVA) in particular built scores of dams and reservoirs throughout the impoverished South, especially in Tennessee, securing the land through eminent domain. Although it brought electricity to areas that had none before, along with clean water flowing regularly and predictably, the TVA was among the most hated of New Deal programs, with long-lived and nurtured resentments among local citizens.

Well before he headed the Manhattan Project, Leslie Groves had experience claiming private land for national use. In early February 1942 the federal government used eminent domain to take 411 acres of land in East Arlington, Virginia, to build the Pentagon. Residents, mainly African Americans, received only fifteen to thirty days' notice to move.[60] When war began in Europe and loomed for the United States in the late 1930s, federal authorities turned to well-established processes to acquire private land for wartime preparation: to build airports and naval stations, to expand the manufacture and storage of war materials, and above all, to establish national defense installations and military proving grounds.

The government's use of eminent domain expanded in response to the needs of the Manhattan Project. One thousand Tennessee families "living in rural poverty" on ninety-two square miles of valleys and ridges lost their homes and land for the Oak Ridge facilities.[61] The speed and the sheer size of the building for that project and the population growth, in the words of historians Johnson and Jackson, struck "with what amounted to hurricane force."[62] Landowners and townspeople received little warning; the army simply posted eviction notices on front doors, gates, or trees in early fall 1942 after securing the legal right to immediate possession of fifty-six thousand acres in two Tennessee counties. The army intended to allow six weeks for people to move, but some residents received only two weeks' notice. Area residents protested that they were not given fair value for their land, and they also protested that there was no way to buy comparable land.[63] But it was wartime. As farmers and townspeople drove down the highway with household goods piled on trucks and wagons, they crossed paths with thousands of construction workers coming in to build the facilities that became the pseudonymous "Clinton Engineer Works" component of the vast Manhattan Project.

Caught up in the legal and political conflicts over the White Sands area ranchers' lands, the army and other entities in the federal government maintained that the ranchers were paid fairly for their property, for damages to their property, and for their grazing leases.[64] The army provided a detailed accounting for the money it had paid to 110 people or ranches from 1942 to 1983 as well as money paid for mining claims. As of July 1, 1983, the army had paid a total of $20,526,645 for the White Sands properties.[65] Representatives of the army (on behalf of the Department of Defense) and representatives from the Departments of Justice and the Interior all argued that the ranchers' claims had been settled in 1988 by the U.S. Claims Court and that suggestions of new legislation would reverse "binding and conclusive federal judicial determinations" on claims that had been addressed and resolved by the courts.[66] They also argued that "merely holding a grazing privilege does not and should not establish a property right in public lands."[67] A Department of Justice deputy assistant attorney general added that the ranchers had been paid millions of dollars "for the use of lands which were not their property but which had been government property."[68]

### The Ranchers' Case

In some respects the ranchers had legitimate grievances. Their most powerful argument lay in the contrast between their treatment and the government's very different process of claiming ranchland in the McGregor Mountain area for expansion of the missile testing area. The White Sands ranchers and the McGregor Range ranchers both in the end received payment from the government for their lands; the McGregor ranchers were paid in 1957 at the time their properties were taken over for the missile range. The government told them that the ranches would never again be theirs, but they were then paid outright in one lump sum, and in some cases the government helped pay relocation costs. Both acts rankled deeply with the protesting White Sands area ranchers.[69] The White Sands ranchers were kept in a state of limbo, in some cases for over twenty years, about whether they would be allowed to return to their land. Because they were not paid lump sums or "upfront money" most could not afford to start again by buying a new ranch.[70]

The rancher-government conflict was marked by very considerable disparities in the evaluations of their ranches in the White Sands area.

The government's appraisals were low and the ranchers' were high; the courts generally took a middle ground. In one example, Wesley L. Walker and others acquired a ranch in 1971. The date suggests that it was one of the properties revaluated in 1970–75 when the government sought to buy outright the ranches formerly kept through the lease and condemnation contracts. The original rancher may have decided not to fight the government and sold it to Walker, who subsequently refused the government's offers. His ranch was taken by condemnation in October 1981, and the condemnation hearing was held in May 1983. At the hearing Walker claimed that the land was worth $12,024; the appraiser he hired stated that it was worth $6,350; the government's appraiser said $1,300. The judges declined to accept the high and low appraisals and ruled the worth to be $6,350.[71]

The White Sands Proving Ground ranchers spent decades in uncertainty. Many clearly hoped that they would be allowed to return to their ranches in 1970 and instead became embittered to learn the army had declared that they were taking over their properties completely, that there would be no further leasing, and that the ranchers had been paid enough in total. In general, the courts agreed with the army or ruled against the ranchers, sometimes because of ranchers' procedural violations (taking too long to bring a case to court). The decades the ranchers were left in limbo should be factored into judgments about the justice of what happened; uncertainty takes tolls on health and well-being. The relatively small number of families who carried out the protests over the years does not mean that others were satisfied; it means that some felt more aggrieved than others. The protesters included some of the wealthiest and most politically connected ranchers, but they also included some of the oldest Hispanic families in the area with ancient ties to land they had treasured over generations.

## The McDonald Family

When the army opens the Trinity site to tourists once or twice a year no one wants to miss the McDonald house, where Manhattan Project scientists did the final assembly on the plutonium "gadget" for the test in mid-July 1945. A few miles away, on another McDonald property, the army created the base camp with barracks to house and feed several hundred men working on site in preparation for the test.[72] The McDonalds' restored ranch house is the one permanent fixture from the Trinity test (apart from the fencing) in the National Historic Site. The National Park Service spent time and effort in the 1980s to restore the house to its 1945 status, although there is remarkably little to see today that captures the taut anxieties and high tension of those final hours of bomb preparation. I conclude this chapter with the McDonald family, whose several ranches in the Tularosa Basin were taken over by the army during World War II and later. The responses of that family varied, and their histories take us back to the complicated mosaic of land use, ownership, and dispossessions that form so much of the bedrock of New Mexican history.

The family patriarch, Michael McDonald, emigrated to the United States from Cork, Ireland, and he fought for the Confederacy in the Civil War. He may have come to that position after having worked on a Southern plantation as an overseer of slaves, as many Irish immigrants did in the antebellum years; he may also simply have been expressing powerful sentiments for states' rights, equating Irish and Southern U.S. resistances to larger federal forces. His sons later held the same beliefs. Michael and his wife, Annie Carter, moved to Texas after the war, and in the mid-1870s the family (eventually including ten children) moved to New Mexico near what is now Alamogordo. For a while, "Indian trouble" in that part of New Mexico forced them to leave and go to Fort Huachuca, Arizona. While there, the oldest son, Tom, helped support the family by working for the army as a butcher. With the capture of Geronimo and the subsiding of Apache resistance in the late 1880s the McDonalds considered it safe to move back to New Mexico. Tom bought land at Mockingbird Spring in the Mockingbird Gap southeast of Socorro and slowly over many years established Mockingbird Ranch, which, to the family, became the "home place." His sons worked for other ranchers and used their earnings to buy land and cattle for their own ranches, which slowly increased in size and worth.

The McDonald family owned numerous ranches and lost control of three to the U.S. military in various ways. One of George's ranches lay on the east side of what became the White Sands bombing range, but he did not fight to retain possession of it because of the intensity of the bombing. He then put together another ranch on the "east side of the lava beds," but the White Sands Missile Range took that over in the 1950s.[73] George's third ranch became the site of the final assembly of the plutonium device in July 1945 and is part of the national landmark today.[74] When the army served an eviction notice in 1942 to the family patriarch, Tom McDonald resisted with a threat of violence. As two military police officers and a U.S.

marshal drove up in a U.S. Army jeep, armed with machine guns, to evict the family, McDonald stood in his yard waving a .45-caliber pistol "crying and cussing the men sent to get him." His son Ross managed to get the gun away, and no one was harmed. The army did not bring charges, but according to his son Dave, Tom McDonald died three years later, a bitter and broken man.[75]

Dave McDonald worked as a ranch hand for wealthy families on the Tularosa during the "drought" years of the 1920s and the Depression while also steadily buying cattle and land. (The McDonalds, like others, preferred staying within family networks in buying land and cattle. Dave, born July 5, 1901, in Tularosa, married Mertes May Townsend in 1921. They bought his sister-in-law's ranch and cattle in 1924, although he also worked for H. O. Bursum.) By the early 1940s Dave and his family owned ranchland in that area sufficient for a Bureau of Land Management grazing permit for 440 head of livestock. He learned in September 1941 that the government wanted his ranch for an "air to air gunnery range." The family was ordered to leave and was allowed to take only household goods, vehicles, and the livestock (many of which were calving).[76] They moved their stock to a ranch near Ancho, New Mexico, and rented a house in Socorro. In 1948 when the family believed they were being allowed to return to the ranch, Dave complained about damage done to the wells, the water tanks, the fencing, and his house when it became part of the Trinity Base Camp. The family was not allowed to remain at the ranch after 1948, however, because the army wanted the area for its expanded missile tests.

Over the next few decades Dave McDonald became one of the most vocal and embittered of the White Sands ranchers, protesting in legal actions, writings to state officials and federal congressmen, and finally, threats of violence. In October 1982 Dave McDonald, then aged eighty-one, and a thirty-two-year-old niece, Mary McDonald, returned to the site of his former ranch and staged a protest. Canny about the value of publicity and public sympathy, the McDonalds persuaded Joe Skeen, the Republican representative from New Mexico, and Senator Harrison Schmitt to be with them at the ranch along with newspaper reporters when the army came to force them to leave. The *New York Times*, as well as local state newspapers, reported the protest along with the congressmen's statements that they planned to investigate whether the federal government and the Department of Defense had dealt fairly with New Mexico ranchers in acquiring land for bombing tests.[77] McDonald's publicity spurred Representative Skeen and Senator Pete Domenici to hold congressional hearings in the spring. Those hearings, as this chapter has described, brought wider public attention to the complaints of ranchers about their treatment by the federal government since 1942, but little final acquiescence.

The conflicts between ranchers and federal authorities in the atomic bomb test area of New Mexico are part of a long history and tradition of western anger stemming from federal activity. The period after World War II saw a hardening and deepening of the earlier political quarrels over who "owned" and who could control activities in the American West. Ranchers and diverse political and business groups opposed expanded federal control over public lands, but beginning in the 1920s and for decades after, the National Park Service, organized hunting groups, wilderness advocates, and a growing number of the American public became more vocal and politically active in promoting protection and public ownership of land. The conflicts and fears about possession and dispossession grew especially intense after World War II. Historian Karen Merrill traces the seeds of modern environmental politics to conflicts about the Taylor Grazing Act and the creation of the Bureau of Land Management.[78] The Taylor Grazing Act changed the way ranchers regarded the public domain; they began to view it as their private property, and they began to fight more forcefully, sometimes violently, for what they regarded as their property rights.[79] The conflicts it created emblematize the growing and deepening anger among western groups toward the federal government.

The White Sands ranchers' protests about the loss of their lands to the military during and after World War II might be considered a preview of the "sagebrush" rebellions of the late twentieth and early twenty-first centuries as groups with diverse political leanings fought in peaceful and nonpeaceful ways against state and federal expansion of the public domain. Land contestations in New Mexico's Tularosa Valley can be seen as a microcosm of centuries of conflicts over land elsewhere in the country, especially in the American West.

One further point I wish to emphasize: the Trinity test site did not force Native Americans from their land. That dispossession, as this chapter documents, occurred much earlier. The creation of a military base in the area and its expansion early in World War II led to the loss of ranches owned by Anglos and Hispanics, and the acreage claimed for the atomic bomb test pushed more such ranchers off of their properties. The one criterion American government officials stipulated for the choice of the bomb test site was that it not displace Native Americans. (See the next chapter.) The nuclear bomb tests of the postwar and Cold War forced Native groups in areas around the world from their land and poisoned their environments with radioactivity. With the establishment of the Nevada Test Site in 1951, the traditional land-use area of the Western Shoshones and South Paiutes became the site of 814 nuclear tests. As numerous observers have observed, the Western Shoshones became the most nuclear-bombed nation on earth.[80] The U.S. bomb tests in the Pacific forced the Marshallese from their homes for decades (some forever) and left radioactive waste that still threatens health and life.[81]

# THREE

## Building the Test Site

Once the decision had been made to hold a test of the plutonium device, frenzied months followed: a site had to be selected, a vast number and range of supplies had to be procured, many men with diverse expertise had to be added to the workforce and, throughout it all, everyone had to work to preserve essential secrecy. After selection of the site in March 1944, the next sixteen frenetic months saw workers create a small town that, at the time of the actual test, housed over three hundred people. They laid hundreds of miles of wire for electricity and telephone communications and for the myriad experiments to be conducted during and after the explosion. They created and then improved several hundred miles of road. They brought in hundreds of tons of materials for the scientific records of the test as well as food, clothing, bedding, eating and bathing supplies, and medical equipment for everyone on site. This had to be done with extreme haste, under adverse weather conditions, and under the strictest rules of secrecy that could be devised by the U.S. military. The tasks and the goals still seem unbelievably daunting: to conduct a complex and completely original experiment detonating a new invention—a plutonium device of unfathomable power—by a new kind of implosion method, and setting up ways to measure and record all of the results, not in a climate-controlled laboratory, but in a harsh outdoor desert.

Before any other aspect of the history of constructing the Trinity site, we must acknowledge the climate. It created hardships for the construction crews who faced ice and snow when they first began work and then scorching dry heat by spring and summer as temperatures soared into the one hundreds. The aridity sucked eyelids and mouths dry, the ferocity of the windstorms caked everything and everyone with red dust, and the afternoon monsoon rainstorms typical of the high desert in the spring and summer often brought fierce lightning and wind along with rain. In those downpours, dry gullies flooded to become raging torrents. Right up to the minutes before the actual test, the weather exerted its commanding presence. Uncertainty about possible rainstorms delayed the test for several days and then hours, and the men making the decision faced deep uncertainty. They decided to go ahead.

## Selecting the Site

Because of the rushed nature, uncertainties, sleeplessness, and secrecy surrounding all aspects of the Trinity test, much about the selection of the area for the test is murky. Records exist about different areas investigated for the test site, but those records differ. The main criteria for the test site were that it be flat, have reasonably stable (or at least predictable) weather, and be extremely isolated so as to preserve secrecy. The selection group explored the possibility of six especially favored areas: (1) the army airfield that was part of the World War II Desert Training Center near the town of Rice in Southern California's Mojave Desert; (2) San Nicholas Island—the most distant of the Channel Islands off the coast of Los Angeles; (3) an area of lava beds south of Grants, New Mexico; (4) Padre Island in the Gulf of Mexico just south of Corpus Christi, Texas; (5) an area near the Great Sand Dunes National Monument in south-central Colorado; and (6), the site finally selected, an area in the Tularosa Valley of south-central New Mexico that was already part of an army air base.[1] Some other areas may also have been under consideration: the bombing range at Wendover Field, located one hundred miles west of Salt Lake City (where the B-29 pilots later did practice runs for the atomic bombing of Japan), the Coconino Plateau (south of the Grand Canyon and north of Prescott, Arizona), and several sites in New Mexico that proved to be too close to Los Alamos for serious consideration.[2]

Accounts differ about other aspects of the decision process, particularly who was involved, how they investigated the various sites, and what their reactions were. In the Los Alamos Historical Society's account, in the spring of 1945 Robert Oppenheimer, Kenneth Bainbridge, Peer de Silva (at that point head of security at Los Alamos), and (army) Major W. A. Stevens (described as being in charge of maintenance and construction "for the implosion project") set out by both plane and car to investigate the possible sites.[3] One biography of Oppenheimer has him "bouncing around the barren, dry valleys of southern New Mexico in a three-quarter-ton Army truck" for three days and nights checking out sites.[4]

The secretary of the interior, Harold Ickes, had warned Groves earlier that no Native American tribes or reservations were to be displaced because of the test, and Groves factored those orders in.[5] Later atomic bomb tests forced the removal of Native peoples around the world, but the people dispossessed of their lands for the Trinity test were not Native Americans. Groves ruled out the Rice site because he did not want to have to deal in any way with its commander, Brigadier General George S. Patton, whom he disliked. Groves liked the idea of a certain proximity to Los Alamos for easier and cheaper transport of men and materials, but he warned that the test site should not be so close that anyone could detect the link between the two projects.

The choices for the test underscore how little concern Manhattan Project officials had at the time about any serious possibility of radioactive fallout. The prevailing winds from several of the possible choices blew toward populated areas. In the month of July the prevailing wind off the small island of San Nicholas, sixty-one miles from the California coast, is west-northwest out of the Pacific, which means it would have blown the radioactive cloud directly toward Los Angeles and Orange County. The prevailing wind pattern from Grants, New Mexico, in July and August is from the southeast, so the radioactive cloud would have blown toward the Navajo lands around Farmington and Shiprock, New Mexico. An official Manhattan District history notes that the choice of what became the Trinity site was made at a time when everyone believed that the nearest habitation was twelve miles away and the nearest town was about twenty-seven miles away.[6] That, for numerous nearby ranchers, turned out not to be the case, but with poor maps and little detailed on-foot investigation, no one preparing for the Trinity test recognized at the time how many New Mexicans would be affected as "downwinders." (The term and the concept, of course, did not yet exist in 1944.)

Berlyn Brixner, one of the chief photographers of the Trinity test, recalled much later a different and little-known version of the selection process. He recalled Bainbridge being in charge of finding the site, which in the fall of 1944 included an area close to Los Alamos near Cuba, New Mexico, "and the most distant one was down in the Gulf of Mexico on some sand islands." Brixner remembered that Bainbridge settled on a site south of Grants, New Mexico, but when he went to look it over before the final decision, he invited Brixner, who had lived and traveled in that area, to accompany the group. When they arrived, Brixner "found a very bad situation there." The area was covered with lava flows with tunnels under them that made them "very unsuitable as a site for roads and hauling over the big bottle, Jumbo." So Brixner told Bainbridge that they needed to find a more suitable site "that didn't have any of these disadvantages and was very easy to use." Thus, the Jornada del Muerto area southeast of Socorro, New Mexico, came into consideration because "it's a large flat area and it doesn't have any trees or lava flows or anything on it." According to Brixner, Bainbridge took one look at the area and decided it would do.[7] Groves concurred. He especially liked the location of the site within an existing army gunnery range that would automatically provide an extra layer of secrecy.

Once Groves approved of the site choice and the governing board at Los Alamos concurred, the appropriate military authorities had to be approached and their permission secured for access to and control over a small portion of the military base for the Trinity test. Much about that process remains speculative. No one at the time appears to have written an account of the discussions and decisions, which were "informal and oral" and vague about the people involved.[8] Groves went to the top, seeking approval from Uzal G. Ent, commanding general of the Second Air Force (still at that point the army air force), who had control over the Alamogordo Base. Groves recalled later that Ent's commanding general, Henry Harley Arnold, had "long since instructed him to give us the utmost cooperation in any of our undertakings."[9] In one account Bainbridge flew to Colorado Springs to secure Ent's permission.[10]

Ent had just risen to become commanding general of the army air force in 1944; he had also just begun working for the Manhattan Project in late August, helping to coordinate and oversee training of the squadron based at Wendover Field—the squadron that would drop the atomic weapons on Japan. Ent must have been back in Colorado Springs in early September, where he approved the Manhattan Project's plan to use a site that was considerably removed from the airfield base itself.[11] Because of security requirements, the agreement reached by the two men about that area of the Alamogordo Bombing Range to be turned over to the MED (Manhattan

Engineer District or Manhattan Project) for the atomic bomb test generated no paperwork. One month after agreeing to the Manhattan Project's use of the Trinity site, Ent was severely injured in a plane crash and was hospitalized for two years before dying of those injuries in March 1948.[12] Possibly because of Ent's injury or because of the ongoing expansion of the Alamogordo Air Base and the changes in commanders, and certainly because of the lack of a traditional paper trail, the MED's acquisition of the parcel of land for the Trinity test came as a surprise to the new commander of the Alamogordo base. In his typescript account of the selection of the test site, Kenneth Bainbridge noted that the commanding officer of the Alamogordo Bombing Base, Colonel Roscoe Wriston, was taken aback when he learned about the plans for that parcel of the land under his command. He objected to Bainbridge's request for a southwest portion of the rangeland that Trinity planners wanted because of prevailing winds. Wriston "reluctantly" allowed the release of a block in the northwest corner of the bombing range.[13]

In his formal account written for Los Alamos in 1947, Bainbridge portrayed the acquisition of the Trinity site as having been more precise and orderly: "The final choice of a site was made after consultation with Gen. Ent of the Second Air Force on September 7, 1944, who gave permission for a party to approach the Commanding Officer of the Alamogordo Bombing Base to seek an area within the base approx. 18 by 24 mi. Four locations were discussed, and finally the northwest corner of the Alamogordo Air Base was selected, latitude 33/28-33/50, longitude 106/22 to 106/41." In Bainbridge's account, the test site's isolation constituted its chief characteristic: the location "permitted separation on the north and west of a minimum of 12 mi to the nearest habitation, which was great enough so that no trouble could be expected from shattering of ranchers' windows by the blast even under conditions of 100% yield. On the east the area under government control extended 18 mil and adjoined the 'Malpais' area. The nearest towns in any direction were 27–30 miles away. The prevalent winds were westerly."[14] Bainbridge's report mystifies in its several serious inaccuracies. Groves feared windows being shattered in towns much farther away than eighteen miles, but much more significantly, the prevailing winds were known to be easterly, which is one reason no bunker was built to the east of the bomb tower.

The lack of formal documentation of these decisions and land transfers caused a further problem later. In the fall of 1945 when the war ended in

Japan and operations at the newly named White Sands Proving Ground (WSPG) were heating up under the missile program, Lieutenant Colonel Harold Turner, the first commanding officer of the White Sands Proving Ground, learned that a predecessor commander of the Alamogordo Bombing and Gunnery Range had transferred control of 432 square miles to the Manhattan Project for the atomic bomb test over a year earlier.[15] Unfortunately, military records don't provide nosy historians with Turner's reactions to that news.

## The Site Itself

The site selected for the Trinity test lies in the north-central area of what is now the White Sands Missile Range but what, as noted above, was the Alamogordo Army Air Field during World War II and was then renamed the Alamogordo Bombing and Gunnery Range. (Some sources say that the site is located in the northeast corner of the bombing range and others say the northwest corner. This probably reflects the changing boundaries of the range over the years.) Built on the desert plain, the site has lava beds to the east and west, the San Andres and Organ mountains to the west (and southwest), and the Sacramento range and the Oscura Mountains to the east. Before the army took over the area just before World War II, what became the Trinity site was identified as Tularosa Grazing District No. 4, where stockmen grazed their cattle.

Accounts differ about the mapping process and the maps that ended up being used for the Trinity site. Wartime secrecy contributed to some of the historical confusion about the actual location of the Trinity site. Good and precise maps existed in the 1940s for the state of New Mexico—grids that marked by latitude and longitude townships and areas with state-granted grazing rights. Nevertheless, obtaining reliable maps of the New Mexico desert areas proved to be an especially difficult problem. Fearing that a sudden call for maps of the New Mexico desert areas would alert spies, Groves ordered more surreptitious acquisition of information via devious channels that included geodetic survey maps for New Mexico as well as Grazing Service and county maps for the state. Other Los Alamos officials persuaded the Second Air Force to make a "6-in.-to-the-mile mosaic" of a six-by-twenty-mile strip that included Trinity's "point zero."[16]

The memories of a young explosives expert from Los Alamos underscore the piecemeal, even somewhat slapdash approach to mapping the area. Jay Wechsler, involved in testing early prototypes of the implosion system that would be used for the Trinity bomb, believed a few months before the test that his group had done everything possible on that project and that there would be little further work on it. Wechsler desperately wanted to be involved more directly with what was going on at Trinity, so he talked to senior people to find out if mapmakers were needed. He had learned some mapping techniques in the infantry, and officials told him to bring a team down to map the Trinity area, although he had to get transportation. Wechsler persuaded a buddy to let him borrow a truck—a World War II Dodge weapons carrier. He and another GI (Bob Ludwick) joined an official convoy in Albuquerque and "that's how I got to Trinity."[17] Wechsler says that they then mapped "any dirt road that led away from the Trinity Site for about twenty miles in all directions." He drew the maps by hand "using a compass, graph paper, and the odometer on that weapons carrier to mark out where those roads went and what was there—cattle, sheep, sheepherders, any buildings, or anything else." He tells nothing more about how, or if, his maps proved useful and to whom, but the work made it possible for him to see the test on the morning of July 16 "from about ten miles away."

## Naming the Test and Its Site

Everything and everyone at Los Alamos—places, work projects, major officials—had disguising pseudonyms, but it took awhile for "Trinity" to become the official code name for the bomb test and its site. How and when that happened, as with so much else about the Trinity test, has differing interpretations. Sometime between spring and early fall 1944, Bainbridge pushed Oppenheimer to come up with a single code word for the test because too many different designations floated about: "Muncy's office calls it 'A.' Mitchell's office calls it Project T but ships things to s-45 and last week it was christened Project J." Bainbridge suggested that it be coded as Project T.[18] In several documents, Stafford L. Warren, a radiologist, head of the MED medical office, and a chief consultant to Groves, referred to the test and the site as "Muriel."

Later, no one could precisely pin down how, why, and when Oppenheimer came up with the name "Trinity." Groves wrote to Oppenheimer in 1962 asking about the name's origins, and Oppenheimer replied that although he had indeed chosen the name, "there is no rational answer to your question about the code name Trinity." He loved the poetry of John Donne, but he had no recollection of why "trinity" had come to his mind in naming the test.[19] In Bainbridge's account he telephoned Oppenheimer in September 1944 requesting a code name for the project, and Oppenheimer, who said he was reading the poetry of Donne at the time, suggested "Trinity." Donne's "Holy Sonnet" 171 refers to a "three-person'd God" that scholars cite as meaning the Trinity of "God, the Father, the Holy Spirit, and the Son."[20] Two of Oppenheimer's major biographers suggest that in naming the site, Oppenheimer drew from the Bhagavad-Gita: "Hinduism, after all, has its trinity in Brahma, the creator, Vishnu the preserver, and Shiva the destroyer."[21] Their explanation makes sense, too, given Oppenheimer's famous response after the Trinity test: "Now I am become Vishnu, destroyer of worlds."

There may be another explanation for Oppenheimer's thoughts turning to a threesome—a "trinity"—when he was pushed to come up with a code name for the test and its site sometime between March and September 1944, this one based on the tangled relationship of the scientist himself, his wife Kitty, and his former lover, Jean Tatlock. Oppenheimer may have been reading Donne because he was thinking of Tatlock, who had introduced him to Donne's poetry years earlier, and according to historian Jeremy Bernstein, he read Donne "in dark times."[22] As the atomic bomb project got seriously underway Oppenheimer experienced "dark times" with his former lover, Jean Tatlock. For reasons no biographer has been able to explain, in the middle of the deeply secret work on the atomic bomb in the spring of 1943 Oppenheimer visited Tatlock in San Francisco and spent the night in her apartment. She drove him to the airport the following morning, and he flew back to his work, his wife, and baby son in Los Alamos. He never saw Tatlock again, for she committed suicide in early January 1944. In their sympathetic account of so much in Oppenheimer's life, Kai Bird and Martin Sherwin are astutely thoughtful about the impact of Tatlock's suicide: "For Oppenheimer, Jean Tatlock's suicide was a profound loss. He had invested much of himself in this young woman. He had wanted to marry her, and even after his marriage to Kitty, he had remained a loyal friend to her in her need—and an occasional lover. He had spent many hours walking and talking her out of her depressions. And now she was gone. He had failed." Jean Tatlock, they suggest, "might be considered the first casualty of Oppenheimer's directorship of Los Alamos."[23]

John Canaday's insightful book of poems about the atomic bomb project provides additional support for the idea that Oppenheimer was thinking of Jean Tatlock when he suggested the code name "Trinity" for the test. In his book, *Critical Assembly: Poems of the Manhattan Project*, the first poem about Oppenheimer does not appear until halfway through the book, and it focuses on Oppenheimer thinking about Tatlock's suicide. He says that Bohr recognizes his grief. The poem also refers to words Oppenheimer fell in love with in his youth—"Le recherche"—a reference to Proust's novel about the search for lost time ("la recherche du temps perdue"). Canaday's poem, focused on Oppenheimer, was specifically about the terrible loss of a loved one and fear about what the lab was creating.[24]

Oppenheimer may also have been thinking about his marriage, which appeared troubled even to outside observers. In the middle of the intense pressures about whether the plutonium bomb would work and Oppenheimer's consequent reorganization of the labs in late summer July 1944 to try to iron out those problems, biographers note the complications in the Oppenheimer marriage. Dorothy McKibben, who helped organize many of the domestic and other details of the scientists' lives from her office and home in Santa Fe and who became for Oppenheimer "a bit of a shoulder to cry on, a support system, a mother figure" observed that the marriage was unhappy and difficult.[25] At Los Alamos, people took note of Kitty's heavy drinking and deepening personal unhappiness. It would not have been out of character for Oppenheimer to turn to poetry for solace about two women in his life and therefore to have a ready, if mysterious, name for the test that, if successful, would shatter worlds.

Oppenheimer may also have read Donne to think about war with its weapons and deaths and loss—the ongoing war with Europe and Japan as well as warring human relationships. The atomic bomb historian Richard Rhodes reminds us that the Donne poems are martial, about destruction and war, but also about dying and death bringing redemption. Rhodes suggests that Oppenheimer might have seen in them a reassuring interpretation that the bomb would end war.[26]

## A Huge Outdoor Laboratory

Although the official Army Corps of Engineers history of the atomic bomb program calls the Manhattan Project "the largest crash construction job in history," the corps does not specifically mention the extraordinary achievement of construction at the Trinity test site.[27] In the spring of 1944 "Project Trinity" became an official organization within the Manhattan Project, granted top priority for requisition of materials and personnel.[28] An official history of Los Alamos notes, "The scope and intensity of the preparations necessary for the Trinity test cannot be overemphasized. To establish a complex scientific laboratory outdoors was novel in the first place, but to do so in a barren desert under extreme secrecy and great pressure added to the difficulties. In addition to the always complex issues of obtaining supplies, too few people were available for the amount of work to be done."[29]

The complexity of obtaining supplies for the atomic bomb test (much less the entirety of the Manhattan Project) staggers the imagination. Everything had to be transported from Los Alamos (with special attention to obscuring that origin) or Albuquerque.[30] Major Stevens of the army sent a detailed memo to Groves about all construction and equipment that would have to be requested for the test. Materials of every sort and in abundance had to be procured from vendors who were already under intense pressure from other military and civilian sectors competing urgently for scarce products in the middle of a world war. Purchase requests had to be rated in terms of their urgency: X, A, B, and C. In the spring of 1945 as the Trinity test supply needs escalated, all requests became "X." Then even that top rating proved insufficient, and a new system was devised (the sources don't say by whom): x1, x2, and xx as highest, super-urgent rating. The Procurement Office for Los Alamos went through the Washington Liaison Office and then straight through to the highest authority—the War Production Board. Special dispatch or cargo planes picked up supplies for the Trinity test anywhere they were available in the United States and flew them directly to Albuquerque. The pressure on the purchasing offices in Los Angeles, Chicago, and New York grew ever more intense; none had enough workers to deal with the dramatic rise in general military procurement requests in 1945 even before the added pressure from Los Alamos. None had been able to hire new workers for over a year, and salaries were too low to retain workers lured by competing wartime jobs at good pay. In May 1945 workers in the main warehouse at Los Alamos received an average of thirty-five tons a day of incoming materials; in June it rose to a daily average of fifty-four tons. The goods were primarily bound for Trinity, but some went on to Tinian Island in the Pacific, where preparations were already underway to assemble the atomic bombs.[31]

The necessity of secrecy increased the inevitable delays in obtaining products because no direct contacts could take place between officials on the Trinity project and the purchasing offices at Los Alamos. Workers in the purchasing offices could not contact the scientists directly about products to discuss substitutions. Items went to fictitious people at addresses in Albuquerque to disguise their actual destination at Los Alamos. Inevitably, the complicated arrangements led to delays and mishaps. Ten thousand feet of simple garden hoses, needed so that sensitive wiring could be encased for protection against the severe heat and rain at the test site, had still not arrived two weeks before the scheduled test.[32] Trucks, always in short supply anyway, became useless when tires, damaged by the rough roads in the desert, could not be readily replaced.[33]

A quick overview illustrates the speed and intensity of the entire construction process at the Trinity site. In the spring of 1944, officials gave Project Trinity its official name, and basic planning began. By midsummer, plans incorporated the layout of the "ground zero" area, including the placement of the tower to hold the bomb and the design and construction plans for the shelters. Scientists busily prepared plans for the myriad experiments that would take place during and after the test, but much of that early work continued to take place at Los Alamos rather than on site at Trinity. By mid-October, as plans for the base camp became finalized, crews scavenged far and wide for old Civilian Conservation Corps buildings and materials that could be used for miscellaneous needs at the test site. In November Groves approved the construction plans, and in December the first military police (MPs) arrived, with their horses, to patrol the site. In a few weeks, by early January 1945, the first of the workforce arrived— hired construction workers from the two outside construction companies contracted to do the major building and a few of the early SEDs (Special Engineer Detachments). The work pace picked up furiously by early spring as men set about building and improving roads, building structures and refurbishing old ones for living and eating, laying electrical and communications wiring, and creating bunkers and small facilities for the experiments. After the "100-Ton Test" in early May the pace intensified even more frantically. Then, in mid-July, came the test itself.[34]

## Early Stages

One of the very first essential construction projects involved the erection of steel observation posts at corners of what would become the immediate test area so that guards could watch for intruders or spies. In December 1944, two months before any other military personnel arrived, a small detachment of about a dozen military police, under Marvin Davis, took up residence in the two dilapidated McDonald brothers' ranch houses that had been taken over early in the war by the army, had fallen into disrepair, and were now part of the Trinity test area. A crucial early project involved improving existing roads and building new ones. An early secret internal report in October 1944 alerted test planners that only ten miles of road existed at the test site.[35] Marvin Davis, with the earliest MPs, noted the appalling condition of the roads and the "alkali dust" so terrible that "fellows couldn't hardly breathe in the back of those vehicles."[36] The dust, the cold in the winter and heat in the spring, and the daily summer monsoons slowed truck travel in serious ways, as did the frequent flat tires. Work crews built new roads and improved miles of older roads linking the test site to nearby towns of Socorro, Carrizozo, Alamogordo, and Los Alamos (in spite of the desire to reduce any connection between Trinity and Los Alamos). Eventually crews laid over two hundred miles of blacktop. After the practice test in May, Oppenheimer and Bainbridge urgently requested materials and additional men to help improve the roads. The terrible quality of the "low grade" roads brought severe damage to valuable heavy equipment forced to travel over them.[37] Crews found gravel for concrete and larger stone available at a mine dump not far from the test site.[38] As the July test approached, urgent requests went out for additional repairmen and for crews to service the roads at night.[39]

Work also began quickly on crucial communications systems. Preparations for the test as well as everything connected to the actual test required the creation of a large and complex system tied together by thousands of miles of electrical wiring.[40] That wiring included telephone communication lines among managers at the site and between Manhattan Project officials at Los Alamos and in Washington DC and all of the "public address systems" on the site. Officials set up a technical stockroom to hold supplies that included electrical cables for lights for the camp and for the experiments that would be conducted during and after the test.[41]

## Creating the Base Camp

Plans for the base camp appear to have first been drafted in mid-October 1944.[42] The Trinity Base Camp's first structures consisted of the two McDonald houses, a few of the ranches' outbuildings, an old earthen reservoir, at least two windmills, and a water tank.[43] The base camp also received buildings scavenged from other military and government entities including, as noted earlier, buildings from the Civilian Conservation Corps in the Albuquerque District that were dismantled, brought to the Trinity site, and rebuilt.[44] One of the camp buildings that became a blacksmith and saddle shop had been at the Mockingbird Gap mine, which until 1920 produced sulphide ores.[45] A 1995 archaeological report sponsored by the White Sands Missile Range contains impressive details about existing buildings on the site and what Los Alamos officials brought in. This included "ten Civilian Conservation Corps portable buildings, including four 20-by-100-ft units, a 20-by-60-ft unit, a mess hall and kitchen, three 20-by-50-ft buildings, and a 150 man latrine." The report noted, "The portable buildings were used as barracks and for supply, shop, and office functions." In addition to the portable buildings, some twenty army hutments, each about sixteen square feet, were set up at the base in the spring of 1945. (Hutments are clusters of huts, usually in a military setting.)[46] By early July 1945, with construction completed, the base camp included housing for up to three hundred men. It included a mess hall, a kitchen, a commissary, a storehouse, and a latrine.[47]

Lack of water and unpotable water were always problems in the desert. The earliest ranchers in the area had quickly laid claim to any land with water, preferably potable, but any water would do, and several of the nearby ranches built wells and windmills to bring up any groundwater. Much of the latter was unfit for human consumption, as the Trinity test officials quickly discovered. At the McDonald ranches that the army used as part of the base camp, the well water proved to be so alkaline that men could not even use it for bathing.[48] Camp Structure No. 35, a two-thousand-gallon water storage tank, did not begin to provide sufficient water for drinking and bathing. Men dug deeper wells and even tried bringing up better water by using one of the ranch windmills, but the gypsum and lime content made the water problematic. As one account lamented, "The hardness of the water at Trinity made it difficult to maintain ordinary sanitary requirements in the mess hall."[49]

Eventually crews began trucking in water from nearby towns, creating one of the many ironies of the history of this top-secret site, as men driving 2.5-ton, seven-hundred-gallon-tank trucks drove regularly to nearby towns to secure potable water. One of the workers interviewed decades later recalled that water trucks went to Socorro about three times a week and brought back water from that town's ice house.[50] Unfortunately, we have no record of what townspeople thought about what drove such high demand. Historian Ferenc Szasz wrote that some twenty trucks hauled water from the Rio Grande twenty-four hours a day.[51]

## Construction at Ground Zero

The actual area for the test itself was constructed simultaneously with the base camp. Construction there included the heavy earth and concrete bunkers (described in an earlier chapter) positioned at 10,000 yards (5.68 miles) north, west, and south of the tower that would hold the bomb.[52] The bunkers held many types of equipment to gauge, measure, and record scores of details about the test. As noted earlier, because the earliest beliefs about wind patterns held that any "blow" would be due east, no East 10,000 bunker was built. This may be one reason for the mistaken idea that Trinity planners very early on took seriously the possibility of radioactive fallout, which, as I argue later, was not so. However, someone paid sufficient attention to prevailing wind patterns in midsummer to worry, so no bunker to the east was built. (Archival records that I have seen do not detail any of those discussions or decisions.) The ground zero area included a tower for Jumbo—a 214-ton steel and concrete cylinder that in the end was not used. The Eichleay Corporation of Pittsburgh, Pennsylvania, provided the one-hundred-foot steel tower from which the bomb was detonated.[53] A few miles from ground zero, the house of another McDonald brother, George, who had also been forced to abandon his property by the war authorities, became the site for the final assembly of the bomb.

By early July 1945 most of the construction had been completed. Regular planning and overview meetings between Los Alamos scientists, military officials, and others both at the Trinity site itself and in Albuquerque and Los Alamos kept everything reasonably on schedule. A month before the May 7 test and then starting a month before the July 16 test, all interested group or section leaders with field construction work underway met nightly, directly after supper, either with Captain Davalos or with a Sergeant Gibson (about whom I have not found further information).[54]

At first, everyone found conditions in the camp to be extremely primitive. The earliest arrivals did their own cooking, although eventually cooks were brought to the base camp to provide regular meals for the growing crew of workers and scientists. By the time Felix DePaula, one of the first Special Engineer Detachment engineers, arrived at the Trinity site in March or April 1945 he found the barracks livable: "People seem to get the impression that the barracks we lived in were nothing but old pieces of lumber put together. But they were really regular World War II type barracks." DePaula thought the barracks were made of new lumber and newly painted, but they weathered quickly in the dry desert heat and the paint quickly peeled off. Even so, DePaula found them "really quite adequate" even without insulation, so they were very hot in summer and were "quite cold in the cooler weather." DePaula recalled that his first job at the Trinity site was bringing in coal for the barracks and hauling most of the trash out of the camp. Laughing, he noted, "I became the sanitation engineer" or, in other words, "a garbage man."[55]

The workdays lengthened seriously after the May test, with men working twelve- and then fifteen-hour shifts. They later recalled that in their scarce free time they slept, gambled at cards, or swam in the metal tubs the ranchers had originally used for watering their livestock. Several histories report that men went antelope hunting with army-issued machine guns, and some also shot rabbits. Personal photographs taken by several enlisted men show some playing polo on the mounted patrol's horses. Some played baseball. In a very surprising lapse in the strict secrecy Groves tried to impose on everything related to the project, Lawrence Antos recalled that the MPs at Los Alamos named their baseball team the "Los Alamos Bombers."[56] All activities, however, were tempered by the extremes of weather, and men came to know what it was like to work when daytime temperatures climbed in the late spring and summer to over 110.

## Workers

The first workers at the Trinity site came from the contingent of military police based at Los Alamos. At Los Alamos those earliest MPs had performed all kinds of tasks, including menial work for the scientists such as delivering ice and hauling furniture (which some MPs found demeaning and irksome).[57] Then, in late December 1944, First Lieutenant Bush told some fourteen or sixteen of the Los Alamos MPs that they were going on "detached duty." To maintain secrecy they took a deliberately roundabout approach to get to the Trinity site. Under the command of Sergeant Marvin Davis, they went first to the Sandia Base in Albuquerque, where they picked up trucks and trailers for the horses. They took one day going south to Socorro and then to San Antonio, then crossed the Rio Grande and arrived at the Trinity Base Camp the night of December 30, 1944.[58]

In one of the ironies of atomic bomb history, some of that first group of guards for the new bomb site came on horseback. Their "horse-mounted unit" included in its history the U.S. Cavalry's defeat by the Sioux and the death of their leader, George Armstrong Custer, at the Little Big Horn. With their history as the first horse-mounted military police outfit in the army, they brought sixteen horses with them to Los Alamos and then to the Trinity site, although Davis remembered that the horses "proved to be kind of useless" and once trucks arrived "were rarely used."[59] It is worth underscoring that the first men to arrive at the site of the world's first atomic test included a "stable sergeant," a blacksmith, a farrier, and a saddler.[60] The earliest buildings at that site included a blacksmithery, a hay barn, and stables for the horses.

Sent to the desert to build a base camp, the early duties of the mounted police involved climbing the newly erected steel guard towers at four corners of the site to watch, with binoculars, for intruders. Other duties were to patrol the back roads and abandoned ranches. They did this in jeeps and other vehicles rather than riding the horses. Davis recalled later, "Sergeants like me traveling from one post to another, why we didn't generally travel the main roads. We traveled through the back country to make sure people were not coming in."[61] They discovered that some ranchers sneaked in at night to open up the windmills for water for their animals, so, as Davis remembered, "we had to go out and shut them down again."[62] Davis also recalled, "The first month or two we were busy hauling beds and mattresses and supplies for the technicians that were to follow. We were here possibly two months before anyone else came." He minimized the hardships: "It was pretty strenuous at first, 'cause we didn't have the cook crew in and we had to do our own cooking. We kept our vehicles going, a lot of different odds and ends. We had another sergeant who got a bulldozer going and dug our refuse pit, to bury the refuse and all things like that." Davis himself ended up occasionally taking provisions (bacon and eggs, peanut butter and jelly) to the men stationed at the outposts. "In the winter time why I had to haul some fuel out for their stoves. One post I rigged up a little oil burner for 'em so the little stove would burn oil instead of the coal."[63]

After the Trinity test, Davis and a few of the other MPs remained at the site to protect it from intruders. "Then after the blast, I don't know how many days it was that we set up the post out here and that was the only time we used the horses." Men and horses wore dosimeters to measure their radiation exposures. Davis reported later, ruefully, "We ended up being just a plain guard outfit at Los Alamos and down here at Trinity Site," but after the war the veterans of that "horse outfit" wore a special ring and insignia created especially for them. The ring displayed the insignia of the Army Corps of Engineers along with the castle and the crossed pistols of the mounted police. It also had a spur with the numeral "1" inside it—a symbol of the unit's pioneering role. Emphasizing yet another aspect of their unit, the ring carried the words "silencio" and "servicio."[64]

The ultimate authority over all civilians and military personnel working for Project Trinity came from the Manhattan Project, and that authority extended to enlisted men from the Alamogordo Army Base and Army Ordnance Corps who were ordered in at times to help.[65] The evidence about who those men were, what specifically they did, and when they did it is sparse. Interestingly, given the rigorous demands for secrecy, Groves permitted the Trinity managers to hire two private companies to do much of the heavy construction at the test site. They must have been well vetted by Manhattan Project officials, but no records illuminate details about procedures, or for that matter, why those particular companies were selected and which workers from the companies did what jobs. Groves's earlier experience with construction companies may have been one reason some were selected, but we know only that some of the construction at the site came from civilian contractor crews.[66] One such crew built the twenty-foot structure for the May test.[67] Workers with the J. D. Leftwich Construction Company from Lubbock, Texas, worked on base camp facilities wiring residence buildings, repairing the ranch houses, and working to install electricity, water, and a sewer in addition to other tasks. An otherwise unidentified "drilling crew" from the small town of Fort Sumner in De Baca County drilled a new well that provided potable water.[68] The men hired by the Theodore R. Brown Company ("the Ted Brown group") built the three large earth and concrete bunkers at ground zero and two towers. By March 1945 the Brown crew consisted of two hundred New Mexicans who worked dawn to dusk, seven days a week, for thirty days. After a brief rest, they worked another week, then another.[69]

### Special Engineer Detachment

Two other significant groups worked at Los Alamos on the Trinity test and at the site itself as scientists and laborers: the Special Engineer Detachment (SED), sometimes called the Special Engineer Division, and the Provisional Engineer Detachment (PED). Although both groups have begun to receive deserved attention, neither is well known in atomic bomb history. The SEDs were generally young men studying engineering or sciences in college or headed toward those fields who were briefly inducted into the army and then sent to Manhattan Project areas to work on the bomb. Charles Bagley, who worked at Los Alamos in the SED program, complained later about how little recognition the group has received in histories of the atomic bomb: "I think General Groves did a dis-service to both the civilians and military, military in particular because he did not, to this day, I don't think ever recognize that the Special Engineering Detachment really were the ones that actually built the bomb. The scientists who were mentioned by the media almost every time you turned around, didn't build anything. . . . The machinists and, as I said, explosive casters and plumbers, electronic engineers, these people built the bomb."[70]

Some of the men came out of the Army Specialized Training Program (ASTP). To avoid the mistakes made by several countries in World War I when authorities drafted men too quickly without strategic concern for the ways that their skills and specialized training would be crucial to the war effort later, the United States created the ASTP early in World War II. Men drafted into the army who had special technical skills went through basic training, but then, instead of being shipped to war, they were sent to posts around the country to use their training for the war effort. The ASTP program was disbanded in early 1944 as the need grew for men to fight overseas. The expansion of the draft in the fall of 1943 worried Manhattan Project leaders especially, as it became harder to claim occupational deferments for younger men with specialized scientific and technical skills, particularly if they had no dependents.[71] Local draft boards proved understandably unsympathetic to Manhattan Project officials' pleas that their workers, whose jobs could not be explained or specified, needed exemption from the new draft rules. Such difficulties spurred the creation of the new military organization within the Manhattan Project: the Special Engineer Detachment.

The SEDs were modeled in part on another new and secret group created early in World War II within the Army Signal Intelligence Service. That group, known as the "Special Signal Corps Detachment" (also called the Second Signal Corps Battalion), had been specially created to handle secret coded messages. It consisted of small groups of technicians—enlisted personnel—scattered all over the country who worked side-by-side with civilians. Groves learned in April 1943 about the creation and functioning of a new kind of unit in the Signal Corps—a "Special Engineer Detachment"—that might work for the Manhattan Project. He received reassurances that there had been no problems assigning the detachment to a regular service command (meaning, to a regular army or navy group), and the men did their jobs without being required "to give any information about the nature of their work."[72] Groves also must have been pleased to learn that the Signal Corps was able to "write their own ticket" in assigning ranks and grades to their men without oversight by the army. The only thing the army insisted on was that all personnel go through limited military training "in case later events should make it necessary for them to participate in combat service." Also, members of the Signal Corps' special battalion were paid a monthly monetary allowance rather than being allotted rations and living quarters.[73] Already interested in the concept but preoccupied with other pressing matters, Graves received a reminder in late April 1943 about the need to establish a Special Engineer Detachment within the Manhattan Project. A colonel and district engineer in the Army Corps of Engineers wrote to urge Groves to create a Special Engineer Detachment of the Manhattan District so as to secure the expertise of technical and scientific personnel before they were drafted into the regular armed forces. As enlisted men in an SED unit, the men would be "returned to their former work" but with ranks from technical sergeant to technician (T-3, T-4, and T-5).[74]

Whitney Ashbridge, lieutenant colonel in the Corps of Engineers (and stationed for a while at Los Alamos), sent Groves a short memo in late May 1943, requesting the creation of several SED units so that "the secret and highly important project conducted by this District" would not lose men to the draft. Ashbridge wanted SED units assigned to several of the Manhattan Project sites, including the Monsanto facilities in Ohio, Oak Ridge, Tennessee, and "Columbia" (presumably Columbia University, where scientists Enrico Fermi and Harold Urey had created the first "atomic pile" before it was moved to the University of Chicago in December 1942).[75] Some men already worked for the Manhattan Project but needed to be protected from being drafted into the regular armed services; other men needed to be brought on board. A commander would oversee the SED "assisted by such officers as may be necessary." For administration, living quarters, and rations, the men would be attached to the service commands where they were stationed, although it was recommended that the SED men receive monetary allowances instead of rations and subsidized living quarters. The SED men would need "a limited amount of basic military training—about two to three weeks before assignment to the MED."[76]

Groves may have worked hard to secure SEDs for the Manhattan Project for reasons beyond fearing the loss of men with invaluable scientific skills. He much preferred dealing with military personnel instead of civilians, and the fact that the SEDs would be part of the army, even if only minimally, may have reassured him. Groves warned the new army colonel, Gerald R. Tyler, who took over from Colonel Ashbridge at Los Alamos in late 1944, "The scientists detest the uniform. They'll make your life a hell on earth and will do everything they can to embarrass you. When you start talking to them about property accountability . . . they'll scream that you are a Fascist and that you are trying to regiment them. Your job will be to run the post. Try to satisfy these temperamental people. Don't allow living conditions, family problems, or anything else to take their minds off their work."[77]

By the end of the war, SEDs made up nearly 50 percent of the technical personnel at Los Alamos.[78] Some of the men who became SEDs were plucked from basic training around the country before they were shipped off to fight in Europe or the Pacific; some were drawn from graduate programs primarily in the technical sciences and engineering. They were not told where they were being sent or, in any detail, what they would be doing. In later reminiscences they recalled receiving army orders to leave wherever they were, to report to a specific place from which they were then sent on to New Mexico. No one informed them about why they had been selected and what the projects would be. Those who ended up in

Los Alamos received assignments based on their skills and training. The army applied the term "engineer" generically; sometimes the term went to men who performed construction and maintenance tasks, sometimes to the famous scientists working on the Trinity project because the designation disguised some of the nature of their involvement with the test and helped to preserve its secrecy. Those detached from the Los Alamos SEDs specifically to work on the Trinity test received the designation of "Special Services Detachment."[79]

The SEDs' work ranged widely. William Spindel happened already to be in the army when he was recruited to be in the Manhattan Project's SED. He recalled later that since he had lived in New York he loved the idea of returning to Manhattan. One can only imagine his disappointment when he learned that the Manhattan Project had nothing to do with New York City and that he was being sent first to Oak Ridge, Tennessee, and then to Los Alamos, New Mexico. He worked in a group "that was doing primarily coatings for the implosion bomb."[80] Roger Rasmussen, with the SEDs at Los Alamos, worked as an electrical engineer, but during the Trinity test he was assigned to help evacuate local civilians if it proved necessary.[81] David Rudolph worked at the Chicago Metallurgical Laboratory on the "pile experiment" when he was drafted into the army but was quickly assigned to an SED unit. At first, as a soldier in the SED, he was sent to Oak Ridge, but shortly after, he was back at the Met Lab "under the same supervision that I had been under before." About six months later the Met Lab began to receive "large numbers of military personnel who were assigned in laboratory tasks. So although I was the first one to go through this metamorphosis, many more followed."[82]

In a 1998 interview, David P. Rudolph (a Tech 3 member of one SED unit) recalled that his unit consisted of some forty specialists including carpenters, plumbers, "high linemen," and "cat-skinners" (operators of caterpillar bulldozers).[83] Rudolph arrived at Los Alamos early in 1945 and was immediately sent to the Trinity site to be an administrative assistant to the post engineer. In a later interview he recalled, "We started to build up a group of enlisted personal [personnel] specialists in various engineering fields. . . . All kinds of specialties were selected to come out there to install the service equipment and the monitoring and measurement equipment for the tests."[84] Robert J. S. Brown, a student at Cal Tech in early 1943, received a draft notice from the army, but instead of being trained for overseas combat, he first studied electrical engineering at Ohio State College for nine months and then went with several other Ohio State students to Oak Ridge, Tennessee. As a private first class in an SED unit, he and some others then went on to Los Alamos. He recalled later that "it became somewhat evident that some people knew about atomic fission," but at that time he did not. Nor did he know anything about the bomb project until his supervisor at Los Alamos, George Kistiakowsky, told everyone on his crew what the project was about.[85] Brown worked at the Trinity site setting up electronic equipment, occasionally driving a pickup truck with electronic materials in it. He remembered having to endure the worst heat of his life. During the test itself he was about ten miles away from ground zero, and a few hours afterward he drove back to Los Alamos. Before leaving Trinity, however, Brown took a souvenir: the largest piece of trinitite he could find. Later his wife had it made into a bolo tie, and Brown wore it proudly. Ironically, given that he wore a radioactive decoration for decades, one of Brown's projects back at Los Alamos was to devise small radiation alarms to be worn like wristwatches.

Like Brown, many of the SEDs worked in the civilian technical areas at Los Alamos, but in most other respects they were considered army, living in the barracks with regular army draftees and eating in the army mess halls. Although not required to wear army uniforms, the army expected the SEDs to conform to army discipline: to participate in the 6 a.m. calisthenics exercises with the regular GIs, to salute officers, and to stand at attention when so ordered. Half a century after the war, former SED Val Fitch (later a Nobel laureate in physics) still lauded his boss in the "implosion" section, physical chemist George Kistiakowsky, for standing up to Groves and refusing to allow his men, almost all SEDs, to be forced to follow all army orders. Their jobs focused on producing lenses for the implosion bomb, and Kistiakowsky did not want his SEDs to be under army discipline and authority. Fitch recalled that Kistiakowsky "was terribly concerned about the way they were treated. He was expecting them to work, you know, twenty-four hours a day, but they had all this other nonsense." Complaining to Groves about the "rather spit-and-polish attitude of the military," Kistiakowsky, "as a matter of fact, threatened to leave the place if it wasn't changed." One week later, in Fitch's memory, the SEDs had an easier life. "We didn't have to get up at 6:00 in the morning [to do calisthenics], and never did we have any KP [kitchen patrol] or anything like that. The mess hall was staffed by indigenous labor, supervised by a mess sergeant. After the Kistiakowsky effect, we no longer had to clean the latrines."[86]

The SEDs and regular army personnel occasionally conflicted. In a long and detailed interview about the early days at Los Alamos, Severo Gonzalez, who was a young boy when the Manhattan Project took over his family's land at Los Alamos, recalled details about the SEDs: "The engineers were the real military people. The SEDs were in a different class, I'd say. They had everything separate from the other group. Seems to me that the regular people and the regular engineers were more friendly to the people around here. The SEDs were—well, most of them didn't have military training whatsoever. They were probably educated people, you know, in their field. They were very knowledgeable in what they were doing. So they were placed in the military and they had them separated."[87] Arno Roensch, who worked as a glass blower in an army unit at Los Alamos, recalled later resentments between the civilians and the GIs: "You are working next to someone doing exactly the same thing, they're getting $450 a month and you're getting $50 once a month as a buck private. Not that it meant anything. We had a job to do and we did it, there was no question about that. But then there were little things like, they would get the better work and we got the crappy work." Roensch recalled that the GIs rebelled a bit, too, about fairer divisions of labor so that one "person doesn't get all the hot work or someone gets all the easy stuff."[88]

A few of the grievances that surfaced during the war remain documented. One in the spring of 1945 records the resentment of some SEDs at Oak Ridge who grew angry about perceived injustices, and their superior reported their unhappiness to Groves. The disgruntled men were all "highly qualified scientists," particularly chemical engineers selected to perform special and extracurricular activities for the Intelligence Division. Their anger stemmed from differences in pay "and privileges" between the SEDs and the ERC (Enlisted Reserve Corps) and the lack of transparency in assigning some soldiers to be SED and some to be ERC. SEDs also complained that some of them had to be shifted from single to double bunks in order to make room for the 170 ERC men who had recently arrived from El Paso. Others complained about the rations.[89] Groves also learned, however, that "the only grievances of any consequence were on lack of promotions."[90] A few of the oral histories also recall resentments toward the scientists who came briefly to the site from Los Alamos and received luxuries and special treatments not offered to the other workers. No reports, however, cited behavior problems, fistfights, or men being punished for breaking the rules. The SEDS' commanding officer, Captain Howard C. Bush, appears in memoirs and later interviews as having been well-liked by the men and thoughtful about their needs. He looked the other way when they shot wildlife for meat; he went out of his way to get them special leaves at the end of the war and to write formal commendations for them.

One document in the archives sheds some light on what an unidentified but apparently close associate of General Groves understood about the kind of men Groves wanted for the Trinity site. The list contains some thirty-five names along with their military rank and comments on the men's personal qualities and their minor or major experience with the Manhattan District. Whitney Ashbridge, a lieutenant colonel with minor and major Manhattan District experience (who served briefly at Los Alamos), was "the third most outstanding officer in the Manhattan District excluding the General." One man "had more decorations than Colonel Farrell." Edward William Benson from Fort Custer was "one of the most outstanding young officers I have contacted in the construction set-up." Another was listed as "very tactful." One major was damned as a West Point graduate who "has never gotten over it." Another, commended for getting work done, "did not have the personality for General Groves."[91]

### Provisional Engineering Detachment

The Provisional Engineering Detachments (PEDs) did some of the heavier engineering and construction work at Manhattan Project sites, particularly after the civilian construction companies hired early on departed. Lieutenant Colonel Whitney Ashbridge, post commander at Los Alamos, recruited some of the earliest PEDs to work as carpenters, plumbers, and other more menial jobs. He assigned them to one of two sections in the Operations Division, one for community maintenance and construction and the second for technical area work employing carpenters, bricklayers, plumbers, painters, electricians, and more general laborers.[92] PEDs also handled heavy equipment, driving the big caterpillar tractors and the huge trucks.

Bob Porton first served in the PEDs at Los Alamos, but then unexpectedly in July 1945 received a transfer into the SEDS. He said later that the transfer changed his life. The SEDS "were treated so much better than the other military units." Many of the "boys" in the SEDs had a bachelor of science degree but some were still merely planning to go on to college after they got out. To Porton, the best thing about being an SED was that promotions came faster and easier. At first at Los Alamos, Porton was a private, but a year and a half after moving into the SED unit he was a technical sergeant. "Some of us in the SEDs would get a promotion every thirty days. That was very unique. That's probably the only place in the entire service that that took place."[93]

### Women Workers and the Trinity Test

Some women worked on the Trinity bomb project, although they have been even less acknowledged historically than the other groups. The Women's Army Auxiliary Corps (WAAC) worked at various Manhattan Project sites, especially Oak Ridge, but also Hanford and Los Alamos. After it was established in August 1943, members of the Women's Army Corps (WAC) also worked for the Manhattan Project, and by August 1945 some 260 were stationed at Los Alamos.[94] The largest contingent of women workers at Los Alamos, the WACs did many kinds of jobs. Some worked as switchboard operators or as clerks, and many were in the secretarial pools for the various divisions at the laboratory—typing, filing, taking dictation, keeping records. A few women did computations by hand or with the era's new electronic calculating machines. The first history of women professional workers for the Manhattan Project, only published in 1999, does not list the actual bomb projects the women worked on. Some of the women scientists' work may well have contributed to the Trinity bomb, but it has not been specifically identified. Myrtle Bachelder, for example, with advanced college degrees in chemistry, worked in one of the Los Alamos labs on chemical and emission spectroscopy (to determine the purity of metals used in the preparation of uranium and plutonium).[95] She joined the army in 1942, and after graduating from Officers' Candidate School in Iowa she received a commission as a second lieutenant in the WACs, where her first job was to escort a company of fifteen to twenty WACs, under secret orders, to Santa Fe and then to Los Alamos.[96]

A few women civilians with degrees in scientific and mathematic fields worked in the Los Alamos labs. Some came with their scientist husbands and were then hired on their own accounts. Male colleagues recruited others directly from universities or private science labs. Joseph Hirschfelder recruited Naomi Livesay to Los Alamos to work "on a war project." With advanced degrees in mathematics, she arrived at Los Alamos in February 1944 and began working on implosion calculations for the Trinity test. In addition to her own calculations, she supervised the GIS and civilians running the new IBM electric calculating machines day and night.[97]

A scant few anecdotes tell us that some women would have at least visited the Trinity site as part of their jobs in the transportation pool. A WAC sergeant, Margaret Swank, oversaw transportation at Los Alamos, so she made sure that at least some WACs received assignments driving cars and trucks for various jobs.[98] The very few anecdotes about the WACs in the driving pool run to stereotypes about women drivers. Kenneth Bainbridge's report of the Trinity test recounts a woman who worked at Los Alamos driving "a five-ton truck at the Trinity construction site. History has not recorded her name, but she is remembered for knocking down the only man who knew the layout of the 500 miles of electrical lines installed for the first test of the atomic bomb."[99] In another anecdote, scientist Philip Morrison, carrying the plutonium core from Los Alamos to the Trinity ranch house, where it was to be inserted into the device, recalled being terrified by the fast driving of the young woman driver.[100] Whether Morrison's terror was caused by the undeniably striking presence of the plutonium core in the backseat next to him or was actually a response to fast driving he did not clarify. In one of the only other anecdotes involving women at the Trinity site, a woman driver who had "trucked gasoline to the Trinity area" told physician Albert Bellamy, who was investigating the area's residual radiation in 1948, that she had suffered a uterine tumor and a "spleen condition" and was "actively wondering" if it might be due to her exposure to radiation in the area. Bellamy reported the query to James A. Jensen at the Atomic Energy Commission as they discussed "public relations and legal liability matters"—coded references to the public's exposure to radiations from the Trinity test. Bellamy presented the woman's statement as ridiculous (putting an exclamation mark after the "uterine tumor"), adding that the woman had, until recently, "a shoebox full of trinitite in her possession."[101]

No accounts in records I have seen name women at the Trinity site before or immediately after the test. The select honored guests invited to watch the Trinity test from a distance included no women. Mary Argo, who worked under Edward Teller in the Theoretical Physics Division, reported much later that she had been "officially invited to see the test." What that turned out to mean, however, was that she learned about the test (possibly from Teller) and she and her husband, Harold, drove to Chupadera Peak near Socorro, "about 30 miles from gz [ground zero]," where they watched the test through binoculars.[102] Some other women's memories about Trinity must also be read with care. In her account (a questionnaire filled out in 1991) for the first history of women workers on the Manhattan Project, *Their Day in the Sun*, Harryette Hunter Emmerson said that she was a WAC company commander at Los Alamos but with a degree in home economics, and that she also worked as a dietitian in the hospital. She recalled being "invited to attend the Trinity test," but she refused because "her sergeants had not been invited." As with Argo, Emmerson may have misremembered suggestions about where to view the test unofficially as an actual invitation to the test. But she also recalled that, although she did not go to the site the day before the test, she was there the day after. She recalled being allowed to walk into the crater carrying a Geiger counter, and she was impressed by the fact that the blast had turned the desert sand into glass of different colors, depending upon its impurities.[103] Although compelling, her account is highly improbable since no one *walked* into the crater the day after the test; those few who went in at all did so in lead-lined tanks. There are no documents about women at the Trinity site right after the test.

### Race and Ethnicity at the Trinity Site and the Manhattan Project

The number of people employed by the Manhattan Project grew very quickly in spite of the other competing demands for wartime labor, including the military draft. At its peak the Manhattan Project employed over 160,000 people. The town of Oak Ridge, originally expected to house 12,000 people, grew to 75,000 by the end of the war. At Hanford, the construction camp eventually housed 24,000 men and 5,000 women, with 900 hutments available for 10,000 more workers.[104] A second town, Richland, twenty-five miles south of Hanford, grew from its prewar population of about 200 farm-related people to 17,000 by the time the war ended, 6,000 of them working to operate the reactors and plants. At the end of the war Los Alamos employed 6,500 civilians and military personnel.

African Americans, Hispanic and Mexican Americans, and Native Americans worked for the Manhattan Project, most frequently as laborers. In Tennessee, the South's prevailing segregation system meant that at Oak

Ridge, whites and African Americans lived, ate, and relaxed in racially separate quarters, and the menial jobs almost always went to nonwhites. The state of Washington did not have legalized segregation, and at first officials at Hanford paid no attention to the practice even though early Manhattan Project officials hesitated to hire nonwhites until the military draft decreased the number of available white workers. As that happened, Manhattan Project officials also came under pressure from the Fair Employment Practices Commission to hire African Americans for the federally funded work. Thus encouraged, the DuPont Company, in charge of running Hanford, began hiring African Americans in the summer of 1943, eventually employing some 5,400.

As increasing numbers of African Americans joined the workforce at Hanford, whites moving up from the South for jobs with the Manhattan Project insisted on racial segregation, and Manhattan Project officials acquiesced. Historian Kate Brown points out that the majority of workers at Hanford did not come from the segregationist South and found the bathrooms, barracks, mess halls, and movie theaters designated for "whites" and others for "coloreds" surprising, even shocking.[105] Although a system of formal, legal segregation was not established at Hanford, officials nevertheless created separate living areas for African Americans in the newly expanding town of Richland, some thirty miles from the plutonium works at Hanford and eventually at Pasco, thirty-seven miles from Hanford. After sunset Blacks were not allowed to cross the bridge to Kenwick, and even in Pasco some places would not serve Blacks. The buses taking workers to Hanford were segregated until the NAACP protested, and finally in February 1944 DuPont integrated the buses.[106]

The African Americans who worked at Oak Ridge during the war lived in segregated quarters so removed from central areas that many of the white residents never realized the "Negro Village" existed. The hutments for Blacks had dirt floors, coal stoves, and no glass in the windows.[107] The civil engineer who oversaw construction at Hanford, Franklin Matthias, for a while resisted hiring Mexican American workers because of the expense of building separate facilities for a third racial group. He believed that the "Mexicans will not live with the Negroes and the Whites will not live with the Mexicans."[108] Only about one hundred Mexican Americans ended up being hired for the Hanford project, and they lived in refurbished buildings in the town of Pasco along with African Americans.

Historian Kate Brown's detailed study of life at Hanford underscores the racism. The DuPont Company worked hard to attract white professional workers during the war (and to retain them after). The company paid more than government wages but also sought to attract desired workers by providing lavish and cheap food and entertainment. For Christmas 1943, celebrations for whites at Hanford included dances in mess halls and a minstrel show with performers in blackface.[109] Work was segregated along with housing and other activities. Most African American and Mexican American men hired for the Manhattan Project sites worked as unskilled laborers on construction projects, and the women generally worked as cooks or maids.

At Los Alamos during and after the war most of the day laborers came from the Hispanic communities of the nearby towns of Española, Chimayo, Santa Cruz, San Ildefonso, Santa Clara, and San Felipe and from the surrounding Native American pueblos, four of which encircled Los Alamos: the Jemez Pueblo, the Pueblo de Cochiti, the Pueblo of San Ildefonso, and the Santa Clara Pueblo.[110] Official racial segregation did not exist at Los Alamos, but structural segregation did. The primarily Hispanic maintenance and construction workers and their families lived in trailers, and the hutment parks where many people squeezed into small spaces and bathrooms were sparse. In other ways, however, groups intermingled. Mexican American families sent their children to the Los Alamos schools, especially after the war. Historian Jon Hunner notes that while residents of Los Alamos demonstrated racial prejudices and nonwhite children in the schools were sometimes taunted, the schools had no official segregation. In the 1950s the children of the two African American families who lived on "the Hill" at Los Alamos already attended the area's schools before the *Brown v. Board of Education of Topeka* decision in 1954.[111] A few examples demonstrate the informal racial integration at Los Alamos. Tony Martinez, son of the famed potter from the San Ildefonso Pueblo, Maria Martinez, worked in the physics group at Los Alamos. Jack Aeby, the photographer, recalled that he "was really quite a good physicist among other things." Ed Rynd bunked below Martinez and they became friends. Popovi Martinez, another son of Maria Martinez and her painter husband, Juan Martinez, sometimes led the ritual dances at San Ildefonso with his face painted half yellow and half green. Drafted in 1944, he became an SED sent to Los Alamos, where he worked on the particle accelerator.[112]

Native American tribal members at first hoped that the new laboratory would provide steady employment for adults, schooling for children, and health care; to some extent those hopes materialized but in severely restricted ways. Early in the morning GI-driven buses drove from Los Alamos to the pueblos and the local villages, where workers boarded to go up the mountain to work for the day. Men worked "as drivers, carpenters, janitors, furnace stokers, plumbers and day laborers."[113] Native American women and Hispanic women worked at first as maids, nursemaids, cooks, and sometimes as food servers in the canteens. Laura Fermi recalled later that all of the men who had not been drafted, "all women who could leave their babies, all girls who could take time off from school, came to work on the mesa."[114] Adrienne Lowry, married to one of the radiochemists at Los Alamos, recalled that her maid, from one of the pueblos, once gave her as a gift one of the prized vases by Montoya Martinez from the San Ildefonso Pueblo.[115] Eventually some of the Native and Hispanic women began to be hired to work in the technical area, much to the annoyance of the scientists' wives, who complained about losing household help.

Some of the Hispanic men and women went to work on the site after the Manhattan Project appropriated their ranchland or small farms. Dimas Chavez recalled being a young boy allowed to enter the gates at Los Alamos, where his father worked for the Zia Company. Chavez spoke no English at first, and he told interviewers that his father never spoke about his work, but Chavez said proudly that nothing could have been accomplished at Los Alamos without "the blood, sweat and tears of all of the personnel, men and women, from the Zia Company." Chavez recalled plumbers, electricians, and workers who took care of the library and the hospitals. Some were ironworkers such as Louis G. Rojas, who later became sheriff of Los Alamos County, and Ben Lujan, who later became Speaker of the House in New Mexico.[116]

Did any of the Native Americans, Hispanics, or Mexican Americans working at Los Alamos contribute to the Trinity test? Some may have been involved with experiments for the test without going to the test site. Some may well have ferried materials to the test site. It is likely that Hispanics were among the two hundred New Mexicans working for the Ted Brown Company hired to construct the Trinity Base Camp. The records are unfortunately silent about names of any of the personnel making such contributions.

# Secrecy

Given the secrecy enshrouding the entire Manhattan Project, every effort was made to mask all relationships between Los Alamos and what was going in the northeast corner of the Alamogordo Bombing Range.[117] Groves, Oppenheimer, and the highest-ranking officials in Washington wanted no one to make a connection with the mysterious lab on the mountain near Santa Fe and the activities in the desert bombing range. Only four officials could have direct communication between Los Alamos and the Trinity site. All other communication had to be routed in complicated ways through several places so as to disguise any linkage between the two projects. Telephone calls between Los Alamos and Trinity went first to Denver, then to Albuquerque, then to San Antonio, New Mexico. In addition to the routing complexities, telephone communication was poor, and it was exceedingly difficult for speakers to hear each other. So, communications worked better via notes sent with truck drivers, especially as the number of trucks commuting between Los Alamos and Trinity increased from two to ten every evening.[118]

As soon as construction began, work crews, military police, scientists, and others at the site needed to communicate by radio. The B-29 crews participating in the test also needed radio frequency. It took months of effort on the part of the MED, but finally officials in Washington DC established what were to be the exclusive radio frequencies for each operation at Trinity. Inevitably, though, there were glitches. The frequency for the ground crew turned out to be the same as a railroad freight yard in San Antonio, Texas. The air crews shared the same frequency as the Voice of America. Bainbridge wrote later, "Anyone listening to the Voice of America from 6 a.m. on could also hear our conversations with the planes."[119]

The work at the Trinity site could not have been kept totally secret. Light in deserts carries far, and for months the construction at the site itself would have been illuminated for miles. With increasing numbers of truck convoys and automobiles driving to the area daily and then nightly, it would have been impossible to disguise that something big was going on. Even if drivers tried to bypass the towns by taking smaller, newly constructed roads, the dark could not entirely hide the dust that would have been stirred up by such traffic on the rough roads. The ranchers and the residents of the small towns surrounding the Trinity site must certainly have become aware of the increased numbers and frequency of truck traffic passing through their areas and back out into the desert. In the spring and summer of 1945, residents in the small towns of Socorro, Carrizozo, and Belen could hardly have overlooked the influx of vehicles coming and going day and night. Socorro had a commercial laundry and a general post office as well as stores selling gasoline, water, miscellaneous food supplies, soft drinks, and beer. The Illinois Distributing Company and Hammel Brewery Building, owned by Socorro residents Marcella and Clarence Hammel, provided beer and sodas to the men working at Trinity; Marvin R. Davis, with the military police, recalled going to Socorro almost every day to get the mail and buy beer to take back to his coworkers.[120] Men from Trinity also went regularly into Carrizozo to fill large gas and water containers and to pick up foods unavailable at the site. They bought beer at a favorite gas station with an attached restaurant and bar. Manhattan Project officials obviously forbade any talk or factual discussions about what was going on at the Trinity site. SED Felix DePaula said later that the servicemen received no explanation about their mission and, even so, had strict orders not to discuss anything about the camp with civilians, especially on their water and food supply runs into towns.[121]

It seems possible, however, that the men, bored with the routine of driving back and forth daily, bored with the scant knowledge allotted to them, grew to know and like the friendly townspeople in the gas station and grocery and liquor store, and they may well have exchanged more than a few noncommittal "hellos" and "goodbyes." The evening before the actual test, some GIS stopped for gas and supplies and advised the owner, Joe Miera, to watch at dawn for something he had never seen before.[122] Whether he watched or not and what he thought about any of it remains unknown.

## Spies

Four spies have been identified as working at Los Alamos during the war, two of them working on the Trinity bomb—Klaus Fuchs and Oscar Seborer—with Seborer actually attending the Trinity test. Fuchs watched it from afar. David Greenglass and Klaus Fuchs have been recognized as atomic spies since the 1950s, but it took until the mid-1990s for Theodore (Ted) Hall's name and involvement to become known and until 2020 before Oscar Seborer's name came to light. Greenglass transferred in August

1944 from Oak Ridge to Los Alamos, where his work included making molds for the lenses to set off the detonation in the plutonium bomb. An army sergeant in an SED group, Greenglass was a skilled machinist. His brother-in-law, Julius Rosenberg, persuaded Greenglass to give him information about the bomb design and its material, which Rosenberg then passed on to the Soviets. When the spying became known in the early 1950s, Greenglass's testimony against his sister, Ethel Rosenberg, helped condemn her to death. She and Julius died in the electric chair at Sing Sing Prison in June 1953. Greenglass served ten years in prison for his spying, the time reduced because of his aid to the prosecutors. Klaus Fuchs, a skilled nuclear physicist, left Germany when the Nazis came to power. He worked in nuclear physics in Canada and Britain, and migrated to America first to work on nuclear fission at Columbia University and then at Los Alamos, where he worked in the Theoretical Physics Division under Hans Bethe. Fuchs did not participate directly in the Trinity test, but he understood its physics and its political meanings, and he passed information about the implosion process and the plutonium bomb designs to the Soviets. Prosecuted in Britain after the war for his spying, Fuchs served time in prison and upon his release emigrated to Russia, where he became an honored scientist.[123]

Theodore Alvin Holtzberg, born in New York, changed his surname to Hall to evade the anti-Semitism rampant in so many American circles in the early twentieth century. One of the youngest scientists to be recruited to the Manhattan Project, Hall worked at Los Alamos on both the uranium and plutonium bombs. He left the United States after the war and worked in science in Britain the rest of his life. During and after the war he provided detailed descriptions to his handlers in the USSR of both atomic bomb designs and the processes for purifying plutonium. Although the American FBI suspected Hall of being a spy when material about him turned up in the Venona Files, they did not prosecute. The Venona Files, a clandestine program run by the U.S. Army's Secret Intelligence Service for thirty-seven years during World War II and the Cold War, decoded thousands of Soviet materials and in the process discovered the existence of spy rings in Britain and in the American Manhattan Project. To protect the Venona program, American authorities chose not to prosecute the suspected spies, so Ted Hall therefore was never charged with giving atomic secrets to the USSR.[124]

Scholars have just uncovered the presence of a fourth spy at Los Alamos: Oscar Seborer, who, using the Russian code name "Godsend," worked first at Oak Ridge and then at Los Alamos from 1944 to 1946. Like all of the spies except Fuchs, Seborer was a U.S. citizen; all of the spies held passionate convictions about left-wing causes, particularly about the need to help the Soviets. He studied electrical engineering at Ohio State College, and when he joined the army in October 1942, he was assigned to an SED unit. Using the alias Stuart Smith, Seborer worked first at Oak Ridge and then from 1944 to 1946 at Los Alamos, where he helped devise the explosive trigger for the plutonium bomb. Unlike the other identified atomic spies, Seborer participated directly in the Trinity test; as a Tech 5, he was part of a unit monitoring seismological effects.[125]

Historians and journalists remain divided about the value of the information the spies passed on to the USSR. Some experts believe that the work of the atomic spies indicates that the Soviets received much valuable information, but most think that the main effect of the American material was to speed up the Soviet atomic bomb by a few years. Just forty-nine months after Trinity, the Soviets detonated a nearly identical device in Central Asia, and both the rapidity of the Soviet bomb and its basic design seem to have come from scientific details spies provided about the Trinity bomb. Klaus Fuchs passed information about the upcoming test to his fellow spy, Harry Gold, in Santa Fe in early June 1945. The packet he passed to Gold included a detailed description and drawing of the plutonium implosion design, and that information was quickly transmitted to the USSR.[126]

The Trinity test remained a secret from the general U.S. public. The greatest factor in preserving that secrecy was undoubtedly the test site's location within an acknowledged and recognized military base. Curious townspeople, ranchers, sheepherders, and even potential spies had ready explanations for the increased traffic and the construction because the area had been in use as a bombing range since before the United States went to war. On an already known army base with ongoing and regular bombing tests, there was little need for local people to question additional activity, even the increasing activity in spring and summer 1945. To American citizens, especially ranching and farming citizens accustomed to minding their own business, it may also have seemed unpatriotic to question any comings and goings too closely. Holm Bursum, who had one of the largest ranches in the area—much of it north and northeast of the test, happened to be in the town of Socorro at the time of the test. Asked later by historian Ferenc Szasz what locals thought was going on at the site, Bursum said he had observed construction there; he had even observed workers erecting a tower. No one knew what was going on, "no one gave a damn. It was just part of the war effort."[127]

# FOUR

## Post-Test Events at the Trinity Site, 1946–67

The three days following the Trinity bomb test saw considerable activity at the test site. Many officials left quickly to return to Los Alamos, Washington DC, and elsewhere, but the focus now turned to the bombs for Japan, and scores of scientists, technicians, and other workers remained briefly on the site to retrieve equipment, conduct additional experiments, and take photographs. Trinity test director Bainbridge and two others designated themselves the "Going-In Board" to approve or deny entry to the area around ground zero. Several groups working on radiation measurements received permission to go to the crater area to collect earth samples that would be taken to labs for assessing the types and amounts of radioactivity. One Sherman tank, specially fitted, carried a new device—rockets "to which retrievable collectors were fastened" so that soil samples did not have to be gathered by humans.[1] In a less sophisticated approach, five men (SEDs and scientists) took turns gathering soil. One man drove the tank and the second scooped up soil samples through a trap door in the bottom of the tank. One unidentified army sergeant made three trips and received the highest radiation exposure officially recorded for anyone at the Trinity test: 13 roentgens per hour.[2] A photographer and radiological safety monitor went near ground zero several times to photograph Jumbo; a photographer went into the test area six times between late July and late October and received an official total count of 12.2 roentgens per hour. Six men went into the test area to retrieve neutron detectors.

In the four months after the test at least forty-six men identified as technical personnel and laborers remained on site gathering test equipment and putting up fencing. An additional seventy-one soldiers took turns on guard duty, many of them on horseback, riding or walking around the ground zero perimeter. Men and horses wore radiation-detecting dosimeter badges. (According to a later report, none received anything but the most minimal amount.)[3] In one account, as many as one thousand people may have been at the test site between July 16 and the end of 1946 as scientists, technicians, and military personnel but also as visitors. Some of the scientists took their wives and children on a tour of the area near ground zero "to view the green glass called 'trinitite' which covered the crater floor."[4] In addition, scientists and technicians who remained at the site conducted various tests and studies of its residual radiation.

## 1947 "Urchin" Experiments and 1967 Cleanup

After the Trinity test some people apparently still expected that there would be a second atomic bomb test. In a mysterious and unidentified memo in the U.S. Department of Energy OpenNet archives, the writer addressed Roger S. Warner Jr. and Henry W. Newson (whom I have not been able to further identify) about the desirability of having a second test soon. He had interviewed as "large a fraction as possible of the people involved in the last Trinity test," and their opinion was "nearly unanimous" that early next summer there should be another test, this time of a "levitated gadget." The bomb should again be mounted on a tower but higher than the original one.[5] No second atomic bomb test appears to have been seriously planned, for there is nothing about such ideas in any material I have discovered. However, the Trinity test area was used intermittently in other ways by Los Alamos scientists, the Atomic Energy Commission (AEC), and the military in the two decades after the test. The army used Jumbo for some kinds of tests (as described below). Many groups came to the Trinity area and environs to investigate the residual radiations (also described below).

One important set of experiments for which detailed evidence remains available involved creating three bunkers with underground compartments to test different kinds of "initiators"—devices designed to set off a plutonium bomb. Los Alamos began to plan the tests in 1946 after Groves secured permission and funding. Men from the H. C. Gee Company (the principal civilian company that had done construction at Los Alamos from the beginning) began digging three bunkers, each forty feet underground, southeast, northeast, and northwest of the crater area. The tests were conducted in the fall of 1947.[6]

Scientists wanted to experiment with different designs of initiators—the small devices containing radioactive materials (polonium in particular) that in the experiments were intended to detonate the high explosives substituted for an actual plutonium core. The chamber in each bunker consisted of an octagon fourteen feet in diameter, with walls two feet thick and twelve feet high, ten feet below ground level. Each was covered with forty feet of dirt and sand; each had a vertical timbered shaft from the top of the dirt mound down to a steel door mounted in the side of the chamber.[7] The bunkers also contained equipment to measure the neutrons released in the experiments.[8]

Los Alamos scientists conducted two tests in the fall of 1947. The experiment in the northeast chamber proved successful; the southeast chamber failed to detonate and scientists dubbed it the "sleeping beauty." Following that failure, the experimenters decided to move the third test to Los Alamos, so they covered all three bunkers at the Trinity site with soil and tried to forget about them. One additional set of actions taken at the time of those experiments but little noted then and forgotten about for twenty years involved gathering up bags of trinitite from the crater area and storing them in the bunkers.

Early in 1952 the commanding officer at Holloman Air Force Base asked if there were still AEC materials or installations at the Trinity site. The query appears to have jolted memories and spurred detailed internal exchanges among Los Alamos officials about the 1947 failed experiments and their bunkers. Given the hopes of Park Service people to preserve the Trinity site and given that authorized and unauthorized people visited the site, official fears about its safety—and possible lawsuits—escalated. Raemer Schreiber, the acting director of the Weapons Division at Los Alamos, reviewed the situation for Donald P. Dickason, the acting director of the Security Division, although with confusingly contradictory statements. Three areas outside of the ground zero fence, each enclosed by its own fence, posed different kinds of danger. One bunker contained no dangerous scientific or classified material, but its open shaft would be a hazard to anyone climbing on the mound. The shafts on the other two mounds had been filled in with sand just before the experiments, so no one considered them dangerous in that respect. The problem was in the second chamber, the one to the southeast, because it still contained materials from the failed experiment, namely a "high explosives initiator."[9] In 1952

Los Alamos scientists remained perplexed about why the experiment had failed: why the high explosive had not been set off in 1947. Adding to the worry, the current condition of the initiator was unknown.

In explaining to Dickason, Schreiber contradicted himself in several places in the memo. He noted that originally, the "Urchin's" radioactive strength was very high, but they now believed that it would have "decayed to be less than a fraction of a curie." However, Schreiber then added, confusingly, "In case the H.E. were detonated, this radioactivity would spread around the chamber. The health hazard due to this amount of radioactivity is such that a person entering the chamber after the H.E. were detonated would be in some danger." He continued: "The principal hazard is due to the unexploded H.E. charge. There is absolutely no hazard due to radioactivity or H.E. as long as the mound is undisturbed." Schreiber said that Los Alamos would support destroying or shutting up the chamber, but he warned that "it is clear that any operations in this area must take into account the H.E. and radioactivity hazards."

Schreiber said that nothing classified remained in the bunker but then contradicted himself again, adding: "The Urchin is a former weapon component. Although it is now obsolete, its description is still classified Secret. The H.E. charge is not a weapon part." Although some remain curious about the reason the experiment failed, he noted that "the techniques used for this experiment are now obsolete." The experiment in the northeast chamber had been a success, and there was little later concern in the AEC about it: "There is no classified material in this area unless the presence of traces of radioactive material (polonium) is regarded as classified information."[10]

However strong the concerns among some high-ranking Los Alamos officials in 1952 were, it is an indication of the general confusion around control and oversight of the Trinity area that it took until 1967 before Los Alamos sent a crew to enter the bunker, test for radiation, examine the unexploded device, and then blow it all up.[11]

### 1967 Excavation of the Bunkers

In February 1967 two men from the nuclear effects branch of the Army Missile Test and Evaluation Directorate at the White Sands Missile Range investigated the external remains of the three 1947 bunkers. They reported that the mounds remained enclosed by a chain-link fence about eight feet high. The fences had no gates, but because of damage in places, entry was not difficult: "One area has sand drifts high enough that one could walk over the fence into either the bunker area or into TS [Trinity site]." They discovered that one of the mounds "has an open vertical shaft about 48 feet deep at the bottom which appears to be an open door to the concrete chamber."[12] Perhaps spurred to action by the White Sands Missile Range report or from the Atomic Energy Commission's own growing fears about possible lawsuits, a few months later a group from the engineering and health departments at Los Alamos, along with men and equipment from the Zia Company that handled construction in Los Alamos, conducted "Operation Sleeping Beauty." The group went to the Trinity site to investigate the 1947 bunkers.[13] They planned to level off the mounds of dirt covering the three underground chambers, to "locate, excavate, and remove ten containers of crater scrapings that were buried over twenty years ago," and to make "a radiation survey of the entire area within the fence surrounding the crater area." In addition, some of the crew had instructions to open the second underground chamber and assess if possible why the "Urchin" had failed in 1947.

The Zia Company, given its longtime ties with Los Alamos, provided men to operate the heavy equipment (Fes R. Gentry, Andrew Red Jackson, and Wayne Wells) and men who were asked to excavate, partly by hand (Tony J. Maestas and Felix E. Maez). Zia workers also included Louis Rojas, Otis Sissel, and Art Sena.[14] The head of Los Alamos, Norris Bradbury, also attended the excavation, along with one woman (otherwise unidentified): Virginia Lees. At the end of the operation they returned to Los Alamos along with Donald P. MacMillan and Robert J. Lanter, both scientists at Los Alamos who had worked on the early initiator tests. The operation included an elaborate procedure with military police mounting roadblocks around the site. Part of the operation involved taking radiation measurements around the Trinity site and within the bunkers. Advisors on radiological safety Fred L. Fey, Charles D. Blackwell, Jack R. Richard, and Gerald D. Eagan conducted a radiological survey within the fenced area; Richard and Eagan surveyed the crater area within the fence.[15] Opening the "sleeping beauty" chamber required great care: "A lengthy process was used to move a large counter across the room to make access to the gadget of concern and to provide an opening for the approximately 100 lbs of HE (high explosives) to be used in destroying the apparatus in the chamber."[16]

Once the bunker had been opened and declared safe and the trini-tite had been removed, explosives experts from Los Alamos entered and strung detonator cords out across the desert to a safe firing location. They placed one hundred pounds of high explosives inside the bunker and blew everything up. The Blackwell report concluded with a reassurance that the area was safe "from an industrial safety viewpoint." The northwest bunker, the intended site of a third experiment, was also blown up because any future experiments would be conducted at a closer and more suitable area at Los Alamos.[17]

A few months later, Bradbury, who had become the director of Los Alamos when Oppenheimer stepped down, sent a short report to L. P. Gise, manager of the AEC's Albuquerque office.[18] He reported that the area had been backfilled, leveled, and left in a presentable condition, and no concerns remained about excessive radiation exposures from the bunkers. Bradbury warned that Los Alamos could not give "informed advice" about the "overall advisability of limited or full public access to the Site." Gise then gave guarded advice to officials at the White Sands Missile Range about the radiation dangers at the Trinity site. He agreed with Los Alamos that "visitors to the proposed national monument would not, under any credible circumstances, receive a significant exposure to ionizing radiation." There was some danger that workmen for the Park Service might conceivably receive more than the allowable limit. Gise suggested alternatively fencing off and restricting access to any areas around ground zero "with radiation levels of 2 mR/hr." He added that the "two small spots of contamination outside of the restricted zone" where radiation levels were above 2 milliroentgens per hour (mR/hr) could be decontaminated or covered with fresh earth, and then all could be opened to unrestricted access as far as radiation hazards were concerned.[19]

## Jumbo

The 214-ton steel container named "Jumbo" exemplifies a low point when the lab scientists expected the bomb test might "fizzle." Leaders debated ways to save the precious plutonium in case the detonation failed, and after rejecting various ideas, their solution was to have a small, scaled-down explosion in a large containment vessel that would capture the plutonium. Although some later accounts attribute the decision to hold the test in a giant containment vessel to scientists' worries about scattering plutonium around the countryside, that was not the reason for Jumbo. Plutonium was so precious and rare as these discussions took place in 1944 that, as Bainbridge recalled, "recovery of the precious fissionable material in case of failure became one of the main preoccupations."[20] This was especially a concern of General Groves, who was always conscious of costs and who grumbled that after the war he would face the wrath of a Senate committee "if he lost a billion dollars worth of plutonium."[21]

Some half dozen Los Alamos scientists worked on early calculations and also on the design and engineering of Jumbo.[22] With those finalized, Oppenheimer wrote to the heads of steel companies with specifications for the size and construction of the object he wanted built but received only negative replies about the feasibility of such a project in the middle of the war, with materials scarce and the reasons for the project so secret. At last the Babcock and Wilcox Corporation in Barberton, Ohio, with experience making boilers for the navy, accepted the job in August 1944. They completed the gargantuan cylindrical steel container (twenty-five feet long, twelve feet in diameter, with walls fourteen inches thick) in the spring of 1945 at a cost of about $20 million. A special train brought Jumbo from Barberton, Ohio, to Pope, New Mexico. Jumbo weighed so much that several of the railroad trestles between the Ohio plant where it was manufactured and New Mexico suffered damage and afterward had to be rebuilt.[23] Jumbo arrived by rail at the little-used railroad siding in Pope, New Mexico, in May 1945, where SEDs unloaded it onto a specially built sixty-four-wheel trailer and oversaw its transport overland to the Trinity site. Local ranchers and townspeople must have caught glimpses of the bizarre sight, and it may have helped provide an explanation for curious citizens to know that the navy was involved in projects at the Alamogordo Army Base, and Jumbo did have resemblances to a submarine. After the war local residents sometimes joked that they had believed the work at the Trinity site had been to build submarines.[24]

Jumbo arrived at the Trinity site well after the decision had been made not to use it. Scientists' confidence in the ultimate success of a larger-scale bomb test increased throughout 1945, and anxieties about the scarcity of plutonium lessened. In the end the scientists who protested that using a containment vessel would interfere with crucial test measurements won out. As Kenneth Bainbridge wrote in his later account, "good blast information was one of the main objectives of the test. It was important to study the blast effects under conditions that could be translated into combat use conditions to obtain the maximum military effect of the bomb."[25] Furthermore, if the detonation blew Jumbo up, the fragments would be a serious hazard to gauge lines, equipment, and personnel.

Although some accounts have Jumbo being raised on a tower, Jim Eckles, a White Sands Public Affairs employee and expert on much of the history of the test site, sets the record straight: in the center of a seventy-foot steel tower eight hundred yards from the tower for the bomb, Jumbo was "lowered onto a concrete pad with a dimple in it" that accommodated Jumbo's curved end. Thus it was standing upright for the test, resting between the legs of the tower.[26] The force of the Trinity blast did not harm Jumbo even though it destroyed the steel tower around it, and the giant container remained standing in the same upended position for almost a year.

Sources differ about what happened to Jumbo next. It was apparently used for eight test firings of five-hundred-pound "general purpose" bombs.[27] Eckles writes that on April 16, 1946, at 11:30 a.m. "with Jumbo still standing on end, eight 500-pound bombs were exploded inside it. It was supposedly done to dispose of the bombs."[28] Another source puts the "improperly conducted explosives test of the container's design" in 1947.[29] The military official who reported the effects of the bombs to his commander wrote that Jumbo lost both ends "and fragments were thrown as far as three-quarters of one mile. A piece estimated to weigh over fifteen tons landed 750 feet from the site."[30] This was done without consulting Los Alamos, and officials there were upset. The commander at Sandia suggested that the steel in Jumbo be salvaged, but no one acted on that. Jumbo remained on the site, partially buried. At some point its steel bands were stolen. In July 1960 Norman R. Banda, an officer at White Sands Missile Range, wrote to the headquarters troop commander at the base about Jumbo: it was a "single cast metal cylinder that resembles a thermos bottle insert. It is approx. 20 to 25 feet in length, 8 to 10 in diameter, and the walls are 8 to 10 inches thick." It currently rested "in a hole in the desert gathering rust" in the northwest corner of the Trinity site, outside the fence surrounding the site.[31]

In 1960 the Chamber of Commerce officials in Socorro, about fifty-two miles from the Trinity test site, wanted to "establish a historical monument to the first atomic or nuclear test" and hoped to include Jumbo among the exhibits at their envisioned "Atom Park."[32] Banda explained to his commander that although Jumbo did not appear in the property records of

White Sands Missile Range, it might be under military jurisdiction. It had little or no monetary value, so he recommended donating it to the Socorro Chamber of Commerce.[33] For reasons unexplained in the records, this did not happen; Jumbo remained at the Trinity site, although in the 1970s someone at White Sands had it moved to a gate outside of ground zero.[34] On visitors' days in the twenty-first century Jumbo remains a historic relic at the Trinity site, although considerably damaged by bombs and weather.

## Trinitite

When the immediate shock and awe of watching the first atomic bomb test wore off, scientists at the site saw that a "very slight saucer-like depression" now surrounded the tower and explosion area, and that crater area was encircled for several hundred yards by a glassy covering, creating the effect of "a lake of green glass."[35] At first scientists called the glassy layer "atomsite" but later changed the name to "trinitite."[36] Aerial photos taken twenty-eight hours after the test showed the trinitite layer extending out with a radius of at least three hundred meters, or maybe as many as four hundred meters. Most of the trinitite was green and some was light blue from iron in the sand, but some was also red and yellow from copper.[37]

Early explanations say the heat of the explosion fused the sand particles in the crater and they hardened into trinitite. A 2005 reassessment from two scientists at Los Alamos presented new arguments: the explosion of the plutonium in the bomb created the trinitite. The force of the blast threw sand into the air where small "semi-glassy agglomerations" were formed, some of which became "solid trinitite beads." This occurred in the air rather than once the materials fell back to the ground. Other "molten droplets" "rained down" to coalesce as the solid layer of trinitite around the bomb site.[38] That report is the first that makes sense of the memory of Rex Edward Keller, who had been a radiation monitor stationed some eighteen miles from the test center. Keller reported in a much later and quite confusing interview that on September 1946, Seth Neddermeyer, who worked in the implosion division at Los Alamos testing explosives, asked him to get rid of the radioactive materials at Trinity. Keller described the materials as "little round balls the size of a golf ball" and recalled that he threw them into a lake.[39]

We have many differing accounts of how the trinitite was handled (or not handled) over the next decades. The muddled and contradictory statements clarify one point at least: no one kept official records of the trinitite even if many wanted it removed. In spite of various removal plans and several actions, the Los Alamos scientists studying the creation of the trinitite found samples of it as small "spheroids" about two millimeters in diameter still at the site in 2005.

After the test, the exotic, colored glass–like material immediately attracted the attention of everyone visiting the site, and people took home samples as souvenirs. Some turned it into jewelry. A New Mexico newspaper just as the war ended carried a photograph of "the lovely Pat Burrage" holding jewelry made of "atomsite."[40] Los Alamos SED Robert J. S. Brown took home a sample of the trinitite and had it fashioned into a bolo tie that he still proudly displayed in a 2017 interview.[41] Former secretary of the interior Harold Ickes asked the National Park Service (NPS) to send him some trinitite as his own personal souvenir.[42] For decades after the test, businesses around New Mexico hawked pieces of trinitite; a Chevron gasoline station in Socorro sold samples to its customers for fifty cents.[43] Even in 2018, homemade signs outside the Trinity site entrance advertised "trinitite for sale down the road."

Official groups tried to collect samples of the trinitite over the years. Late in 1945 Park Service officials sought samples to include in an exhibit in the hoped-for museum on the site, but army officials refused.[44] In another account, the NPS tried to obtain one hundred pounds to be sent "in a safe and suitable container for preservation" to the NPS Regional Office in Santa Fe.[45] Johnwell Faris, superintendent of the nearby White Sands National Monument, wrote several times to NPS officials in hope of obtaining permission to display trinitite in the museum at the monument, but NPS superintendent M. R. Tillotson rebuked him: the trinitite was "entirely extraneous to the story of the [White Sands] monument. . . . It would be just as illogical to exhibit a small model of an atomic bomb at Bandelier National Monument, simply because the area is close to Los Alamos."[46]

## Radioactivity of the Trinitite

The radioactivity of the trinitite worried many different groups for decades, but the numerous studies contained little agreement about its radioactivity and any dangers it posed. In the 1967 project that blew up the decades-earlier experimental bunkers on the Trinity site, investigators removed bags of trinitite from the underground bunkers. They found that the pieces with the highest counts of beta, gamma, and alpha activities were those with the dullest surfaces; those with the highest glass (the ones most desirable as souvenirs) produced the lowest counts.[47]

In late March 1967 a Los Alamos investigator "pushed for time" sent a cursory handwritten note by telecom to his bosses reporting that he had found "10 garbage cans in bunker. Pretty high count. Contents looks like ashes. Cans are deteriorated. Propose bringing 50 gal drum from Los Alamos, placing cans in drum and returning it to Los Alamos."[48] A few months later another investigation by Los Alamos officials indicated that "at true ground zero (buried beneath approximately 14″ of top soil) radiation levels as high as 12 m/r continue to exist."[49] A different investigation and report from the spring of 1967 focused on radiation within the fenced area and concluded that all "activity" at Trinity came from the trinitite, not from the air or soil.[50] Those investigators reported that the highest rates of radioactivity (gamma radiation) were "proportional to the amount and depth of trinitite in that area." They found "large quantities of trinitite on the surface" and noted that it was conceivable "that a person visiting Trinity Site could pick up as much as 1 kg of trinitite in less than an hour. If he were to take this quantity of trinitite home, it would constitute a source of radiation." But the report's final conclusions sought to reassure: it would be virtually impossible to receive enough external or internal exposure from alpha or beta-gamma radiation from the trinitite to be harmful. (One official report did advise guides who spent forty hours or more a week within the fenced areas to wear a radiation dosimeter and keep a record of exposure.)[51]

### Trinitite Removal History

The responses of Manhattan Project officials and then Atomic Energy Commission officials pertaining to the trinitite are not easily traced in the records. The officials worried about possible radiation dangers from the fused glass and organized several attempts over the years to collect and remove all of the trinitite. The records of those attempts are often unclear or inaccurate about when and how much was actually dug up and what was done with it. Apart from Rex Edward Keller's memory of throwing some trinitite into a lake, the earliest report about digging up the trinitite comes from Jack Aeby, best known for his dramatic color photographs of the fireball as it expanded in the seconds after the bomb's detonation.

In an interview decades later Aeby recalled that a few weeks after the test "one of our jobs was to go down and mine the crater, [be]cause the idea was that there were probably enough neutrons there to produce some very interesting isotopes. So we mined all that nice surface material—that glassy stuff that was formed as much as we could—and we mined a truckload of barrels of that. I suspect it was a couple of tons actually, of material. We went down with shovels and put it in." The film badges Aeby and the crew wore "got blacker than the ace of spades."[52] Unclear about what happened to the trinitite next, Aeby remembered that it was "stored in a bunker at GZ and then the Army bulldozed it under." At that same time someone from Los Alamos dug up a sample to be preserved for a future museum at the Trinity site. They then covered the sample with a simple, small roof shelter (about 20 by 50 feet) approximately 250 feet from ground zero.

In December 1948 a small group from Los Alamos and two representatives of a contractor company visited the crater area to investigate the radioactivity of the trinitite. Harry O. Whipple from the Los Alamos Health Division reported that 90 percent of the total radioactivity in the crater area could be found in the fused trinitite layer occupying a rough circular area of about 250 yards in radius, averaging about one-third inch thick.[53] His report proposed that two subcontractors who wanted experience before attending the upcoming hydrogen bomb test at Eniwetok in the Pacific be assigned the job of raking up the "fused layer." Whipple expected this to yield about 1,500 cubic yards of material that would then be mixed into concrete, and the concrete would be poured as a slab "either in the central excavation or in a separately dug hole." The contractors would then place earth over the concrete to "reduce radiation intensities to negligible levels. Presumably one foot of earth will be sufficient." After that, they would plow the entire area within the fence, burying "all material remaining on the surface to a depth of 12 to 14 inches." They would compact the soil and seed it with "some plant capable of maintaining a ground cover under the climatic conditions existing in this desert area." They estimated that this would "lock up permanently" 90 percent of the radioactivity in the area, and the remaining 10 percent would be rendered safe by being covered with soil and plants.

That project was never carried out (for reasons unexplained in any sources I have located), and for several years the trinitite continued to cause occasional worry at the AEC. When the army resumed control of the Trinity area in 1948, AEC lawyers warned that the commission might still have legal liability if the trinitite caused people harm. The general manager of the AEC wrote a warning to the secretary of the air force in December 1950: "Within the crater and extending for a radius of about 600 feet from the crater, there is enough radioactivity to present a strong presumption of a hazard. Dust-borne radioactive trinitite from the crater is being scattered by wind over an area extending several miles from the crater. Inhalation of this radioactive material could constitute a significant hazard to humans."[54] The AEC asked his approval for "appropriately disposing of the trinitite in the bomb crater and adjacent area." Nothing was accomplished at that time, however, and two years later, in the spring of 1952, AEC worries about the radioactivity at Trinity became more acute.[55]

In April 1952, at a conference in Washington DC attended by New Mexico members of Congress, representatives of the Department of Defense, the AEC, and the National Park Service decided unanimously that the test site area should be preserved as a National Monument. However, they also agreed that it would not be feasible to develop the monument for public use quickly because it was surrounded by an actively used bombing range and also "because of the hazards to public health and safety of the test site itself."[56] They meant the trinitite, some of which would be preserved for tourism while the rest would be disposed of. Conference members decided that the modest shelter then protecting the small sample of trinitite needed to be improved. The roof would be repaired and siding would be added all the way to the ground; the siding would then be banked with sand for at least one foot above ground level. Debris such as cans and thistle would be removed. Tourists would not be allowed to enter the shelter shed, but it would be designed to allow scrutiny of the "best remaining sample of trinitite."[57] The next month, on May 20, 1952, the same representatives toured the actual Trinity site to firm up their plans.[58]

Conference attendees approved a plan that the following year, in the spring of 1953, the AEC would bulldoze the first six inches of trinitite and haul it away to be buried (in a place unspecified in the report). Then the AEC would seed the ground with native grasses.[59] The entire crater around ground zero was to be enclosed with a tight fence "at the earliest practicable date," and no one would be permitted to enter the grounds within the fence. The air force would protect the area.[60] Work on those plans began and was completed that summer of 1953. The AEC hired an Albuquerque construction company, Campbell and Kay, to scrape up and bury the trinitite. The company then planted grass and rehabilitated the small shed, sheltering a small sample of the trinitite. When that work was completed, the AEC regarded its activity at the Trinity site as ended.[61]

In the summer and fall of 1953 letters between National Park Service officials and the AEC as well as a few newspaper articles expressed hopes that the Trinity site would be opened to the public.[62] As chapter 6 documents, the site was not turned over to the National Park Service but remained under the jurisdiction of the War Department (with some rights still allocated to the AEC).[63]

The plans and actions in the early 1950s continued to raise grumbling and objections.[64] Thomas Shipman, irascible head of the postwar Health Division at Los Alamos, consistently insisted that there was no reason to spend money decontaminating the crater area since there was no danger "from having people pick up pieces of trinitite as souvenirs and carry them away in their pockets."[65] According to Shipman, sometime around 1949 members of the Health Division had collected ten to twenty pounds of the trinitite in cardboard boxes, and he assured the AEC's worried attorney that storing ten to twenty pounds of the trinitite in individual metal containers posed no health hazards whatsoever.[66]

Confusion remains about what actually happened to the trinitite. In February 1967 two officials from the "Nuclear Effects Branch of the Army Missile Test and Evaluation Directorate" at the White Sands Missile Range visited the Trinity site to locate the trinitite and measure its radioactivity.[67] They contacted people in the AEC's Albuquerque office, AEC people at the Nevada office, people at Los Alamos, and the vice president of what had been the Campbell and Kay Construction Company (later renamed the Allen Campbell Construction Company) to try to recreate the history of the trinitite removal. Those sources recalled that the "hottest" material had been placed in steel drums and buried shortly after the test, so "it may be advisable to determine where this material was buried and if it is reasonably accessible, it should be excavated for analysis."[68] In the course of their historical research, the two investigators also learned the story of the trinitite material that had been left underground in the three bunkers built for "Urchin" tests in 1946, bunkers that still existed as earthen mounds around the Trinity fence. Finally, they were also told that "topsoil" and trinitite gathered up in a 1953 operation had been buried in "mounds" around the site. They explored and found thirty-two mounds around ground zero with trinitite in all, but not in significant quantities because "it appears that the attempt to bury the trinitite was not too successful as the deposition of the trinitite in the mounds is probably less than what is remaining dispersed on the top of the ground in certain areas within the fence."[69]

As memories were jarred about the earlier "Urchin" experiments (and their failure), so were memories about the high explosives that had been part of those experiments and the storage of substantial amounts of the radioactive trinitite in those bunkers. This underscores how poorly certain kinds of records were kept in the months (and years) after the Trinity test. The pressure to quickly calculate the test results and to improve the bombs being readied for Japan mitigated against careful reports of some aspects of the test, especially the resultant trinitite. No one kept careful track of what happened to that trinitite in the ensuing decades, and it was primarily the memories of the few persons who participated in the early tests and who were still around Los Alamos in the late 1960s that helped reconstruct some of what had happened.[70] When investigators opened the "sleeping beauty" bunker in 1967, they discovered ten thirty-gallon cans "filled with contaminated waste" (e.g., trinitite) stored in the chamber. They then excavated those cans and trucked them to the "contaminated dump" at Los Alamos.[71] Trinitite, however, still remained at the ground zero area because, as noted above, scientists were able to study samples in 2005.

## Radiological Warfare and the Trinity Site

By August 1948 the AEC no longer gave the Trinity site serious consideration for further atomic bomb tests. Noting vaguely that it had "served its useful purpose," the AEC agreed that the area could be returned to the military. The Pacific Ocean now seemed a better site for bomb tests, but a continental "proving ground" also stirred official interest especially in the western United States. By 1951 the Nevada Test Site opened for its decades of nuclear testing.[72] Although official desire to use the Trinity site for bomb tests dwindled, the site attracted considerable interest for some years among those interested in radiological warfare (RW).

When American civilian and military leaders realized that the new radiological products from fission might be used as weapons of war even if not in the form of an atomic bomb, institutions old and new began intensive investigation into how that could be achieved. The very early interest in the possibilities of using fission products as weapons developed simultaneously with the creation of the Manhattan Project. Among its several responsibilities, the Metallurgical Lab ("Met Lab"), created early in 1942 on the University of Chicago campus, oversaw research into atomic chain reactions for an atomic bomb.[73] Its Health Division, established that summer, studied the hazards of radiation and toxic chemicals, developed radiation detectors and dosimeters, and sought ways to measure workers' radiation exposures. As its focus expanded, the Met Lab gained four additional sections: biological research, medical research, health physics, and a military section that studied radiological warfare.[74] Met Lab scientists simultaneously studied the military uses of fission products and also how to protect soldiers from those products. With obvious uses in defense and offense, much of its research centered on the inhalation of radioactive materials—especially dusts and aerosols.[75]

After the war, civilian and military groups in astonishing array and diversity studied the potential of RW. Interest and funding soared in the United States from early 1947 until the early 1950s among civilian officials (especially at the Atomic Energy Commission), army and navy officials, elected political leaders, universities across the nation, and civilian agencies such as the RAND Corporation. As soon as it was created in January 1947, the Atomic Energy Commission devoted attention and money to RW. At its October 1948 meeting the Advisory Committee in the Division of Biology and Medicine had an "extensive discussion of radiological warfare" during which "the importance of intensive work in this field in a relatively short time was stressed."[76] To reduce competition, key officials in the AEC and the military created a new group to study radiological warfare in 1948. The AEC-NME (National Military Establishment) RW panel (shortened to the "Joint Panel") met several times a year, investigating different types of radiation as weapons, dispersion methods, and testing sites until it was disbanded in 1950.

Research into radiological warfare meshed readily with older and expanding programs in chemical warfare and biological warfare.[77] A dense tangle of civilian and military institutions participated in chemical, biological, and radiological warfare (in the shorthand of the day, "CBR warfare"); the groups paid close attention to each other and followed developments attentively as generous funding flowed. Sometimes the groups worked together, especially in field trials of their "munitions."[78]

The frenzied interest in radiological warfare began to decline in the mid-1950s as the army lost interest because of its hopes now placed in the military potential of the hydrogen bomb, as the navy focused on the potential of nuclear-bomb-carrying submarines, and as the air force focused on its growing fleet of nuclear bombers. In the spring of 1950 the Joint Chiefs of Staff recommended against any further major investment in RW, and the Joint Panel disbanded; experts generally concluded that radiological warfare held too little promise and should be reduced in scope or even be abandoned altogether. One reason that the appeal of radiological weapons waned is still shocking today: because they did such long-lasting damage to industry and to buildings. Chemical weapons held greater appeal because they did not poison the land long for the victorious occupying forces. An article in the *Denver Post* in 1954 noted that the "potential military value of GB [sarin] gas . . . is greater in some respects than even the atomic weapons. . . . An invader can wipe out life in a city and take it over intact—its industries, utilities, transportation and power plants are ready to be used again in a few hours, instead of being ruined and radioactive."[79]

Evidence linking the Trinity site to this short spurt of interest in radiological warfare is sketchy. One compelling piece of evidence, however, is the involvement of Joseph Hamilton in the very earliest Trinity radiation studies. Hamilton, one of the best-known radiation experts in the country, became one of the most vocal promoters of radiological warfare research and testing during World War II until his untimely death from leukemia in 1957.[80] Hamilton's early work emphasized the importance of inhalation as a radiological weapon. His 1943 study included five pages titled "A Brief Review of the Possible Applications of Fission Products in Offensive Warfare" that gave special attention to inhalation: "The two principal channels by which humans may become internally infested are the lungs and digestive tract. It has already been demonstrated experimentally that a very large proportion of the long life fission products are retained for protracted periods of time in the lungs." A secret report he wrote in spring 1943 summarizing "some of my notions concerning the military application of the long life fission products," concluded with him urging "tests with relatively large quantities of fission products."[81] In 1946, in the transition from the wartime Manhattan Project to the civilian AEC, Hamilton argued that the military needed to conduct a full-scale investigation into radiological warfare. He urged particular attention to the uses of "RW agents" through inhalation, ingestion, or external exposure.[82]

The Trinity test provided exactly what Hamilton and other early radiological warfare researchers wanted: a site to study the residual quantity of fission products in the dust, soil, plants, and animals of the surrounding desert. Hamilton sent a four-page memo in the fall of 1947 to Stafford Leake Warren urging serious study of the Trinity test site's radiation.[83] He reminded Warren that as much as one kilogram of plutonium might have been spread over a one-hundred-square-mile area from the Trinity site. It was exceedingly important, he argued, to understand and to be able to predict the chain of events if large land areas became contaminated with fission products because of accidents "or military action."[84]

Warren, after his medical work for the Manhattan Project, became the first dean of the new medical school at UCLA that was founded just after the war. He focused many of his earliest energies on creating and finding funding for a secret "atomic energy project" (AEP) at the medical school. Studying the radiation remaining from the Trinity bomb became some of the earliest investigations of the aptly named "Alamogordo" division of the AEP.[85] In his later oral history, Warren recalled that the AEC was reluctant to fund that study of the residual Trinity radiation because "they were afraid we might find something. And I said, 'Well, you've got to look, because if there is something, you'd better find it and prevent further things, or pay off, and face it before there is some scandal.'"[86] The UCLA AEP does not appear to have been involved in any way, certainly not directly, with radiological warfare interests. But their half dozen studies of the Trinity radiation over the next two decades would have held considerable interest for groups with such concerns. (I provide more details about those reports in the final chapter of this book.) The only remotely direct link I have found between radiological warfare research and the UCLA AEP is that Warren, always interested in increasing funding, persuaded Brigadier General James McCormack Jr. of the Military Application Division of the Atomic Energy Commission to fund some of the studies of the radiation at Trinity. McCormack's approval began, in the words of nuclear medicine pioneer and historian J. N. Stannard, "a decades-long association of the [UCLA atomic energy] project with the weapons-testing program, especially in the area of terrestrial phenomena."[87] It is also worth noting in the context of radiological warfare interests at the time that one of the earliest studies conducted by the AEP group, published as UCLA-32 Trinity report, noted that one of their field assignments was to collect "data useful to Military and Defense organizations."[88]

At its October 1948 meeting the AEC decided that any radiological warfare work not done at the Chicago Toxicity Lab would be parceled out elsewhere.[89] The sites first considered included several of the early Manhattan Project work. Oak Ridge became one of the sites of some early tests of radiological warfare materials, and Edwin McMillan, who headed the "initiator section" of the Weapons Physics Division at Los Alamos after the war, maintained considerable interest in radiological warfare.[90] In 1948 Los Alamos showed its greatest interest in radiological warfare. The AEC's Advisory Committee in Biology and Medicine discussed the continuing radioactivity at "Alamogordo" at their October 1948 meeting, and a few months later, in March 1949, Los Alamos Health Division and AEC Division of Biology and Medicine members exchanged information about the plutonium and other "long-lived fission products" in Trinity earth samples.[91] Communications between Los Alamos and the AEC about radiation at the Trinity site contain hints of continuing radiological warfare interests. For example, the Weapons Test Division at Los Alamos took an active role in some of the decontamination of the fenced-in area at the Trinity site. It is intriguing, too, to note that carbon copies of Trinity radiation reports were sent to the highest-ranking military men in the military's radiological warfare bureaucracy, such as James Cooney, who in 1948 headed the Air Force Special Weapons Project.[92] In the end, however, among the AEC and U.S. military leaders, radiological warfare interests declined; those that remained shifted to sites other than the New Mexican desert.

In the frenzied days from the Trinity test until the uranium bomb exploded over Hiroshima and the plutonium bomb exploded over Nagasaki, those Manhattan Project men and women who had contributed to the reality of the weapons had little time to contemplate their roles. When the war ended, however, their reactions differed. Some expressed joy that they could return home, having contributed to the Allied victory and the defeat of the despised Japanese enemy. Others, over the years, preferred to let amnesia take over—or at least silence about their work on the bomb project. Others, as time passed, agreed to be interviewed and spoke more openly about their contributions to the bomb, their memories and responses varying from the celebratory to the contemplative. Even immediately after the Trinity test, its significance resonated in spite of the official secrecy and requisite silence. Some believed that the Trinity test created a division at Los Alamos: those who had been at the lab before the test and those who came after, with the latter never being accorded the same stature as the pioneers. Others argue for a more dramatic before and after, believing that the Trinity test marked the start of the Cold War.[93]

At the site itself, however, the physical remains of the first atomic bomb gradually disappeared. For a few weeks some men remained at the site to remove telephone wires, posts, and all equipment that could be used elsewhere in the war effort. Since the site was surrounded by miles of desert, miles that were also part of an army and air force base, only modest fencing and a few mounted police guards seemed necessary. The army salvaged some materials in 1952: insulators, copper wire from communication and instrumentation lines, and steel and iron fragments. Over the next few decades some buildings were removed to be used elsewhere while others fell into disrepair; roads returned to their prewar states of varying degrees of impassability. The handwritten notes scribbled by some of the scientists on the walls of some bunkers disappeared.[94] A few official forays took place over the years to removed failed experimental equipment and the trinitite—as noted in this chapter. Otherwise, the relentless entropy, the heat, the desiccating winds, and the blowing dust of the southwestern desert contributed to the eradication of the physical remains of the test site.

1. Trinity area landscape, 1945. Courtesy of LANL.

2. Windmill, water pump, and water storage tank on platform; unidentified ranch. Courtesy of LANL.

3. (*top*) Transporting old ranch water tank to Trinity Base Camp. Courtesy of LANL.

4. Trinity Base Camp. Note the windmill for futile attempts to increase amounts of potable water. Courtesy of LANL.

5. (*opposite top*) Men at Base Camp in line for food. Courtesy of LANL.

6. Transporting Jumbo from the railroad siding to the Trinity site. Courtesy of LANL.

7. Jumbo en route. Courtesy of LANL.

8. (*above*) Jumbo, unscathed after the Trinity test. Courtesy of LANL.

9. Stacking explosives for the 100-Ton test in May 1945. Courtesy of LANL.

10. Constructing the 100-Ton test; a wooden platform to support the cases of TNT. Courtesy of LANL.

11. (*above*) Posing before the 100-Ton test, May 1945. Courtesy of LANL.

12. Desert landscape and trucks near the Trinity site. Courtesy of LANL.

13. Hoisting "the gadget" up into the tower the afternoon before the test. Courtesy of LANL.

TR-310

14. The bomb being hoisted up into the tower. Courtesy of LANL.

15. Unidentified soldier setting up experiments before the Trinity test. Courtesy of LANL.

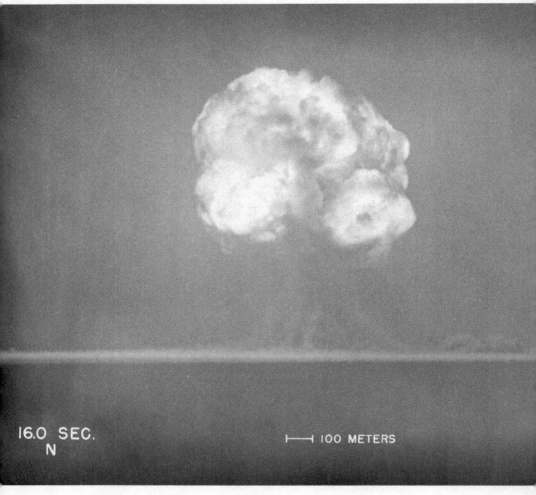

16.0 SEC.
N

⊢——⊣ 100 METERS

16. The Trinity explosion at sixteen seconds.
Courtesy of LANL.

17. (*top*) Debris in the desert after the test. Courtesy of LANL.

18. Debris and decaying bunker after the Trinity test. Courtesy of LANL.

19. (*above*) Ruined bunker, possibly destroyed by the test or perhaps an example of later ruin. Courtesy of LANL.

20. Open House 1965. Tularosa Basin Historical Society/ Museum, Archives and Special Collections.

21. Crowd at Open House 1965. Tularosa Basin Historical Society/Museum, Archives and Special Collections.

22. (*above*) Open House 1968 parking lot and "Keep Out" sign. Tularosa Basin Historical Society/Museum, Archives and Special Collections.

23. Cars at Open House 1968. Tularosa Basin Historical Society/Museum, Archives and Special Collections.

24. Downwinder protest at the entrance to the Trinity site, Open House 2016. Photo by author.

25. (*above*) Ring created for the mounted military police detachment at Trinity. It carried special insignia and words: "Silencio and Servicio" along with the traditional spur and number 1 for the first mounted military police in the army. Photo by Jenn K. Jett. Courtesy of White Sands Missile Range Museum.

26. SED Robert J. S. Brown's bolo tie made of trinitite. Photo by author.

27. Nagasaki, September 1945, destroyed by the plutonium
bomb first tested at Trinity. Courtesy of LANL.

# FIVE

## The Army, the Air Force, the Navy, the Atomic Energy Commission, and the Trinity Site

Men and women seeking historical preservation of the Trinity site faced complications because of its location within what became a major missile testing area of the Cold War and by its proximity to other U.S. military sites. It lay in the northeast area of what was for several decades after World War II one of the nation's major missile testing areas—at first called the White Sands Proving Ground (WSPG) and later renamed the White Sands Missile Range (WSMR). For decades as different groups sought official preservation of the Trinity site, the army and the air force resisted relinquishing control over the area and indeed generally opposed public access to the area. This chapter explores some of the complicated history of the military's use of the land surrounding the Trinity atomic bomb site.

### The Growing Military Presence in New Mexico during World War II

In 1940 and 1941, as the United States faced a broadening two-front war in Europe and Asia, military preparations increased dramatically throughout the nation. In addition to expanded production for bombers, ships, and armaments to be sent to help the British and French, the War Department began what would turn into a massive expansion of U.S. national defense installations, new and expanded "proving grounds," naval stations, military airports, and facilities to manufacture and store war materials. The federal government acquired over twenty million acres of land for these purposes, often by using the established legal mechanism of condemnation through the government's right of eminent domain.[1]

In the 1940s, even before the United States officially entered World War II, the National Military Establishment began to expand its already sizable holdings in New Mexico, which had supported military forts and bases established in the nineteenth century as army outposts in the "wild west." War Department plans in 1940–41 included a "premobilization" program of expanded personnel and training in remote regions of the nation.[2] After the war the military-controlled land in the Tularosa Basin of New Mexico expanded exponentially, fueled by army, air force, and navy demands for their own separate facilities for testing weapons and delivery systems, especially in the new areas of rockets and missiles. Today the state of New Mexico hosts four massive military bases ranging from 50,000 acres to 3,200 square miles (the largest military base in the continental United States).

When the United States entered the war, the southern area of New Mexico experienced an immediate and massive increase in the military's presence. Franklin Roosevelt signed an Executive Order in January 1942 withdrawing public lands in New Mexico (as elsewhere) "for use of the War Department as a General Bombing Range." In addition, the government established at least ten areas in Texas and New Mexico specifically for fighter pilot practice.[3] Names of military bases changed frequently in the war and postwar years, as did their functions. The Alamogordo Army Base became the Alamogordo Army Air Field, then the Alamogordo Air Field, then the U.S. Army Air Force's Alamogordo Bombing and Gunnery Range and, finally, the Holloman Air Force Base. Established in April 1941, six miles west of the town of Alamogordo, New Mexico, the base became an important site for bomber pilots' flight practice and actual bombing practice for pilots training to fight in Europe and the Pacific. Army air force (AAF) units began to move onto the base on May 14, 1942, and from then until the end of the war it served as the training ground for over twenty different groups of airmen, flying primarily B-17s, B-24s, and B-29s. Two years later the Second Army Air Force was stationed there.[4]

Before the United States entered the war, the base provided a practice area for some of the British Royal Air Force pilots and planes that had come to the United States as a safety measure in case, as British and American authorities feared would happen, the Axis powers conquered Europe.[5] After the United States declared war, the airfield came under full control of the U.S. Army Air Corps, and it expanded quickly with new runways, hangers, administrative buildings, and barracks to house the growing number of enlisted men. A year after the war ended, the base experienced a brief period of deactivation in February 1946, but it was quickly reactivated when the U.S. Air Force became the separate third component of the new Department of Defense (DOD). In January 1948 the name of the base changed to the Holloman Air Force Base in honor of the late Colonel George V. Holloman, a pioneer in early rocket and pilotless aircraft research.

The army's Fort Bliss just across the border in Texas also expanded in both size and functions during the war and in the following Cold War decades. Home of all antiaircraft training in the United States at the end of the war, Fort Bliss soon also became the site of some of the earliest U.S. missile tests. A new Antiaircraft and Guided Missile Center was established there in July 1946, and the acquisition of land in the southeast Tularosa Basin and on the Otero Mesa—the McGregor Range Complex—provided significant new areas for military testing.[6]

With the growth in military spending and the increasing size of the army and the navy during World War II, interservice rivalry also increased. During the war, that rivalry included the army air force, whose leaders had long sought its independence from the army. The president and his advisors would not take steps for air force independence during the war, but the "flying arm" of the army gained considerable autonomy in those years. Army air force leaders determined air policies and issued orders without having to go through the army chief of staff. This autonomy and clout stemmed mainly from the prestige of the army air force leader, General Henry "Hap" Arnold (who was also a member of the Joint Chiefs of Staff).

As the war ended in Europe in spring 1945, and then in the Pacific in September 1945, the American military feared reduced funding; every military branch faced serious concerns about how the anticipated "drawdowns" would affect their service branches, bases, and finances. Military officials were right to worry because the immediate postwar years did see significant retrenchment in funding that brought the closure of bases, the return of millions of enlisted men to civilian life, and the slashing of budgets in every service. Drastic demobilization in the AAF brought the discharge of officers, the closure of installations, and the sale and storage of aircraft. The army's Chemical Corps headquarters, for example, sent notices about demobilizing bases and arsenals even as President Truman announced the end of the war.[7] Navy historian Harvey M. Sapolsky notes that late in 1949 the navy was "desperately searching for ways to reduce expenditures" since it had just lost a bitter political struggle with the air force and the Truman Administration over the structure of U.S. forces.[8] In 1949 navy leaders had been open and vocal in promoting a larger role for their service in strategic bombing missions through a new "super carrier." Instead, the Truman administration reduced the navy's budget and used the savings to build B-36 bombers for the air force. Sapolsky made the point that "several senior officers including Admiral Denfeld, the Chief of Naval Operations, were forced to retire early because of their public protest of the budget cuts and the dashing of the Navy's strategic ambitions."[9]

The reductions (and the anxieties about the future) furthered historic rivalries among American military forces and also spurred new ones as leaders of the AAF renewed efforts to make it an independent third military force, which both the navy and the army bitterly opposed. Then the end of the war also brought the most significant reorganization of the U.S. military in its history. In July 1947 Congress passed the National Security Act, which combined the military services as the newly named National Military Establishment under a civilian secretary of national defense. (It later became the U.S. Department of Defense, which included the army, navy, air force, and marine corps.) Two months later, in mid-September 1947, the U.S. Air Force officially became the separate "aerial and space warfare" branch of the U.S. Armed Forces.

The military retrenchment after World War II did not last long. The Soviets tested an atomic bomb in August 1949, which alarmed many powerful groups in the United States and now advocated stepped-up American atomic preparedness. The beginning and then the deepening of a "Cold War" also encouraged Congress to provide more funds for all military needs. The outbreak of war in Korea in 1950 fueled demand for an expansion of the armed forces, for more atomic weapons, and for more conventional weaponry.

Adding to already significant national spending on military matters, the early Cold War funding grew exponentially for research and development of the promising military use of missiles. Research into the peaceful uses of rocket propulsion began at the California Institute of Technology (CIT) in Pasadena, California, in the mid-1930s, but as Frank J. Malina, one of the early participants in that program, recalled later, "World developments by 1938 dictated our participation in the military application of rocket propulsion."[10] Malina recounted being drawn into "councils of those with military responsibilities [and] I participated more and more in discussions of what should be done in the next war with long-range rocket missiles."

During and immediately after World War II, therefore, the U.S. Army turned in significant ways to missile research and development; the navy, too, and then, logically, the new air force wanted roles in creating, testing, and deploying the promising new weapons. German missile attacks on England spurred Allied research not only in how to protect against such weapons but in how to replicate them quickly for offense against an enemy.[11] As it became evident that piloted planes could be challenged by missiles and as hopes grew that missiles could carry nuclear bombs, the air force wanted ever-greater funding and control over research and development of such weapons systems even though under the terms of the 1947 military reorganization, both the navy and marines continued to be allowed their "air arms." Since neither the army nor the navy would relinquish oversight and control in the vastly promising new area of missile development, vying for funding and contracts in those fields deepened the intense rivalries between the three branches of the American military.

Even during the war, by late 1944 American military and defense officials began to make concrete plans for testing long-range and high-altitude missiles, and the desert Southwest seemed ideal for all such work. In early December 1944 the War Department worked to create an area that would be under its control but would also establish joint use areas so the army and army air force could test long-range and high-altitude missiles. War Department officials contacted Manhattan Project head Leslie Groves because of concern that one of the areas under consideration "might interfere with certain highly important projects of a different nature which are under your cognizance."[12] The unidentified author of that memo sought to reassure Groves: "Actual test use of the area by Army Service Forces will not be required until approximately May 1945. Prior to that time, however, there might be a small amount of activity connected with the construction of structures for observation and instrumentation." (Groves's reactions are not preserved in the archives.) Two months later, in February 1945, the War Department created the White Sands Proving Ground in New Mexico's Tularosa Basin. Other areas in the U.S. West also came under consideration as potential missile ranges, including the Muroc Bombing Range in California, the Tonopah Bombing Range in Nevada, the Wendover Bombing Range in Utah, and a site in western Florida.[13] The White Sands Proving

Ground grew as the army pieced together parcels of other military sites in the region, including acreage from the Alamogordo Bombing Range, some territory that was already part of the ORDCIT (Ordnance–California Institute of Technology) long-range ballistic missile project, and portions of the army's Fort Bliss.

In November 1943 Malina and a colleague at Cal Tech prepared a study of rockets based on reports from overseas interviews with German POWs: "Our results showed that although ranges in excess of 100 miles could not be reached with engines then available, rocket missiles could be constructed that had a much greater range and a much larger explosive load than rocket projectiles then being used by the Armed Forces."[14] The AAF did not respond to the proposal from Malina and his colleagues, but the Army Ordnance Department did, with alacrity. The army wanted Cal Tech to undertake an intensive program for the development of a missile with a minimum payload of one thousand pounds of explosives and a range of up to 150 miles.[15] By mid-January 1945 Cal Tech and the Army Ordnance Corps signed a contract for its development, instituting the ORDCIT program.[16] The first tests under ORDCIT took place in various areas but especially in the early days at the Hueco Range at Fort Bliss, Texas, where, as Malina later explained, everything had been too rushed and the missiles were not constructed with enough precision, so several of the early tests failed.[17]

The captured v-2 rockets brought from Nazi Germany required longer testing grounds than those that existed at the army's main site in Aberdeen, New Jersey. To lengthen the testing range for the new weapons, the army began taking over new areas in New Mexico in December 1944. Along with the ranchers evicted for the planned atomic bomb test, others received eviction notices because of the army's new missile projects.[18] In May 1945 the Army Corps of Engineers warned the superintendent of the White Sands National Monument, Johnwell Faris, that test firings might require evacuation of his personnel for indefinite periods. That was how Faris learned that "the vast stretch of the Tularosa basin (from Socorro to Carrizozo, then south to the Texas state line) had become part of the 'ORD-CIT' project."[19] To get an area sufficiently large for testing missiles required piecing together portions of other sites.[20] In March 1948 the secretary of the army, writing to the AEC head, Lilienthal, added a comment about the expansion of the shared range for the ORDCIT program: in "the existing range used by all elements of the National Military Establishment . . . action has been initiated to acquire approximately 33 miles additional land to the north of this area for the purpose of extending the test range."[21]

While conducting the early missile tests at Fort Bliss under the ORDCIT Project, Malina and others visited the "nearby missile test range being newly prepared for the Ordnance Dept at White Sands, New Mexico." At that site the army had begun constructing facilities for tests of an early experimental sounding rocket built by the United States, named the "WAC Corporal." In September 1945 its launch inaugurated the White Sands Proving Ground.[22] In May 1952 an additional 40-by-117-mile area was added to this "joint range"—including sections of the Alamogordo Bombing Range and Fort Bliss's antiaircraft range. The area for missile testing expanded yet again with the creation of the McGregor Missile Range out of Fort Bliss. In the early 1960s, while John Frederick Thorlin served as commander of White Sands Missile Range, he inaugurated the "off-range" firing of the long-range missiles. Through a massive effort and constant coordination with the governors of Utah, Colorado, and New Mexico, the off-range launch program was approved.

It is fascinating, and little explored by historians, that the sites for these new forms of warfare—missiles, rockets, and atomic bombs—were being constructed at the same time and essentially next door to each other in the waning days of World War II. The tests of the new weapons also took place very closely together in time and geographical area. The overlapping dates of the creation of the White Sands Proving Ground and the first atomic bomb test are startling: WSPG received official authorization three days before the Trinity test.

In mid-June 1945, as preparations for the atomic bomb test became increasingly frenzied at the Trinity site, work also began in earnest at the nearby WSPG. Officers from the army's Office of the Chief of Ordnance, members of the ORDCIT project, the Army Corps of Engineers, and men from the Army Signal Office laid out elaborate plans at the new WSPG— plans for roads, water, electrical systems, and sewers. One of the very first tasks required drilling water wells. In one of the few histories of the construction process, Peter Eidenbach notes that the new commander "selected base camp and launch site locations, erected wood-floor squad tents, established generator and line power, drilled the first wells, and re-erected the three relocated barracks."[23] The army claimed three former New Deal Civilian Conservation Corps (CCC) buildings from Sandia Air Base along with "a relocated hangar, Dallas-type hutments, a missile-assembly building, and a building for the Fire Department."[24] Electrical power at the camp came from lines strung between Las Cruces and Alamogordo. Generators from the Elephant Butte Dam created electricity.[25] Construction of an army blockhouse at the Army Launch Area began on July 10. Given that the primary purpose of the new White Sands Proving Ground centered on testing missiles, within two and a half months, by late October 1945, the "1st Guided Missile Battalion" had been constituted and the men were stationed on the site. Ironically, someone among the leadership made the decision that the U.S. soldiers should not live with or next to the German/ex-Nazi scientists who had been brought to the United States to aid American military missile development. According to New Mexico researcher William Boehm those men lived at Fort Bliss and commuted to the WSPG for participation in the test firings.[26] It may also have been a decision based on army authorities' fears about conflicts if the two groups commingled too closely, given the Nazi past of so many of the Germans.

Initially, the new proving ground had three sections, each (on paper at least) to be governed by a separate branch of the military. The army air force (the air force as of 1947) held jurisdiction over the northern portion, the central portion came under the jurisdiction of the Office of the Chief of Ordnance of the Department of the Army, and the navy held a third section.[27] However, with the lines of authority and the mapping ambiguously drawn and the financial stakes high, disagreements and competition prevailed. The original idea of shared joint military control over the White Sands Proving Ground deepened interservice rivalries from the start. In January 1949, hoping to reduce the tensions, the secretary of defense created a "Joint Range Coordination Committee" composed of the commanding general at WSPG, the naval officer in charge of navy activities at the WSPG, and the commanding officer at Holloman Air Force Base (formerly the Alamogordo Army Air Force Base). The "Joint Range" committee was supposed to resolve problems of cooperation and jurisdiction, but instead the army's commanding general at Fort Bliss claimed that he had sole authority over the entire area. The air force, the navy, and army officers at White Sands opposed his claim (and each other), and the three years from 1949 to July 1952 saw, in the words of historian Peter Eidenbach, a bitter and protracted "interservice debate about the Proving Ground chain of command."[28]

Finally, with no diminution of the conflicts, the secretary of defense in mid-August 1952 sent a memo to the air force and navy authorities authorizing the army's commanding general of the wspG to be the central authority having formal control over the "Integrated Range."[29] At the same time, however, he allowed the air force to retain title to and command of the Holloman Base and the navy to retain administrative control and title over all navy facilities located at Holloman.

Congress expanded funding for the joint military long-range proving ground in the spring of 1949 for more research into and testing of guided missiles and other weapons, although that work saw few successes and numerous failures in the early days. Intensive work in ballistic missile development accelerated from 1954 to 1956, when the DOD assigned the air force responsibility for all ground-launched missiles with ranges of more than two hundred miles (later changed to five hundred miles). On March 31, 1958, the Department of the Army created the Army Ordnance Missile Command (AOMC) with headquarters at the Redstone Arsenal complex in Alabama. Its elements included the Jet Propulsion Lab at Cal Tech and the wspG in New Mexico.[30] At that time the wspG was renamed the White Sands Missile Range (wsMR). In early January 1962 the wsMR came directly under the command of the army's chief of ordnance.[31]

In addition to testing missiles, uses of the wsMR expanded in the 1960s and 1970s. By the mid-1970s the Defense Nuclear Agency had established its own testing ground for "nuclear simulations" south of the Trinity site area.[32] Testing of large-scale nonnuclear bombs took place in the 1980s, with an eight-kiloton bomb being tested near the Trinity site in 1986.[33] By 2014 the White Sands Missile Range site hosted multiple entities: NASA's White Sands Test Facility, the Goddard Space Flight Center Tracking and Data Relay Satellite Systems Facility, and the National Reconnaissance Office (NRO) Aerospace Data Facility. At that date, the wsMR, along with nearby Fort Bliss (then home of the army's First Armored Division, used for heavy armor training) constituted the two largest military installations in the United States—some five thousand square miles of land.

## The Navy in New Mexico

In October 1945 the army's chief of ordnance formally invited the navy to participate in the new guided-missile program at the White Sands Proving Ground. The navy accepted the offer and in May 1946 established the

U.S. Naval Ordnance Missile Test Facility there.[34] This unusually cordial relationship between historically jealous rivals stemmed in part from the navy's serious research and development work with rockets in the preceding decade as well as aid that the navy gave to the Manhattan Project during the war. At times during World War II the army and the navy demonstrated rare interservice cooperation. Both had been engaged separately in missile and rocket research and development since the 1930s (indeed, both worked separately with different groups of scientists at the California Institute of Technology). The navy became steeped in rocket research in the years before the war; Cal Tech scientists and navy personnel worked together on rocket research, design, and testing. Much of the early work took place in East Pasadena, California, in some twenty-nine small buildings that were not far from the Cal Tech campus but had no official linkage with or acknowledgment of being part of that university. Cal Tech scientists worked at the East Pasadena site with navy personnel under navy contracts. Some of the research involved studies of jet propulsion, some involved other studies of rocketry, and some may have included weaponry work such as torpedo designs. Although the site remained in use until the 1970s, there is little specific information about what went on there.[35] With its rocketry work expanding, the navy needed much more open space for testing, especially space far from the urban area of Pasadena and Los Angeles. An area in the Mojave Desert in eastern California near the small town of Inyokern (adjacent to the later town of China Lake) seemed ideal, and the army agreed to transfer its property there so the navy could establish the Naval Ordnance Test Station (NOTS).[36] According to navy historians, NOTS gained a speedy position of leadership in weapons testing, and it became recognized as one of the new postwar proving grounds for missile and rocket research. Throughout the postwar period the nation's ordnance community turned to NOTS experts to answer questions about missile testing such as the types of testing ranges needed, how many, where, and how large.[37]

At first the program at NOTS continued (and furthered) the Cal Tech/navy work in rockets. As with other navy entities, including the Naval Research Laboratory, all work on nuclear power was independent of the Manhattan Project.[38] According to historian Richard Rhodes, President Franklin Roosevelt specifically instructed Vannevar Bush, head of the Office of Scientific Research and Development (OSRD), to exclude the navy from atomic bomb work. (Rhodes does not explain why FDR gave this order.) Shortly after he was put in charge of the Manhattan Project, Groves visited the Naval Research Laboratory in September 1942, but the few other contacts between the navy and the Manhattan Project remained little publicized. Rhodes notes that the "official flow of information on nuclear energy research ran from the Navy to the Army one-way only."[39] The navy's work on aspects of nuclear power for submarine propulsion— the work to invent small nuclear-powered reactors that would extend the depth submarines could go underwater and also the time they could stay below the surface—had no linkages to the Manhattan Project.

In spite of FDR's injunction, however, in 1943 and 1944 the navy came to be quietly drawn into atomic bomb work for the Manhattan Project. In June 1943, with U.S. Navy captain W. S. Parsons appointed leader of the Ordnance Division at Los Alamos, the navy's historic involvement and expertise in ordnance work of all kinds was recognized and sought after for the atomic bomb project; the navy began to be given more significant roles in Manhattan Project ordnance, implosion, "gun design," and testing designs.[40] When Oppenheimer learned in fall 1944 that the California Institute of Technology (CIT) rocket program had completed most of its research and the development period and was ready to enter the production phase, he saw an opportunity for the Manhattan Project to make good use of several of the CIT groups' "high professional scientific ability with practical wartime experience in weapon engineering."[41] Oppenheimer recognized as an added bonus that the navy group also had its own labs and equipment. So that November he sought out C. C. Lauritsen, head of the California Institute of Technology's physics group, to discuss possible collaboration on the bomb project. With approval from OSRD officials Vannevar Bush and James Bryant Conant, as well as Leslie Groves, the Camel Project was created to help with the design of the atomic bomb.[42]

Furthermore, two navy plants helped produce the bomb components: the Naval Gun Factory made the gun and breech components, and the Naval Ordnance Plant in Centerline, Michigan, made various other parts.[43] According to an official history of the Manhattan Project, Project Camel work was confined to "problems of the bomb assembly mechanism and its combat delivery, specifically implosion design and delivery."[44] The navy also took part in practice tests for the atomic bomb drops over Japan. NOTS included a nearby airfield built by the New Deal's Civilian Conservation

Corps as a small emergency airfield in 1935. The army air force acquired the field in 1942 but transferred it to the navy as part of the NOTS exchange. During the war the navy did some rocket testing at that airfield, but when the rapprochement between the Manhattan Project and the navy occurred, the three runways also became a place for practice, with B-29 bombers carrying different sizes and shapes of mock atomic bombs.[45]

After the war, the navy deepened its earlier wartime research into developing a nuclear-powered submarine force. Nuclear propulsion, with its promise of longer submarine submersion time and faster maneuvering, became the personal project of navy captain Hyman G. Rickover, who with the generous postwar funding for the new Office of Naval Research (signed into law by Truman August 3, 1946), became director of a collaborative project with the AEC to develop nuclear propulsion systems for naval vessels.[46] The AEC supported the nuclear-powered submarine project and established a Naval Reactors Branch that worked with the navy's Bureau of Ships to build them.[47] Rickover set up collaboration with Westinghouse Electric Corporation at Bettis Airport, thirteen miles southeast of Pittsburgh, and the AEC footed the bill for Westinghouse to develop the technology.[48] An AEC facility in Idaho tested "precise-scale prototype models," and the navy proudly launched the USS Nautilus, the first nuclear submarine, in January 1954.[49] The costs associated with that program may partly explain the sudden and dramatic escalation in the navy's budget from allocated total funding of $44.9 million in 1950 to $82.2 million in 1951.[50]

As for navy activities at the White Sands Proving Ground, they expanded. In the spring of 1947 the director of the White Sands National Monument, adjacent to the proving ground (which was at times forced to shut down because of the overhead missile tests) learned, in shock, from the WSPG commander about ongoing negotiations with the navy that "would virtually close down our area." Johnwell Faris noted bitterly that it appeared that the national monument was "just an existing evil and not necessarily to be considered by such priority agencies as the War and Navy Departments."[51] That feared forced closure did not happen, but relations between the National Park Service and the WSPG did not become more cordial, and those animosities contributed to the problems in securing historical recognition of the Trinity site.

## German Rockets and Missiles

As the war waned in Europe, the Allies conducted intensive searches in Germany for the factories producing the v-2 rockets that had so damaged London and Antwerp and had threatened a dozen other European cities. They searched for hidden caches of Nazi materials as well as for the Axis scientists and technicians who had created the materials. Several excellent histories document those searches, and the historical record is ample about the German scientists' work in underground secret labs in Germany during the war, using slave laborers to produce the rockets.[52] Major James P. Hamill, an intelligence officer with the American Army Ordnance Corps in Germany at the end of the war, received orders to locate enough rocket parts "to reconfigure one hundred of them at the White Sands Proving Ground."[53] Already immersed in inventing and testing their own missiles, the National Military Establishment followed with great interest reports that the Allies (predominantly the Americans) had discovered a cache of v-2 components hidden in caves in Germany. There was much (quiet) excitement about the German models being sent to the United States, so the army, army air force, and navy began serious lobbying for land and funding to test the German products and to improve the American ones. Thus, the capture of the German missiles and the quick way that U.S. Army officials secreted them out of Germany and into the United States may help explain some of the urgency about creating new and expanded proving grounds, including the area in the New Mexico desert. When the army captured the v-2s, officials recognized that the United States would need a larger testing area than the Aberdeen Proving Ground in Maryland permitted. Expansion of the New Mexico military sites became more attractive. As frenzied construction took place at the new White Sands Proving Ground in late July 1945, three hundred freight-car loads of v-2 missile parts were en route there.[54] By early November the German materials had arrived in New Mexico, carefully guarded by American troops at railway sidings near Las Cruces.[55]

In addition to the captured v-2s, the United States brought captured German scientists and technicians, most of them former Nazis, quietly and secretly to the United States beginning in May 1945 under "Operation Paperclip." Eventually some 1,600 Germans (and their families) came to the United States and became citizens. Historians differ in their analyses of the roles those emigres had held as Nazis in Germany and what work they had engaged in besides inventing and testing v-2 missiles. Many had worked on rockets, chemical and biological weapons, and aviation and space medicine. In her voluminous history of Operation Paperclip, reporter Annie Jacobsen focuses in detail on twenty-one of the men, most of whom had been major Nazis.[56] After Hamill helped discover the German v-2s, he conveyed the German scientists themselves to the United States and then to the areas where they would live for the next few years. Most of the early-arriving Nazis went to Fort Bliss, Texas, and the nearby White Sands Proving Ground. In early October 1945 Hamill escorted Wernher von Braun by train from the East Coast to Fort Bliss, a journey that Hamill later described as particularly fraught because of the scores of American soldiers also riding in the railway car. Returning from the war, many had been in Germany fighting Nazis. Hamill did not want von Braun's identity or past to be discovered.

American officials had long, discreet, highly guarded discussions among themselves about bringing in the Nazis. Their presence remained a secret from the U.S. public for over a year. As the war ended in Europe the Allied Supreme Commander, Dwight Eisenhower, very explicitly ordered that German POWs not be given special privileges: "Detained German officials, civilian and military, regardless of rank will be cared for on a scale normally accorded prisoners of war . . . there must be nothing in the appointments which suggest in any way that these Germans are being treated as guests or accorded any honors or special privileges."[57] So American officials recognized some political danger in bringing select Germans to the United States well before they had undergone any of the full, formal "denazification" process. Not until December 1946 did the American public learn of their presence, and at that time Americans had mixed reactions. Some prominent citizens sent telegrams of "profound concern" to Truman, including Albert Einstein; the Federation of American Scientists also objected strongly.[58] Democratic congressman John D. Dingell of Detroit "said the army was nuts for bringing in Nazis." On the other hand, according to one von Braun biographer, the Rotarians in El Paso, Texas, invited him to give a talk, and he received a standing ovation.[59]

The sources and facts differ considerably about many aspects of the Nazi scientists' work in the United States, especially about what they worked on: the most publicized and celebrated being their role in helping to develop

America's rockets, missiles, and later, satellites. At first some worked at Fort Bliss and the WSPG as consultants and then as technicians and teachers in assembling and launching the reconstructed V-2 rockets.[60] By mid-1947 the German team there numbered about 200; they shared work at White Sands and at Fort Bliss with some 125 employees of the GE company and with some U.S. soldiers who had engineering and scientific degrees.[61] Von Braun worked under the civilian title of "Project Director of Operation Paperclip." One White Sands source claims that in May 1946 the Nazi scientists launched the first V-2 from the White Sands range; it misfired. The next month, however, saw the first successful launch from White Sands. The Germans remained at White Sands until 1949 and 1950, after which most moved to Alabama to work in the Redstone Arsenal.[62] Some rose to exalted positions in the following years. Von Braun, for instance, became head of a satellite division at NASA, and four or five other early Nazi/German arrivals also moved to important positions at NASA.

In one action not explored in the histories of the ex-Nazi scientists brought to America, Hamill's first act when they arrived was to conduct a few of them to the Aberdeen Proving Ground in Maryland. This received little notice when the Germans' presence in the United States became public knowledge a year later and in the histories about the ex-Nazis in America, but it is worth a passing consideration. The Aberdeen Proving Ground was one of the nation's oldest and most important ordnance testing facilities. As a destination for a handful of Nazis it seems to have elicited few questions. But questions remain: Who, specifically were the ones who went to Aberdeen instead of Fort Bliss with the other rocketeers especially if von Braun, the acknowledged expert in rockets and missiles, went to Fort Bliss? Was their actual destination the Edgewood Plant, adjacent to Aberdeen, which had become in World War II the nation's oldest and largest chemical and biological weapons facility? (In 1971 the Edgewood Arsenal and the Aberdeen Proving Ground were consolidated into what became the Edgewood Area of Aberdeen Proving Ground.)

Throughout the war, interest among different groups of American military and civilian officials grew ever greater in the Nazi chemical and biological warfare programs (and in the Japanese programs as well). Agents working under Operation Alsos from 1942 to 1945 investigated how far the Nazis had proceeded in creating an atomic bomb and in their pursuit of new biological and chemical weapons.[63] In the aftermath of the war in Europe, the Allies found a stockpile of German chemical weapons, some 296,100 tons, which they divvied up and shipped home to England, Russia, and the United States, ostensibly to be destroyed. Many of those weapons sent to the United States would have ended up at the Edgewood Plant, since it had already been formally designated as a Chemical Warfare Service (CWS) arsenal designated to receive captured German chemical weapons. At Edgewood and other American proving grounds, officials eventually buried the confiscated Nazi biological and chemical weapons in pits dug in isolated areas and also threw thousands of pounds into the sea. That disposal took decades, however, and it is quite likely that before all were destroyed, some were dispersed for further study among the burgeoning postwar American biological, chemical, and radiological research facilities.[64] As soon as the Allies discovered an unexpected cache of newly invented German organophosphate nerve agents, for example, the Americans' Chemical Warfare Service shipped samples to facilities in the United States to be studied.[65] Some of the "Paperclip" Nazis who came to America had expertise in biological and chemical weapons. Were they the men who went to the Aberdeen Proving Grounds?[66]

## The White Sands National Monument

As the army and army air force expanded operations in New Mexico, they encountered problems with the National Park Service (NPS) over the White Sands National Monument (WSNM). The anger generated on all sides resonated for decades and may have added to the military's resistance to discussions of any kind of historical protection of the Trinity site.

The White Sands National Monument is now formally a National Park. Its designation as a National Monument attested to changing American attitudes toward seemingly barren spaces; it symbolized a growing respect for deserts. Preserving a spectacular area of natural beauty and the largest gypsum dune field in the world, the monument had begun to attract growing numbers of tourists when the threat of war brought a growing and chafing military presence to the Tularosa Basin. In his history of the monument, historian Michael Welsh notes that in three years the War Department transformed southern New Mexico and "altered the course of the Monument's history."[67] It became wedged between two large and growing military bases: to the east the Alamogordo Air Base (later, Holloman) and to the west the White Sands Proving Ground. Beginning in the spring of 1945 and expanding through the postwar years, the military's ORDCIT project claimed even more land in the state and imposed new military demands on the monument.

Initially hoping to find ways to work with the military, WSNM officials became frustrated and at times intensely angry over military actions and the disregard for their site. Johnwell Faris, the longtime superintendent of the monument, hoped that White Sands could coexist with the military even though he recognized that the dunes were "in the very heart of the new [bombing] area."[68] The army quickly disabused those with such optimistic hopes. In the spring of 1942, with the expansion of the Alamogordo Air Base, the army needed new and greater supplies of the area's scarcest resource—water. Construction of the base's runways required large quantities of water for mixing with the concrete. The National Park Service authorized access to the monument's main source of water, the Garton Well, which at first seemed plentiful. Judging the army's petition for the water to be a "critical defense project," the NPS authorized the monument director to grant a permit for up to 75,000 gallons of water per day. As Welsh notes, that very quickly rose to 175,000 gallons daily.[69] Monument officials then had to supplement their own water needs elsewhere and turned for help to the Alamogordo Air Base. In July 1945, as preparations for the Trinity test intensified, Faris learned that even that access had been lost because of the needs of the Trinity project.[70]

Dwindling water supplies were far from the only problem. Army vehicles crossed WSNM boundaries and drove on the delicate gypsum dunes, causing considerable, long-lasting damage. The army erected towers for running electrical wires across WSNM land without prior permission from the Park Service or anyone at the monument. The bombing practice runs also caused problems, as pilots occasionally miscalculated and bombs actually fell on the monument. The environmental damage continued after the war. In June 1959 a Nike rocket capable of carrying a nuclear warhead over one thousand miles crashed in the dunes. The Nike contained classified material that had to be destroyed immediately, so it was blown up with five hundred pounds of TNT that left a gaping crater full of black water and a wider area three hundred yards across, black as coal, in the white gypsum dunes.[71]

By the spring and summer of 1945 WSNM Park Service personnel had begun to frequently experience the scale of changes in the area. In May, the Army Corps of Engineers warned Faris that test firings might require the actual evacuation of monument personnel for indefinite periods.[72] Local park officials wrote to the head office, expressing fears about the army's plans. E. T. Scoyen, associate director for the NPS's Region 3 (which included New Mexico), wrote to Arthur E. Demaray (then probably the acting director of the NPS) citing testimony from a hearing in Albuquerque of the U.S. Senate Committee on Public Lands: "One is let [led] to conclude that the activity must be of great importance in the conduct of the war . . . as there could be no other adequate justification for breaking up ranch homes which have been going concerns for well over 50 years with severe financial losses in many instances."[73]

For a while during the war some WSNM officials hoped that the military's actions might ultimately prove to be a benefit. When the Army Corps of Engineers filed condemnation papers on land around the monument in the spring of 1945, the NPS's acting director of Region 3, James Lassiter, hoped that after the war those formerly private lands would be transferred to WSNM.[74] Those proved to be pipe dreams, and as missile testing proceeded in the years after the war, the military wanted ever-larger parcels of the Tularosa range. The army expanded its acreage there even before the end of the war. Faris learned that "the vast stretch of the Tularosa basin (from Socorro to Carrizozo, then south to the Texas state line) had become part of the 'Ordcit' project," which began to supersede environmental protections the NPS had negotiated for the monument. Colonel Pitcher of the WSPG came to talk to Faris, explaining that it would "damage military calculations if missiles could not travel north to south in the basin," so Faris ended 1945 by negotiating a second memorandum of understanding allowing the army "intermittent use of the lands included in the White Sands National Monument within the exterior boundaries of the Ordcit Project."[75]

After the war, the military's expanded presence in the Tularosa Basin continued to affect the national monument next door. In 1948, when the army tried to obtain a permanent permit for its use of WSNM (again seeking to expand the ORDCIT project), park officials, Bureau of Land Management officials, and local ranchers raised such objections at a public meeting in Las Cruces that the army softened its immediate demands. The outcry did not, however, actually change the military's long-term plans about use of the Tularosa Basin. Hillory A. Tolson, acting director of the NPS from 1945 through at least August 1950, wrote that a "permanent permit" for army use of the monument was out of the question "since it would amount to virtual disestablishment of the monument." John K. Davis, acting Region 3 director, also protested the military's damage to the fragile ecology with its "close gridiron pattern traversed with many jeeps."[76] Welsh notes that the Park Service people either were very naive or had few options in the face of national security claims in the years after World War II and before the Korean War.

In November 1949 Faris warned the NPS to see the handwriting on the wall. He had learned of plans for over 500 new homes within 35 miles of WSNM; a year and a half later, he reported that the army now proposed the construction of some 2,500 new housing units within a 125-mile radius of White Sands. He also alerted the NPS to recent visits from the army to survey the monument's boundaries and to research the legal titles of the private holdings of ranchers.[77] The Kennedy-era space program as well as weapons testing brought new threats to the White Sands National Monument. In 1963 the military—flush, powerful, and popular—floated ideas about transferring the manned space flight center at Cape Canaveral, Florida, to the Tularosa Basin.[78] New Mexico officials, including the governor, supported that transfer even though it would have essentially meant the end of the White Sands National Monument.

Other forces, however, also began to play into decisions about WSNM. The coalescing environmental movement gave more clout to park officials and more voice to citizens anxious to protect areas of natural beauty. The secretary of the interior, Stewart Udall, in the late 1960s took the radical stance that the military should be forced to leave the dunes altogether. Military officials at the WSMR also had to deal with shifting environmental politics. For the first time ever they had to answer to Park Service officials about violations of new environmental impact laws and, increasingly, they had to fill out forms and write reports about the environmental impact of their programs on the adjacent monument. WSMR officials responded at times unhappily and unwillingly to the new demands. At a meeting in October 1974, Tom Ela (otherwise unidentified but officially connected with the new environmental impact rules) asked at a meeting with missile range personnel whether anyone at the base had given consideration to moving the missile range activities to another location, for example, to Nevada. Whether he made the query in jest or anger is unclear from the written report, which also neglected to report their reactions.[79]

It seems likely that the conflicts about the White Sands National Monument between the National Park Service and the army (especially its component, the army air force) became a reason for the military's reluctance to pursue the creation of a formal historic site at Trinity. Army annoyance at having to share the border of a national monument may well have helped convince commanders that they did not under any circumstances want a repetition of those complications with another national site.

## The Atomic Energy Commission and the Trinity Site

In January 1947, after much contentious, even acrimonious debate within Congress and the country at large, the U.S. military was required to relinquish control over the nation's nuclear energy production facilities and its nuclear stockpile and transfer everything to the civilian Atomic Energy Commission, created by Congress and signed into law by Truman in August 1946. Executive Order 9816 required that on January 1, 1947, "title to plants, facilities, land, etc. then in possession or custody of the Manhattan Engineer District would be transferred to the [Atomic Energy] Commission."[80]

Atomic Energy Commission (AEC) commissioners informed General Groves in early December that as of January 1, 1947, they would take over the atomic project, and all property and functions were to be transferred to the AEC by that date. The AEC would then "retransfer such property and functions deemed more appropriate for armed services control."[81] Groves and Kenneth D. Nichols objected, arguing that certain properties, including all ordnance works, the Sandia Base at Albuquerque, and "all weapons storage sites," should not be transferred even temporarily; furthermore, "the raw materials function should remain under Army control . . . and intelligence operations and records should be transferred directly to the new Central Intelligence Group."[82] The commission disagreed, and even though Nichols met with AEC officials several times in December, the AEC commissioners would not relinquish their new power of total civilian custody of atomic weapons. Thus, the AEC assumed oversight and control of researching, manufacturing, and testing nuclear weapons in a complex scattered over thirteen states, with two thousand military employees, four thousand government employees, and thirty-eight thousand civilian employees or contractors.[83] In addition to Los Alamos, Hanford, Oak Ridge, and the scores of lesser-known and smaller materials-procuring, producing, and processing sites, the AEC gained authority over the acreage at the Trinity site.

The civilians appointed by President Truman to manage the AEC found fierce resistance not only from Groves and other Manhattan Project military officials but also from within the War Department (soon to be the Department of Defense). Eventually the AEC mitigated some of the animosities by adding a Military Liaison Committee, but conflicts continued especially in the early postwar years as many interested parties wrangled over access to and control of nuclear weapons and the nuclear weapons complex. In their desire for a complete break with the Manhattan Project personnel, the AEC rebuffed Groves's suggested names for the first members of the AEC's Military Liaison Committee. Groves also tried to designate Kenneth Nichols as a liaison between him and the AEC, but that, too, fell through. In one of the ironies that sometimes happens in such antagonisms, the AEC was housed in the New War Department Building in Washington DC with offices adjacent to Groves's headquarters.[84]

As the AEC prepared to take control of all atomic bomb sites and materials from the army in the official transfer of power in January 1947, the army worked to secure an exception for the Trinity test site area. Army officials did not base their efforts on the site's historical importance but rather on army and air force officials' fear that their expanding joint program to test missiles would be hampered if they lost control over the strip of land that had been used for the atomic bomb test. In late March 1948 the assistant secretary of the army wrote to the head of the AEC that retention of the Trinity site area by the AEC "would seriously limit the ability of the Military Establishment to execute its responsibilities for research and development in the field of guided missiles and would reduce the overland test range for guided missile testing by one-third of the area required."[85] Furthermore, since that area of the range had become a testing area shared by "all elements of the national Military Establishment," there were plans to add thirty-three miles of additional land to the north.[86]

In mid-April the head of the AEC, David Lilienthal, replied. "The Commission now foresees no major obstacles which will prevent use of the bombing range by the National Military Establishment." He agreed with the army's suggestion that there be cooperative arrangements over the safety and security of "portions of the area in which the Commission has a continuing interest." The next month (on June 24, 1948) the AEC approved the return of "operational control" of the Trinity test site area of the Alamogordo Bombing Range Test Area to the Department of the Army "subject to the condition that the Department of the Army must accept responsibility for continuing security and health safety requirements over the crater and satellite initiator test areas."[87] The AEC agreed to relinquish control over the Trinity area because it "had served its useful technical purpose." They now had "new and adequate test sites for both full scale weapon and component testing" at the Nevada Test Site as well as in the proving grounds in the Pacific. Furthermore, the AEC believed that the security and health safety requirements at Trinity could be entirely fulfilled by "proper fencing and posting of test areas and conducting periodic technical and security surveillance inspections."[88]

The AEC expected the army to maintain the fence, to conduct periodic inspections "to guard against the security and health hazards involved in unauthorized entry," and "to control any use and disposition of the crater and satellite test areas consistently with security and health safety requirements." The AEC stipulated that they would conduct occasional inspections to assure adequate oversight by the military. Everyone involved apparently expected details to be worked out by representatives of the AEC and the military, but there is little documentation of when or how often those meetings took place, who was involved, and what specifics anyone agreed upon. In fact, there was initial confusion about which branch of the military actually held jurisdiction over the Trinity area after the AEC relinquished control. Three days after the AEC's decision to return the area to the army, the assistant secretary of the army responded that "the crater area" actually fell within the geographical limits of the Holloman Bombing Range and was therefore under the jurisdiction of the Department of the Air Force.[89] The army then notified the AEC that it accepted all stipulations but warned that control "of the Range" would soon be transferred to the air force.

The confusion is understandable: in July 1948 the Alamogordo Bombing Range became the Holloman Bombing Range overseen by the air force. Part of the area had become the joint White Sands Proving Ground, which as noted above, became a "common range for the testing of guided missiles" by the army, the air force, and the navy. The army's sole interest at the time appears to have been continuance of the "joint use arrangement that now exists between the two Departments." In other words, as of July 1948, the army only wanted to be able to maintain the agreement with the air force. The air force agreed to accept the transfer of the Trinity area to its jurisdiction and agreed to accept responsibility for "guaranteeing the security of the crater area."[90] Under the agreement, therefore, the AEC would continue to have some involvement at the Trinity site proper until they could rest more easily about public safety (and the fear of potential lawsuits) from the residual radiation. On August 10, 1948, the commanding officer of the Holloman Bombing Range and the chief engineer of the AEC's Office of Santa Fe Directed Operations signed a memorandum of understanding, which established agreements about shared obligations without completely transferring control over the Trinity site to either agency. The AEC would remove all personal property from the tract and make some restorations; it would also erect fences and post signs warning trespassers to stay off the property. The air force would maintain the fencing and would conduct periodic inspections "to guard against the security and health hazards in unauthorized entry upon said tract."[91] The next day Carroll L. Tyler, manager of the AEC office in Santa Fe, publicly announced that the National Military Establishment would now reclaim 275,000 acres of the northeast corner of the Holloman Bombing Range (formerly the Alamogordo Bombing Range), including the site of the world's first atomic bomb explosion. It had been under the jurisdiction of the AEC since December 31, 1946, but now the "air forces" would have jurisdiction over the tract. The air force would maintain the site and conduct "periodic inspections." The air force would also allow the AEC "to use certain portions of the site for further research, if desired," specifically "the crater resulting from the Trinity blast . . . as well as certain satellite test sites."[92]

## Deserts as Sacrifice Zones

Environmental historians, among others, have long pointed out the ways in which the world's deserts and the Native peoples inhabiting them came to be regarded as "sacrifice zones" whose destruction seemed to have little consequence, but indeed was often justified as contributing to the perceived greater national good. This has been especially true for much of modern U.S. history: deserts have been devalued as worthless, unsuited for modern development, and unpeopled (or, rather, inhabited by groups given little societal worth and lacking power and respect from national authorities).

Increasingly in the twentieth century, however, those same deserts came to hold increasing attraction as sites for military training and weapons testing. The Trinity test established the precedent of the desert as a nuclear testing area and soon, during the Cold War, other deserts of the American West became established areas for nuclear weapons tests, biological and chemical warfare tests, and militarized missile tests.[93] Historian Patricia Limerick noted astutely decades ago the many reasons the American West appealed to the military: secrecy could be easily maintained, the wide-open spaces allowed large-scale testing of planes, tanks, guns, and bombs, and because the underdeveloped deserts "were already by popular consensus vacant and useless, bombing could hardly hurt them."[94]

Even when late nineteenth-century railroad travel and then the transformations in travel by mid-twentieth-century air-conditioned cars made deserts more appealing to tourists, earlier views often prevailed. Historian Andrew Kirk demonstrates the ways that official early photographs of the Nevada Test Site's nuclear tests deliberately emphasized the Mojave Desert's barrenness and desolation (as well as erased the long history of the Western Shoshones in the area).[95] The world's oceans also bore the brunt of nuclear tests, turning areas of the seas and their islands into some of the most polluted places on earth. Immediately after the Trinity test, some of the largest American atomic bomb tests took place in the Pacific Ocean, but the logistics of getting ships, materials, and people such distances, as well as concerns about maintaining secrecy, soon made continental sites more appealing.[96]

Some voices praise the ways that military control has preserved large swaths of the desert by making vast areas off limits to the general public, to tourists and developers alike. Drivers on Highway 70 in New Mexico observe mile after mile of the seemingly timeless, pristine beauty of the White Sands Missile Range desert. One sees no billboards, no roadside stalls offering souvenirs and miscellaneous goods, no gas stations and truck stops, no motels, no abandoned shacks, no tracks from off-road vehicles marring the sand hills. Any areas pockmarked by bomb tests are far enough removed to be invisible. Military officials thus defend the desert lands they control in the United States, arguing that they are engaged in environmental preservation. In some respects it is hard to differ. The petroglyphs within the China Lake Military Preserve in California, for instance, are indeed undamaged by human vandals, unlike those in many western areas open to the public.[97]

That argument, however, overlooks the often invisible damage done to animals, plants, and humans from the atomic tests (as well as biological and chemical tests). Richard Rhodes's history of the atomic bomb devotes some twenty-four pages of powerful and moving accounts of the horror of the human pain and deaths caused by the bombs in Hiroshima and Naga-saki. His chapter about the Trinity test concludes with a simple observa-tion: "A bomb exploded in a desert damages not much besides sand and cactus and the purity of the air." Searchers looking for lethal effects at the Trinity site found only some "partially eviscerated rabbits" and wildlife killed by the blast.[98]

No one could argue for an equivalence between the bomb test in the New Mexico desert and the leveling of two cities, the firestorms, the tens of thousands of human lives instantly obliterated, and the lingering hor-rors of radiation sickness, sometimes for lifetimes. Yet, in recent years we have seen significantly growing attention to the human costs of the Trinity bomb, costs paid by the surrounding ranchers, farmers, townspeople, and Native Americans in New Mexico and other areas of the West for their initial exposures to immediate fallout and the longer exposures to residual radioactivity. The seemingly unspoiled landscape has different meanings with such sacrifices in mind.

# SIX

## The Trinity Radiation and Its Afterlives

Aged eleven, Henry Herrera was helping his father fill the radiator of their truck outside their ranch near Tularosa, New Mexico, when he saw the Trinity test. At about 5:30 a.m. on that July 16 morning, as he remembered the experience over fifty years later, he "heard a very large blast and saw a very big flash of light. I got so scared I thought The World Is Coming to an End. Then I saw what looked like a large big black gray ball of smoke going higher and higher in a north easterly direction." He watched the "cloud of dirt, smoke, and debri[s]" for hours as it traveled northeast toward the small towns of "Capitan, Ruidoso, Hondo, Roswell." After a few hours the cloud began to come back toward Tularosa. He ran inside the house, calling to his mother, "Aqui viene la bola patras" (The ball is coming back toward Tularosa). His mother, disbelieving, went outside. She had washed clothes that morning and had hung them outside to dry. "Because of the dirt, dust, debris, black ash that fell on her clothes she became very angry, because she had to take all her clothes down and wash [them] again." Henry recalled: "The filth . . . was on our roofs, our gardens, milk cows, rabbits, pigs, turkeys, and chickens." The Herrera family, like most others in that part of arid New Mexico, relied on rain water collected from the roof into a cistern, so the debris from the roof was collected in their cistern water after the first rainfall.[1] A congressional hearing in 2019 noted that Henry Herrera and two sisters survived cancers, but a brother, a niece, and a nephew died of the disease.[2]

In recent years, more details have emerged about people affected at the time by the radiation from the Trinity test. A group of twelve young girls from a dance class and their teacher, enjoying a camping trip near Ruidoso, woke up about 5 a.m. the morning of the test. Barbara Kent reported to the *Santa Fe New Mexican* in 2015 that "all of us in the upper bunks fell to the floor when the bomb went off. Nobody could understand what was going on." Later that day the girls were startled to see what seemed like snow falling from the sky. Kent recalled thinking, "Oh, my gosh. It's July and it's snowing . . . yet it was real warm." That "snow"—which no one of course realized at the time—consisted of fallout from the atomic bomb test. Kent said that other campers nearby came to watch as the snow covered the grass and the gently flowing river: "We put it on our hands and were rubbing it on our face. We were all having such a good time in that river, trying to catch what we thought was snow. There was a lot, let me tell you."[3] Of the twelve girls who played in the "snow" that morning only two lived to be forty. The dance teacher's daughter died of cancer, the teacher died, Barbara Kent survived skin cancer and several other types of cancer, and her mother, who had been staying in a lodge near the camp, died of a brain cancer.

A 2019 study published in the *Bulletin of the Atomic Scientists* observed that "the first victims of the first atomic explosion might have been American children." Kathleen M. Tucker and Robert Alvarez drew on vital statistics collected by the state of New Mexico and the U.S. government in the 1940s and found "a sharp rise in infant deaths following the Trinity explosion." From 1940 to 1960 infant mortality in New Mexico declined steadily and deeply, with the exception of 1945 "when it shot up." Infant mortality rates in the state between 1943 and 1948 peaked in the late summer after the Trinity test "with a significant peak in September."[4] Tucker and Alvarez could find no other explanations for the spike in infant deaths; there was no unusual heat, heavy rains, or natural disasters such as floods. What they found was that, as we have already seen, the fallout "snowed down" for several days after the test, affecting the milk from dairy cows and the rainwater collected from roofs into cisterns.

This chapter focuses on the complex issue of the radioactive fallout from the Trinity test: the decades of studies attempting to measure the radiation and understand the consequences, the diverse responses of authorities and citizens in the decades of growing publicity about the consequences of exposure to radioactive materials, and the impacts on the test's "downwinders."

## Monitoring and Measuring Radiation from the Trinity Test

The Manhattan Project scientists had several reasons for focusing on the radioactivity that would be released by the blast; early on they wanted to understand, to measure, and to trace the gamma, beta, and alpha radiations and the neutrons produced from the explosion. Early test planning included obtaining (and even building) radiation-measuring equipment to be placed around the site and around the state. As we have seen, early plans included groups of human monitors to oversee the equipment at the test site and in the surrounding countryside. Histories of the test include detailed analyses of who those monitors were, what equipment they carried and read, how it worked (or malfunctioned), and what the results were (although some of the scientific data remained highly classified for years). As we have seen, equipment and trained monitors were set up around ground zero for this purpose, tracking and measuring radiation for hours and days after the test. Heavily shielded army tanks with portable ionization chambers went about the test site measuring radioactivity and radioing data back to the control shelter.[5] Test officials set up equipment and monitors around the state to record important data about the different types of radiation from the explosion. Manhattan Project scientists and government officials wanted those measures and records as scientific knowledge for future atomic bombs. Some of the immediate post-test radiation study may also have been spurred by the growing radiological warfare interests of various U.S. military and civilian officials.

Accounts written after the war try to make it appear that officials from the beginning had deep concern about possible danger from the Trinity test's radiation and that preparations were thorough and careful in order to protect workers and the local population. Few actual records bear out such accounts. Planning for the test certainly included thinking about the possibility of fallout dangers to the men involved in the test, and secondly to nearby communities, but that attention came late in the planning stages and remained quite minimal. Groves, for example, grew angry a few months before the test when some on his medical staff suggested the need for emergency evacuation crews. Always obsessed with preserving the project's secrecy, Groves feared arousing suspicions among townspeople if suddenly scores of men appeared ready to help them leave in an emergency. Accounts from the time present him as far more fearful of giving away the secret of the bomb than worrying about the public's safety. "What are you, some kind of Hearst propagandist?" he barked after physician James Nolan warned him about the possible radiation danger to New Mexican residents.[6] Groves in fact provides a good example of the "retrospective falsification" around the radioactive fallout from the Trinity test. His autobiography presents untrue pictures of his actions and his fears about the test's fallout in New Mexico.[7] Groves was far from alone in such misrepresentations.[8]

Certainly, several of the scientists thinking about the atomic bomb and some working to create it understood early on (if dimly) that radiation hazards might spread following the detonation. Physicists Otto Frisch and Rudolf Peierls, who fled Nazi Germany for Britain and later worked as part of the "British Mission" for the Manhattan Project, warned as early as March 1940 about the dangers of radioactive fallout after a nuclear explosion.[9] In an October 1944 memo chemist George B. Kistiakowsky, who, as noted in earlier chapters, oversaw implosion work in the Ordnance Division at Los Alamos, warned Oppenheimer that the bomb would produce radioactive residue that would fall to the ground. However, Kistiakowsky expected incorrectly that the major radiation would come from the immediate blast, so his memo may have actually helped to minimize concern about possible later radiation dangers. Attuned to the growing military interest in the possibilities of radiological warfare, Kistiakowsky did note that the military would be very interested in "where and how such products are precipitated, what intensity of radiation they create on the ground."[10]

In the early spring of 1945 another scientist gave a slightly more public warning about the possible dangers of radioactive fallout from the test. John Magee was working for B. F. Goodrich Company in Akron, Ohio, when he was persuaded in 1943 to go to Los Alamos along with his colleague Joseph Hirschfelder to work with Hans Bethe on the possible effects from the blast. In an interview many years later Magee stated that very few Los Alamos scientists had seemed concerned about any radioactive residue from the bomb. In Magee's memory, Hirschfelder came dashing into their office one day in the early spring of 1945 saying, "What about the radioactivity?" Hirschfelder answered, "Lots of radioactive materials will be produced by the explosion. What'll happen to it? It'll sweep up dirt from the ground. . . . It will eventually be brought down to the ground." To Magee this suddenly seemed "elementary," so they "told people about it, to prepare for it." Magee, however, remembered, "I don't think anyone took this seriously. It was not that they were frivolous. Nobody thought there would be any problem there."[11] Magee and Hirschfelder did worry, however: "So we did studies about the composition of sand and calculation about the fallout—the medical implications."[12] They sent a memo to test director Kenneth Bainbridge on June 16 expressing concern about "the possibility of a dangerous amount of active material sedimenting down onto nearby towns."[13] The timing of their memo suggests that they were influenced by Anderson's May test discoveries about the high radioactivity in smaller "dust" particles, and those findings may have helped overcome the reluctance of Groves and others, spurring some of the preparations for emergency evacuations, minimal as they were.[14] In a surprising and little-explained action, Hirschfelder and Magee sent a second memo on July 6 to Bainbridge that minimized their earlier fears about post-test radioactivity.[15] In it they revised their earlier fears and now stated that they did not expect much of a problem from radiation. Sources do not clarify what they based this new assessment on and how Bainbridge reacted.

Other evidence also attests to a general lack of concern about fallout dangers to test workers and to the New Mexican citizens during preparations for the Trinity test. In an important technical history of the atomic bomb, four historians of science and technology touch only cursorily on the scientists' thinking about the possibility of danger from radioactive fallout, noting briefly the expectation that optimum winds "would draw the radioactive cloud away from nearby towns and break it up as rapidly as possible."[16] In nearly seven pages at the end of the chapter reviewing the results of the Trinity test, the sole paragraph addressing its radiation focuses on the radiation at ground zero.[17] Scientists' considerable immediate interest in the fission fragments remaining in the soil at ground zero came primarily for what those fragments revealed about the explosion rather than for the radioactivity itself.[18]

As chapter 1 documents, radiation monitors positioned around New Mexico (with a few in other nearby states) recorded information from the blast, in some places taking measurements for days afterward. They conducted "dust-borne product surveys" with portable alpha and gamma ionization chambers and Geiger counters. They took readings at the explosion site, and some of the men who remained at Los Alamos in the next few weeks, months, and even years after the test participated in occasional surveys of the residual radiation even at remote sites up to two hundred miles away. Only a few sources document the panic and fright some of those monitors experienced. In 1947 Los Alamos released Joseph Hoffman's official account of the radiation monitoring, including three appended reports amplifying the details about the radiation-measuring instruments, a radiation monitoring trip three weeks after the test to the "Hot Canyon," and a third monitoring trip five months after the test to record radiation measurements around the state.[19] Several other monitors' reports from the same time, however, were left out of the official printed version Los Alamos released for public consumption. Those reports contained more alarming descriptions of monitors' experiences with high radiation readings and their fear.[20]

As I have argued throughout this book, later memories about the test's radiation need special critical scrutiny. Louis Hempelmann, who headed the medical group at Los Alamos during the war, recalled in an interview in the 1960s his intense fear about the unexpectedly high levels of radioactivity in some areas after the test. Fallout readings as high as 20 rems per hour were "very frightening."[21] In that interview Hempelmann overlooked his earlier bravado about radiation as in his blithe 1947 note to a colleague: "I think that the plutonium from the thousand bombs scattered universally over the earth would do us all good (stimulates the spermatocytes—not for publication). . . . Plutonium, next to alcohol is probably one of the better things in life. We are using it for toothpowder out here."[22] Similarly, five days after the test, Stafford Warren wrote an eight-page memo for Groves with details about the unanticipated fallout "intensities," tracking in pages of maps of where and when radiation fell to earth. The memo, meant only for Groves, does not seem to have been read by anyone else for decades after the war. Groves stored it in the "top secret" files of the Manhattan Project, where it remained with other highly classified materials in his possession for years and then in the National Archives for decades.[23] Warren emphasized that populated areas around the Trinity site had not been endangered: "The highest intensities fortunately, were only found in deserted regions. . . . Intensities in the deserted canyon were high enough to cause serious physiological effects."[24] Warren observed that radioactive dust "could be measured at low intensities 200 miles north and northeast of the site on the 4th day [after the test]. There is still a tremendous quantity of radioactive dust floating in the air."[25] He also noted, "While no house area investigated received a dangerous amount, i.e., no more than an accumulated two weeks dosage of 60r, the dust outfall from the various portions of the cloud was potentially a very dangerous hazard over a band almost 30 miles wide extending almost 90 miles northeast of the site."[26]

Warren never referred to the memo in his later voluminous papers and writings, although his career centered for decades on the study of radiation effects. For forty years after the war, Warren's professional responses to radiation dangers fluctuated from considerable early fear to an appearance of later nonchalance. His frightened concern about the Trinity fallout appears to have had no effect. Not only did Groves bury the memo, but he ordered Warren himself to go to Japan within a week of the test to measure radiation at Hiroshima and Nagasaki. In a boost to his career and in fascinating juxtaposition to his fright after the Trinity test, Warren reported that he found little to worry about on the ground in either nuclear-bombed city.[27]

Fears about the test's radioactive fallout were also tamped down by the press of events. Immediately after the test, the majority of scientists returned quickly to Los Alamos to evaluate results, their evaluations intensified by knowledge that the bomb assembly on the Pacific island of Tinian had begun and that it would be dropped on Japan as soon as possible. Thus, concern about ranchers and townspeople in the areas of New Mexico and elsewhere who might possibly have been affected by the fallout came to be minimized or entirely ignored.

## Radiation Research from the Trinity Test

For decades, experts from diverse institutions in different fields in the sciences and medicine studied the radiation from the Trinity test and wrote it up in memos and reports.[28] Different agencies measuring and evaluating the residual radiation in soil, plants, and animals produced several dozen—perhaps as many as forty—studies. Since most of the studies were classified, their circulation is impossible to document even within the scientific communities increasingly interested in fallout and its effects. The investigators came from different institutions: from Los Alamos, from the Crocker Radiation Lab on the campus of the University of California at Berkeley (later renamed the Lawrence Radiation Lab), and from the Atomic Energy Commission (AEC), especially those in its Division of Biology and Medicine (DBM), and many came from the laboratory at the newly funded postwar medical school at UCLA: the UCLA Atomic Energy Project (AEP).[29] In the 1970s and 1980s scientists from the Office of Radiation Programs at the Environmental Protection Agency (EPA), and later from the Defense Nuclear Agency also produced reports about the radiation from the Trinity test.

Fields of expertise of those conducting the studies varied. Traditional radiologists and those who during the war began to identify themselves as "health physicists" wrote some of the reports as they expanded their knowledge from traditional medicine to the impacts of atomic radiation.[30] Quickly, however, specialists in new fields emerged in "radiochemistry," "radioecology," "radiobiology," and by the 1960s "environmental radiation." At UCLA at the newly founded Atomic Energy Project in the late 1940s and early 1950s, scores of personnel worked in new fields revolving around ionizing radiation: eighteen in radiobiology, eighteen in pharmacology and toxicology, fourteen in radioecology. In addition, eleven worked in "Special Problems," particularly the section blandly titled "Alamogordo," which was founded to study the Trinity radiation.[31]

The first extensive report about the fallout from the Trinity test came in 1948, conducted by scientists from the UCLA AEP who studied a six-hundred-foot-diameter area around "the crater" (ground zero), the fenced area around the crater, and an unfenced area that they did not further detail.[32] They also conducted a detailed radiological survey of 1,130 square miles around the test site to determine the "remaining activities in the path of the initial maximum fall-out."[33] They paid close attention to the soil because it constituted "the reservoir of the remaining contaminants including plutonium." The report noted that rains and occasional "flash floods" created runoff with large amounts of red clay and sand that filled the arroyos "so fall-out from the fission products and plutonium change constantly."[34] The study looked at "the original deposition of fission products and [indecipherable] particles during the fall-out" but, importantly, it also looked at the "redistribution of activity due to wind and water erosion," noting the significance of wind erosion in the desert. Wind carried some of the greatest radioactivity in any sample collected outside the "fence area" in 1948.

Three years later, in 1951, another UCLA AEP report contained little to soothe those fearful of the continuing radioactivity from the bomb test.[35] The abstract began by stating, "Plutonium has been found in soil and plants collected from various locations along the line of Fall-out for at least a distance of eighty-five miles from the Fenced Area." The study scientists found the maximum readings on the Chupadera Mesa, twenty-eight miles from ground zero. They found alpha activity (that they assumed to be plutonium) in the bone, liver, muscle, and connective tissue of all rodents collected twenty-eight miles from the crater, but nothing in rodents collected in and around the fenced area. Even more worrisome, researchers found that the radioactivity increased with distance from ground zero, becoming especially high thirty-five to forty miles away. The surprisingly high levels of radioactivity in juniper bark they attributed to fallout from the original radioactive cloud.[36] Although vegetation was exceedingly sparse in many areas, the researchers measured significant amounts of beta-gamma radioactivity in the thistle that accumulated as tumbleweeds against the fence around ground zero. Even on the calmest days, they found that "air-borne dust in the Crater Region contains significant amounts of alpha emitters, presumably plutonium."[37]

It is not at all clear how widely UCLA circulated any of the Trinity studies, but if the AEC read the 1951 report it is no wonder they grew alarmed. The report warned in its conclusion that outside the fenced area around ground zero "there are many potential long-term insidious hazards from the present low level contamination which is the focal point of these studies. Evidence is beginning to accumulate from these annual Biological Surveys that such hazards exist."[38] They found some annual increase in "fission product uptake by grass." Referring to the fenced area: "It is abundantly clear that the entire area is in a state of flux with respect to distribution and biological availability of radioactive fission products and unfissioned material. Evidence is accumulating . . . that many years may pass before a biological equilibrium with respect to residual contamination is reached."[39]

A 1951 UCLA study (UCLA-140) resurveyed three areas studied in 1948, and the three (unidentified) authors found continuing—even increasing—radioactivity (which they minimized). Their language reads in places as convoluted and confusing: "It was demonstrated that vegetation is the most important influence in decreasing the removal of wind-borne material." In other words, vegetation appeared to aid in the persistence of radioactivity. Investigators found that radioactivity from dried plant material in soil samples had increased, but they expressed the findings in technical language: the ratio of soil to plant beta-gamma radioactivity of residual fission products in Area 21. In 1949 the activity of a gram of dried plant material was 3.85 percent of the radioactivity in a gram of soil, but in 1950 it was 5.59 percent.[40]

A 1957 UCLA report gave even less reassurance as the investigators resurveyed areas studied earlier and corrected earlier findings.[41] They found that the area originally contaminated by fallout from the Trinity detonation "was greater than the 1,100 square miles estimated in the 1948 survey." They also found that "the relatively slight change in plutonium level from 1948 to 1956 in these locations indicates that no appreciable decrease in plutonium content of the soils is occurring due to erosional factors."[42]

In his one-thousand-page history of post–World War II research into internally absorbed or ingested radiation, radiologist J. Newell Stannard managed to obtain a few of the UCLA studies but, to his annoyance, far from all of them. He noted that the UCLA scientists found that radioactivity outside the crater sometimes increased with distance up to eighty-five miles, although the maximum radiation was found at about twenty-eight miles from ground zero. This was true of the surface soil and in animals and plants: "Even after many years and scores of rainstorms, activity deposited on the leaves of some plants was almost impossible to remove."[43] The data also suggested some sort of accumulation process because "concentrations in animal tissues that were very low in the first two years began to be detectable in 1949 and 1950. . . . Activity in plants rose similarly, but somewhat earlier."[44]

While some reports drew alarming conclusions about the persistence of different types of radiation from the Trinity test, others downplayed any danger. The AEC, while authorizing some studies of the Trinity radiation, became much more defensive about the nation's nuclear weapons testing and the dangers of fallout. Such shifts stemmed from new and more politically conservative (and pro-nuclear weapons) leadership within the AEC, broad changes in the nation's political responses to nuclear weapons as the Cold War deepened, and dawning public awareness of, and fears about, nuclear fallout. At Los Alamos over the years different groups conducted studies of the Trinity test radiation and came to differing conclusions. Two and a half months after the test, Los Alamos radiologists traced "a swath of fairly high radioactivity on the ground covering an area of about 100 miles long by 30 miles wide."[45] On the other hand, Joseph Hoffman's official report about the Trinity radiation stated in 1947 that no alpha radiation had been detected from the Trinity test, adding, "While it is possible that a localized 'hot spot' might have occurred, none was found, and the actual contamination indicated a uniform distribution at a concentration which is considered not to constitute a health hazard."[46] Even some of the UCLA AEP reports took care not to sound alarms: "Due to the low levels of activities found in the animals from the Alamogordo Area and the absence of controlled laboratory data for such activity levels, no conclusions can be reached at this time concerning the presence or absence of biological hazards in the contaminated areas."[47]

At Los Alamos, too, many disagreed about the dangers. In 1950 the general manager at Los Alamos told the secretary of the air force that at Trinity's "ground zero" and for six hundred feet there was "enough radioactivity to present a strong presumption of a hazard."[48] In June 1952, the director of security and a lawyer for Los Alamos wrote a memo expressing concern about public safety and legal liability if the site were to become a National Historic Site.[49] A little-circulated 1972 Los Alamos study found contamination of the soil at the Trinity site and claimed that the "increasing migration of Pu [Plutonium] into the soils" constituted a major change.[50]

The UCLA AEP reports about Trinity (and later about the Nevada Test Site) were among the first studies to describe the unpredictability of where radiation fell back to the ground after a bomb test. Radiation from atomic bombs surprised the early experts in not being dispersed in predictable patterns; it could not be traced in ever-smaller amounts in concentric circles from ground zero. Large amounts sometimes fell hundreds of miles from the detonation site, creating what came to be known as "hot spots." Kermit Larson of the UCLA AEP said later, speaking of the 1948 Trinity study, that they found no "hazard from external total body exposure to ionizing (gamma) radiation" in the fenced area. What they discovered was an area in "flux with respect to distribution and biological availability of radioactive fission products and plutonium." And they had no idea how many years would pass before some kind of biological equilibrium would occur.[51]

Understanding of the eccentricities of radioactive fallout from nuclear tests came slowly and sporadically. Many experts, especially in the Atomic Energy Commission and within the U.S. military, spent much time and energy in the late 1940s and 1950s trying to understand fallout—its characteristics and its sometimes strange patterns in falling back to earth. Their work was hampered by the secrecy and the politics surrounding all aspects of nuclear tests. The many civilian and military officials who wanted the United States to have a prolific and vigorous nuclear weapons testing program did not relish public worry about the consequences of such tests.[52] Thirty years after the Trinity test, federal government agencies continued to study its residual radiation. In 1973, for reasons unexplained in the extant document, the Environmental Protection Agency's Office of Radiation Programs in Las Vegas measured plutonium in soil samples in some seventy-five areas around the Trinity test site. What they found they described as negligible.[53] In 1982 the Defense Nuclear Agency issued an equally reassuring study that found no residual radiation in surrounding areas.[54]

The dozens of reports about the Trinity radiation with their divergent conclusions about the types and amounts of radiations, its mapping, and its toxicity illustrate important issues about post–World War II nuclear energy studies. First, the differing reports underscore the novelty and complexity of trying to map and measure different kinds of radiation over decades in a remote high desert environment. Just as the Trinity test scientists faced challenges mounting complex experiments in a desert rather than a laboratory, the early Trinity reports came from experts not yet deeply trained in field investigations, which were quite new in the sciences in the postwar decades. Environmental radiation research personnel, equipment, methodologies, and terminologies, changed significantly over the years.[55]

For decades investigators found the existing radiation-measuring machines, even the latest models, to be insensitive and generally inadequate. Kermit Larson, who cowrote many of the UCLA reports, recalled numerous problems with the equipment, but he especially singled out the instruments to measure alpha radiation. To get even minimally useful measurements, investigators had to crawl on their hands and knees close to the source. No one, said Larson, wanted to do that.[56] It is important to note, however, that over the years as more sensitive equipment became available and began to be used more widely, investigators conducting field research in New Mexico drew new and often more alarming conclusions about the persistence of plutonium.

The politics surrounding the bomb's radiation also played a major role in the production and circulation of information, in the censorship of information, and even in the conclusions drawn in diverse reports. Studies of fallout and residual radiation carried political consequences; civilians and military officials in the nuclear establishment feared that public alarm threatened funding. Conflicts over these issues became sharp and frequent in civilian and military groups, not least within the AEC. The stark disagreements among experts about whether the radiation at Trinity posed safety hazards also importantly foreshadowed decades of bitterly divisive conflicts about the medical dangers from nuclear fallout and about the dangers of exposure to low-level radiation.[57] Secrecy and its requirements became ever more stringent. As historians have long argued, some of the secrecy surrounding nuclear fallout stemmed from officials' fears of lawsuits. Studies of the Trinity radiation, like much about the nuclear tests at the Nevada Test Site and in the Pacific, remained undercover so as not to inflame public fears; officials also hoped to minimize any legal problems that might emerge based on downwinders' health claims.[58]

The reports and their divergent conclusions about the Trinity radiation did not receive open circulation or debate, and the degree to which any groups of officials may have discussed them behind closed doors, or whether they were ever actually discussed at all, remains unknown. Profoundly important issues about the effects of atomic fallout reached no public forum. Some of the reports, particularly those issued by Los Alamos personnel, remained classified and extremely hard to obtain for decades; many are still hard to find or are available only in highly censored form.

The controlled circulation of the Trinity studies provides insights into the evolving culture of Cold War secrecy in the United States. A full-blown system for classifying nuclear material did not emerge instantly even though the Atomic Energy Act of 1946 declared that everything pertaining to nuclear matters was "born secret."[59] The Trinity radiation studies illustrate the different paths that limiting circulation of nuclear information could take in the early decades of the Cold War. Some of the Trinity radiation studies were stamped "secret" when first issued, a few were stamped "confidential," and others were treated as "gray" literature—that is, reports, memos, and conference proceedings that were not subjected to classification procedures, whose printing came from government funds, but whose information was restricted simply by the reports not being made readily available. Sometimes such gray literature was not catalogued or was shelved in obscure places, its circulation deliberately circumscribed.[60]

The circulation of reports was also controlled by the often-used expedient of printing only a few limited copies and safeguarding distribution lists.

The secrecy surrounding so many of the Trinity radiation studies is a particularly important part of the Trinity story because it was from that test that U.S. military and civilian officials first tried to understand and, quickly, to contain knowledge about the effects of nuclear radiation from atomic weapons. Trinity served as a pioneering site for such studies in the decade after the war before "fallout" was well understood and as the United States increasingly put its military hopes in nuclear weapons. Gradually, as the culture of deepening and more pervasive secrecy crystallized, new ways of communicating knowledge emerged. New ways emerged for experts with equivalent levels of security classification to talk and write to each other at classified conferences or by circulating classified reports through approved classified channels.[61] But this took time to evolve. Very little knowledge about fallout from atomic bomb tests circulated outside of closely guarded networks in the United States until the mid- (and some would argue, the late) 1950s, and even then, knowledge about the Trinity radiation remained little known and little publicized.[62] So, for many years after other aspects of atomic radiation entered into the public realm to be discussed, debated, and argued about, the issue of the Trinity test radiation remained quietly cloaked. Investigated in many studies, it nevertheless remained a secret issue arousing little public discussion.

These politics surrounding the Trinity test radiation continue today. The issues continue to be contentious and unsettled as experts publish disparate findings. Radiation epidemiologist and health physicist John D. Boice Jr. argued in 2020 in the journal *Health Physics* that "no transgenerational effects occurred as a result of exposure to fallout from Trinity." He also argued that there is no evidence "of increased cancer rates among scientific, military, and professional participants at the Trinity test . . . who received much higher doses than NM residents downwind from the Trinity site."[63] In 2016 and 2017 the National Cancer Institute (NCI) conducted a field investigation "to inform a study to estimate cancer risk from Trinity already underway." In collaboration with NCI radiation dosimetrists, a multidisciplinary team began "to collect data and derive estimates of lifestyle factors that could be applied to the dose assessment methods for the Trinity test." Dr. Steven Simon summarized the major findings from that and several other studies and presented conclusions that are in striking contrast to earlier Trinity radiation studies.[64] One of the surprises: "The findings indicate that only in small geographic areas immediately downwind of the detonation site were the exposures substantially higher than naturally occurring background radiation." The largest doses (which the researchers did not regard as having been dangerous) occurred in areas that are not mentioned in other records before or after the Trinity test: Torrance and Guadalupe Counties (somewhat north and east of the bomb site). Another study cited by Simon found reassuring results. Even in the areas where the most unfissioned plutonium fell, "the concentration of plutonium in the topmost layer of soil (that is, the layer most available to contaminate persons in the vicinity) was below the level at which action was required for it to be reduced for health protection." Additionally, the study found that over successive years, the concentration of plutonium originally at the surface of the ground had been reduced "because of natural processes that continually move the contamination downward to deeper levels of the soil below the surface." These findings contrast significantly with what the UCLA AEP studies found in earlier decades. The current study concluded that the plutonium levels did not require remediation by the EPA. Earlier in this chapter I noted that politics led to censorship or silencing of some of the earlier reports about the Trinity radiation. Is it possible that similar censoring, self or otherwise, took place with the NCI radiation studies during the Trump Administration?

## Native Americans and the Trinity Test

Native Americans rarely appear in the histories of the atomic bomb, although many worked at Los Alamos. As I note earlier, some men from the nearby pueblos worked as laborers—and, as time passed, as workers—in the Los Alamos labs; Native American women worked as housekeepers, maids, and nannies at Los Alamos. In general, though, the actions and even the presence of the many Native Americans whose pueblos and villages surrounded Los Alamos are among the most glaring lacunae in the histories of the atomic bomb. In spite of this omission, as I have written earlier, the very choice of the Trinity test site involved Native Americans. General Groves smarted over the warning from Secretary of the Interior Harold L. Ickes that no Native peoples were to be moved for the Trinity test, but he complied. Ickes was one of the few high-ranking political figures in American history to take strong stances toward protection of

Native peoples. His wife may have been an important influence because she had lived in New Mexico and Arizona, respected its Native peoples, studied the Navajo language, and wrote a book, *Mesa Land*, focused on life and culture in the Southwest.[65]

Given that Groves deferred to Ickes's stipulations in choosing the site of the bomb test, did he and other Trinity test leaders have concerns about the test's effects on the nearby pueblos or the Mescalero Apache Reservation? Specifically, did they worry about any possible radiation falling on the reservations and pueblos? Nothing that I have seen in the archival records focuses on this, but the possibility sheds light on some otherwise odd actions and one particularly strange concern of the test's planners. Joseph Hoffman, already often cited as head of the offsite radiation monitors during and after the test, explained that as pre-test planners speculated about the likely path of the radioactive cloud right after the explosion, expectations centered on it going either northeast or southeast. He then notes: "It was deemed necessary to choose a weather condition which would not blow the cloud over the town of Carrizozo which lies slightly north of due east of zero."[66] Why did the test leaders "deem" it necessary to avoid any fallout over Carrizozo? Furthermore, why was their ideal wind condition the "North Blow," which would take the radioactive cloud well north of Carrizozo? They ruled out conducting the test if weather would take the cloud south of Carrizozo or if the weather made the cloud's direction "indeterminate." Thus, the ideal date for the test was July 16, when, according to the meteorologists, the most likely wind direction blew to the north.

What was this about? The town of Carrizozo had no larger population than other towns nearby.[67] Was the focus on Carrizozo a way to avoid overt mention of the need to protect the Mescalero Apache Reservation, some sixty miles *southeast* of Carrizozo, from fallout?

In the detailed accountings of where radiation monitors (humans with equipment and in some cases only equipment) were placed and what their machines recorded in terms of fallout in the hours after the test, none appear to have been placed in, or even near, the Mescalero Apache Reservation. Hoffman's report includes handwritten (unfortunately, often illegible) lists of where offsite monitors took readings, but none seem to have been near the reservation. No monitoring went on at Ruidoso, for example, where, as I noted earlier, a girls' camp received significant fallout. Monitors were placed in areas quite a distance from ground zero but always east or north of the reservation (at Roswell for instance). Either test planners had considerable confidence about their wind-direction predictions or else they simply wanted to minimize any focus on the Native peoples in the area. (Perhaps they sought permission from the reservation leaders to monitor the radiation and it was refused; it seems more likely, given the broader history of Los Alamos's disregard for the neighboring pueblos, that Trinity leaders preferred to leave the reservation as invisible as possible.)

New Mexican Native Americans had so few cancers that, for a while, medical personnel in the mid-twentieth century believed them immune. Cancer rates among Native Americans in the U.S. Southwest, however, soared in the decades after World War II, largely attributed to the upsurge in uranium mining and the presence of uranium pilings in Native American territories as demand grew for the material so precious for nuclear weapons. In his history of the often fraught relations between Los Alamos and the pueblos, Joseph Masco pays close attention to the illnesses caused by the radiation from Los Alamos, especially from the "RaLa" tests to improve implosion designs for the atomic bomb. That testing generally took place at Bayo Canyon, three miles east of the town of Los Alamos and bordering the San Ildefonso Pueblo. Averaging one test a month for eighteen years, "from September 1944 through March 1962, Los Alamos scientists conducted 254 implosion experiments using high explosives around a core of lanthanium-140."[68] The test protocols required that experiments only take place when the wind blew away from the town of Los Alamos in a north or northeasterly direction toward "unpopulated areas." Winds in that direction may have protected Los Alamos residents, but they took the fallout toward the pueblos of San Ildefonso, Santa Clara, and Pojoaque, as well as the town of Española.[69] Masco's scrutiny of the impacts of Los Alamos radiation on neighboring Native American tribes makes no mention of radiation from the Trinity test.[70]

It is a powerful reminder of the linkages between nuclear bombs, the poisoned environment, and Native groups that the worst radiation accident in U.S. history, a dire disaster for citizens in many western states but catastrophic for the Navajo people downstream and downwind, occurred on the thirty-fourth anniversary of the Trinity test. The Church Rock uranium disaster released the largest amount of radioactive material into the environment in U.S. history, including that of the much-more publicized event several months earlier at the Three Mile Island nuclear plant in Pennsylvania.[71]

Immediately after World War II, demand for uranium for atomic bombs created mining frenzies in many parts of the globe, but nowhere more so than areas of the southwestern U.S. encompassing Navajo lands in New Mexico and Arizona. Mines small and large appeared across the landscape, poorly regulated and laxly policed during operations and even more ignored once mining operations ceased. Some Navajos benefited from jobs in the mines or processing the dirt and rocks to obtain the uranium, but in general the post–World War II and Cold War uranium boom brought environmental pollution and escalated radiation dangers throughout the West. Mines dotted the landscape and were worked for brief periods before being abandoned with no regulatory oversight for the mounds of debris remaining piled about, much of it radioactive. Winds blew the radioactive dirt far; precious groundwater became contaminated. In the summer of 1979 at a private mill outside Church Rock, New Mexico, a disposal pond containing the waste rock and fluids remaining after the removal of uranium accidentally overflowed. No one sounded an emergency alert, and for two days over one thousand tons of radioactive waste and ninety-four million U.S. gallons of acidic, radioactive tailings and other toxic materials flowed into the Puerco River, a major source of drinking water and irrigation for the neighboring Navajo Nation. In recent years historians and environmentalists have paid careful attention to the Church Rock disaster; no longer ignored, it has become part of a growing history of radiation disasters. I include it here because of the irony of its occurrence on an anniversary of the Trinity test that created the original demand for ever more uranium for ever more nuclear bombs.[72]

## The Trinity Test Downwinders

In the decades in which so many groups studied the Trinity test's residual radiation, the focus remained almost entirely on plants, soil, mammals, birds, and reptiles in the Tularosa Basin. Few experts raised concerns or paid attention to the human toll of the Trinity radiation. One reason, as noted in the preceding pages, is that so little information became available to the public. Over the years a few articles in local New Mexico newspapers referred to the radiation from the test, almost never in alarmist ways but with reassurances that officials understood and oversaw any possible danger. On a broader scale, as I have noted several times in this book, based on historian Paul Boyer's classic cultural history of American public reactions to the bomb, Americans' attitudes in the early years toward the radioactivity from nuclear weapons altered dramatically. The intense fear that followed the earliest sensationalized reports of deliberate radiation "poisoning" at Hiroshima and Nagasaki and the reports in newspapers about how "it could happen here" turned surprisingly quickly into a kind of numbed public amnesia that lasted nationally until the mid to late 1950s, when public consciousness took a new turn and Americans began to pay attention to the seemingly new issue of "fallout" and be alarmed about reports of fallout from the Nevada tests. That public concern became sufficient to spur Congress to hold well-publicized hearings about "the nature of radioactive fallout and its effects on man" in 1957 and 1959.[73] (In 1959 the AEC's Division of Biology and Medicine created a "Radiation Effects of Weapons" branch.)

Even as the U.S. public began to express growing concern about fallout and other dangers of bomb-related radiation, little of that attention focused on the Trinity area. Public reactions (and lawsuits) centered on the Nevada Test Site "downwinders," the victims of the U.S. nuclear tests in the Pacific, and later (although to a far lesser extent) the Navajo uranium miners in the Southwest. The ranchers and townspeople directly affected by radiation from the Trinity test received little attention from any authorities, and the same is true for the workers at the test. All were ignored by the researchers I have discussed above, who, from 1945 on, studied the Trinity bomb's effects, as well as by government agencies that, beginning in the 1970s and expanding in later decades, began to conduct formal investigations into early Cold War radiation exposures of soldiers, sailors, and U.S. civilians. Even as those studies expanded, Los Alamos and AEC officials did not (in any public way at least) study any possible human ill effects from the first atomic bomb.

The Ratliff family illustrates this. The pre-test mapping of local ranches and farms overlooked that family—a ranching couple and their grandson. Several reports document radiation monitors' surprise at discovering an otherwise unknown and unidentified family living in what Trinity officials came to call "the Hot Canyon" because of its high radiation readings. Stafford Warren's handwritten notes about the test's radiation included the comment that the "house (with family)" located 0.9 miles beyond the canyon received "an accumulated total dose" of 57–60 roentgens.[74] After radiation monitors' initial shock at finding a family living near areas that read 15 roentgens per hour (R/hr) a few hours after the test, two Los Alamos health physicists returned in the next weeks and months to investigate that family, their health, and to take radiation readings of their property, including inside the adobe house. Joseph Hoffman and Harry Whipple reported that the fifty-year-old couple living on the property with their ten-year-old grandson had been asleep on the morning of the shot, and they reported hearing, feeling, and seeing absolutely nothing out of the ordinary. They were aware of nothing unusual until the grandson returned home from Bingham late in the afternoon. He had left early in the morning to go to school, probably riding his horse, and had reached Bingham around 9:00 a.m., where he heard the fabricated innocuous explanation for the explosion. Hoffman and Whipple wrote in their report that the boy, by being at Bingham during the day and indoors at night, missed most of the heavy exposure that fell that first day at his grandparents' place.

They showed surprisingly little concern with the senior Ratliffs. They wrote that "Mr. X" (they blacked out the surnames, but later reports included them) spent most of the time outdoors the day of the test, but his wife worked mainly indoors. For the next two weeks the couple apparently kept to their usual routine, arising at 6 a.m., working about the ranch, coming indoors for dinner about 7 to 8 p.m., and listening to the evening news broadcast. They lived in a "well built two room adobe structure" with walls about fifteen inches thick and a tin roof. Water fell from the roof into a cistern until drawn up for use. It rained the night after the test, so "some of the [radio]activity was carried into their drinking water and may have been drunk on the following day and thereafter." The Los Alamos investigators took samples of drinking water and soil from various places in the Ratliff yard and inside the house. The war raged on in Asia and secrecy remained tightly controlled, so the two Manhattan Project investigators said nothing to the Ratliffs about radiation dangers (including about the drinking water). Nowhere do the records document how Hoffman and Whipple explained their personal questions, their measuring instruments, and their repeated visits.[75]

At a certain point, the Ratliff family moved away and disappeared from public records, only to reappear in recent years as knowledge about the Trinity downwinders' experiences became more publicized. Similarly, although the experiences of the Herrera family during the Trinity test, with which I began this chapter, received little attention for many years, recently Henry Herrera has been interviewed by newspapers and television reporters worldwide, including Al Jazeera and Japan. In one interview he vividly recounted "ash as large as snowflakes" falling for hours.[76] He was interviewed by people from the National Cancer Institute since his medical history included a diagnosis of cancer of the salivary gland at age sixty-three and the loss of life savings to pay for the medical treatments five hundred miles away in Albuquerque.

Not until the mid-1950s did people in Utah and Nevada who lived downwind of the Nevada Test Site begin to go to court seeking compensation for damage to their livestock and for their own medical problems that they had come to believe were caused by the radioactive fallout from the tests. The Atomic Energy Commission consistently claimed that the bomb tests did not cause cancers; few claims made by downwinders made it to trial, and in the rare times when there was a trial, juries accepted the government's positions of national security and innocence of wrongdoing.[77] Very gradually, however, public and official responses became more sympathetic to downwinders' claims. In the 1980s, the Department of Energy's "dose reconstruction" studies attempted to chart the radiation exposures experienced by military personnel during previous decades' nuclear maneuvers. In 1995 reports about officially sponsored and condoned human radiation experiments during and just after World War II spurred the secretary of energy to establish the Advisory Committee on Human Radiation Experimentation (ACHRE). That committee and its four-volume report, along with tens of thousands of now-public declassified documents, opened the door for serious historical investigation into many aspects of American nuclear history.[78] In 2010, fifteen years after the groundbreaking work done by ACHRE, the Center for Disease Control funded a detailed study of the Trinity radiation: the Los Alamos Historical Document Retrieval and Assessment report (LAHDRA). For the first time, a publicly available government report provided explanations, tables, and maps of the post-test radiation. Some of the findings remain shocking; the report asserted that radiation exposure rates in "public areas" near the Trinity blast "were measured at levels 10,000 times higher than currently allowed."[79] Joseph Shonka, one of the lead researchers for the LAHDRA study, gave a paper in 2019 at the annual Health Physics Society meeting arguing that the

Trinity test produced the equivalent of a "dirty bomb" because less than 20 percent of the plutonium was fissioned in the explosion and the rest, unfissioned, fell back to earth, becoming part of the heavily contaminated soil and debris that spread over thousands of square miles.[80]

The LAHDRA report's conclusions disappointed the growing number of activists who wanted official recognition and compensation for the suffering they believed they and their families had endured because of the Trinity radiation. The report concluded, "Too much remains undetermined about exposures from the Trinity test to put the event in perspective as a source of public radiation exposure or to defensibly address the extent to which people were harmed."[81] The report found that there was not enough evidence to draw conclusions about radiation effects because no one at the time and in subsequent decades paid sufficient attention to the internal doses "received by residents [near the Trinity test] from intakes of airborne radioactivity and contaminated water and food."[82]

*Compensation for Downwinders*

On a research trip to the National Archives in Maryland, I found a folder labeled "Disposition of Holloman Bombing Range" with a bright red piece of paper attached: "SECRET. This is a cover sheet for Classified Information. National Security Information." The bottom of the folder had another label, "secret," bordered in red. In looking through the folder's contents I could only deduce that the secret information may have pertained to hazards from the radioactivity in the crater area at the Trinity site since many of the remaining documents mention that hazard.[83] I was also intrigued to find that two items had been removed entirely because they contained "security classified information." Although censors had removed the actual documents, their titles remained. One, removed in August 1994, was a memo written June 18, 1948, from Roy B. Snapp, secretary of the AEC, to the AEC, titled "Disposition of Alamogordo Test Area," and the second item, removed in April 1997, was a memo dated July 31, 1948, from Gordon Gray, assistant secretary of the army, to David E. Lilienthal, chairman of the Atomic Energy Commission, labeled "Disposition of Holloman."[84] Although the most significant issue pertaining to the Trinity area in the spring through the fall of 1948 remained its transfer from the AEC back to the army (and then to the air force), officials in all three agencies shared concerns about "the contaminated portion" of the area or, when being more forthright, the health hazards created by the radiation.[85]

Why were those two documents pulled in the 1990s? It seems likely that NARA had only received the materials in 1993 since that is the date marked on the outside of box 64. Therefore, the archivists charged with checking for material needing censorship could not have begun earlier. In thinking about the politics surrounding downwinder compensation, the dates and the censorship began to make possible sense. In October 1990, in the midst of the growing demands for redress from America's decades of nuclear testing, Congress passed the "Radiation Exposure Compensation Act" establishing a system by which U.S. citizens who believed they had suffered from radiation exposure during official U.S. bomb tests could seek federal compensation. The act also covered Native Americans and others affected by the fevered-era of uranium mining in the 1950s.[86] The 1990 bill followed an earlier but weaker 1979 bill providing a pathway for civilian downwinders to claim compensation for exposure to radiation from atmospheric weapons testing at the Nevada Test Site.[87]

The original act only offered compensation to nuclear test downwinders in very specific areas: ten counties in Utah, five counties and part of a sixth county in Nevada, and five counties and one added area in Arizona.[88] No provisions offered compensation for downwinders in New Mexico. This omission gave new force to existing organizing and political lobbying that sought to expand the coverage offered to downwinders, including those from the Trinity test. Could individuals in the federal government or the National Archives have been sufficiently concerned about that expansion to censor evidence about the radiation hazard from the Trinity test?[89]

The censoring of the NARA documents, therefore, may be evidence of some officials' growing concern about New Mexico downwinders' exposures, a response to the Radiation Exposure Compensation Act (RECA) of 1990. In the mid-1990s the Trinity test's effects began to receive sustained attention from New Mexican downwinders claiming damages from exposure to the test's radiation. The newly founded Tularosa Basin Downwinders Consortium (TBDC) began to advocate for members' inclusion in RECA.

Amendments to the RECA law over the years added new geographical areas of compensation eligibility for residents in parts of Nevada, Utah, Arizona, and "a small part of Inyo County, CA." The 1990 RECA bill expanded the geographic area and list of cancers that would make someone eligible for government-funded compensation. The list included the Trinity test site but covered only people who had been present at the site during and after the test as employees of the government, the military, or the AEC. Thus, Trinity test scientists and other workers (as well as the radiation monitors) met the eligibility criteria and could appeal for compensation, but the amendment specifically ruled as ineligible New Mexicans who lived downwind of the test. In 2000 Congress added further geographic areas in which residents during the years of nuclear testing could petition for compensation if they now suffered from certain kinds of health conditions. Again, the Trinity test downwinders were excluded.

The history of the RECA legislation includes numerous bills to further expand "the downwinder eligibility area." Some passed but others failed. One, for instance, sought coverage for people who had been alive during the years of atmospheric testing at the Nevada Test Site—people in the states of Arizona, Nevada, and Utah and in specified areas of Colorado, Idaho, Montana, and New Mexico. In 2001, for the first time, the wording of the proposed amendment included Trinity downwinders: "Additional legislation would have created downwinder eligibility for persons living in Guam during atomic weapons testing in the Pacific and for persons affected by fallout from the initial Trinity test in NM."[90] That amendment did not pass.

In 2002 Congress asked the Board on Radiation Effects Research of the National Research Council (NRC) to give advice about whether the RECA downwinder area should be further expanded. The NRC issued a report three years later with the astonishing conclusion that fallout from the Nevada Test Site "covered the entire country" and that "people living far beyond the current downwinder eligibility area may have been exposed to higher amounts of radiation."[91] The committee recommended changing the criteria for determining eligibility and compensation. The government should move from geography as a basis for compensation consideration to an "alternative science-based approach" that would take many factors into account to calculate an applicant's "individual absorbed dose of radionuclides." The estimated dose would then be used to calculate the probability "that the individual's specific type of cancer was caused by his or her exposure to ionizing radiation." The Congressional Research Service report about the proposal concluded that a large number of people in the United States would therefore be eligible to apply for compensation under RECA, but concluded that the NRC model would probably result in fewer successful claims. In the end, however, Congress did not vote on the proposed new model. To this day, downwinders from the Trinity test remain left out of the compensation processes.

As publicity about nuclear fallout and its dangers widened in the decades of the late twentieth century, as citizens of other states sought redress, men and women who now had a name for their situation—"Trinity test downwinders"—organized, created publicity, and sought government compensation. It took them many years to work up to such political actions and to learn how to gain public recognition and momentum. When the Trinity downwinders failed to be included in the original RECA and its amendments in 2000, some of them and their family members formed the Tularosa Basin Downwinders Consortium to advocate for inclusion in the compensation policies. They sought from the government, first of all, money to help defray the medical expenses their families had paid for decades because of illnesses they believed stemmed from exposure to the 1945 test. They also wanted the federal government to apologize to them and their families for their decades of health suffering as well as loss of lands and animals.[92]

To date there has been little to no financial compensation and no apologies to the New Mexicans affected by the Trinity test even though, in the conclusion of two historians with the U.S. Department of Energy, the Trinity test posed "the most significant hazard of the entire Manhattan Project."[93]

In her pathbreaking 2014 book, *Downwind: A People's History of the Nuclear West*, historian Sarah Alisabeth Fox argues that failure to address radiation-affected people continues their marginalization, and she criticizes the way such groups were overlooked even by historians working on the "Atomic West."[94] The past two decades, however, have seen a growing attention to and acknowledgment of downwinders' claims of having been harmed by nuclear tests. Few historians today could say that those claims lack scientific or historic validity, and downwinders are no longer presented, as they were sometimes in the recent past, as examples of local color "in the historical narrative of the Cold War American West."[95] As this chapter argues, the Trinity bomb's radiation has, since the test itself, preoccupied different groups of scholars, scientists, and government and military officials. Much of the attention was kept secret and most of officials' concerns focused on distant effects of the radioactivity or its impacts on animals, birds, and plants rather than on human "downwinders." At times some officials had fears that radiation remained at the Trinity test site, but those fears were not a significant factor in the delays and problems in historical preservation of the site.[96]

One of the ironic consequences of the silencing and secrecy documented in the preceding pages is the growth of a mythology to fill the vacuum left by a lack of specific knowledge. Interviews conducted by anthropologist Jake Kosek reveal a widely held suspicion among New Mexican residents that the scientists who for decades collected data for their reports about the Trinity radiation were also responsible for hundreds of cattle mutilations in the areas around Los Alamos in the 1970s and 1980s. Kosek found that New Mexicans believed that the scientists used the soft tissue to test radiation levels. New Mexico citizens associated the removal of the cattle's sexual organs, udders, and tongues with the long history of environmental studies of radiation.[97]

The Trinity test has never become simply a historical event. The National Park Service marks its site as a National Historic Landmark, but its legacies live on in deep controversies about the bomb's radiation. Tourists at the site during its once-or-twice-a-year opening sometimes joke about the radiation by lining up for photos in front of the big yellow sign warning of "radiation." Such lightheartedness appears as well just outside the entrance to the site in a road sign unlike anything else on the highways depicting an oddly malformed animal of some sort, presumably misshapen from radioactivity. But the citizens of New Mexico affected by fallout from the Trinity test—the "downwinders"—do not joke about the radioactivity. To them the impacts remain.

# SEVEN

## Historical Preservation of the Trinity Site

As part of the White Sands Missile Range, the Trinity site is carefully guarded and closed to the public. However, because it is also a National Historic Landmark the army opens the area to tourists once a year under carefully controlled conditions. (It has been open twice a year in recent years, but this has varied.) A chain-link fence surrounds the ground zero area, which remains a slightly indented area with a radius of several hundred feet. For some years a small, twisted remnant of one of the tower's steel legs remained, but at some point it vanished. A few miles away during the open house event, tourists can visit the George McDonald house, where the final assembly of "the gadget" took place. Otherwise, apart from miscellaneous materials the army sets up at the site the few times it is open to the public, only the fence and an obelisk distract from the space and silence of the surrounding desert.

For decades different groups tried to preserve the site to commemorate the invention of the atomic bomb and the achievements of American science and later, in vaguer language that at times tried to minimize the fact of the atomic bomb, as an important part of the nation's history. The numerous preservation attempts over decades, the changing cast of key players, and the varying terminology complicate presenting a disentangled narrative. Even before the official end of World War II, some Americans sought official commemoration of and preservation of the Trinity site as significant in the development of America's atomic bomb. At times the efforts became a long, often contentious series of campaigns, but at other times efforts languished. The single major obstacle that the National Park Service and politicians faced over the decades remained the Trinity site's location in what continues to be an active missile range, carefully protected by the Department of Defense. For twenty years supporters focused on preserving the site as a National Monument—a high-status designation, second only to a National Park.[1] When that failed, efforts shifted to preserving the site as a National Historic Landmark (officially achieved in 1975) and also as a National Historic Site (not achieved). The new Manhattan Project National Historical Park, for which serious planning began in the early 2000s, included the novel concept of a park consisting of several noncontiguous units. The early plans included the Trinity site as one of the units (discussed later in the chapter).

This chapter looks first at attempts by diverse people and agencies to gain formal recognition and preservation of the Trinity site and then at the "atomic tourism" and public meanings attached to it.

## Early Attempts to Preserve the Trinity Site as a National Monument

Immediately after the atomic bombing of Hiroshima and Nagasaki, in mid-August 1945 the Alamogordo, New Mexico, Chamber of Commerce envisaged turning the Trinity site into a National Monument. The White Sands National Monument, adjacent to the White Sands Missile Range, may have spurred those state officials' enthusiastic hopes for another tourist-attracting, revenue-generating official park area, but in the next five to six years other groups enthusiastically echoed the idea. Representatives of the Department of the Interior, the Department of War, the National Park Service (especially its Region 3, which included New Mexico), New Mexico state legislators and congressional representatives, and numerous individual citizens participated in meetings and other talks and wrote and circulated memos and reports enthusiastically supporting the creation of a National Monument in the atomic test area. The attempts underscore the high value early supporters placed on such official recognition.

Plans for a new National Monument to the atomic bomb test progressed slowly in the late fall of 1945, hampered by several problems. National Park Service (NPS) officials worked to get the information needed for a formal report as well as supplementary materials for the actual preserved site. M. R. Tillotson, director of the NPS's Region 3 (which covered New Mexico), became seriously involved in the effort. He tried to get photos of the site from *Life*, he tried to get the army's specially built tanks used before and after the test to be part of the monument, he wrote numerous letters to the state tourist bureau. Newton B. Drury, the head of the NPS, wrote in December to Tillotson to say that the secretary of war had authorized a small group of Park Service officials to investigate the site. It was to be arranged through General Groves. Drury also passed on a warning from the War Department that a National Monument "might interfere with the continued use of the Alamogordo Bombing Range."[2] A little later, Drury explained to New Mexico governor John J. Dempsey the growing enthusiasm for a National Monument at the Trinity site, noting that the NPS would investigate and issue a report about what lands and features should be included in the monument. The secretary of war had given the NPS permission to study the area. It is startling to read how Drury imagined the monument because it was so at odds with the official report created a little later by others in the Park Service. Drury said that there would be no need for a large area of land and that "land requirements for site preservation, access, and development of facilities will be modest." He added a warning for the governor: because so much about atomic energy was still "a closely guarded secret," the army might want to keep the area closed off for some time and that might delay the creation of the monument.[3] Another reason for possible delay, Drury noted, came from Congress, which was working on legislation "concerning the entire field of atomic power and energy," and not even the secretary of war nor the secretary of the interior quite knew what to expect. He was referring to the legislation that resulted in the creation of the Atomic Energy Commission (AEC), but in mid-October 1945 he did not have a clear idea of what Congress envisioned.

In the fall and winter of 1945 various groups continued attempts to secure National Monument status for the test site. One problem that continued for years involved getting a precise description of the actual area being considered. In early October 1945 the General Land Office at the Department of the Interior claimed not to know the precise location of the Trinity test area. Groves probably contributed to this confusion because, although he agreed that the War Department should send the Park Service photographs of some aspects of the Trinity site (the "scientific aspect and personnel"), he urged that the surrounding countryside not be pictured.[4] This may have stemmed from Groves's congenital secretiveness, but it also reflects his awareness of ongoing plans to expand the missile program and the need to keep the entire area little known. M. R. Tillotson, the Park

Service's regional director for the New Mexico area, apologized for the delay in completing the formal proposal, a delay he said was caused by problems in securing and then preparing the maps, difficulty in securing "land status," and delays in clearance from the army for the photos the Park Service had already taken for the report.[5] The NPS completed a formal report on the proposed National Monument in late November, and in December Drury sent a memo to the secretary of the interior about the proposal to designate the "site of first explosion of an atomic bomb" as a National Monument. Ickes agreed to accept the report, and the NPS forwarded it to him that month.[6]

The proposal for an Atomic Bomb National Monument began with the attention-grabbing statement that the test was "the climax of what was probably the most dramatic and significant scientific venture in history. This was the test explosion of the first atomic bomb." The authors explain that the site deserved preservation "because of the effect that the atomic bomb had in hastening the termination of World War Two and will undoubtedly have on the entire future history of the world." The report proposed that the National Monument should be a large area covering "everything of historical significance" with "ample room" for "visitor accommodations" in the way of parking areas and comfort stations as well as an administration building and residential and utility areas. The report envisioned the monument having "three separate isolated sections with connecting right-of-ways"[7] The walkways would connect the bunkers and the crater area around "Zero." The plan specified that it was "particularly desirable that the remains of the steel tower at point 'C' be untouched. From the public standpoint this will be one of the most spectacular exhibits of the entire monument."[8] All roadside wiring, bunkers, and observation posts should also be left untouched as part of the visual display visitors would walk past. The report also specified the construction of some water diversion ditches east of ground zero near the foot of the Oscura Mountains to protect the area against flooding, and some roads should be redirected, envisioning that "perhaps the ultimate plan would involve the construction of a modern park approach road to connect with U.S. 380."

The planners assumed that "the story could best be told" in a museum since, apart from the remains of the tower at ground zero and the "atom-site covering the ground in the vicinity of Zero," they believed "there is little to be seen of a spectacular nature" at the Trinity site. Disparaging the desert area, the planners said that the surrounding landscape would not "adequately convey the momentous event that had taken place." The report also viewed the George McDonald house as unworthy of inclusion: "the bomb might just as well have been assembled at any other house in the vicinity or a temporary structure erected for that purpose." The house could be pointed out to tourists who would view it from a distance. (NPS officials also understood that the army was involved with ongoing legal problems acquiring the properties.)

Visitors would have "to be very carefully controlled during their entire time spent in the monument" because, as the report's authors stated, visitors allowed to "roam at will and unattended over the area" could not possibly gain "a full and proper understanding of the event" that the monument would commemorate.[9]

Asserting mindfulness of the need to limit the amount of acreage to be withdrawn from the military, the plan emphasized that only a total of 3,531 acres would be needed for the monument.[10] The report clearly noted that it was well understood that the area would not be put under NPS administration until it was "fully released by the Army," which might take a number of years, but the report emphasized that such a delay should not affect the early establishment of the monument. Ironically, given later criticisms of the army for destroying materials at the Trinity site, the report added that as long as the army remained on the site and as long as army authorities understood what the National Park Service wanted in terms of "protection and preservation," the site could "be assured of full 100 per cent protection."[11]

Although the December 1945 report gained the support of various important people and groups who then worked hard for years to secure their goal, the Trinity site never became a National Monument. The reasons deserve scrutiny.

Some Americans objected to honoring the atomic bomb, expressing fears that the atomic bomb had crossed a crucial moral threshold and it represented an ethically unacceptable weapon. In his classic study of early reactions to the atomic bomb in America, historian Paul Boyer traces complicated, far from straight shifts of early public fear and revulsion to later celebration and pride.[12] Certainly, numerous Americans expressed moral qualms about celebrating an atomic bomb, particularly in the early years when the effects in Hiroshima and Nagasaki remained horrifying to many. Even a few Park Service officials expressed reservations. Hillory A. Tolson, who served as acting director of the NPS from late 1945 through at least August 1950, said that the Park Service wished "to emphasize in contrast to [the bomb's] destructive potentialities . . . the medical and other constructive gains which atomic energy makes possible." Tolson added that the monument would "determine mankind to use atomic power only for peaceful ends."[13]

Ben Thompson, who in the 1950s was chief of the Division of Recreation Resource Planning for the NPS, wrote a carefully worded memo to the director in November 1947: "I believe that this Country should not establish a national monument to commemorate a bomb—any more than we would want to commemorate the use of poison gas. Perhaps what we are trying to do with the Atomic Bomb National monument project is to commemorate the first controlled and dramatic use of atomic energy outside the laboratory. The fact that controlled atomic energy was first used for bombing purposes would seem to be incidental to the main fact that man is learning to control atomic energy." Thompson suggested that the site be named the "Atomic Energy National Monument" and that "in the development and interpretation of the area, we treat the military use of atomic energy as an incidental use."[14] Thompson emphasized that he objected to the name of the monument and "the emphasis to be given or not to be given to the bomb," but he hastened to say that he did not intend his suggestion to interfere in any way with the establishment of the proposed National Monument.

Other people had no qualms about wanting to commemorate the atomic bomb test at the New Mexico site, but for many reasons formal efforts to preserve it did not crystallize in the late 1940s and 1950s. General Groves became involved in the historical preservation attempts, offering to lend his help to the NPS. He must have been pleased to hear from the director of Region 3 that once the army "completes its activities" at the site "we hope to make this area available to the public as one of the most significant historical sites not only in the U.S., but in the entire world."[15] Groves helped organize a permanent committee to oversee the proposed Atomic Bomb National Monument, but he dropped out quietly from serving on that committee following his conflicts with Truman and congressional leaders about the establishment of the AEC.[16]

In general, in 1946 and into 1947 interest in the National Monument proposal remained high and generated meetings and exchanges of memos. Some hoped to include permanent exhibits such as the *Enola Gay* (the B-29 bomber that dropped the Hiroshima bomb). The secretary of war liked that idea but in early spring said that neither of the two B-29s that dropped the atomic bombs in Japan could be made available, as they were being modified to participate in the planned atomic tests in the Pacific— the Bikini tests. In addition, he warned (without further elaboration) that official concerns about secrecy would limit the availability of equipment "and other historical objects used at the test bomb site." In particular, the *Enola Gay*, although certainly in a "special interest" category because of its historical value, would have to be stripped of all secret equipment.[17] By midsummer, after meetings between army personnel stationed at Los Alamos and NPS officials, those involved decided that the army would assemble material (approved by the Los Alamos Security Section) and turn it over to NPS Region 3 director Scoyen, who had established good relations with Howard C. Bush, the army officer in charge of the Trinity camp after the war. The materials would include the lead-lined tanks originally brought to the test site for sampling the radioactivity at "Zero" right after the test. The material would also include Jumbo, any remains of the tower, pictures of the project, and names of people associated with it. A section of the trinitite would be moved and put under a temporary shelter. The memo declared firmly, "No further changes or destruction is to take place at the site."[18]

From early January 1946 through 1948 various Park Service officials drafted versions of what they hoped would be a presidential proclamation to create a National Monument at Trinity. The drafts exist in the archives but with no details about why President Truman never issued a proclamation. One version contained the intriguing language that this was to be a monument to the "first non-laboratory use of atomic energy."[19] For reasons not explained anywhere that I have found, Truman never issued the proclamation if it even reached his desk.

Sometimes in offering historical explanations we need to draw back and look at the bigger picture, and this is certainly important with this issue. As much as some people wanted the Trinity site to be approved as a National Monument, no one could work steadily and solely on a single issue in the tumultuous late 1940s and 1950s. Efforts for a memorial at the Trinity site waned in those years in part because all of the contending agencies had newly pressing demands that took time and attention and diverted their focus from the preservation attempt. The army, air force, and navy, as we have seen, fought internal problems over their identities, roles, and funding in those years. They also had the obvious preoccupation of fighting a war in Korea. The radiation at Trinity preoccupied other groups and agencies, particularly the Atomic Energy Commission.

The National Park Service underwent serious internal reorganization in the years immediately following World War II, and its new focus on an expanded mission challenged its traditions, its funding priorities, and its leaders' attention. The shifts in leadership at the national and regional levels within the Park Service underscore why some earlier issues lost momentum. In some accounts Newton B. Drury served as director of the entire NPS from 1940 to 1952, but in other sources Hillory A. Tolson served as acting director from 1945 to 1950, Arthur E. Demaray as acting director in 1948, Conrad L. Wirth as director in 1952, and E. T. Scoyen as acting director in 1957.[20] Region 3's directors often took action in the years when preserving the Trinity site was most in the public eye, and the revolving door in leadership affected them. M. R. Tillotson served as director of Region 3 from November 1945 through 1952, E. T. Scoyen as acting regional director 1945 to 1947, and P. P. Patraw became associate regional director in 1949 and then served as assistant regional director from 1951 through at least July 1953 (although other sources list Hugh M. Miller as assistant Region 3 director in 1952). That kind of instability did not facilitate consistent attention to complicated (and troublesome) projects and almost certainly contributed to the delays and confusion about preserving the Trinity site.

Given the wider national debates about historic preservation in general and differences about the role the NPS should take in such preservation, records illustrate ongoing uncertainty about the Trinity site preservation. One significant issue continued to be confusion about the exact area to be included. Groups also differed over what type of preservation to seek. Well through the 1950s many people continued to hope that the Trinity site would be formally designated a National Monument. This included the governor of New Mexico, who met in 1952 with the secretary of the interior, AEC officials, and some in the (newly named) Department of National Defense to pursue efforts to establish a National Monument at what some now referred to as the "Trinity A-Bomb explosion site." The

AEC responded with the alarming statement that it was under contract to destroy the "vestiges of the site" but would delay that action until the Department of the Interior had a chance to review the issues.

In the spring of 1952 congressional representative A. M. Fernandez (Democrat from New Mexico) introduced HR 6953 to establish the Trinity Atomic National Monument. Congressional members, however, quickly modified the bill so that no action would occur until the site was "no longer useful to the DOD."[21] On July 29, 1952, demonstrating continued interest in the site as a monument, several officials made a formal inspection: NPS director Conrad L. Wirth, New Mexico governor Edwin L. Mechem, and Region 3 park director Tillotson, among others. Two months later the assistant director for Region 3, P. P. Patraw, distributed yet another preliminary NPS report detailing hopes about preservation and public access to the Trinity area, this time sending it to Brigadier General George G. Eddy (commanding general of the White Sands Proving Ground), Colonel Don R. Ostrander (commanding officer of Holloman Air Force Base), and Carroll Tyler (AEC manager for New Mexico). It produced no results.

For the rest of the decade the NPS met with no success from any of its preservation efforts at Trinity. Ben H. Thompson (chief of the NPS's Division of Recreation Resource Planning) noted in 1957 that five years earlier they had reached "substantial agreement" with the Department of Defense (DOD) and the AEC about including the site in the National Park Service but "it is not feasible in the present circumstances since the area lies within the Alamogordo bombing range which is still in active use by the Army and is not open to the public." Thompson reported that the proposal had not been abandoned but is "quite dormant and is likely to remain so for the indefinite time."[22] These reduced efforts are reflected in the archives, which contain almost no material about preservation attempts for the Trinity site in Park Service or army records from the mid to late 1950s.

## The Trinity Site as a National Historic Landmark or a National Historic Site

By the 1960s Trinity site promoters deployed several new options for its historic preservation. Acknowledging the difficulties in trying to secure the area as a National Monument, some groups worked in that decade to preserve it as a National Historic Landmark (NHL) while others wanted it officially designated as a more prestigious National Historic Site. The history of these efforts is not easily disentangled. Some of the complications stem from terminology because words relating to preservation of historic sites in the United States are used both loosely and precisely. "National historic site" is sometimes used very generally to refer to any number of places considered for preservation in some way. The United States preserves places for diverse reasons: their natural beauty, their historical value, and their artistic and archaeological value.[23]

The number of nationally preserved sites and areas in the United States has changed over the years, as has the terminology; new categories have been added and others have been altered or removed. At times the list has included National Parks, National Parks and Preserves, National Historical Parks, National Monuments, National Historic Landmarks, National Historic Sites, National Memorials, National Battlefields, National Preserves, National Seashores, National Lakeshores, National Grasslands, National Wildlife Refuges, National Rural Scenic Roads, National Recreation Areas, National Parkways, the National Trails System, Wild and Scenic Rivers, Historic Trails, Memorial Parkways, and Frontier Military Roads. The National Park Service administers some of these historical entities, while others are managed by other sections of federal or state government such as the U.S. Forest Service or the Bureau of Land Management. Some are managed by private organizations.

Areas considered for status as National Historic Landmarks are sometimes referred to loosely as national historic sites, and this contributes to the confusion because the nation has a formal designation for National Historic Sites and a strict procedure for nominating and selecting them. A National Historic Site (NHS) usually has one historical feature. (A related designation is a National Historical Park, and that involves more than a single property or building.) Many NHSS had been the homes of famous people such as Clara Barton, Edgar Allan Poe, Carter Woodson, and several U.S. presidents—or they commemorate significant occurrences, such as *Brown v. Board of Education* (elevated from a National Historic Site to a National Historical Park in 2022).[24] Any place receiving official approval as a National Historic Site will have gone through carefully designated formal procedures, which can be (and often were) lengthy, time-consuming, and challenging.

In the materials about preserving the Trinity test area this loose terminology causes no little confusion. In a 1952 memo clearly titled "Proposed

Trinity Atomic National Monument," a writer at the Pentagon referred several times to the "proposed national historic site." He seemed unaware that a National Monument and a National Historic Site were two different kinds of preservation.[25] In the late 1960s there continued to be confusion or at least contradictory language about what kind of historic recognition was being sought. The Senate bills introduced in 1967 and 1968 aimed to preserve Trinity as a National Historic Site, but one official at the White Sands Missile Range still reported erroneously in a memo that "s-291 proposes to make the TS into a National Historical Monument."[26]

During the New Deal years Congress passed significant new preservation laws. The Historic Sites Act of 1935 created the Historic Sites Survey to identify nationally significant sites and buildings that needed protection and that might be considered as eventual additions to the National Park System.[27] The Historic Sites Survey, discontinued during World War II, slowly revitalized in the late 1940s and early 1950s and was then incorporated into the National Register of Historic Places created by Congress in 1966 as part of the National Historic Preservation Act. That act established the National Register of Historic Places and the criteria and steps needed for a site to be listed in it. At the same time, a second program was created to evaluate sites that seemed worthy of more prestigious status: the National Historic Landmark program.[28] The National Register of Historic Places lists thousands of sites, buildings, and areas. Once listed on the National Register some sites may be proposed for further recognition as NHLS or, more selective still, as National Historic Sites. The National Park System Advisory Board reviews proposed National Historic Sites and National Historic Landmarks and, if approved, forwards them to the secretary of the interior, who makes the final decisions. The whole rigorous process has often taken two to five years.[29]

As the new 1960s programs took root, judging committees abandoned some of the earlier criteria for historic preservation. Several earlier stringent rules changed in the 1960s to take into consideration buildings less than fifty years old as well as those with architectural originality. Architectural beauty as well as the political fame of the owner now counted.[30] One of the reasons for the relaxation of the fifty-year rule came from the desire of members of the advisory committee in the 1960s to include atomic energy sites.[31] Several of those sites did indeed receive NHL designations in the 1960s including several from the Manhattan Project: the attic rooms in Gilman Hall at the University of California, Berkeley, campus, where plutonium was identified as a new element; the x-10 uranium processing reactor at Oak Ridge, Tennessee; and the entire Los Alamos Scientific Lab in New Mexico. The Trinity test site made it to the original list but, as documented below, the date of its official recognition as an NHL is open to question.[32]

Given the numerous and long-lived efforts by so many groups and individuals to secure formal historic recognition for the Trinity site, it is ironic that there remains confusion about just when and how it actually happened. Some of that confusion surely comes from the twelve-foot granite obelisk at ground zero. The plaque on the obelisk reads simply (with missing punctuation): "Where the world's first Nuclear Device was exploded on July 16, 1945 Erected 1965 White Sands Missile Range J. Frederick Thorlin, Major General, U.S. Army, Commanding." Ten years later, on the thirtieth anniversary of the atomic bomb test, a second plaque was added below the first, carrying the official seal of a designated National Historic Landmark along with the date of 1975. The wording is especially noteworthy because it in no way acknowledges or celebrates the atomic bomb or the Trinity test. Instead, the message reads simply that "the site possesses national significance in commemorating the history of the U.S.A."[33]

The two plaques reflect confusion and problems in the process of gaining official recognition of the bomb test site. In the autumn of 1965 NPS and army officials began to take new interest in obtaining formal recognition of the Trinity site; the army noted that the site was eligible for registration as a National Historic Landmark, and someone in the army or the regional park service (the records are unclear) submitted the application form to enter the Trinity site into the new National Register of Historic Places. Everyone apparently believed that all procedures had been followed correctly, and two years later, in 1967, the NPS declared the Trinity site including ground zero and the George McDonald ranch to be an official National Historic Landmark.[34] The White Sands Missile Range (WSMR) erected the stone obelisk and the general at the base, as noted, proudly included his name and rank in the plaque's wording.

All seemed fine until new and more stringent federal rules began to be applied to the nation's historic and cultural properties in the early 1970s. New environmental protection rules began to be implemented, and oversight agencies gained new power. Within the NPS, a Landmark Review

Task Force discovered problems with the Trinity site's official historic status because, apparently, the National Register nomination had not been properly completed earlier. To rectify that problem, park personnel took action, sending in a modified nomination form, and on March 15, 1972, the Trinity site was listed as a National Historic Landmark in the Federal Register of Historic Places.[35]

Other problems continued. In April 1974 the landmarks specialist with the Southwest Region of the NPS (formerly Region 3) pointed out that the boundaries of the Trinity National Historic Landmark had never been officially established. The army considered the NHL to be the area at ground zero within the current chain-link fence, but the Park Service held a much more expansive vision based on the master plan of 1970.[36] As the new director of Region 3, Joseph C. Rumsberg Jr., observed in a note to the White Sands National Monument superintendent, who was overseeing the preservation effort, there would be no memorandum of understanding with the army about the Trinity site until the boundaries of the landmark were defined and the correct procedures had been followed for the National Register nomination process.[37] So Rumsberg enlisted the help of the commanding officer at the WSMR and asked him to file a formal application for a certificate and bronze plaque designating "this historic property as a Registered National Historic Landmark."

Some of the backstory about the attempts in these years comes from archaeological specialists including Bill Godby with the Cultural Resource Program at the White Sands Missile Range.[38] Godby explained that in 1974 a "landmarks specialist" (presumably with the Park Service) pointed out problems with the exact boundaries of the historic site. According to Godby, although that original boundary remains officially on record in Washington, it is not actually the boundary managed by the WSMR since the 1970s. Although the 1970 master plan (for turning the Trinity area into a National Historic Site) proposed a diamond shape, the management plan drafted by the NPS modified the diamond shape to become more of a block shape. Godby points out, however, that nothing was made official, including the modified boundary. Bob Burton, Godby's predecessor archaeologist at White Sands, worked on a draft version of the "National Register of Historic Places Registration Form" in 2001, but according to Godby, "it never moved forward." Everything since then hit "a wall of bureaucracy," and nothing changed. At a certain point the WSMR hired the outside firm Human Systems Research Inc. to conduct a study of the archaeological remains at the Trinity site.[39]

In spite of (perhaps ignorant of or perhaps simply uncaring about) the technical problems with the formal recognition of the Trinity site, the commanding officer at the WSMR, Major General Robert J. Proudfoot, submitted the formal application to the director of the NPS in March 1975 explaining that he was acting in response to a Region 3 representative's request. Proudfoot noted that since the Trinity site was already listed in the National Register of Historic Places "the certificate and plaque will officially designate the site itself as the Registered National Historic Landmark." Proudfoot promised three things: WSMR would preserve "as far as practicable and to the best of our ability the historical integrity" of the site, they would use it only for purposes "consistent with its historical character," and they would permit an annual visit by representatives of the NPS. If the three were not upheld, "it is agreed that the Registered National Historic Landmark status shall cease" and neither the registered NHL certificate nor the plaque would be displayed.[40] Thus, finally in October 1975, the second plaque was mounted on the obelisk and the Trinity site received formal acknowledgment as an NHL.[41]

One irony is that if today's rules had been in effect, the Trinity site would probably not have met the criteria for NHL status because so much had been destroyed by 1972. By current standards if a proposed site has deteriorated or been modified since its period of national significance—if it does not retain "to a high degree the physical features that made up its historic character and appearance"—it might not meet NHL standards. This certainly happened with the Trinity site between 1945 and its being awarded NHL status in 1972.[42]

### Efforts to Preserve the Trinity Site as a National Historic Site

In the spring of 1974 as NPS Region 3 director Rumsberg sought to get agreement with the army about the Trinity site boundaries and to follow the correct procedures for registering the site on the National Register, he added a comment to a colleague that further complicates this already far-from-transparent history. He said that it was now time to more actively pursue establishment of the *Trinity National Historic Site* (emphasis added). Rumsberg thus failed to recognize that for years some people had been actively trying to achieve just that. Even as NPS agents (along with New

Mexico political figures and diverse federal officials) worked to secure recognition of the Trinity site as a National Historic Landmark, others worked in the 1960s through the 1980s to get it acknowledged as a National Historic Site. It is a great honor for a U.S. place to be officially recognized as an NHS, and diverse officials worked to secure that honor for Trinity. They ultimately failed, but not without considerable effort from the mid-1960s through the 1980s. The NPS's Advisory Board endorsed the possibility of Trinity becoming an NHS at its fifty-sixth meeting in October 1965.[43] In January 1967, New Mexico senators Anderson and Montoya introduced Senate Bill 288 "to establish Trinity National Historic Site." The bill was primarily intended to identify and protect the historic resources at the Trinity site pending its establishment as a National Historic Site. Under the bill, the Trinity site would be transferred to the Department of the Interior "when DOD determined it was consistent with national security to do so."[44] Referred to the Committee on Interior and Insular Affairs, the bill died.[45] At some point also in 1967 the New Mexico senators introduced another bill, S-291, to establish the Trinity National Historic Site in the state of New Mexico, but it too died in committee.

Meanwhile, the NPS continued efforts in the late 1960s through the 1970s to identify areas and structures at the test site that would become part of the official historical site; they worked with the army on interim protection plans and they drafted development concepts and preliminary master plans. By September 1970, they had created a third draft of the master plan for the Trinity National Historic Site, a very ambitious plan involving 51,500 acres, any instrumentation bunkers that were still extant, Jumbo, the McDonald ranch house where the scientists assembled the bomb, remaining structures at the Trinity Base Camp, and several nearby ranches.[46] The plan did not, however, bring Trinity official status as an NHS.

Relations between park officials and staff at the missile range in those years were generally cordial although interspersed with occasional flare-ups and misunderstandings. Emboldened by Executive Order 11593, "Protection and Enhancement of the Cultural Environment," five months earlier, park officials criticized the WSMR leadership in October 1972 for not having legally protected the area. A misdirected memo from Theodore E. Thompson, associate director of the Southwest Region of NPS in July 1973, raised the ire of Carcie Clifford, chief of staff at the WSMR. Thompson claimed to have intended the memo only for NPS eyes, but it ended up on

Clifford's desk, and he became enraged at the charge that his installation was destroying a National Historic Landmark. In a memo that added fuel to the growing controversy, Ken Tapman, compliance officer for the NPS's Advisory Council on Historic Preservation in Washington DC, sent a stern letter to the director of real property management, Office of the Assistant Secretary of Defense, Installations and Logistics, at the Department of Defense demanding information about the army's mistreatment of the site and asking for an investigation. Colonel Clifford defended the actions of the WSMR with a mid-July 1974 memo sent to three high-ranking army officers in different branches of the service. He pointed out that the McDonald house and Camp Trinity remained under private ownership although they were under "exclusive use agreements" with the army and nothing could be done with them until the government formally acquired the property. He stated that his headquarters would continue to "protect and preserve all items related to the Trinity Test," but release of the area was not feasible at that time. He offered a plan to protect and preserve various parts of the site by "fencing and posting."[47]

In the end, the Trinity test site did not gain National Historic Site status. The military uses of the missile range expanded as it acquired large chunks of additional land throughout the 1970s. In 1980 the NPS showed brief renewed interest in adding the Trinity site to the National Park System but abandoned the notion when the new director of the Southwest Region argued against the plan.[48] After that, efforts to expand the status of the Trinity site abated for twenty years. Much of what park officials had hoped to preserve at the Trinity Base Camp, on the outlying ranches, and at the bunkers around the test area itself could not be salvaged. The army opened the site to tourists once or twice a year, but little else changed.

*The Trinity Site and the Manhattan Project National Historical Park*

For a brief while the Trinity site was considered for inclusion along with Los Alamos, Hanford, and Oak Ridge as the fourth entity in plans for a new national park honoring the Manhattan Project. In 2001 the Advisory Council on Historic Preservation convened a panel of experts that recommended creating such a park, and the next year Congress took up the matter, spurred by congressional members from Washington State and New Mexico who introduced the "Manhattan Project National Historical Park Study Act of 2003." It directed the secretary of the interior to conduct a study "on the preservation and interpretation of the historic sites of the Manhattan Project for potential inclusion in the National Park System."[49] The bill made its way through Congress. On September 30, 2003, S-1687, the Manhattan Project National Historical Park Study Act continued to include the Trinity site as a fourth component of the proposed park, but a companion bill introduced at the same time included a significant change: an amendment removed the Trinity site area from the plan. A Senate committee adopted that amendment a year later without any explanation for the deletion of the Trinity site.[50] The most likely explanation for the removal of the Trinity site from the park is its continued location within the White Sands Missile Range. As has been the case since 1945, the U.S. military uses the areas around the Trinity site and has no desire to contend with the added number of tourists who would visit a national park, much less the federal rules governing a national park.[51]

Interestingly, following the removal of the Trinity site, the Manhattan Project's plutonium-producing plant in Dayton, Ohio, received brief consideration as a new fourth component of the proposed park. A draft report says that it was added to the study "by Congressional colloquy" but with no explanation of how it came to be added or how it soon came to be dropped.[52]

## American Nuclear Tourism

Atomic tourism is big business in the United States, attracting tens of thousands of visitors annually to sites around the nation. Nuclear accidents have generally received little public attention in the United States, so American tourism at nuclear sites has been more nostalgic and patriotic and less tinged with the macabre than in other places in the world. For example, tours at the vast wartime uranium processing complex in Oak Ridge, Tennessee, for decades (and continuing now) used to emphasize the charms of a "secret city" and "atomic triumphalism." Tourists could take a driving tour while listening to narratives on CDs as they encircled the "World War II Secret City."[53] At the equally gigantic wartime plutonium-producing plants in Hanford, Washington, a reporter in 2014 described one guided tour beginning with a forty-five-minute bus ride across the desert to the gate patrolled by armed guards.[54] Barbed wire fences and tumbleweeds lined the 586-acre site. Although all of Hanford's nine weapons reactors were closed, the bus stopped at the B Reactor, where the tourists were allowed inside. The reporter, Rick Hampson, explained, "I checked out the control room, which was like stepping inside the mind of a mad scientist, circa 1950. The primitive computers and other machines, painted a government green-gray, bristled with a bewildering array of switches, dials, screens, knobs, gauges, buttons and lights, with cryptic labels such as 'Deadman Test Switch' and 'Work Area Fog Spray.'" Hampson's article ended with the observation that although the B Reactor "may have been an agent of Armageddon, and Hanford may be the most polluted place in America," the on-site facilities manager told the tour group, "We do have fun here."

Nuclear tourists also flock to decommissioned missile silos and launch sites such as the Minuteman Missile National Historic Site in Philip, South Dakota; the Titan Missile Silo site in Royal City, Washington; and the landing beaches on Tinian Island in the Marianas, where the U.S. team assembled the bombs dropped on Japan in August 1945. Cold War sites of U.S. bomb production popular with tourists also include the plutonium reactors along the Savannah River in South Carolina; the Arco, Idaho, site of the first experimental breeder reactor (and the site of a serious nuclear accident in 1961, but that is often minimized); and the newly opened nature preserve created from the site at Rocky Flats, Colorado, where plutonium triggers for America's nuclear bombs were produced in the 1950s and 1960s. Tourists also flock to sites of nuclear bomb tests, especially the Nevada Test Site outside of Las Vegas, although it is open only occasionally to tourists who go through serious vetting before being bused around the site. Bikini Island in the Pacific has begun to attract tourists intrigued by the remnants of the series of devastatingly radioactive naval tests from "Operation Crossroads" in 1946. Tourists can scuba dive or snorkel among the sunken, irradiated ships. Among the scores of U.S. nuclear-weapons-related museums some focus broadly on Cold War exhibits or memorabilia while offering displays and descriptions of nuclear weapons production. Museum features include nuclear submarines, nuclear bombers, and the casings of "Fat Man" and "Little Boy" (the bombs dropped on Hiroshima and Nagasaki).

Atomic bomb tourism has mirrored tourism at American military museums in many ways. Tourists at such places react to the displays of fighter aircraft, military missiles, and information about nuclear bomb productions with scientific interest, national pride, and measured curiosity. In their many varieties of public displays, American wars have generally remained sacrosanct from deeply disturbing challenges. Traditional military and war museums in the United States, although sometimes acknowledging the devastation and painful civilian and military losses of wartime, have also generally continued to focus on battles, strategies, daily life for soldiers, military campaigns, and life on the homefront. Museums in that genre update by adding exhibits with new art such as life-size battle dioramas, depictions of new weapons, or technology such as virtual reality combat simulations. In the late twentieth century, some American history museums did begin to focus on increasingly somber topics including the horrors of wars, genocides, mass deaths, and other kinds of traumatic events such as famines or tsunamis, but this was rarely true of American war museums.

America's atomic tourist scene celebrates scientific achievement, American know-how, and, generally, civilian rather than military exploits. It is rare for any site to note an accident or to refer to any past or ongoing dangers such as radioactive waste even when the problems still exist. There is little focus on the fear, horror, death, and destruction from nuclear weapons; museums counteract the sobering potential of nuclear weapons and the problems of radioactive fallout and nuclear proliferation with approval of the brilliance of nuclear scientists and the peaceful prospects of nuclear knowledge. As historian Lindsey Freeman observes, many American nuclear tourist sites blend nationalism and a celebratory stream of what she calls "scientism." She also notes that in the United States, sites of nuclear tourism tend more to the nostalgic, whereas elsewhere in the world the "doom-tinged" attractions of dark tourism prevail (and sell tickets).[55]

In many American nuclear museums the solemn celebration of science coexists with atomic nostalgia and patriotic pride. American tourists appear to be drawn to the lighter sides of nuclear history and seek sites that evoke—or are overlaid with—atomic kitsch, which has been part of American popular culture since the end of World War II, as citizens tried to mitigate their fears about atomic bombs with movies about invasions of giant, irradiated ants or atomic gadgets. Visitors to nuclear museums can smile at the 1950s humorous electric mushroom clouds, "Miss Atomic Bomb" contests, atomic cocktails, and replays of duck-and-cover drills, while taking pride in America's nuclear arsenal and the belief that with such strength the nation won the Cold War. The Las Vegas Atomic Bomb Museum illustrates this well: a separate section (formally, the Nuclear

Test Archive) holds an archival treasure trove of historical documents of the atomic era—invaluable scholarly materials ranging from official reports to scribbled pencil notes on the backs of envelopes—all available to researchers. But most visitors do not come for the archived treasures; instead they enjoy celebratory photographs of atomic bomb explosions and a large and inviting store full of tempting items of atomic nostalgia and humor. Tourists can also visit the world's first experimental breeder reactor in Idaho on a carefully guarded site surrounded by ten thousand acres of desert. They can then drive up the road to the nearby small town of Arco, celebrated as the world's first city lighted since 1951 by atomic power, and they can eat "world famous atomic burgers" at the local café.

Some American historical sites and museums increasingly grapple with how to depict fraught and controversial topics. Museums have begun experimenting with new ways to present frightening or shocking topics to museum visitors. History museums attempting to challenge publicly accepted views about wars, battles, victories, and losses began to run into controversies early on. The most well known of these was the firestorm that engulfed the Smithsonian's *Enola Gay* exhibit in 1995. That attempt to depart from World War II celebratory culture by including a focus on the human suffering caused by the atomic bombings in Japan caused such protest that the entire exhibit had to be withdrawn.[56] The *Enola Gay* fiasco has had long-lasting impact, but American history museums today are tackling controversial topics in new ways, such as attempting to bring visitors into direct emotional contact with the stark and harsh horrors of recent wars by using space itself dramatically, by using light and sound in new ways, and of course by depicting horrors through photographs and films. Maya Lin's Vietnam War wall on the Washington Mall, installed in 1982, is a forerunner of the new approach, although its shock comes from its size and the number of names of young men killed rather than more graphic depictions of that war. Examples of the new approaches include the U.S. Holocaust Memorial Museum opened in April 1993, followed by sixteen other Holocaust museums in the United States and Holocaust museums worldwide, including the Berlin Holocaust memorial, which opened in April 2005.

Very few of the nuclear sites that tourists visit in the world publicize anything controversial about the site's history. Certainly almost none note any history of antinuclear protests, very few raise ethical or moral concerns, and very few provide information about environmental impacts of nuclear weapons past and present. Many such sites, of course, have seen protest demonstrations, but no markers record those historical events.[57]

Many people who are engaged with history, memory, and preserved national spaces hoped that the new Manhattan Project National Historical Park would present to the public some of the complex issues surrounding the birth of atomic weapons. The senators sponsoring the bill in Congress fueled such hopes. After praising the contributions of the Manhattan Project to victory in World War II, Senator Jeff Bingaman of Washington added that its legacy also "includes the deaths of hundreds of thousands of Japanese, and the sacrifices of the homesteaders that were forced off of the sites to make way for the project, its thousands of workers and their families, and the uranium miners, 'downwinders' and others." He acknowledged that the legacy of the Manhattan Project had been the subject of hot debate for decades and added that although the "enormous significance" of the Manhattan Project was abundantly clear, the greatest challenge "has been and will continue to be—interpreting this history in a sensitive and balanced way." U.S. history, he noted, included aspects that brought mourning, "anguish," and embarrassment over "senselessness." Washington senator Maria Cantwell, another sponsor of the bill, celebrated the significant contributions made by Hanford, especially the B Reactor, but she also acknowledged the importance of recognizing "the complicated and weighty issues arising from the production and use of nuclear weapons, their impact on world history as well as their human and environmental costs." She noted that farmers and tribes were displaced and that the Department of Energy (DOE) "continues its work to clean up the Hanford site, the country's most contaminated nuclear reservation." She emphasized the importance of honoring the achievements of the Manhattan Project, but also the need to commemorate "the tremendous sacrifices made by workers, displaced families and tribes, and this era's environmental legacy."[58]

To date, the new historic park has not embodied the hoped-for complications of celebratory nuclearism. The shutdown of many NPS sites during the COVID-19 pandemic affected plans for the new Manhattan Project National Historical Park; since its founding in November 2015, little has been done to create new exhibits or tours or to provide more critical analysis of the downsides of nuclear weapons. Tourists are given none of the shocking details about the environmental damage at Hanford, such as the existence on the site of fifty-six million gallons of radioactive waste products stored in rusting and leaking metal barrels. The historic racial disparities among workers at the Manhattan Project sites have begun to receive more direct historical assessment, but it is still tentative and paltry. The displacement of Native Americans from their lands because of atomic bomb creation and testing has yet to be fully documented in a national historical park.[59] No tours at all are available presently at Los Alamos; tours at Hanford and Oak Ridge are sparse. The relatively few interpretive materials online about the new park sites maintain celebratory rhetoric along with a few important critical recognitions of human and environmental costs. Since the new park is overseen jointly by the Department of Energy and the National Park Service, their divergent missions help explain some of the lacunae. The current official explanation is that the limited public access is due to "ongoing national security requirements and cleanup activities" and because the park has to be consistent with the mission of the Department of Energy, which is to "enhance U.S. security and economic growth."[60] The "Legacy" section, with three short paragraphs, is sparse but telling. Its first paragraph acknowledges the "enormous physical and economic toll" on the people in Hiroshima and Nagasaki and the "significant number of people displaced from their homes, lands and waters" as well as traditional use areas—and sacred sites. One statement glosses briefly over the serious health effects: "Nuclear processing and testing activities had impacts on human health and the surrounding environment."[61] The legacy section ends on an upbeat focus on the "monumental advancements" in science, engineering, technology, and nuclear medicine pioneered by the Manhattan Project. The foundation document notes that the park "lacks an overall interpretive framework" and the uncoordinated visitor centers (not managed by the NPS) tell only "portions of the overall story of the Manhattan Project." It acknowledges that more interpretive stories are needed about the diverse groups involved in the Manhattan Project, including the role of women. The document notes the need for more detailed focus on the bomb projects' impacts on displaced groups, on Manhattan Project workers, and on the Japanese people.[62] There is no mention of the radioactive legacies.

### Early Tourism at the Trinity Site

All of the decades of efforts to preserve the Trinity site were based on expectations that visitors would come to see the area to learn about the world's first atomic bomb test. As with the preservation efforts for the site itself, visions about the tourists—how many should be permitted to visit, when and how they should visit, what they should see, and how extensive their experience would be—all such issues aroused intense discussion and controversy over the decades.

The Trinity site attracted the world's first atomic tourists. Two young scientists from Los Alamos who had not been involved with the test, overcome by curiosity, drove in unauthorized in 1946. Lawrence Bartell and Paul Barker had both worked at Los Alamos with high-security clearances, but when the war ended, the two frisky twenty-two-year-olds wanted to see the site of the first atomic bomb explosion. Bartell recalled in a much later interview that they drove around in an old 1937 Ford, asking for directions to the site, and people "would point vaguely out into the desert." Without maps or any real sense of where they were going, they finally saw a sign—"U.S. Government Property. No trespassing"—so they knew they were on the right track. At one point they drove up a hill and found "there in front of us, a sea of green glass about a half a mile across, surrounded by red desert mud." They understood that they were looking at the site of the bomb's detonation. Bartell told the interviewer that he still owned a "little piece" of the trinitite. They were surprised not to see any kind of crater: "The ground was just pushed down because the bomb was set off on the top of a tall tower which wasn't there anymore."

At that point White Sands Missile Range police swooped in and arrested Bartell and his friend. After many telephone calls they were "thrown in the back of a truck and driven to the nearby military base." The enraged commanding officer told them that they were the first unauthorized people "ever to have been at this site" and their car was the first unauthorized vehicle to have been there (none of which was likely). But when the commanding officer learned that both men had worked at Los Alamos—both holding the high-level Q clearances—he apparently realized that "we were just a bunch of smart-aleck young twenty-two-year-olds" and permitted the two to drive back to Los Alamos, although still under watchful military guard.[63]

In the next few years, before any official historic recognition of the site, local ranchers and herders seem to have come quietly to look it over or they may simply have wandered in unaware of where they were. Military officials and park officials inspecting the area in the early years after the war occasionally found spent rifle shells, which they thought might have come from locals shooting rabbits. Small pieces of equipment left on the site disappeared—wire especially. The army's records do not provide details about such unwarranted visits in those early postwar years. General Groves orchestrated the first official tour of the site for thirty-one writers and photographers just as the war formally ended in September 1945. A famous photograph of that visit shows a group of men in and around the mangled remains of the steel tower that held the bomb. The two immediately recognizable are Oppenheimer and Groves, both men wearing cloth coverings over their shoes to protect them from the radioactive dirt.[64] It took eight more years before a group from Alamogordo visited the site on September 9, 1953. The visit took place during the period of often fraught negotiations among the Atomic Energy Commission, the army at the surrounding White Sands Missile Range, and the National Park Service about who controlled the site. A newspaper photograph depicts about a dozen people standing on or near a dirt mound about three feet tall near the twisted remains of the metal tower. Although the photograph documents one woman turned around, laughing at someone behind her, the other visitors are unsmiling, listening to the uniformed local White Sands army major explain the test.[65]

Occasionally in the next decades the army gave permission for National Park Service personnel to visit the area, generally to make a quick study of some aspect they wanted to include in a report arguing for the preservation of the site. Sometime in those years the Alamogordo Chamber of Commerce began to sponsor an annual tour of the test site, sometimes attracting more than one thousand visitors.

The October 1972 annual tour turned into a public relations disaster and spurred panicked restrictions on future tourists. Bill Ferdig, who worked in "facilities" in Range Engineering at wsmr, described what happened: "One of the tour's participants picked up a piece of trinitite and caused quite a furor by announcing to the press that that trinitite was dangerous to the public. Since this man held a PhD, this sensational announcement caused considerable reaction."[66] Angered by that furor and hoping to preclude such problems in the future, wsmr officials devised new procedures (many of which disappeared in subsequent years). All requests for visits to the Trinity site would now have to go through the wsmr Command Group. The army constructed a new fence from the outside gate to the long-established inner fence surrounding ground zero. Under other new procedures, the army would increase the number of guards watching visitors during open house at the site; no visitors would be allowed to pick up objects, especially the remaining trinitite. No visits would be longer than one and a half hours. No food would be consumed at the site. In addition the "Facilities Engineering Up-Range Division" installed a new corridor fence, installed warning and directional signs, removed sand, weeds, and other debris from around the fence, and repaired the fence and gates "to preclude unauthorized entrance."[67]

In spite of such restrictions and the basic difficulty of simply getting to the area, visitors continued to flock to the Trinity site the few times it was officially opened. Conducting research for her master's thesis, Kristel Wills visited in April 1998 along with several thousand other tourists. She found the scene like a carnival with people selling books, videos, pins, postcards, magnets, and T-shirts from tent shops along with vendors of hamburgers and drinks. At one tent shop an enthusiastic man demonstrated radiation levels with a Geiger counter. The general level of radiation, he explained, was comparable to simply being in the sun for a while, but the glaze on an old Fiestaware plate caused a "frantic clicking" of the Geiger counter and a small sample of trinitite caused it "to go crazy."[68] Wills expected to find "a sort of quiet veneration for this radioactive ground. I thought there might be tears. I believed that people came to this site as a pilgrimage . . . I thought that this place might actually serve as a kind of American Dachau that would remind people, 'Never again.'" Instead, she found "a kind of carnival" of gift shop tents, "colorful blue port-potties lined up neatly nearby, a large food counter, and a quarter mile walk to the most exotic attraction of all: nothing."[69]

## A Personal Visit to the Trinity Site

In 2015, the seventieth anniversary of the Trinity, Hiroshima, and Nagasaki atomic bombs, a record 5,534 people visited the site. A year later, on April 2, 2016, when I visited the site, by 7 a.m. over thirty cars waited in line one hour before the Stallion Gate entrance was scheduled to open.[70] By 8 a.m. several hundred cars were lined up along the narrow two-lane road outside the chain-link fence surrounding the White Sands Missile Range and then filed slowly past guards, some carrying machine guns, and past soldiers scrutinizing drivers' licenses and car registration papers. Four hours later the line of cars stretched several miles. In addition, army buses brought in scores of tourists from the Alamogordo area, southeast of the official drive-in entrance. Based on car license plates, tourists in April 2016 came primarily from local western states, especially Arizona and California; many were local New Mexicans. But others came from Texas, Iowa, New York, and even British Columbia.

The ways that officials from the White Sands Missile Range staged the Trinity site for the open house in October 2016 reveal a lot about the meanings they hoped tourists would take away from the visit. They trucked in items to provide tourists with a narrative to absorb. Some years the props have included a replica of the bomb itself: deceptively small in its roughly three-foot circularity. In 2016 a replica of Jumbo, brought to the site and displayed inside the fence, provided very little explanation of what the original plans for Jumbo had been and why they were eventually scrapped. Nor was there an explanation of what happened to Jumbo following the success of the test.[71] Reproductions of photographs, blown up to poster size, lined the chain-link fence. Those photos showed some of the Army Corps of Engineers men who built the site and some of the well-known scientists who designed the bomb. They showed hardworking American men employed in primitive and challenging surroundings; the photographs depict sturdy American grit and diligence, scientific know-how, and integrity. The Trinity open house traditionally includes the famous photographs of the fireball expanding from second to second with its growing mushroom stem. These have become iconic even though photographs of later, ever-larger nuclear explosions have become even better known to the American public.

Nothing at all controversial was displayed during my visit. It is noteworthy, however, that even though controversies are avoided, the Trinity site does not celebrate American triumphalism in inventing the atomic bomb or its role in Japan's surrender in World War II. That triumphalism— "Victory Culture," in the words of one historian, so long a part of the nation's reactions to and memories of World War II, celebrated by many citizens and criticized by others—does not hold the stage at the Trinity site commemorations. Nor did any photographs depict the destruction of Hiroshima and Nagasaki.[72] The atmosphere at the site that October morning could only be described as toned-down, casual, apolitical. Tourists wandered about gazing at the photographs, standing in line to have a turn to be photographed next to the obelisk commemorating the test. None of the tent stores of earlier years remained except for a display table with samples of trinitite and one author selling his history of the test. Many visitors simply wandered about almost desultorily. Visitors who had seen enough at the ground zero area could take a short bus ride to the nearby restored McDonald ranch house to imagine the bomb being assembled. And after that, they headed home.

For some time people studying museums and historical sites have begun to try to understand how visitors react to museum exhibits and what tourists think of the sites they visit. It is challenging to determine what visitors see, understand, and feel; it becomes especially a problem when we try to understand what tourists take away from the Trinity site. The White Sands base staff provides no guest books for recording reactions, and they truck in for the day almost everything at the site, so it all seems ephemeral. What do the tourists think about what they see? How much do they absorb about the test and its consequences? In spite of decades of attempts to create a memorial site, what remains today is emptiness rather than explanation, nothingness rather than the science or the historical explanations of the bomb and the reasons for its use in Japan. The Trinity site is in many ways unique among the proliferation of areas attracting atomic tourism because of its isolation, the harsh desert surround, its sparse exhibits, and its only occasional accessibility. It is a site to which visitors must bring their own sensibility. Perhaps some tourists have a dawning appreciation for the area's stark beauty, as did Ronald F. Lee, the chief historian of the National Park Service, after an early autumn visit to the site in 1947. Lee wrote, somewhat in surprise, "It is difficult to describe the strong appeal of this barren spot. Some persons might find the area disappointing; to me the visit was unforgettable. The approach is long, desolate, and forbidding. . . . There is a certain near grandeur in the wide valley setting with low rolling mountains a few miles off, ranging around on all sides. The abandoned landscape, unfriendly near at hand, but appealing in the larger [?] provided a sort of wild and appropriate stage, on a huge scale, for the atomic explosion."[73]

Noting the ironies surrounding the historic preservation of the Trinity area, historian Ryan Edgington observes that the site "has become a place largely defined by imagined encounters with nuclear weapons," and although it lacks "a narrative history that connects its ecological past to its modern value as a monument to the nuclear age," the site has become an "international site of remembrance" that has emerged from the contaminated desert.[74] The Trinity site does not fit the mold of "dark tourism" sites that draw tourists in other parts of the world (the Chernobyl and Fukushima sites, for example, or the Holocaust and other genocide sites). As I have argued, American atomic tourism seems motivated by patriotism, a fascination with technology, or simply a love of American history more than any particular lure of "darkness." Nevertheless, darkness is inherent in the history of the site, as Japanese atomic bomb survivor Kyoko Hayashi discovered on her visit in 1999. The surrounding desert may seem colorless, but the history of Trinity is definitely not beige.[75]

# NOTES

### PREFACE

1. Kyoko Hayashi, "From Trinity to Trinity," *The Human Experience of Long Time Being Spent* (2000), quoted in Yoshida, "From Atomic Fragments," 62.
2. Muraki's documentary was influenced by Kyoko Hayashi's "From Trinity to Trinity." It is also based on writer Mary Palevsky's account of her parents' work at Los Alamos, *Atomic Fragments*, particularly the last chapter, "Running to Ground Zero." Detailed in Yoshida, "From Atomic Fragments," 62.

### INTRODUCTION

1. Rieder and Lawson, *Trinity at Fifty*, 10.
2. Kuletz, "Invisible Spaces, Violent Places," 237, calls the southwestern U.S. deserts the "largest peacetime militarized zone on earth."
3. Edgington, "Fragmented Histories," 189.
4. *Empire Magazine*, *Denver Post*, July 6, 1967, cited in Szasz, *Day the Sun Rose Twice*, 167.

### 1. THE TRINITY TEST

1. Fine and Remington, *U.S. Army in World War II*, 701. At 2 a.m. the weather improved; at 4 a.m. the rain stopped. They called off the 4 a.m. shot. At 4:45 there was a good report, and Groves decided the test would take place at 5:30. See also Groueff, *Manhattan Project*, 354.
2. Frank Oppenheimer, quoted in Rhodes, *Making of the Atomic Bomb*, 675.
3. Joe Lehman, interview by Theresa Strottman, 1992, "Remembering Los Alamos: World War II," M1992-112-1-13.
4. Bernstein, *Oppenheimer*, 199. I. I. Rabi also had a sober reaction: with other invited VIPs at the Campania Hill site some twenty-nine miles northwest of ground zero, he recalled that at first the men gathered were jubilant and they congratulated each other. "Then, there was a chill, which was not the morning cold; it was a chill that came to one when one thought, as for instance when I thought of my wooden house in Cambridge, and my laboratory in New York, and of the millions of people living around there." Rhodes, *Making of the Atomic Bomb*, 675. James Bryant Conant (then chair of the National Defense Research Council and thus

an overseer of the Manhattan Project), according to his major biographer, was "traumatized" by the "transcendentally terrifying vision" at the Alamogordo test. Hershberg, *James B. Conant*, 240.

5. Rhodes, *Making of the Atomic Bomb*, 675.

6. Rhodes, *Making of the Atomic Bomb*, 675.

7. Brigadier General Thomas Farrell, interview by Lansing Lamont, tape 12, transcript, Lamont Papers.

8. Schwartz, *Atomic Audit*, 15.

9. Hoddeson, *Critical Assembly*, 13.

10. Good explanations of this can be found in Hoddeson, *Critical Assembly*, chap. 2; and in compelling detail in part 1 of Rhodes, *Making of the Atomic Bomb*.

11. Norris, *Racing for the Bomb*, 233. Szilard said in 1939 that if a chain reaction could be created with graphite and uranium, a bomb was possible. Rhodes, *Making of the Atomic Bomb*, 302.

12. Rhodes, *Making of the Atomic Bomb*, 314.

13. Fermi, *Atoms in the Family*, 166–67.

14. Plutonium was discovered in February 1941 at UC Berkeley by Glenn T. Seaborg based on work done by Edwin M. McMillan, Philip M. Abelson, Emilio Segre, Joseph W. Kennedy, and Arthur C. Wahl. Schwartz, *Atomic Audit*, 54n36.

15. Rhodes, *Making of the Atomic Bomb*, 284.

16. To underscore the speed with which American officials moved, all of this happened before December 2, 1942, when refugee Italian physicist Enrico Fermi and half a dozen other scientists achieved a controlled chain reaction with natural uranium, which, among other things, demonstrated the feasibility of a fission bomb. The experiment, involving what Fermi labeled "a pile" of graphite threaded with uranium, took place under the football stadium at the University of Chicago, where scientists at the "Metallurgical Laboratory" studied many aspects of nuclear energy.

17. Schwartz, *Atomic Audit*, 55. Groves had almost finished overseeing the Army Corps of Engineers' construction of the Pentagon—the massive new headquarters for the War Department in Arlington, Virginia. The Army Corps of Engineers, with its experience building and overseeing large-scale construction projects both in the United States and overseas, began construction of the giant Pentagon project in 1941—on September 11 (which decades later became another powerfully meaningful date in U.S. history)—just three months before Pearl Harbor. The war emergency pushed the Pentagon project to completion in less than sixteen months. Groves, who wanted an overseas assignment closer to actual combat, negotiated a promotion to brigadier general before accepting the job of supervising the entire bomb project.

18. Groves, "Some Recollections of July 16, 1945," 47.

19. Fine and Remington, *U.S. Army in World War II*, 200.

20. Bobbie Ann Mason, "Fallout: Paducah's Secret Nuclear Disaster," *New Yorker*, January 10, 2000.

21. Schwartz, *Atomic Audit*, 56n41.

22. Carroll, *House of War*, 68.

23. Carroll, *House of War*, 27.

24. Malloy, "'A Very Pleasant Way to Die,'" 515–45.

25. Harold Agnew, interview by Theresa Strottman, 1992, "Voices of the Manhattan Project."

26. Fermi, *Atoms in the Family*, 226.

27. Fine and Remington, *U.S. Army in World War II*, 663.

28. One of the best sources about this is McMillan, *Ruin of J. Robert Oppenheimer*.

29. Bernstein, *Oppenheimer*, 76.

30. Bernstein, *Oppenheimer*, 83.

31. McMillan, *Ruin of J. Robert Oppenheimer*.

32. Schwartz, *Atomic Audit*, 9n12.

33. Schwartz, *Atomic Audit*, 6.

34. Schwartz, *Atomic Audit*, 53–54.

35. Schwartz, *Atomic Audit*, 58–59 and 60, table 1-1. This included the costs of the NDRC, OSRD, and MED.

36. Rieder and Lawson, *Trinity at Fifty*, 25, citing Bainbridge, *Trinity*.

37. Rhodes, *Making of the Atomic Bomb*, devotes little space to the May test. Army historian Vincent Jones wrote that the test "provided a likely indication of the amount of radioactive materials needed for the final test." Jones, *Manhattan*, 512. Rieder and Lawson, *Trinity at Fifty*, 27, provide a good description of the test.

38. Hoddeson, *Critical Assembly*, 361.

39. Tolman to Groves, memo, May 13, 1945, RG 77, Box 55, Folder 319.1, NARA Maryland.

40. Tolman to Groves, May 13, 1945.

41. Bainbridge, *Trinity*, 2.1.

42. Hoddeson, *Critical Assembly*, 361; Jones, *Manhattan*, 512.

43. Bainbridge, *Trinity*, 2.3.3.

44. Hawkins, *Project Y*, 237.

45. Tolman to Groves, "Report on First Trinity Test," May 13, 1945, RG 77, Box 56, NARA Maryland.

46. Bainbridge, *Trinity*, 2.4.

47. H. L. Anderson, "Radioactivity Measurements at the 100-Ton Trial," May 25, 1945; H. L. Anderson, "100-Ton Test; Radiation Above the Crater after 41 Days," June 22, 1945, available online at Los Alamos National Laboratory Research Library.

48. Hoddeson, *Critical Assembly*, 358.

49. Laura Fermi, *Atoms in the Family*, provides warm and admiring accounts of the professional relationship and friendship between Anderson and her husband. Although still a doctoral student, Anderson worked with senior, world-famous scientists in ways that reminded Laura Fermi of much that she found especially laudatory about American democracy. In the carefully neutral explanation of David Hawkins, *Project Y*, 237, the Los Alamos scientist who wrote one of the early histories of Los Alamos, the information "secured by the Fission Studies

Group of F Division, was essential in planning for equipment recovery, bomb efficiency measurements and personnel protection for the final test." It should be noted that the "personnel protection" was for the workers at the test site, not the citizenry of New Mexico.

50. Nagle, "Memorial Colloquium Honoring Herbert L. Anderson."
51. Anderson, "Radioactivity Measurements," May 25, 1945, Los Alamos Research Library online version.
52. Anderson, "Radioactivity Measurements," May 25, 1945, Los Alamos Research Library.
53. Hirschfelder and Magee to Bainbridge, memo, June 16, 1945, U.S. Department of Energy OpenNet, https://www.osti.gov/opennet/, accession no. NV0059784.
54. Anderson to Bainbridge, memo, "Operational Plan for Trinity," June 14, 1945, U.S. Department of Energy OpenNet, https://www.osti.gov/opennet/, accession no. ALLA0001781. The men were Sergeant Brothers (6.11 roentgens per hour), Sergeant Smith (5.0), G. Weil (4.83), M. Gentry (4.83), J. Tabin (1.67), Sergeant Hanas (0.3), and L. D. P. King (0.3). Darragh Nagle received 2.41 roentgens per hour and Anderson himself 2.34.
55. Nagle, "Memorial Colloquium Honoring Herbert L. Anderson." Nagle, a graduate student at Columbia, worked with Anderson and Fermi there, went with them to the University of Chicago for the fission experiments, and then went with them to Los Alamos.
56. Kistiakowsky to Oppenheimer, memo, October 13, 1944, Szasz Papers, Box 8, Folder 21.
57. Pierce to Groves, memo, May 18, 1945, RG 77, Box 56, Folder 319.1, NARA Maryland.
58. To Major Claude C. Pierce, memo, "Security and Intelligence Operations in Connection with Trinity," July 30, 1945, RG 77, Box 56, Folder 319.1, Trinity Test Reports Misc., NARA Maryland.
59. Hoddeson, *Critical Assembly*, 353–54, citing Bainbridge, *Trinity*. Bainbridge provides extraordinarily detailed lists of which men did what preparations for the test, but he does not always identify the numbered sites, such as the two men with seismographs at "9000N" and the geophones at "N9000." In the final "arming" of the test, Bainbridge drove Joseph McKibben to "W900," where the timing and sequence switches were located. This location, too, is not further identified in sources. See Rhodes, *Atomic Bomb*, 667.
60. Bainbridge, *Trinity*, 86.
61. Groves, *Now It Can Be Told*, 286 and 291. Groves portrays himself and others as deeply worried about the radiation from the test and its effects on ranchers and towns, but his claims seem after-the-fact.
62. Hoddeson, *Critical Assembly*, 354.
63. Hoddeson, *Critical Assembly*, 354.
64. Lamont, *Day of Trinity*, 220. After the national anthem the Delano, California, radio station played a waltz from Tchaikovsky's "Serenade for Strings," which apparently was also broadcast, at least in part, over the loudspeakers at the Trinity site.

Confirmation of this is in Los Alamos Historical Society, *Los Alamos 1943–1945*, 54. Carr, "Thirty Minutes Before the Dawn," 7n65, says that "The Star-Spangled Banner" played over the camp radio.

65. Bainbridge, *Trinity*.

66. The officials at the base camp included Vannevar Bush (head of the U.S. Office of Scientific Research and Development); James Bryant Conant (then chair of the National Defense Research Council and thus an overseer of the Manhattan Project); scientists Richard Tolman, Cyril Smith, I. I. Rabi, Kenneth Greisen, and Enrico Fermi; physician Stafford Warren; and Groves himself.

67. Lamont, *Day of Trinity*, 219.

68. Lamont, *Day of Trinity*, 223–25. The others included British detonation expert Ernest Titterton, who had sole responsibility for the "thyratron" tube that would activate the bomb detonators.

69. Val Fitch, interview by Cindy Kelly, 2008, "Voices of the Manhattan Project." See also Lamont, *Day of Trinity*, 221.

70. Warren Nyer, interview by S. L. Sanger, 1986, "Voices of the Manhattan Project."

71. Lehman, interview. Lehman is unlikely to have known about chain reactions at that time, so this is a good example of some of the complexity of later oral histories.

72. Nyer, interview.

73. Maag, *Report*, 3.2.

74. To Major Claude C. Pierce, memo, July 30, 1945, NARA Maryland.

75. Fitch, interview.

76. Fitch, interview.

77. Lamont, *Day of Trinity*, 209.

78. E. O. Lawrence, handwritten note about his responses to the test, "Report on Test II at Trinity, 16 July 1945," Roll 1, Subseries 1, Files 1–7D, Scans 101–200, 0103TIF, Top Secret Correspondence MED 1942–46, Digital File, Center for Research Libraries. See also Rhodes, *Making of the Atomic Bomb*, 668–76.

79. Bernstein, *Oppenheimer*, 80. William L. Laurence, reporter for the *New York Times*, also attended. For a critical analysis of Laurence's reporting, especially about the radiation, see Keever, *News Zero*, 73–74.

80. Charles and Jean Critchfield, interview by Theresa Strottman, n.d., "Remembering Los Alamos: World War II," M1992-112-1-2.

81. T. O. Jones to Groves, memo, "Eye Witness Accounts of Trinity Test," July 30, 1945, RG 77, Box 56, Folder 319.1–319.2, NARA Maryland.

82. Joseph G. Hoffman, "Health Physics Report on Radioactive Contamination Throughout New Mexico Following the Nuclear Explosion 16 July 1945," Los Alamos-626, 1947, p. 7, Los Alamos Historical Document Retrieval and Assessment Study (LAHDRA) materials, Folder 1580.

83. Among the Trinity radiation monitors who later monitored radiation in Japan were Barnett, Hornberger, Whipple, and Tybout. Richard A. Larkin (USN) observed the Trinity test and then went to Japan. See Reports Pertaining to the Effects of the Atomic Bomb 1945–56, RG 77, Box 92, NARA Maryland.

84. Hoffman, "Health Physics Report," Los Alamos-626. William McElwreath's name is also spelled McElreath and McElevreath in different sources, but this book uses the McElwreath spelling for consistency.

85. Lamont, *Day of Trinity*, 227. Also, Howes and Herzenberg, *Their Day in the Sun*, 48–49.

86. Hoffman, "Health Physics Report," Los Alamos-626. The group included Langham, Magee, Levine, Barnett, Anderson, and Hirschfelder.

87. Arthur Breslow to J. G. Hoffman, memo and personal notes, "Radiation Monitoring and Itinerary," Szasz Papers, Box 8, Folder 38. Barnett's account was about a mistaken reading, but Breslow's account is more harrowing, raising questions about why it is not better known in the post-test sources.

88. Breslow to Hoffman, "Radiation Monitoring and Itinerary."

89. Capt. H. Barnett, "Field Notes by Radiation Monitor on 16 July 1945," Szasz Papers, Box 8, Folder 38.

90. Jones, *Manhattan*, 512.

91. Jones, *Manhattan*, 511.

92. Assistance of 8th Service Command in Evacuation Plans, Farrell, memo to file, June 26, 1945, RG 77, Box 56, Folder 319.1, Trinity Test Reports Misc., NARA Maryland. Handwritten at top: "Gen. Groves." The estimate raises questions about who was to be evacuated. According to the state's 1940 census, Vaughn "village" had 1,331 people, Carrizozo "village" had 1,457, and Tularosa "village" had 1,636. Socorro, Belen, and Alamogordo populations totaled 3,000 to nearly 4,000.

93. Assistance of 8th Service Command, memo to file, June 26, 1945, NARA Maryland.

94. For information about Los Alamos PEDS serving on an evacuation team, see "Provisional Engineer Detachment," Atomic Heritage Foundation, August 10, 2017, https://atomicheritage.org/history/provisional-engineer-detachment. Other information is that an evacuation detachment of 144 to 160 enlisted men and officers was established, with at least 94 of those personnel drawn from the Provisional Detachment Number 1, Company "B" of the 9812th Technical Service Unit, Army Corps of Engineers. "Fact Sheet: Project Trinity," Defense Nuclear Agency, December 15, 1982, U.S. Department of Energy OpenNet, https://www.osti.gov/opennet, accession no. NV0760126.

95. Lehman, interview.

96. W. J. McElwreath and Robert R. Leonard, memorandum (secret), "To the Officer in Charge," July 16, 1945, Szasz Papers, Box 8, Folder 38.

97. Maag, *Report*, 37.

98. Louis Hempelmann, interview by Ferenc Szasz, December 22, 1981, Szasz Papers, Box 7, Folder 23. Szasz added a note to the Hempelmann interview in which Hempelmann affirmed that test officials had been "more concerned with sound and blast—fallout wasn't [a] concern." Hempelmann also told Szasz that he had not been allowed to see numerous reports about the test and its effects.

99. Roger Rasmussen, interview by Cindy Kelly, 2015, "Voices of the Manhattan Project."

100. To Major Claude C. Pierce, memo, July 30, 1945, NARA Maryland. See also "Fact Sheet: Project Trinity," Defense Nuclear Agency, December 15, 1982, U.S. Department of Energy OpenNet, https://www.osti.gov/opennet, accession no. NV0760126. Men were posted at Alamogordo, Albuquerque, Amarillo, Artesia, Belen, Capitan, Carlsbad, Carrizozo, Carthage, Cloudcroft, Clovis, Deming, Denver, Elephant Butte, El Paso, Fort Sumner, Gallup, Hatch, Hobbs, Las Cruces, Las Vegas, Lordsburg, Magdalena, Mountainair, Nogal, Oscura, Roswell, Ruidoso, Silver City, Tucson, Socorro, and Tucumcari.

101. "Field Notes 16–18 July, 1945," Szasz Papers, Box 8, Folder 38.

102. Moynihan, *Secrecy*. For a more recent and richly detailed study of Manhattan Project secrecy, see Wellerstein, *Restricted Data*, chaps. 2 and 3.

103. Specifically identified vista sites included Sawyer's Hill, the Jemez Mountains, and the Chupadera Mesa.

104. Laura Fermi, *Atoms in the Family*, 62–63, for example, recalled that she and a few other "snoopy wives" went to the top of a hill "somewhere between Los Alamos and Trinity" and watched the test. She wrote in her account that she heard Hempelmann mention "Trinity" and asked him what he meant. He told her to ask her husband. She was a "blue-badge" worker and Hempelmann was a "white-badge" worker who stuck by the rules.

105. Lilli Hornig, interview by Cindy Kelly, 2011, "Voices of the Manhattan Project." After Joe McKibben threw the switch at minus forty-five seconds, the only way to stop the test was if Don Hornig pressed his stopwatch. Groueff, *Manhattan Project*, 356.

106. Meta Newson, transcript of earlier interview, S. L. Sanger collection, 1986, "Voices of the Manhattan Project."

107. Pat Krikorian, interview by Cindy Kelly, 2003, "Voices of the Manhattan Project."

108. Fermi, *Atoms in the Family*, 237.

109. Fermi, *Atoms in the Family*, 161.

110. Adrienne Lowry, interview by Cindy Kelly, 2014, "Voices of the Manhattan Project."

111. Beckie Diven, interview by Theresa Strottman, 1991, "Remembering Los Alamos: World War II," M192-1.

112. Kay Manley, interview by Theresa Strottman, 1992, "Voices of the Manhattan Project." Her husband was probably J. H. Manley. Similarly, Beverly Agnew says that her husband, Harold, who left the Met Lab for Los Alamos in March 1943, with her joining him a month later, never said anything about what the project was, although she knew it was some kind of secret weapon. Beverly Agnew, interview by Theresa Strottman, 1991, "Remembering Los Alamos: World War II," M1992-112-1-6.

113. To Major Claude C. Pierce, memo, July 30, 1945, NARA Maryland. The men listed were "James Buchanan, Tomas Sena, John G. McChesney, Edward C. Farrell, Thomas Van Winkle, Eugene Selmanoff, Harold Hirsch, Edward C. Herman, Jack H. Smith, Ernest R. Martin" (p. 8). This document includes the military police report from July 15, 1945.

114. Charles and Jean Critchfield, interview.
115. Ruth Howes, interview by Cindy Kelly, 2016, "Voices of the Manhattan Project." Howes drew on her personal knowledge of Hinton in writing about her life.
116. Elsie McMillan, lecture, 2016, "Voices of the Manhattan Project."
117. Ed Rynd, interview by Theresa Strottman, 1991, "Remembering Los Alamos: World War II," M1992-112-1-190.
118. Lamont, *Day of Trinity*, 229, reports Fuchs "alone on a saddle between two hillocks" but provides no further details.
119. Hans Courant, interview by Cindy Kelly, 2015, "Voices of the Manhattan Project."
120. Rasmussen, interview. Also, Los Alamos Historical Society, *Los Alamos 1943–1945*, 51, reinforces this point about awareness among even those not supposed to know details of the test. Bainbridge recalled later that when the military convoy brought the plutonium to Trinity he directed the men to deliver it to the McDonald ranch house. He remembered that the crew "seemed awfully eager to get rid of their strange cargo even though they weren't supposed to know the real significance of it."
121. Bob Porton, interview by Theresa Strottman, 1992, "Voices of the Manhattan Project."
122. Porton, interview. The memo sent to Major Claude C. Pierce, July 30, 1945, RG 77, NARA Maryland, cites the case of Bartlett Long on July 14 "shooting his mouth off at the La Fonda Bar."
123. Rosario Martinez Fiorillo, interview by Willie Atencio, 2009, "Voices of the Manhattan Project."
124. Los Alamos Historical Society, *Los Alamos 1943–1945*, 59, source not identified.
125. To Major Claude C. Pierce, memo, July 30, 1945, 7, NARA Maryland.
126. Holm Bursum Jr., interview by Ferenc Szasz, 1981, Szasz Papers, Box 7, Folder 16. This interview, almost illegible, consists of scrawled words on a yellow pad about local citizens' reactions to the test.
127. Rhodes, *Making of the Atomic Bomb*, 692–93.

## 2. DISPOSSESSIONS

1. U.S. Senate, "White Sands Missile Range, New Mexico," 284.
2. U.S. Senate, "White Sands Missile Range, New Mexico," Laura E. McKinley letter, 284–86.
3. Ebright, *Advocates for the Oppressed*, introduction.
4. Rieder and Lawson, *Trinity at Fifty*, 8–9.
5. Schneider-Hector, *White Sands*, 31.
6. Ebright, *Advocates for the Oppressed*, chap. 1.
7. Dunbar-Ortiz, *Roots of Resistance*, 12.
8. Hämäläinen, *Comanche Empire*, 13.
9. Hämäläinen, *Comanche Empire*, 30.
10. Hämäläinen, *Comanche Empire*, 18. I have tried in this chapter to point out an especially complex narrative involving many tribes and Native groups contesting with each other and then with complex new groups of Hispanic and Anglo-American

would-be settlers. Thus, although the early history of the Tularosa Basin of New Mexico obviously fits into the scholarly framework known as "settler colonialism," it is also a more complicated history than encounters strictly between Natives and Euro-Americans. See, for example, Veracini, *Settler Colonialism*.

11. Ebright, *Advocates for the Oppressed*, xv.

12. Ebright, *Advocates for the Oppressed*, xii–xv.

13. Dunbar-Ortiz, *Roots of Resistance*, 93.

14. Ebright, *Advocates for the Oppressed*. Various chapters focus in detail on specific land grants.

15. Dunbar-Ortiz, *Roots of Resistance*, 8.

16. L. Gomez, *Manifest Destinies*, 16, clearly labels it an aggressive war. She also argues that one crucial legacy of American colonization was to establish Mexican Americans as a racial group (p. 17).

17. L. Gomez, *Manifest Destinies*, 47.

18. L. Gomez, *Manifest Destinies*, 47.

19. Sources differ: some Mescalero Apaches were sent to Fort Marion in Florida in 1886. Others were sent to the reservation near Fort Stanton in New Mexico. Today that reservation of 720 square miles is home to four different Apache tribes and lies southeast of the Trinity site.

20. Johnson, *Writing Kit Carson*, engagingly retells much about Carson and his actions.

21. Caffey, *Chasing the Santa Fe Ring*, 107. See also Klein, "Treaties of Conquest."

22. Bradfute, *Court of Private Land Claims*. The book provides rich details of numerous cases.

23. Belnap, review of Bradfute, *The Court of Private Land Claims*. Belnap criticizes the book for not looking into how the court decisions affected people in the Southwest.

24. The Treaty of Guadalupe Hidalgo, signed by the United States in 1848, ending the brief war with Mexico, promised in Article VIII that "property of every kind now belonging to Mexicans now established there shall be inviolably respected. The present owners, the heirs of these and all Mexicans who may hereafter acquire said properties by contract, shall enjoy with respect to its guarantees equally ample as if the same belonged to citizens of the United States." Dunbar-Ortiz, *Roots of Resistance*, 98–99.

25. Dunbar-Ortiz, *Roots of Resistance*, 16.

26. Caffey, *Chasing the Santa Fe Ring*, 112 and chap. 6 overall.

27. Caffey, *Chasing the Santa Fe Ring*, 109. The attorney for the United States in the Court of Private Land Claims, Matthew Givens Reynolds, according to Caffey, "seemed dedicated to the defeat of as many claims as possible. If he could not defeat them, he strove to reduce the acreage confirmed as much as possible."

28. Carpio Chavez appears in the 1900 federal census for Socorro, New Mexico, District 0142. Ancestry.com provides links to the U.S. federal census and then images of the federal census pages for the individual: U.S. Federal Census Collection, Ancestry.com, https://www.ancestry.com/search/categories/usfedcen/.

29. Information on Geronimo Baca and family and neighbors is in the 1880 U.S. federal census for San Antonio and Socorro, New Mexico, Roll 804, p. 166C. U.S. Federal Census Collection, Ancestry.com.

30. Baca information is also in the 1920 U.S. federal census, Socorro, New Mexico. U.S. Federal Census Collection, Ancestry.com.

31. U.S. Senate, "White Sands Missile Range, New Mexico," 48.

32. U.S. Senate, "White Sands Missile Range, New Mexico," 83.

33. A "patent," also known as a deed, was a legally binding document for land ownership and was filed with various appropriate courts. Patents were often 320 acres, suggesting that this was part of the legal process relating to the Homestead Act. Other terminology notes this as "deeded" land. One Isaacks brother patented the northeastern half and the southwestern quarter of section 21 while the other patented 120 acres nearby in the northeastern "14" and southwestern "14" of section 21.

34. The Isaackses' land was in the ORDCIT (Ordnance–California Institute of Technology) section of the White Sands Missile Range. Robert Isaacks received $4,184 for his federal lands, but Myrtle Isaacks, with no private land, received $630 in "rent." U.S. House, "White Sands Fair Compensation Act of 1989," 259.

35. U.S. Senate, "White Sands Missile Range, New Mexico," 307.

36. The Ascarates show up in the 1920 federal census for Dona Ana County, New Mexico, in the 0027 district of Las Cruces. U.S. Federal Census Collection, Ancestry.com.

37. Eidenbach and Morgan, *Homes on the Range*, 2. His reminiscences are also vague about how some ranchers managed to buy the areas with water: "A series of homesteads had the water, had a well, so all of your deeded land in this part of the country controlled the water."

38. Holm Olaf Bursum: 1910 federal census for Socorro, New Mexico, Ward 3, District 0242. U.S. Federal Census Collection, Ancestry.com.

39. U.S. Senate, "White Sands Missile Range, New Mexico."

40. Sinfuriana Apodaca appears in the federal censuses for 1850 and 1910, Pablo Apodaca is in the federal census for 1920, Melecio Apodaca is in the 1920 federal census for Bernalillo, Los Giregos District, all in Ancestry.com. From 1910 to 1920 the people listed on the census as the Apodacas' nearest neighbors primarily had Mexican surnames and worked as "laborers," farmers, shepherds, laundresses, and "houseworkers." U.S. Federal Census Collection, Ancestry.com.

41. U.S. Senate, "White Sands Missile Range, New Mexico," William Cronin's testimony, 26.

42. U.S. House, "White Sands Fair Compensation Act of 1989." One commentator stated that "150 or so ranching families were displaced by the creation of the White Sands Missile Range." Laura McKinley's statement at the 1983 hearing claimed that expansion of the White Sands Missile Range affected about 110 ranchers. An army official at the 1990 congressional hearing stated that the army eventually took four thousand square miles and one hundred ranches for the White Sands Missile Range.

43. U.S. House, "White Sands Fair Compensation Act of 1989," 258.

44. An exhibit at the Farm and Ranch Heritage Museum in Las Cruces, New Mexico, seen in January 2020, included photos of some ranchers and maps pinpointing the ranches near the test site. Unfortunately, because of the COVID-19 pandemic, museum officials were not able to provide me with copies of any of the maps.

45. LAHDRA, *Final Report*, figure 10-15, is a very useful map. I have located no information about the Millers-Watch property, which the LAHDRA report cites as being within the ten-mile radius of ground zero.

46. Rieder and Lawson, *Trinity at Fifty*, 59.

47. LAHDRA, *Final Report*, table 10-3, p. 10-42. The report notes that all of the sheepherders were Hispanic.

48. U.S. Senate, "White Sands Missile Range, New Mexico," 321.

49. U.S. Senate, "White Sands Missile Range, New Mexico," 72, testimony by Charlie T. Lee. He explained his family's experiences when the army wanted their land in the McGregor Range in 1956: there was never a question that payment would be for the total ranching unit, meaning that the grazing leases were included in the calculation.

50. U.S. Senate, "White Sands Missile Range, New Mexico," 279.

51. The federal government has the legal right through its power of eminent domain to take possession of privately owned and state-owned property. Federal officials have the legal right to seek condemnation proceedings for any public purpose. Court cases challenged this law in the 1940s when New Dealers began a vast expansion of land acquisition for national parks and natural resource acquisition and when the War Department began its eventual acquisition of twenty million acres for war-related work. The Supreme Court upheld the federal power. During World War II the Land Acquisition Section of the Environment and Natural Resources Division of the Department of Justice grew so large that a separate "Condemnation" Section was created along with a separate "Title" Section. "History of the Federal Use of Eminent Domain," United States Department of Justice, updated January 24, 2022, https://www.justice.gov/enrd/history-federal-use-eminent-domain.

52. U.S. Senate, "White Sands Missile Range, New Mexico," 28.

53. U.S. Senate, "White Sands Missile Range, New Mexico," 36.

54. In the legal documents included in the appendix of the 1983 hearing, a letter from one of the lawyers representing the ranchers noted that Section 315q "seems to have been enacted primarily to take care of the White Sands problems." See U.S. Senate, "White Sands Missile Range, New Mexico," 273.

55. U.S. Senate, "White Sands Missile Range, New Mexico," 14.

56. The most valuable sources about the New Mexican ranchers and their land claims come in the two congressional hearings of 1983 and 1990 cited above. Skeen persisted in introducing bills, but they went nowhere. He introduced HR 1954, the White Sands Fair Compensation Act of 1991, to the House in April 1991. It was referred to the House Committee on the Judiciary the same day. On June 7, 1991, the Judiciary Committee referred it to the Subcommittee on Administrative Law

and Governmental Relations, and that appears to have been the end of it. As of 2018 the Congressional Budget Office had provided no cost estimates for such bills. Domenici's Senate Bill 867, "White Sands Fair Compensation Act of 1991," met a similar fate. It was read twice and referred to the Committee on Energy and Natural Resources. On April 19, 1991, it was referred by the Committee on Energy and Natural Resources to the Subcommittee on Public Lands and National Parks. On June 6, 1991, the Committee on Energy and Natural Resources requested executive comment from the Department of the Interior's Office of Management and Budget. There is no reported activity on the bill after that.

57. The 98th Congress, 2nd session, in 1984 passed Senate Resolution 405 directing the court to consider a bill, s2761, "A Bill for the Relief of the White Sands Ranchers of New Mexico."

58. 98th Congress, 2nd session, Senate Resolution 405 for bill s2761, "A Bill for the Relief of the White Sands Ranchers of New Mexico," 1984.

59. "History of the Federal Use of Eminent Domain," United States Department of Justice, updated January 24, 2022, https://www.justice.gov/enrd/history-federal -use-eminent-domain.

60. Perry, "Eminent Domain Destroys a Community," 141–61. Residents filed complaints and legal claims about the inadequate compensation, including the lack of compensation for moving or replacing possessions that had to be left behind but received little recompense.

61. Rhodes, *Making of the Atomic Bomb*, 486.

62. Johnson and Jackson, *City Behind a Fence*, 47.

63. Johnson and Jackson, *City Behind a Fence*, 41. Families also lost their ranches and homes for the development at Los Alamos. Lydia Martinez's family had a 160-acre homestead at what became Los Alamos; after "the taking" they moved to San Ildefonso. She refers to their properties as farms and "homesteads" rather than ranches. Other Hispanic families who lost their property to Los Alamos included the Manuel Lujan family, Harold Valencia and family, Adolfo Montoya, the Gomez family, the Roybals, and the Sernas. Some ended up working at Los Alamos. Harold Valencia became an area manager, Pat Roybal worked at the x7 area for a long time as a janitor, and Rosario Martinez Fiorillo's family moved to San Ildefonso "after the taking." Lydia Martinez, interview by Cindy Kelly, 2017, "Voices of the Manhattan Project."

64. U.S. Senate, "White Sands Missile Range, New Mexico," 26.

65. U.S. House, "White Sands Fair Compensation Act of 1989." "$17,386,000 has been made to the ranchers, which includes rental payments, payments for damages to improvements, compensation for fee acquisition of the lands." An additional $3,140,000 went to the state. Some payments went to old mining claims.

66. U.S. House, "White Sands Fair Compensation Act of 1989," 265 and 266.

67. U.S. House, "White Sands Fair Compensation Act of 1989," 98.

68. U.S. House, "White Sands Fair Compensation Act of 1989," 92, statement by Myles E. Flint.

69. U.S. Senate, "White Sands Missile Range, New Mexico," 12.
70. U.S. Senate, "White Sands Missile Range, New Mexico," 9 and 16. A Government Accountability Office (GAO) official testifying at the 1983 hearing acknowledged that the McGregor Range ranchers benefited from receiving their money up front.
71. U.S. House, "White Sands Fair Compensation Act of 1989," 215. Another example comes in a ruling by the Court of Land Commissioners in 1977. The issue was some eighteen thousand acres of land "more or less" situated in Otero, Sierra, and Socorro Counties, New Mexico, taken by condemnation by the government in late June 1975. The hired appraiser evaluated its fair market value as $112,000 on the day of the taking, whereas the appraiser hired by the Corps of Engineers said the land was worth a total of $32,000. The commission ruled for a total worth of $51,200 (p. 218).
72. U.S. Senate, "White Sands Missile Range, New Mexico," 126.
73. U.S. Senate, "White Sands Missile Range, New Mexico," 125.
74. U.S. Senate, "White Sands Missile Range, New Mexico," 125. George McDonald also co-owned the Murray ranch with his wife. The 1990 hearing included extensive documentation about George's ranches. Rieder and Lawson, *Trinity at Fifty*, 47, list the Cicero Green ranch, which was close to the Trinity test, as belonging to Tom's daughter and her husband. Emma McDonald married Cicero Green.
75. U.S. Senate, "White Sands Missile Range, New Mexico," 115, statement from Dave McDonald.
76. U.S. Senate, "White Sands Missile Range, New Mexico," 126.
77. "Rancher and Niece End Missile Range Protest," *New York Times*, October 17, 1982.
78. Merrill, *Public Lands and Political Meaning*, 171.
79. Merrill, *Public Lands and Political Meaning*, 173, notes that there were "serious tensions written into the act" and "competing interpretations of its early administration" that led to the later developments.
80. "Nuclear War: Uranium Mining and Nuclear Tests on Indigenous Lands," *Cultural Survival Quarterly Magazine*, September 1993, https://www.culturalsurvival.org/publications/cultural-survival-quarterly/nuclear-war-uranium-mining-and-nuclear-tests-indigenous.
81. France tested nuclear weapons in the Sahara, in Algeria, and in French Polynesia; England tested on islands in Western Australia; the USSR's nuclear bomb tests affected indigenous peoples in Kazakhstan and Siberia. See Brown, *Plutopia*, and Hahn, "Between the Devil and the Deep Blue Sea."

### 3. BUILDING THE TEST SITE

1. Bainbridge, *Trinity*, 1.3.
2. Loring, *Birthplace of the Atomic Bomb*, 30–31. He provides an extensive discussion of the different sites under consideration and the reasons for their rejection. Unlike much of the book, this section includes good, traditional footnotes, but troubling unexplained contradictions remain in the text.
3. Los Alamos Historical Society, *Los Alamos 1943–1945*, 36.

4. Bird and Sherwin, *American Prometheus*, 304.

5. Norris, *Racing for the Bomb*, 396.

6. Hawkins, *Project Y*, 233.

7. Berlyn Brixner, interview by Yvonne Dalameter, 1992, "Voices of the Manhattan Project."

8. George P. Kraker to McCraw, memo, "Trinity Site Status of and Study on What To Do," August 26, 1952, Szasz Papers, Box 8, Folder 48. This document is confusing because it is labeled McCraw to Kraker, but Kraker wrote it and sent it to McCraw. Szasz mislabeled the folder.

9. Groves, "Some Recollections of July 16, 1945," 52.

10. Lamont, *Day of Trinity*, 70.

11. Groves, *Now It Can Be Told*, 289. Rieder and Lawson, *Trinity at Fifty*, 20, state that in early fall 1944, "arrangements were made with Second Army Air Force, Alamogordo Army Air Field" for use of an eighteen-by-twenty-four-mile area within the Alamogordo Bombing Range for the Trinity test.

12. "Uzal Girard Ent," Wikipedia, accessed February 15, 2021, https://en.m.wikipedia.org/wiki/Uzal_Girard_Ent.

13. Szasz, *Day the Sun Rose Twice*, 31.

14. Bainbridge, *Trinity*, 1.3.

15. Eidenbach, *Star Throwers of the Tularosa*, 7.

16. Hawkins, *Project Y*, 234.

17. Jay Wechsler, interviewer not identified, 2003, "Voices of the Manhattan Project."

18. Los Alamos Historical Society, *Los Alamos 1943–1945*, 37.

19. Norris, *Racing for the Bomb*, 397; Alex Wellerstein, "The First Light of Trinity," *New Yorker*, July 16, 2015. "No one seems to know precisely why JRO named it Trinity," Wellerstein notes. He also says that Tatlock introduced Oppenheimer to the poetry of Donne, and he notes her suicide in 1944.

20. Lamont, *Day of Trinity*, 70, says that this took place late in 1944. Rhodes, *Making of the Atomic Bomb*, 571, says the naming occurred sometime between March and October 1944. The poem is in Shawcross, *Complete Poetry of John Donne*, 344.

21. Bird and Sherwin, *American Prometheus*, 304. In 1976 Marjorie Bell Chambers, in a PhD dissertation about Los Alamos, also suggested the importance of the Hindu concept of Trinity as Brahma (the creator), Vishnu (the preserver), and Shiva (the destroyer); see Szasz, *Day the Sun Rose Twice*, 40.

22. Bernstein, *Oppenheimer*, 59.

23. Bird and Sherwin, *American Prometheus*, 252.

24. Canaday, *Critical Assembly*, 78. It is also noteworthy that the very next poem is about Kitty Oppenheimer and her unhappiness.

25. Jennet Conant, interview by Cindy Kelly, 2017, "Voices of the Manhattan Project." Jennet Conant was the granddaughter of James Bryant Conant. McKibben became a hostess for Oppenheimer later in his life; she became very close to the Oppenheimer children, especially Peter, who was married in her home in Santa Fe.

26. Rhodes, *Making of the Atomic Bomb*, 571, has considerable empathy toward Oppen-

heimer: "Whatever his burden of morale and work in those years, Oppenheimer also carried his full share of private pain. . . . His home life cannot have been happy." When Tatlock committed suicide her note said she became "paralyzed somehow." Rhodes notes, empathically, that it "was a paralysis of the spirit Oppenheimer seemingly had to resist in himself." Scholarly interpretations of Donne's "holy sonnets" differ considerably and provide little clarity about how Oppenheimer might have interpreted them in 1943. The first has stanzas about the devil usurping the divine in the writer. The second (no. 163) speaks of the poet's "black soul" and sin and remorse, and yet the poem also has words about love, about being "to another due," and about being betrothed to one's enemy; it includes the words "divorce me," "untie," and "break that knot againe." English literary critic Dr. Oliver Tearle reads the Trinity poem as containing images "at once deeply spiritual and physically arresting" and, like Donne's earlier love poems, "teeming with erotic language." To Tearle, the imagery in at least one poem is violent and sexual, and the estrangement from God "is shocking as a holy poem." Oliver Tearle, "A Short Analysis of John Donne's 'Batter My Heart, Three-Person'd God,'" Interesting Literature, March 2017, https://interestingliterature.com/2017/03/a-short-analysis-of-john-donnes-batter-my-heart-three-persond-god/.

27. Fine and Remington, *U.S. Army in World War II*, 668.
28. At the same time "Project Alberta" also began with the goal of organizing and overseeing the "combat delivery" of the two atomic bombs in Japan. Los Alamos Historical Society, *Los Alamos 1943–1945*, 39.
29. Hawkins, *Project Y*, 238.
30. Hawkins, *Project Y*, 238.
31. Los Alamos Historical Society, *Los Alamos 1943–1945*, 40.
32. Los Alamos Historical Society, *Los Alamos 1943–1945*, 40.
33. Hawkins, *Project Y*, 238. Loring, *Birthplace of the Atomic Bomb*, 394, notes a typographical error in Palmer's report: the evacuation team had 40 vehicles, not 140.
34. Los Alamos Historical Society, *Los Alamos 1943–1945*, 38.
35. Merlan, *Life at Trinity Base Camp*, 14.
36. Eckles, *Trinity*, 142.
37. Farrell to Groves, memo, May 26, 1945, RG 200, Box 1, NARA Maryland.
38. Merlan, *Life at Trinity Base Camp*, 15. They found a source of micaceous gravel near ground zero, so they spread it six inches deep on the roads, then watered and primed it with asphalt. Rieder and Lawson, *Trinity at Fifty*, 30.
39. Bainbridge, *Trinity*, 13; Merlan, *Life at Trinity Base Camp*, 28. Among the road crew were two heavy-equipment operators (Tech 4 Lester A. Wilhite and a man identified only as Sigler). They "bladed and maintained the system of roads."
40. Hawkins, *Project Y*, 238.
41. Hawkins, *Project Y*, 238.
42. Los Alamos Historical Society, *Los Alamos 1943–1945*, 38, credits Major Stevens.
43. These were the properties remaining on the former cattle ranch of Rube and Dave McDonald and their families. Rieder and Lawson, *Trinity at Fifty*, 53.

44. Merlan, *Life at Trinity Base Camp*, 18 and 20, cites an October 1944 memo from Davalos that six twenty-by-one-hundred-foot buildings and four smaller buildings, twenty by fifty feet each, were dismantled, transported, and reassembled at the site.

45. Merlan, *Life at Trinity Base Camp*, 77.

46. Rieder and Lawson, *Trinity at Fifty*, 55.

47. Szasz, *Day the Sun Rose Twice*, 32.

48. The water was alkaline and could not be drunk. The first MPs dug a new well, but it too proved so alkaline that the men couldn't even bathe in it.

49. Bainbridge, *Trinity*, 13.

50. Merlan, *Life at Trinity Base Camp*, 97.

51. Szasz, *Day the Sun Rose Twice*, 34. The Rio Grande runs through Socorro, New Mexico, so that may have been where the trucks picked up its water.

52. Szasz, *Day the Sun Rose Twice*, 32–39.

53. Fine and Remington, *U.S. Army in World War II*, 700. The Eichleay Corporation of Pittsburgh, Pennsylvania, was known for moving large structures. It created the container for transporting Jumbo, the tower to hold Jumbo, and the tower from which the bomb detonated. Grinnell, "Eichleay and the Atomic Bomb," 8.

54. Bainbridge, *Trinity*, 27, credits H. Williams "to whom the TR Project owes much for the successful completion of the July 16th operation."

55. Felix DePaula, interview by David Schiferl, 2008, "Voices of the Manhattan Project."

56. Lawrence Antos, interview by Yvonne Delamater, 1992, "Voices of the Manhattan Project."

57. Merlan, *Life at Trinity Base Camp*, 25.

58. Merlan, *Life at Trinity Base Camp*, 26, citing Davis.

59. Merlan, *Life at Trinity Base Camp*, 46. The MPs rode the horses to play polo using soccer balls and broom handles.

60. Merlan, *Life at Trinity Base Camp*, 28–29. In February 1945 more MPs arrived including Tech 4 Dillard D. Maher, who was a blacksmith and farrier, and Tech 5 Angelo J. DeBello, a saddler.

61. Marvin R. Davis, interview by Theresa Strottman, 1992, "Remembering Los Alamos: World War II," M1992-112-1-67.

62. "We got to know some of the ranchers over west and visit around these old abandoned houses, kind of established a routine of traveling the trails and keeping an eye on the country. . . . We kept most of the cattle off of the immediate area, but on the outskirts, they still came in. There really wasn't much we could do about it 'cause we had so many other things to do. And like I said before, we set up roadblocks on these different roads. At times they were working on certain projects and they didn't want to be disturbed by other people coming in [so] we had to make sure that the right people were going in to work. Say the camera men or something like that one place or another. We had to keep everybody else out of there. It didn't improve the tempers any, but we had to do it." Davis, interview.

63. Davis, interview.

64. Davis, interview. The end of the interview is confusing because of interference with sound from the wind. Davis told Strottman that only after the war could the men who worked at the test site be given any recognition. "This was a ring that was created especially for the remaining members of the horse outfit that stayed here after the test. It has the insignia of the engineers, the castle and the cross pistols of the MP. Plus it has a spur with a one in it. Which is a symbol of the first provisional MP detachment that came from Ft. Riley, Kansas originally to Los Alamos. It was the first mounted MP outfit that the Army ever had. We ended up being just plain guard outfit at Los Alamos and down here at Trinity Site. It was paid for by the company funds that we had amassed down here when they sold the soda and the beer at the PX in the evening. Which by the way was our only recreation, sitting around drinking beer and soda, playing volleyball. This is possibly, there was only maybe dozen and a half of 'em made." See the photograph of the ring in this volume.

65. "Fact Sheet: Project Trinity," Defense Nuclear Agency, December 15, 1982, U.S. Department of Energy OpenNet, https://www.osti.gov/opennet, accession no. NV0760126.

66. Merlan, *Life at Trinity Base Camp*, 50 and 67.

67. Merlan, *Life at Trinity Base Camp*, 67.

68. Merlan, *Life at Trinity Base Camp*, 81. He notes that one person on the crew was a "Coe" from Lincoln County.

69. Fine and Remington, *U.S. Army in World War II*, 700. They interviewed the company president, Theodore R. Brown, in October 1969 and note that a Colonel Cole instigated the company's work in mid-December.

70. Charles Bagley, interview by Theresa Strottman, 1991, "Remembering Los Alamos: World War II," M1992-112-1-1. Groves doesn't mention the SEDs in his memoirs, nor does Richard Rhodes. Lamont, *Day of Trinity*, 93–97, notes that an SED detachment consisted of technically trained enlisted men put into the Manhattan Project. Bainbridge, *Trinity*, notes that the Provisional Detachment No. 1, Company "B" of 9812th Technical Service Unit, U.S. Army Corps of Engineers helped build the Trinity site in spring and summer 1944–45. Merlan, *Life at Trinity Base Camp*, has rich details.

71. Jones, *Manhattan*, 367.

72. Major L. W. Devereux to Col. J. C. Marshall and Lt. Col. Nichols, memo, April 1, 1943; Devereux to Groves, confidential memo, April 24, 194[3], both in RG 77, Box 55, Folder 319.1, NARA Maryland.

73. Devereux to Marshall and Nichols, memo, April 1, 1943, NARA Maryland; Devereux to Groves, confidential memo, April 24, 194[3], NARA Maryland.

74. J. C. Marshall to Brigadier General Groves, memo, April 24, 194[3], RG 77, Box 55, Folder 319.1, NARA Maryland.

75. Marshall to Ashbridge, memo, May 18, 1943, RG 77, Box 55, Folder 319.1, NARA Maryland. The SED men would be assigned geographically: Company A to the East (Columbia?), Company B to the South (Oak Ridge?), Company C to the Midwest (Monsanto?), and Company D to the West (Los Alamos? Hanford?).

76. Marshall to Ashbridge, memo, May 18, 1943, NARA Maryland.

77. Fine and Remington, *U.S. Army in World War II*, 699.

78. Val Fitch, interview by Cindy Kelly, 2008, "Voices of the Manhattan Project."

79. Merlan, *Life at Trinity Base Camp*, 31.

80. William Spindel, interviewer not identified, 2002, "Voices of the Manhattan Project."

81. Roger Rasmussen, interview by Cindy Kelly, 2015, "Voices of the Manhattan Project."

82. David P. Rudolph, interview by Stephane Groueff, 1965, "Voices of the Manhattan Project."

83. Merlan, *Life at Trinity Base Camp*, 31. Lamont, *Day of Trinity*, 93–97, calls them an "SED Detachment of technically trained enlisted men put into the Manhattan Project, early in 1945."

84. Rudolph, interview.

85. Robert J. S. Brown, interview by Janet Farrell Brodie, March 2019, Claremont CA.

86. Fitch, interview.

87. Severo Gonzalez, interview by Theresa Strottman, 1991, Los Alamos Historical Society Archives.

88. Arno Roensch, interview by Theresa Strottman, 1992, "Voices of the Manhattan Project."

89. Curtis A. Nelson to Groves, memo, "Grievances of Special Engineer Detachment at CEW," April 5, 1945, RG 77, Box 56, Folder 319.1, NARA Maryland.

90. Nelson to Groves, memo, April 5, 1945, NARA Maryland.

91. List (untitled) of men Groves could work with on the Manhattan Project, unidentified author, date indecipherable, RG 200, Box 1, NARA Maryland. Unfortunately, given the paucity of names given for the men who were assigned work at the Trinity site, I have not been able to trace which, if any, of the men on the list actually ended up with the crews preparing the Trinity site.

92. Jones, *Manhattan*, 469 and 498.

93. Bob Porton, interview by Theresa Strottman, 1992, "Voices of the Manhattan Project."

94. Howes and Herzenberg, *Their Day in the Sun*, 164.

95. Howes and Herzenberg, *Their Day in the Sun*, 150.

96. Howes and Herzenberg, *Their Day in the Sun*, 149.

97. Howes and Herzenberg, *Their Day in the Sun*, 106.

98. Howes and Herzenberg, *Their Day in the Sun*, 164. Howes provides a few names of the female motor pool drivers: Mary J. Whiting, Elsie Pierce, and Marjorie Powell Shjopp.

99. Howes and Herzenberg, *Their Day in the Sun*, 152.

100. LAHDRA, *Final Report*, 10-15. Another account is that the "two hemispheres on plutonium made the trip to Trinity from Los Alamos on July 11, accompanied by soldiers in a convoyed sedan." Los Alamos Historical Society, *Los Alamos 1943–1945*, 51.

101. Bellamy to Jensen, memo, October 6, 1948, Szasz Papers, Box 8, Folder 48.

102. Howes and Herzenberg, *Their Day in the Sun*, 51.

103. Howes and Herzenberg, *Their Day in the Sun*, 151.

104. Norris, *Racing for the Bomb*, 221 and 227.

105. Brown, *Plutopia*, 27.

106. The Atomic Heritage Foundation website now includes a short segment about African Americans and the Manhattan Project. The focus is on Hanford, although the site acknowledges that "tens of thousands" of African Americans worked at other sites for the Manhattan Project, including Oak Ridge, the University of Chicago, and Columbia University. "African Americans and the Manhattan Project," Atomic Heritage Foundation, March 1, 2016, https://www.atomicheritage.org/history/african-americans-and-manhattan-project.

107. Fermi and Samra, *Picturing the Bomb*, 58–59, which also includes photos of the "Negro Hutments" and segregated privies.

108. Brown, *Plutopia*, 27.

109. Brown, *Plutopia*, 30–31.

110. San Ildefonso shares a direct border with the lab, and in early days Area E in Site Y literally bordered the Santa Clara Pueblo.

111. Hunner, *Inventing Los Alamos*, 207.

112. Hunner, *Inventing Los Alamos*, 30. He may have been the same young man who became a celebrated artist like his parents, but he died young of alcoholism; see Merlan, *Life at Trinity Base Camp*, 51.

113. Hunner, *Inventing Los Alamos*, 30.

114. Fermi, *Atoms in the Family*, 231.

115. Adrienne Lowry, interview by Cindy Kelly, 2014, "Voices of the Manhattan Project." Lowry remembered that some of the scientists and their wives were invited to dances at the pueblo, suggesting a degree of cordiality, perhaps even friendship, between some.

116. Dimas Chavez, interview by Cindy Kelly, 2013, "Voices of the Manhattan Project." He noted that John Mench, a Hispanic man, was in the SED and worked in the Los Alamos foundry.

117. Everyone tried to keep the connection between Los Alamos and Trinity secret, but this wasn't entirely successful. Construction workers recognized some of the men, probably the scientists. Szasz, *Day the Sun Rose Twice*, 32.

118. Los Alamos Historical Society, *Los Alamos 1943–1945*, 40–41.

119. Los Alamos Historical Society, *Los Alamos 1943–1945*, 37–38.

120. Merlan, *Life at Trinity Base Camp*, 53.

121. Merlan, *Life at Trinity Base Camp*, 63.

122. Lamont, *Day of Trinity*, 209, says that the Army Corps of Engineers rented cabins behind Miera's Owl Bar and Café and set up equipment there but that the men provided no information to Miera.

123. Fuchs and the Rosenbergs are well documented in Rhodes, *Dark Sun*; and in Herken, *Brotherhood of the Bomb*, especially 87–99 and 118.

124. Albright and Kunstel, *Bombshell*. The book focuses on Ted Hall.

125. Haynes and Klehr, "On the Trail of a Fourth Soviet Spy," 5. Also William J. Broad, "4th Spy Unearthed in U.S. Atomic Bomb Project," *New York Times*, November 24, 2019. I have not located his name in any of the lists of men at the test, however.
126. Rhodes, *Dark Sun*, 168.
127. Holm Bursum Jr., interview by Ferenc Szasz, 1981, Szasz Papers, Box 7, Folder 16.

4. POST-TEST EVENTS

1. Maag, *Report*, 2.2.
2. Maag, *Report*, 2.2.
3. Maag, *Report*, 2.3. See also G. R. Tyler, Colonel, CE, Commanding, to Oppenheimer, memo, "Activities at Trinity," September 4, 1945, U.S. Department of Energy OpenNet, https://www.osti.gov/opennet, accession no. NV0310226. "At present time this office has 2 officers and about 109 enlisted men assigned to the Trinity Project." He asks if there is likely to be "any renewal of activity at that station," and he has not been informed if there will be further tests. If not, he wants to withdraw the soldiers except for a small force "for guarding of the crater which would be rotated about once every week or ten days."
4. Maag, *Report*, 2.3.
5. Henry W. Newson, "A Second Trinity," U.S. Department of Energy OpenNet, https://www.osti.gov/opennet, accession no. ALLA0004526.
6. MED (Manhattan Engineer District) memo authorizing installation of three subsurface test firing chambers, Folder Tabs G and F, included with George P. Kraker to McCraw, memo, "Trinity Site Status of and Study on What To Do," August 26, 1952, Szasz Papers, Box 8, Folder 48. Approval was granted on September 25, 1946, with $79,500 allocated. For an engaging, breezier account covering some of this post-test activity, see Eckles, *Trinity*, 73–77.
7. Schreiber to Dickason, memo, Folder Tab D, April 5, 1952, Szasz Papers, Box 8, Folder 48.
8. Hawkins, *Project Y*, 244.
9. Schreiber to Dickason, memo, April 5, 1952, Szasz Papers.
10. Schreiber to Dickason, memo, April 5, 1952, Szasz Papers.
11. Blackwell to Mayer, "Preliminary Report," April 17, 1967, Szasz Papers, Box 8, Folder 5.
12. Don J. White and John P. McDougall, memo for the record, Nuclear Effects Directorate of the White Sands Missile Range (NED), February 23, 1967, 15.006.232, White Sands Missile Range archive, New Mexico (henceforth, WSMR archive).
13. Blackwell to Mayer, "Preliminary Report," April 17, 1967, Szasz Papers.
14. Blackwell to Mayer, "Preliminary Report," April 17, 1967, Szasz Papers. Los Alamos sent W. Clarence Courtright (H-3) and C. W. Trask (ENG-1) to supervise the excavation work along with two men to supervise radiological safety. Don P. McMillan and Robert Lanter, who had participated in the 1947 tests, watched from the sidelines twenty years later. Lees, "Sleeping Beauty Awakens," 8–13, Szasz Papers, Box 8, Folder 5, provides other names: Wes Trask, ENG-1 (Engineering);

Phil Reinig (Engineering); Clarence Courtright, H-3; Charles Blackwell, H-1; Jerry Eagan, H-1; Jack Richard, H-1; Fred Fey, H-1.

15. They used Ludlum Model 14 Geiger-Mueller (or G-M) beta-gamma survey meters with probes attached to long handles "enabling the health physics surveyors to reach the surface of the ground from an upright position." This refers to a problem earlier radiation surveyors had found. Kermit Larson remembered that early field instruments for measuring alpha radiation were so inadequate that investigators had to measure on their hands and knees to get close enough to the source. Quoted in Kermit Larson, interview by J. Newell Stannard, 1979, U.S. Department of Energy OpenNet, https://www.osti.gov/opennet, accession no. NV0702908.

16. Blackwell to Mayer, "Preliminary Report," April 17, 1967, Szasz Papers.

17. Schreiber to Dickason, memo, April 5, 1952, Szasz Papers. Later explosives tests took place at the TA-33 site at Los Alamos.

18. Bradbury to L. P. Gise ("Manager" of AEC in Albuquerque Operations Office), memo, June 1, 1967, 15.006.228, WSMR archive. He copied H. E. Roser, L. P. Reinig, and T. L. Shipman, all at Los Alamos.

19. L. P. Gise to Commanding Officer, Department of the Army, June 23, 1967, 15.006.227, WSMR archive. Gise forwarded his letter to Bill H. Ferdig, assistant chief of the Planning and Installations Branch and Logistics, of the Nuclear Effects Lab at the missile base.

20. Bainbridge, *Trinity*, 4–5.

21. Hoddeson, *Critical Assembly*, 175.

22. Bainbridge, *Trinity*, 4–5. Engineering and design of Jumbo was done by two men from Section X-2A at Los Alamos, R. W. Henderson and R. W. Carlson. Early testing was carried out by Lieutenant W. F. Schaffer, who headed Section X-2B. Measurements of "pressures and deformations" were done by G. M. Martin, B. Bederson, J. A. Hofmann, and R. W. Henderson "of Fussell's section under P. B. Moon's direction." R. W. Carlson "made a more complete analysis of the dynamic mechanics of the vessel and of the stresses involved in the walls. R. W. Henderson completed the new, final detailed design for Jumbo."

23. Roger Allen Meade, "The Inglorious Death of Jumbo," Technical Report, LA-UR-17-23523, p. 6, https://www.osti.gov/biblio/1356107 or https://doi.org/10.2172/135610. There is also information about Jumbo in Szasz Papers, Box 8, Folder 11.

24. Barbara Wieneke, wife of one of the scientists, recalled that she knew nothing about what was going on at the Trinity site because her husband never discussed it. "The people in Santa Fe thought we were building a submarine. I remember that vividly." Wieneke, interview by Theresa Strottman, 1991, "Remembering Los Alamos: World War II."

25. Bainbridge, *Trinity*, 2.1.

26. Eckles, *Trinity*, 38. Loring, *Birthplace of the Atomic Bomb*, provides many little-known details about Jumbo although with sparse documentation.

27. R. W. Henderson, "Destruction of Jumbo," U.S. Department of Energy OpenNet, https://www.osti.gov/opennet, accession no. ALLA0003853. Henderson of Group

z-4 wrote a memo to Lieutenant Colonel A. J. Frolich (stationed at Sandia Base) about the tests, but little is known about what he said.

28. Eckles, *Trinity*, 38.

29. Rieder and Lawson, *Trinity at Fifty*, 48.

30. Eckles, *Trinity*, 39, quoting First Lieutenant Richard Blackburn from Sandia Base to his commanding officer, Lieutenant Colonel A. J. Frolich.

31. Norman R. Banda, Capt. Ord C, to Commanding Officer, Hdts. Troop Command, memo, no date, envelope labeled 15.006.196, WSMR archive.

32. Banda to Commanding Officer, memo, no date, WSMR archive.

33. Banda to Commanding Officer, memo, no date, WSMR archive.

34. Rieder and Lawson, *Trinity at Fifty*, 48.

35. Hermes and Strickfaden, "New Look at Trinitite." Rieder and Lawson, *Trinity at Fifty*, 23, has a discussion of the trinitite.

36. Report on Proposed Atomic Bomb Monument, December 20, 1945, 7, RG 200, Box 1, NARA Maryland.

37. Hoddeson, *Critical Assembly*, 374.

38. Hermes and Strickfaden, "New Look at Trinitite."

39. Rex Edward Keller, interview by Alexandra Levy, 2015, "Voices of the Manhattan Project." Seth Neddermeyer is credited with coming up with the idea and design for the implosion bomb in Groueff, *Manhattan Project*, 200 and 320.

40. Newspaper clipping of photograph of "lovely Pat Burrage of Fort Worth, TX, holding jewelry made of atomsite." *Albuquerque Journal*, September 15, 1945, clipping in RG 79, Box 382, NARA Denver.

41. Robert J. S. Brown, interview by Janet Farrell Brodie, March 2019, Claremont CA.

42. Welsh, *Dunes and Dreams*, chap. 4, note 52 (this online book is unpaginated).

43. Welsh, *Dunes and Dreams*, chap. 5, note 65.

44. To "Tilly," memo, November 16, 1945, RG 79, Box 382, Folder L58, NARA Denver.

45. Welsh, *Dunes and Dreams*, chap. 5, note 67.

46. Welsh, *Dunes and Dreams*, chap. 5, note 65.

47. Blackwell to Mayer, "Preliminary Report," April 17, 1967, Szasz Papers.

48. Handwritten note via telecom, from "Mr. Cartright," Los Alamos Scientific Laboratory (LASL), n.d., 15.006.232, WSMR archive.

49. Vernon R. Rottstedt, "Brief Sheet," July 14, 1967, 15.006.228, WSMR archive.

50. Frederic L. Fey Jr., "Health Physics Survey of Trinity Site," June 1967, Szasz Papers, Box 8, Folder 5.

51. Fey, "Health Physics Survey," June 1967, Szasz Papers.

52. Jack Aeby, interview by Cindy Kelly, 2003, "Voices of the Manhattan Project."

53. Whipple to Jensen, memo, January 5, 1949, Szasz Papers, Box 8, Folder 48.

54. Boyer, General Manager of Los Alamos, to Finlatter, Secretary of the Air Force, December 1, 1950, Szasz Papers, Box 8, Folder 5.

55. Dean to Mechem, telegram, March 7, 1952, RG 79, Box 382, NARA Denver. Dean says that according to Bugher (deputy director of biology medicine, AEC) and Carroll Tyler (manager of Santa Fe operations of AEC), "There is a potential hazard at

the site which with the passage of time will become aggravated. The AEC feels an obligation for elimination of this hazard and we are acting at this time to minimize the hazard." That month Mechem met with Tyler and other AEC personnel. After that meeting he asked Oscar L. Chapman, secretary of the interior, to meet with representatives of the AEC and Department of Defense (DOD) to establish best methods for creating a monument to the "Trinity-A-Bomb explosion site." The AEC said that it was under contract to destroy the "vestiges of the site" but would delay that action until the Department of the Interior had a chance to review the issues. The AEC had "particular interest in dissolution of any health menaces." This referred to the AEC's concerns about lingering radioactivity at the site but may also have been a specific reference to the trinitite.

56. "Report of Field Conference at Trinity Atomic Site," May 20, 1952, Szasz Papers, Box 8, Folder 48.

57. "Report of Field Conference," May 20, 1952, Szasz Papers.

58. "Report of Field Conference," May 20, 1952, Szasz Papers. The official representatives were three from the DOD (the commanding general, a major from the White Sands Proving Ground, and the commanding officer of Holloman Air Force Base), two representatives of the AEC (one unidentified and one from the Engineering and Construction Division of the AEC's office in Albuquerque), and four representatives of the National Park Service's Region 3 in Santa Fe.

59. "Report of Field Conference," May 20, 1952, Szasz Papers. The company also rehabilitated a shed that had been there since 1946 as a shelter for the trinitite. It was about four feet high and twenty by fifty feet. Information about the shed is found in a newspaper article in the *New Mexican*, July 14, 1954, RG 79, Box 381, Folder L58, NARA Denver.

60. "Report of Field Conference," May 20, 1952, Szasz Papers.

61. Tyler to Mechem, July 16, 1953, RG 79, Box 381, Folder L58, NARA Denver.

62. Letters between NPS and AEC and newspaper clippings from the *Albuquerque Journal* and *Denver Post* in September 1953 are in RG 79, Box 381, Folder L58, NARA Denver.

63. Tyler to Mechem, July 16, 1953, RG 79, Box 381, Folder L58, NARA Denver.

64. Eckles, *Trinity*, 75, notes that some people in New Mexico didn't want it cleaned up, thinking that the crater had more importance as a historical site if it was not changed. He also notes that Los Alamos fought the cleanup on the grounds that there were no risks and no scientific reasons to do so.

65. Shipman to Kraker, interoffice memo, January 24, 1952, Szasz Papers, Box 8, Folder 48. Shipman added that AEC actions in burying the trinitite foolishly alarmed the public and were "inconsistent with previous publicity releases." He also reported, without further details, that in the late 1940s he had boxed up trinitite in cardboard boxes and shipped it to Los Alamos.

66. Shipman to Kraker, interoffice memo, January 24, 1952, Szasz Papers. He also reminded Kraker that the NPS would prefer that the area be left "in its present form."

67. To ARMTE Deputy and Ferdig, Director of NED, memo, n.d., 15.006.232, WSMR archive.
68. Don J. White and John P. McDougall, memo for the record, February 23, 1967, 15.006.232, WSMR archive.
69. John P. McDougall and Don J. White, memo for the record, February 14, 1967, 15.006.232, WSMR archive.
70. Rottstedt, "Brief Sheet," July 14, 1967, 15.006.228, WSMR archive. A little-known Los Alamos report states that in 1947 the trinitite "containing the most radioactivity" was placed in twelve drums and buried inside the ground zero area: Hansen and Rodgers, *Radiological Survey and Evaluation of the Fallout Area.*
71. Bradbury to L. P. Gise, memo, June 1, 1967, 15.006.228, WSMR archive.
72. Sumner Pike, Acting AEC Chair, to Senator Hickenlooper, memo, August 9, 1948, RG 77, Box 56, Folder 319.1, NARA Maryland, explaining the return of "operational control" of the Trinity test site to the Department of the Army.
73. Herken, *Brotherhood of the Bomb,* 49. "Met Lab" was the shortened name for the code-named "Metallurgical Lab" at the University of Chicago, where early research into nuclear energy, especially uranium and plutonium and their health effects, was conducted. It became the Argonne National Nuclear Laboratory after the war.
74. Westwick, *National Labs,* 242.
75. Stannard, *Radioactivity and Health,* 516, notes that the University of Chicago's Met Lab conducted much more research into inhalation than was ever made public and that essentially none of the findings were ever published.
76. Minutes, AEC Advisory Committee for Biology and Medicine, October 8–9, 1948, 12th meeting, Advisory Committee on Human Radiation Experimentation (ACHRE) Collection, Box S09F01B194, DOE 082294-B, Folder 8, NARA Maryland.
77. Russell, *War and Nature,* 178. There is also extensive material in Chemical and Biological Warfare Collection, Box 2, "Radiological Warfare Documents, 1940s" Folder. In 1949, three years after its name changed from the U.S. Army Chemical Warfare Service to the Chemical Corps, the agency's official mission broadened to include, along with chemical warfare, both biological warfare and radiological warfare.
78. Appendixes to Stevenson Report, Ad Hoc Committee on CBR Warfare, June 20, 1950, Chemical and Biological Warfare Collection, Box 12, Record 54791. In 1950, for example, the secretary of defense created the Ad Hoc Committee on Chemical, Biological, and Radiological Warfare, replacing an earlier secretary of defense's Ad Hoc Committee on Biological Warfare, which issued reports in May 1949 and July 1949. This committee, also known as the Stevenson Committee for its chair, E. P. Stevenson, worked with the Joint RW Committee. There was occasional overlap between the work in one area with the work in another. For example, in the summer of 1948 data from a biological warfare project about experimental shells was made available to the Noyes radiological warfare panel: Third Report, Military Application of Radioactive Materials, D7673 DOD, Human Radiation Experimentation Database (HREX). Sometime in the spring of 2005, this Department of Energy (DOE) full-text database of Cold War documents recently

declassified by federal agencies and the military suddenly disappeared from the internet. I have copies of some of the materials but far from all.

79. Russell, *War and Nature*, 197.

80. Hamilton worked for over a decade at Ernest O. Lawrence's radiation laboratory on the Berkeley campus conducting some of the earliest human and animal medical experiments using radioactive isotopes. In 1943 he joined his colleague, University of California at San Francisco Medical School physician Robert Stone, at the Chicago Met Lab to provide health and safety oversight in the pioneering work with nuclear fission. Hamilton correspondence can be found in Carton 1, AR97–123, UCSF Human Radiation Committee Administrative Records 1993–19, University of California San Francisco Medical School; the Ernest O. Lawrence Papers at the Bancroft Library, UC Berkeley; and the Birge Papers at the Bancroft Library.

81. Hamilton to Stone, letter and report, May 26, 1943, document no. 724782, U.S. DOE, Nevada Site Office. It was originally in the Ernest O. Lawrence General Files, Carton 8/18, Folder 25, J. G. Hamilton Reports, Bancroft Library.

82. Hamilton to Nichols, memo, "Radioactive Warfare," December 31, 1946, quoted in Welsome, *Plutonium Files*, 182.

83. Joseph Hamilton to Stafford Leake Warren, memo, November 20, 1947. This document used to exist on the website of what was formerly called the Coordination and Information Center in Las Vegas (now the Nuclear Testing Archive): CIC Radiation 95082.042. However, it is no longer available online. I copied the document before it was removed. Hamilton discusses the Trinity site contamination; he thinks studies are advisable.

84. Other sources are the Joseph Gilbert Hamilton Papers, Carton 8, Folder 25, University of California San Francisco Medical School archives, as well as many citations in the Advisory Committee on Human Radiation Experimentation, *Final Report*.

85. Typewritten, nine-page alphabetical list of UCLA Atomic Energy Project personnel ca. 1951–52, n.d., Stafford Leake Warren Administrative Files, Box 31, Folder 1951–1952, UCLA Archives. Research priorities shifted quickly. By 1956 two divisions not even listed in the earliest 1950s budget now received the largest percentages of the total: radioecology (17 percent) and biophysics (15 percent).

86. Stafford Leake Warren, "An Exceptional Man for Exceptional Challenges," 1983, p. 1089, UCLA Special Collections.

87. Stannard, *Radioactivity and Health*, 929.

88. Larson and Bellamy, *Radiological and Biological Survey of Areas of New Mexico Affected by the First Atomic Bomb Detonation*, parts I and II, 1948, published 1949, copied in Szasz Papers, Box 8, Folder 40, UCLA Trinity Reports. See also Brodie, "Contested Knowledge."

89. Minutes, AEC Advisory Committee for Biology and Medicine, October 14, 1948, Advisory Committee on Human Radiation Experimentation (ACHRE) Collection, Box S09F01B194, DOE 082294-B, Folder 8, NARA Maryland.

90. One early radiological warfare investigator, D. T. Griggs, sent to E. M. McMillan at Los Alamos in March 1948 the "Preliminary Study on the Effectiveness of Pile Fission Products as Agent of RW." The document is cited as DOE-072694-B38 in *Advisory Committee on Human Radiation Experiments*, supplemental vol. 2a, appendix E, p. E94.

91. Whipple to Jensen, March 18, 1949, Szasz Papers, Box 8, Folder 48. Whipple sent a copy of the letter to Buettner at the UCLA AEP and enclosed a table of "Plutonium Content of Trinity Earth Samples" and "Long-Lived Fission Product Activity in Trinity Earth Samples."

92. Whipple to Jensen, January 5, 1949, Szasz Papers, Box 48, Folder 8. He copied the letter to Shipman, Dr. Algraves (probably Al Graves), Dr. T. N. White, Colonel Cooney, and C. L. Tyler.

93. Melnick, *They Changed the World*; Malmgren and Matthews, *Los Alamos Revisited*.

94. Rieder and Lawson, *Trinity at Fifty*, 48. When NPS chief historian Ronald F. Lee visited the Trinity site in September 1947 he found "unexpected evidence of the human side" with some scientists' names in pencil "on the unpainted wood above their stations inside the bunkers" and penciled notes that were "possibly last minute notes of things to attend to." Noted in Welsh, *Dunes and Dreams*, chap. 5, note 64.

### 5. THE TRINITY SITE

1. "History of the Federal Use of Eminent Domain," United States Department of Justice, updated January 24, 2022, https://www.justice.gov/enrd/history-federal-use-eminent-domain.

2. Schneider-Hector, *White Sands*, 133.

3. Eidenbach et al., *Brief History of White Sands Proving Ground*, 1–2. Eidenbach notes that 1942 brought new construction at the Alamogordo Army Air Field as well as Carlsbad, Deming, Clovis, and Roswell Army Air Fields. Eckles, *Pocketful of Rockets*, has rich material about the WSMR; chapter 9 is especially focused on the early years.

4. At some point some sources began to call it the U.S. Air Force Alamogordo Guided Missile Test Base. Some documents say that it became part of the White Sands Missile Range, but others note it as sharing some borders with the nearby White Sands Missile Range. Although needing work, there is good information in "Holloman Air Force Base," Wikipedia, accessed March 15, 2021, https://en.wikipedia.org/wiki/Holloman_Air_Force_Base.

5. Eidenbach, *Brief History of the White Sands Proving Ground*, 1.

6. Western Regional Partnership, "Military Asset List: Fort Bliss Training Center, New Mexico," 2016, https://wrpinfo.org/media/1191/fort-bliss-training-center-wrp-mal-final-2016.pdf. The Fort Bliss Training Center in New Mexico is one of the largest Department of Defense–controlled airspaces in the world and includes the McGregor Range complex and the Dona Ana Range complex.

7. Brophy, Miles, and Cochrane, *The U.S. Army in WWII*, 417.

8. Sapolsky, *Science and the Navy*, chap. 4.

9. Sapolsky, *Science and the Navy*, chap. 4.

10. Malina, "America's First Long-Range Missile and Space Exploration Programme," 442–56. Malina, an aerospace engineer and a pioneer in rocketry, cofounded the Guggenheim Aeronautical Lab at California Institute of Technology (GALCIT) and, eight years later, the Jet Propulsion Lab.

11. S. A. Musser to Groves, memo, December 12, 1944, RG 200, Box 1, NARA Maryland.

12. To Groves, memo, "Proposed Area for Testing Long-Range and High Altitude Missiles," December 12, 1944, RG 200, Box 1, NARA Maryland. The map mentioned in the memo is not included with the other material.

13. Schneider-Hector, *White Sands*, 132; also Malina, "America's First."

14. Malina, "America's First," 446. The documents Malina forwarded to officers of the Army Ordnance Department carried for the first time the name "Jet Propulsion Laboratory" (JPL). According to Malina, JPL did not technically separate from the Guggenheim Aeronautical Lab and did not come under administration of Cal Tech until 1949. This may explain some confusion in the sources about whether early work at the WSPG was conducted under GALCIT or ORDCIT.

15. Malina, "America's First," 445.

16. Malina, "America's First," 446. The new and expanded program, renamed "ORD-CIT" (an acronym for Ordnance–California Institute of Technology), came from an earlier program—the Air Corps Jet Propulsion Research Project, known as "GALCIT" for its association with the Guggenheim Aeronautical Lab at California Institute of Technology. Malina explained that the ORDCIT Project required a rapid expansion of staff and facilities of a part of the GALCIT Project known as the Jet Propulsion Lab: "The scope of the ORDCIT Project posed to the administrators of Caltech novel problems" in terms of the range of activities, size of staff, and amounts of money involved. The ORDCIT Project quickly became one of four major projects at JPL.

17. In late 1944 tests of "rocket propulsion" to assist large aircraft takeoff were also conducted at Camp Irwin near Barstow, California.

18. Laura McKinley's statement at the 1990 hearing claimed that WSMR hurt about 110 ranchers. The ORDCIT project required additional land: the Caldwells were told to leave on April 9, 1945, "for an ORDCIT project"; Mrs. Lupe Bernal Robertson's land was within the ORDCIT portion of the missile range, as was Barbarita Baca's. As of July 1, 1983, the army had paid $17,386,000 to New Mexico ranchers for the White Sands Missile Range properties. U.S. Senate, "White Sands Missile Range, New Mexico," 24.

19. Welsh, *Dunes and Dreams*, no pagination but this is chapter 4 near note 42. In January 1947 White Sands Proving Ground needed still more land for its ORDCIT Project.

20. To Commanding Officer S. A. Musser, memo regarding transfer of Albuquerque Air Field, August 2, 1945, RG 77, Box 82, Decimal Files 1942–48, NARA Maryland.

21. Gordon Gray to David Lilienthal, March 31, 1948, RG 77, Box 56, Folder 319, NARA Maryland.

22. Malina, "America's First," 446. There is much engaging material about the missile and rocket firings at White Sands in Eckles, *Pocketful of Rockets*, including even a photograph of Frank Malina (p. 166). Some of the scientists during the war and right after made little distinction between missiles and rockets, and both were tested in New Mexico during and after the war. Sources refer to "German V-2 products," German V-2 rockets, and even V-2 missiles. German rocket scientists brought to the United States worked on early missile tests as well as rocket tests. See, for example, Hamilton, *Blazing Skies*.

23. Eidenbach, *Brief History of the White Sands Proving Ground*, 6.

24. The CCC buildings may have come from a base camp near Las Vegas, New Mexico. Eidenbach, *Brief History of the White Sands Proving Ground*, 6. Trinity, too, used former CCC buildings at its base camp: Merlan, *Life at Trinity Base Camp*, 18.

25. Boehm, *From Barren Desert*, 9.

26. Boehm, *From Barren Desert*, 5.

27. Eidenbach, *Brief History of the White Sands Proving Ground*, 7.

28. Eidenbach, *Brief History of the White Sands Proving Ground*, 14.

29. Eidenbach, *Brief History of the White Sands Proving Ground*, 14.

30. Baker, *Redstone Arsenal*, 13.

31. Baker, *Redstone Arsenal*, 14.

32. Rieder and Lawson, *Trinity at Fifty*, 48. The Defense Nuclear Agency was an off-shoot of the original Armed Forces Special Weapons Project, created in 1947 after the Manhattan Engineer District was disestablished. The AFSWP was transformed over the years into other agencies, including the DNA.

33. Telephone statement to author from Darren Court, museum director at White Sands Missile Range, October 2019.

34. Eidenbach, *Brief History of the White Sands Proving Ground*, 7–9. In July construction began on what became the Navy Cantonment Area at the proving ground.

35. Brian Day and David Cross, "History, Progress and Toxic Chemicals. Council Weighs Future of Former Naval Weapons Research Facility in East Pasadena," *Pasadena Now*, July 9, 2018, https://www.pasadenanow.com/main/history-progress -and-toxic-chemicals-council-weighs-future-of-former-naval-weapons-research -facility-in-east-pasadena.

36. Christman, *Sailors, Scientists, and Rockets*, provides details of the establishment of the Naval Ordnance Test Station (NOTS) in Inyokern, California, in 1943 and some of the work shared there by Cal Tech scientists and navy personnel.

37. Gerrard-Gough and Christman, *Grand Experiment at Inyokern*, 331.

38. Rhodes, *Making of the Atomic Bomb*, 549. The Naval Research Laboratory opened in 1923, one of the first scientific research and development labs funded by the U.S. government and the first research institution within the navy. After World War II it became the Office of Naval Research.

39. Rhodes, *Making of the Atomic Bomb*, 551.

40. Hawkins, *Project Y*, 111–12. At NOTS in Inyokern the navy and Cal Tech undertook a new project for the Manhattan Project under the code name "Project Camel." The name is said to have come from a remark by a Los Alamos scientist that once a camel (meaning Cal Tech) got its nose under a tent flap it was hard to dislodge. "Project Camel," Wikipedia, accessed March 2021, https://en.wikipedia.org/wiki/Project_Camel.

41. Hawkins, *Project Y*, 159.

42. Hawkins, *Project Y*, 159.

43. Hawkins, *Project Y*, 194.

44. Hawkins, *Project Y*, 159.

45. Hawkins, *Project Y*, 273, says that the Salton Sea base, "which had been of some use during the spring and summer of 1945, became the main location of the Ordnance Engineering (Z) Division drop test program" after the war. NOTS in Inyokern produced mock atomic bombs, called "pumpkins," loaded with high explosives, many of which were intended for use in bombing practice at the Naval Proving Ground at Dahlgren, Virginia, and at the Salton Sea Navy Base in California, where the navy had conducted tests of small rockets earlier in the war. Traci Brynne Voyles, *The Settler Sea*, adds stunning details to the ways the Salton Sea became a "military sacrifice zone." Her research corroborates that the Manhattan Project dropped fake nuclear bombs there in order to develop knowledge about the actual atomic bombs being built at Los Alamos (p. 185). She also describes how after the war and through 1952 the Sandia Corporation conducted more test bomb drops at the Salton Sea. Voyles found evidence that although the AEC denied using radioactive materials in those tests, 1993 Environmental Protection Agency reports cited Department of Energy employees claiming that uranium was used in some bomb tests at that site (pp. 185 and 188, note 31).

46. Sapolsky, *Science and the Navy*, 28.

47. Ford, *Cult of the Atom*, 37.

48. Hewlett and Duncan, *Nuclear Navy*, 98–100.

49. Ford, *Cult of the Atom*, 40.

50. Sapolsky, *Science and the Navy*, 132.

51. Welsh, *Dunes and Dreams*, chap. 5, note 27.

52. Crim, *Our Germans*; and Jacobsen, *Operation Paperclip*.

53. Jacobsen, *Operation Paperclip*, 180. Hamill's later career is detailed in Eckles, *Pocketful of Rockets*, 207 and 295.

54. Eidenbach, *Brief History of the White Sands Proving Ground*, 6.

55. Eidenbach, *Brief History of the White Sands Proving Ground*, 8.

56. Jacobsen, *Operation Paperclip*.

57. Eisenhower (Paris) to Major Francis J. Smith, War Dept., Washington DC, memo, May 17, 1945, RG 77, Box 56, Folder 319.1, NARA Maryland.

58. Lasby, *Project Paperclip*, 374, says that the American nuclear scientists at first opposed the Germans being brought to the United States because they had "a keen sensitivity to the meaning of guilt." Their opposition, however, was short-lived.

59. Gimbel, "German Scientists," 441–65. He disputes the arguments that government officials kept the Nazi scientists' presence secret. He argues that there was a double standard for denazification and that German specialists were allowed entry to the United States without formal denazification in Germany (p. 451). The news in December 1946 about their presence in the United States caused some protests, particularly that they were taken out of Germany before denazification.

60. The best sources are Jacobsen, *Operation Paperclip*; Lasby, *Project Paperclip*; Crim, *Our Germans*; Ward, *Dr. Space*; and Eidenbach, *Brief History of the White Sands Proving Ground*.

61. Ward, *Dr. Space*, chap. 8, near note 15.

62. The army operated the Redstone Ordnance Plant until it became the Redstone Arsenal in 1943 and became one of the nation's major producers of chemical weapons. After the war, rockets were developed and tested there. Baker, *Redstone Arsenal*.

63. Jacobsen, *Operation Paperclip*.

64. DENIX: DOD Environment, Safety and Occupational Health Network and Information Exchange, "History of United States' Involvement in Chemical Warfare," DOD Recovered Chemical Warfare Material (RCWM) Program, accessed October 12, 2020, https://denix.osd.mil/rcwmprogram/history/. For histories of the expanding chemical, biological, and radiological warfare research and development after World War II, see Brophy, Miles, and Cochrane, *U.S. Army in World War II*; Endicott and Hagerman, *U.S. and Biological Warfare*; and Hersh, *Chemical and Biological Warfare*.

65. Between 1945 and 1947, more than 40,000 bombs with 250 kilograms of tabun, 21,000 mustard bombs of various sizes, 2,700 nitrogen mustard rockets, and about 750 tabun artillery shells of various sizes were shipped to the United States from Europe. From this, the Chemical Corps developed and eventually produced both tabun (GA) and sarin (GB), with GB adopted as a standard chemical agent by the United States. For a short account of the U.S. involvement in chemical warfare, see DENIX, "History of United States' Involvement in Chemical Warfare."

66. Rominiecki, "Chemical and Biological History." The article is very carefully worded to focus almost entirely on the defensive work and protective equipment done on the site rather than on any of the weaponizing. See also Regis, *Biology of Doom*.

67. Welsh, *Dunes and Dreams*, chap. 4, note 1.

68. Welsh, *Dunes and Dreams*, chap. 4, note 41.

69. Welsh, *Dunes and Dreams*, chap. 4, note 30.

70. Two days before what he called the bomb test "on the White Sands Proving Grounds" Faris discovered that the army planned "not only a twelve-inch water-line from [the base] but also a 115,000-volt power line and massive airplane runways." He told his superior, "It is a project that is being rushed from all angles and things break fast." Welsh, *Dunes and Dreams*, chap. 4, note 44.

71. Welsh, *Dunes and Dreams*, chap. 5, note 42.

72. Welsh, *Dunes and Dreams*, chap. 4, near note 42.

73. Welsh, *Dunes and Dreams*, chap. 4, note 42.

74. Welsh, *Dunes and Dreams*, chap. 4, note 41.

75. Welsh, *Dunes and Dreams*, chap. 5, note 30.

76. Welsh, *Dunes and Dreams*, chap. 5, note 31.

77. Welsh, *Dunes and Dreams*, chap. 5, note 35.

78. Welsh, *Dunes and Dreams*, chap. 5, note 53.

79. James Thomson, memo, October 15, 1974, Szasz Papers, Box 8, Folder 5.

80. Jones, *Manhattan*, 596. President Truman signed the Atomic Energy Act on August 1, 1946. It established civilian control of atomic energy with a dual mandate: to promote atomic energy and to protect the public from its harmful effects. The AEC had a general manager and five commissioners, appointed by the president and approved by the Senate, serving five-year terms. As of January 1, 1947, "title to plants, facilities, land, etc., in possession of the MED would be transferred to the AEC." With many delays, it took until the end of October 1946 for Truman to name all five commissioners.

81. Jones, *Manhattan*, 599.

82. Jones, *Manhattan*, 599.

83. Hacker, *Elements of Controversy*, 10–11. He notes that seven out of eight of the workforce was paid by private companies or universities under government contract.

84. Jones, *Manhattan*, 598.

85. Gray to Lilienthal, March 31, 1948, RG 77, Box 56, Folder 319.1, NARA Maryland.

86. Gray to Lilienthal, March 31, 1948, NARA Maryland.

87. Lilienthal to Gray, April 13, 1948, and a half dozen other notes and memos from AEC personnel in the spring and summer of 1948 regarding "disposition of Alamogordo Test Area," RG 77, Box 56, Folder 319.1, NARA Maryland.

88. Sumner Pike, Acting AEC Chair, to Senator Hickenlooper, memo, August 9, 1948, RG 77, Box 56, Folder 319.1, NARA Maryland.

89. Gray to Lilienthal, July 31, 1948, RG 77, Box 56, Folder 319.1, NARA Maryland.

90. Gray to Lilienthal, July 31, 1948, NARA Maryland. Details were to be worked out between the commanding officer at Holloman Air Force Base and the AEC.

91. Department of Air Force and AEC, memo of understanding, "Disposition of Trinity Site," August 10, 1948, RG 77, Box 56, Folder 319.1, NARA Maryland.

92. Draft of Tyler announcement, RG 77, Box 56, Folder 319.1, NARA Maryland.

93. Childers, *Size of the Risk*, documents the changing ways public lands in the Great Basin, especially in Nevada, were managed from the last half of the nineteenth century through the late 1970s. She pays close attention to weapons testing by the military and the ways that nuclear tests reified views of them as sacrifice zones. Voyles, *Wastelanding*, details how Navajo lands came to be mapped as wastelands, as "sacrificial land." Pasternak, in *Yellow Dirt*, notes the remarkably similar patterns around the globe for atomic testing: places deemed as "wastelands" remove from awareness the indigenous and other residents, obscuring the deeper earlier human histories.

94. Limerick, *Desert Passages*, 167.

95. Kirk, "Rereading the Nature of Atomic Doom Towns," 635–47.

96. For a broad overview, see Hamblin, *Poison in the Well*.

97. Pasqualetti, review of Kirk, *Doom Towns*, 476–80, notes that in one way the military's removal of land from public use has preserved it: "Closed to public use, vast areas of the western states consist of largely undisturbed desert set aside in largely natural states." He adds that at least 95 percent of the Nevada Test Site land has been left undeveloped.

98. Rhodes, *Making of the Atomic Bomb*, 839.

### 6. THE TRINITY RADIATION

1. M. Gomez, "Unknowing, Unwilling, and Uncompensated."

2. U.S. Senate, "America's Nuclear Past." No other information was provided about the Herrera family in the hearing.

3. Dennis J. Carroll, "Lost in the Fallout," *Santa Fe New Mexican*, July 13, 2015.

4. Tucker and Alvarez, "Trinity." The data, collected by the New Mexico health department, showed an unusually high infant mortality rate in counties downwind of the atomic bomb text, but that evidence was ignored for decades.

5. Hawkins, *Project Y*, 246. There had also been plans to measure airborne products by B-29 planes with special air filters, but this proved unsuccessful.

6. James Nolan, interview by Ferenc Szasz, 1983, Szasz Papers, Box 7, Folder 45. The interview consists of virtually incomprehensible handwritten jottings from a telephone conversation. See also Nolan, *Atomic Doctors*.

7. Groves, *Now It Can Be Told*, 286 and 291, emphasizes his concern about radiation over populated areas of New Mexico; Groves, "Some Recollections of July 16, 1945," 53–61, gives details of his radiation concerns before the test, although most are false. Norris, *Racing for the Bomb*, 440, confirms that Groves had little understanding of the effects of radiation at Hanford, Oak Ridge, Hiroshima, or Nagasaki.

8. Stafford Warren's responses (and memories of his responses) regarding the test's radiation varied in complicated ways over the years. See Brodie, "Radiation Secrecy and Censorship," 842–64.

9. Otto Frisch and Rudolf Peierls, memo, "The Properties of a Radioactive 'Superbomb,'" March 1940, cited in Tucker and Alvarez, "Trinity," note 18.

10. Kistiakowsky to Oppenheimer, memo, October 13, 1944, Szasz Papers, Box 8, Folder 21. In July 1941 the British Maud Report apparently warned about dangerous radioactive effects. Groves, however, reported later that he had never read that report.

11. John Magee, interview by Ferenc Szasz, April 1982, Szasz Papers, Box 7, Folder 29. Interestingly, Magee says that he served at the time as an advisor to Stafford Warren, so he must have alerted Warren to the new concerns, but Warren does not seem to have taken action or to have alerted Groves at that time.

12. Magee, interview.

13. J. O. Hirschfelder and John Magee to K. T. Bainbridge, memo, "Danger from Active Material Falling from Cloud," June 16, 1945, U.S. Department of Energy OpenNet, https://www.osti.gov/opennet/, accession no. NV0059784.

14. Nolan, interview; also, Szasz, *Day the Sun Rose Twice*, 65. After the meeting at Oak Ridge, Groves reluctantly granted permission for Nolan to order additional vehicles and to establish an emergency crew.

15. Hirschfelder and Magee to Bainbridge, memo, "Improbability of Danger from Active Material Falling from Cloud," July 6, 1945, sent to author by Martha DeMarre, Nevada Nuclear Testing Archive, NV0059903.

16. Hoddeson, *Critical Assembly*, 363. An early May 1945 memo to Bainbridge illustrates the minimal early concerns about radiation from the upcoming practice test. The main fear was that the blast would damage local mines. There was some concern that the area around the blast site might be contaminated for a while and would need to be fenced in. Captain T. O. Jones to K. Bainbridge, memo, May 2, 1945, Szasz Papers, Box 8, Folder 21.

17. Hoddeson, *Critical Assembly*, 374, notes that local fallout had been heavy enough "to affect some animals on nearby ranches, but apparently no people." Another account in one of the official histories of the test notes that in July and August 1944, preparations for the test included "a certain amount of planning for the measurement of nuclear radiations." The latter was not high on anyone's list of priorities. *Manhattan District History*, Book VIII, Los Alamos Project Y, vol. 2, Technical, Oct. 15, 1947, chapter XVIII Project Trinity, no page, U.S. Department of Energy OpenNet, https://www.osti.gov/opennet/, accession no. MEDBOOK8VOL2, document no. D00030274.

18. Hoddeson, *Critical Assembly*, 358.

19. Joseph G. Hoffman, "Health Physics Report on Radioactive Contamination Throughout New Mexico Following the Nuclear Explosion 16 July 1945," Los Alamos-626, 1947, p. 7, Los Alamos Historical Document Retrieval and Assessment Study (LAHDRA) materials, Folder 1580.

20. H. Barnett's account included his description of a hasty evacuation of the emergency crew at L-8. Robert R. Leonard (S/Sgt, SED) and William J. McElwreath (G-2 S/Sgt), Field Notes, July 16–18, 1945. Their measurements suggested radiation levels "dangerously close to the evacuation limit" about four miles outside of Bingham in midmorning. Szasz Papers, Box 8, Folder 38.

21. Louis Hempelmann, interview by Ferenc Szasz, Szasz Papers, Box 7, Folder 23.

22. Welsome, *The Plutonium Files*, 180, quoting Hempelmann to Don Mastick, July 23, 1947.

23. Stafford Warren to Major General Groves, "Report on Test II at Trinity, 16 July 1945," 2, Roll 1, Subseries 1, Files 1–7D, Scans 101–200, Top Secret Correspondence of the MED, Center for Research Libraries. The document is confusing because the subject line makes it appear to have been written July 16, one day after the Trinity test of July 15. But in the body of the report Warren comments about measuring

radioactive dust four days after the test. See Brodie, "Radiation Secrecy and Censorship," 842–64.

24. Warren to Groves, "Report on Test II," 2.
25. Warren to Groves, "Report on Test II," 2.
26. Warren to Groves, "Report on Test II," 3.
27. Brodie, "Radiation Secrecy and Censorship," 842–64.
28. There are well over two to three dozen reports and memoranda written over six decades containing information about the radiation from the Trinity test from both the initial blast and studies of the residual radioactivity. Some documents exist only from references in other documents; others are still formally classified and unavailable without the lengthy process of a FOIA request. Some appear on the internet but in mangled format with pages, authors, and other pertinent information missing. Others are available through traditional historical research methods in archives and special collections. For a listing, see Brodie, "Contested Knowledge."
29. The UCLA Atomic Energy Project remains little known even today because officials and project personnel so successfully kept its activities unpublicized and little scrutinized for decades. It brought the campus at least $1.5 million annually (and often more in 1950s dollars) for over three decades for research into the impacts of radiation on humans, plants, and animals. I have pieced together information about the UCLA AEP from the Warren Administrative Files and Warren Papers in Special Collections as well as the Jeanne Williams files. There is also material in Box 22, CU-5 Series 4, Inventory of Records of President of UC, Special Problem Folders, 1899–1954, at the Bancroft Library. The only other historical account of the project is in Lenoir and Hays, "Manhattan Project for Biomedicine."
30. This group included Joseph Hamilton, MD, working at the UC Berkeley Crocker Lab, Stafford Warren (physician and radiologist), and physicians at Los Alamos such as Louis Hempelmann and Thomas Shipman. Westwick, "Abraded from Several Corners," is especially helpful about the lack of clear genealogical lines in biophysics, molecular biology, molecular genetics, microbiology, nuclear medicine, and radiobiology after World War II.
31. Typewritten, nine-page alphabetical list of UCLA Atomic Energy Project personnel ca. 1951–52, n.d., Stafford Leake Warren Administrative Files, Box 31, Folder 1951–1952, UCLA Archives. Research priorities shifted quickly. By 1956 two divisions not even listed in the earliest 1950s budget now received the largest percentages of the total: radioecology (17 percent) and biophysics (15 percent).
32. Bellamy et al., "1948 Radiological and Biological Survey," 12.
33. Bellamy et al., "1948 Radiological and Biological Survey," 23.
34. Bellamy et al., "1948 Radiological and Biological Survey," 16.
35. Larson et al., UCLA AEP Interim Report 108, January 5, 1951, Szasz Papers, Box 7, Folder 34, Kermit Larson Environmental Reports 1951–1980.
36. Larson et al., UCLA AEP Interim Report 108, 59, Szasz Papers.
37. Larson et al., UCLA AEP Interim Report 108, 71, Szasz Papers.

38. Larson et al., UCLA AEP Report 140, 76, Szasz Papers, Box 14, Folder 5, "Field Reports of Trinity, 1951."
39. Larson et al., UCLA AEP Report 140, 81–82, Szasz Papers.
40. Larson et al., UCLA AEP Report 140, n.p., Szasz Papers.
41. J. H. Olfason, H. Nishita, and K. H. Larson, "The Distribution of Plutonium in the Soils of Central and Northern New Mexico as a Result of Atomic Bomb Test of July 16, 1945," UCLA no. 406, 1957, Szasz Papers, Box 7, Folder 34. Many pages are missing. Perhaps Szasz only photocopied parts of the report.
42. Olfason, Nishita, and Larson, "Distribution of Plutonium in the Soils."
43. Stannard, *Radioactivity and Health*, 930.
44. Stannard, *Radioactivity and Health*, 930.
45. Weisskipf, Hoffman, Aebersold, and Hempelmann to Kistiakowsky, interoffice memo, September 5, 1945, Szasz Papers, Box 8, Folder 48.
46. Hoffman, "Health Physics Report," Los Alamos-626, Szasz Papers, Box 8, Folder 39.
47. Bellamy et al., "1948 Radiological and Biological Survey."
48. Boyer, General Manager of Los Alamos, to Finlatter, Secretary of the Air Force, December 1, 1950, Szasz Papers, Box 8, Folder 48.
49. Chester Brinck, Counsel, to James L. McCraw, Director of Security, AEC, memo, June 25, 1952, Szasz Papers, Box 8, Folder 48.
50. Thomas E. Hakonson and LaMar J. Johnson, *Radioecology; Distribution of Environmental Plutonium in Trinity Site . . . after 27 Years*, Szasz Papers, Box 8, Folder 48.
51. Larson, "Continental Close-In Fallout," 19–25.
52. U.S. Congress, Joint Committee on Atomic Energy, "The Nature of Radioactive Fallout and Its Effect on Man," is illuminating about governmental and military—as well as scientific and medical—beliefs concerning the safety of exposure to different types of radiation. It sought to be reassuring and to soothe public fears, especially about fallout.
53. U.S. Protection Agency, Office of Radiation Programs, Las Vegas Facility, "Trinity Site Soil Sampling Locations and Results," map figure 2, 1973, U.S. Department of Energy OpenNet, https://www.osti.gov/opennet/, accession no. NV0051304. The highest record was at Trinity ground zero with a reading of 1,100 measured in nanocuries per square meter, which roughly converts to 0.0092 roentgens; they measured 86 nanocuries (0.00072 roentgens) at the Monte Prieto ranch (never before identified in any Trinity-related literature); and they received several readings from 48 to 64 around the small community of Bingham, twenty-three miles south-southwest of ground zero.
54. Defense Nuclear Agency, *Final Report*, Report no. DNA 6028F, December 15, 1982. The DNA was identified at that time as the "Executive Agency" for the Department of Defense.
55. Nash, *Inescapable Ecologies*, chap. 5, points out that California health officials in the late 1940s and 1950s faced complex problems when dealing with the toxicity of pesticides that could contaminate an entire landscape: they had to rethink

procedures when there were no borders to the spatial aspects of some diseases and when the studies had to be conducted out of doors.

56. Kermit Larson, Kelshaw Bonham, and Art Welander, interview by James N. Stannard, 1979, U.S. Department of Energy OpenNet, https://www.osti.gov/opennet/, accession no. NV0702908. The problems of measuring plutonium created particular demand for reliable alpha particle detectors, although a commentator in 1949 complained, "Even today the ideal alpha survey instrument is far from a reality." See also Lapp, "Survey of Nucleonics Instrumentation Industry," 101.

57. Among the most controversial were British physician Alice Stewart, who argued in the 1970s that exposure to low levels of radiation was far more dangerous than officials acknowledged. Stewart challenged the reliance on the linear dose-effect model: the assumption of a proportional relationship between dose and effect. See also the controversies around Thomas Mancuso, a professor of occupational health at the University of Pittsburgh, and John Gofman, who headed a division at the Livermore Nuclear Lab. Both became pariahs for arguing that no level of exposure was safe. See Greene, *Woman Who Knew Too Much*. More sympathetic to the AEC, Hacker, *Elements of Controversy*, neglects the AEC-sponsored biomedical research in the 1950s and dates the fears about low-level radiation and I-131 to the early 1960s, overlooking concerns in the 1950s.

58. Ball, *Justice Downwind*.

59. Brodie, "Learning Secrecy in the Early Cold War," 643–70.

60. Eden, *Whole World on Fire*, states that she could not have completed her study without the invaluable gray literature that informants told her about.

61. Gusterson, "Secrecy, Authorship and Nuclear Weapons Scientists."

62. Not until the 1954 accidental exposure of Japanese fisherman to fallout from the Bikini test did widespread public knowledge emerge. Congressional hearings into fallout in 1957 also provided fuller public understanding. Yet, even as knowledge reached the public about fallout from the Nevada and Pacific bomb tests, knowledge about the Trinity radiation remained little known and little publicized.

63. Boice, "Likelihood of Adverse Pregnancy Outcomes and Genetic Disease," 494–503.

64. Simon et al., "Estimated Radiation Doses Received by New Mexico Residents," 428–77.

65. Crum, "Harold L. Ickes."

66. Hoffman, "Health Physics Report," Los Alamos-626, Los Alamos Historical Document Retrieval and Assessment Study (LAHDRA) materials, Folder 1580.

67. Carrizozo in 1940 was an unincorporated area with about 1,457 people; other towns that could have been affected by fallout had similar numbers. Fort Sumner had 1,669, Tularosa had 1,446, and Vaughn (which actually did receive considerable radiation) had 1,331. The largest town in the area was Socorro with 3,712 people, and there was no mention of concern about it receiving undue radioactivity.

68. Masco, *Nuclear Borderlands*, 136.

69. Masco, *Nuclear Borderlands*, 137–38. Furthermore, Pueblo people were hired in 1963 to clean up Bayo Canyon from the RaLa experiments. Teams spent weeks

picking up debris from eighteen years of tests, taking ninety truckloads from the canyon floor to Area G—one of the lab's radioactive waste burial sites (three canyons southwest of the test site).

70. Masco, *Nuclear Borderlands*, 136–37, 141–44.

71. Pasternak, *Yellow Dirt*, 148–51.

72. Carroll, *House of War*, 29, takes note of the conjunction of momentous events; history "is the appreciation of how events relate to each other, if not causally, then mythically." Carroll reminds us that ground was broken for the Pentagon, America's new "house of war," on September 11, 1941, although that day did not take on its new and horrific meaning until sixty years later on September 11, 2001.

73. Paul Boyer, *By the Bomb's Early Light*, documents the unpredictable shifts in American public consciousness about the bomb and its fallout. He notes the popular cultural fascination with comic book heroes whose superpowers came from atomic energy and the popularity of horror films with irradiated monsters.

74. Warren to Groves, "Report on Test II." The report included five unnumbered pages of maps depicting the trajectory of the radioactive cloud, the wind patterns, and velocities. The final map, hand-drawn, depicts the location of the "hot canyon" (twenty miles northeast of ground zero). Warren wrote, "By 0800 hours the monitors reported an area of high intensity in a canyon 20 miles northeast of zero. . . . At no house in this whole north and northeast area between 20 miles and 40 miles from zero was a dangerous intensity found."

75. Warren, Whipple, and Hempelmann, "Itinerary of Trip, 12 August 1945," Los Alamos-626, appendix II.

76. Henry Herrera has been quoted frequently in recent years concerning ongoing demands for legal redress over the Trinity radiation exposures. See, for instance, Susan Montoya Bryan, "Study Examines Cancer Risk from 1st Atom-Bomb Test," Associated Press, *Las Vegas Sun*, September 29, 2014, https://lasvegassun.com /news/2014/sep/29/study-examines-cancer-risk-1st-atom-bomb-test/.

77. Rich evidence about lawsuits is in Ball, *Justice Downwind*; Fradkin, *Fallout*; and Schwartz, *Atomic Audit*. The federal Price Anderson Act of 1957 forbade private citizens' lawsuits against atomic weapons contractors who were exempted from any claims against them and their activities.

78. Advisory Committee on Human Radiation Experimentation, *Final Report*.

79. LAHDRA, *Final Report*, chap. 22, 31.

80. Shonka, "First Dirty Bomb, Trinity," footnoted in Tucker and Alvarez, "Trinity." Widner and Flack, "Characterization of the World's First Nuclear Explosion," argues that 4.8 kilograms of unfissioned plutonium was dispersed from the test.

81. LAHDRA, *Final Report*, chap. 10, 50.

82. LAHDRA, *Final Report*, chap. 10, 50.

83. RG 326, Records of the Atomic Energy Commission, Office of the Secretary, General Correspondence 1946–1951, 682–723, Box 64, NN3-326-93-007, H. M. 1993, NARA Maryland.

84. The item removed August 23, 1994, was in RG 326, Box 64, Folder 326 (684.2 [4-2-48]), NARA Maryland. The second removed item was in the same folder and box.

85. Lilienthal to Gray, April 13, 1948, RG 77, Box 56, Folder 319.1, Trinity Test Reports, Misc., NARA Maryland. See also the mention of "health hazards" in the fenced area of the site: Lilienthal to Gray, June 1948, RG 77, Box 56, Folder 319.1, Trinity Test Reports, Misc., NARA Maryland.

86. "The Radiation Exposure Compensation Act (RECA) is a federal law originally passed by the United States Congress in 1990 to award financial reparations to Nevada Test Site Downwinders, on-site test participants during atmospheric nuclear weapons tests, and uranium miners and millers who developed cancer and/or other specific illnesses as a result of radioactive fallout or radon gasses to which they were exposed." Amendments were added in 2000. See M. Gomez, "Unknowing, Unwilling, and Uncompensated." For an overview, see also U.S. Department of Justice, "Radiation Exposure Compensation Act."

87. Congressional Research Service, *Radiation Exposure Compensation Act (RECA)*, 10. Schwartz, *Atomic Audit*, 415. As of January 13, 1998, 1,375 downwinders had received $72.1 million in compensation while 1,121 had claims denied. Also in 1998, 155 on-site participants in tests at the Nevada Test Site received money under RECA, but 659 claims were denied. Schwartz, *Atomic Audit*, 404.

88. U.S. Department of Justice, "Radiation Exposure Compensation Act."

89. An important 1948 source noting radiation concerns at Trinity is Kraker to McCraw, memo, "Trinity Site Status of and Study on What To Do," August 26, 1952, Szasz Papers, Box 8, Folder 48.

90. Congressional Research Service, *Radiation Exposure Compensation Act (RECA)*, 10.

91. National Research Council, "Radiation Exposure Screening and Educational Program."

92. M. Gomez, "Unknowing, Unwilling, and Uncompensated."

93. Fehner and Gosling, *Battlefield of the Cold War*, 25, quoted in Tucker and Alvarez, "Trinity."

94. Fox, *Downwind*, 214.

95. Fox, *Downwind*, 223, points out the past marginalization and even caricaturization of radiation-affected people of the Southwest, and her book is a tribute to and contemporary acknowledgment that downwinders' histories "are the products of a complex, historically constructed system of experiential, local knowledge."

96. Historian Ferenc Szasz apparently claimed that the Trinity site "was too heavily contaminated to be made into a national historic site." He made the remark as a critical rebuke to panelists speaking on "The Atomic Southwest" at the 2005 Western History Association meeting. Quoted and repeated in Fox, *Downwind*, 223.

97. Kosek, *Understories*, 256.

1. Early on, the National Park Service leaders' strategy had been to create National Monuments first and then proceed to creating a park at the site. Rothman, *On Rims and Ridges*, 171.

2. Tillotson, Region III Director NPS, to Director of NPS, December 21, 1945, RG 79, Box 382, NARA Denver.

3. Newton Drury, Director of NPS, to John Dempsey, Governor of NM, October 31, 1945, RG 79, Box 382, Folder L58, 1945 Trinity Site, NARA Denver.

4. Demaray to Tillotson, telegram, November 6, 1945, RG 79, Box 382, Folder L58, 1945 Trinity Site, NARA Denver. In the telegram Demaray reported that General Groves's office warned that the surrounding country should not be shown "except as aerial photograph of area and picture of firing location."

5. Tillotson to Demaray, memo, November 6, 1945, RG 79, Box 382, Folder L58, 1945 Trinity Site, NARA Denver.

6. M. R. Tillotson, E. T. Scoyen, H. H. Cornell, and Willard Bradley, *The Report on the Proposed Atomic Bomb National Monument*, RG 200, Box 1, NARA Maryland. Three maps and numerous photographs are appended to the report. Tillotson was Region 3 director of the NPS, Scoyen was Region 3 associate director, Cornell was regional landscape architect, and Bradley was an engineer.

7. Tillotson et al., *Report*, 15–16.

8. Tillotson et al., *Report*, 10.

9. Tillotson et al., *Report*, 17.

10. Tillotson et al., *Report*, 10.

11. Tillotson et al., *Report*, 12.

12. Boyer, "First Reactions," part 1 of *By the Bomb's Early Light*.

13. Welsh, *Dunes and Dreams*, chap. 5, note 62.

14. Ben Thompson to NPS Director, memo, November 1947, RG 79, Box 2982, NARA Denver. The folder includes an intriguing handwritten note dated November 12, 1947, by someone with undecipherable initials: "Good idea. Refer to Advising Board. Also please draft letter to Dr. Bush, whom I know quite well. He would, I think, sympathize with your point of view."

15. Scoyen to Groves, August 9, 1946, and September 12, 1946, RG 200, Box 1, NARA Maryland.

16. Norris, *Racing for the Bomb*, 498–510, illustrates Groves's troubles with the AEC and with Eisenhower.

17. Secretary of War (no signature) to Secretary of the Interior (unnamed), n.d., RG 200, Box 1, NARA Maryland. He concurs with the NPS plan to include the B-29s.

18. Record of Meeting with Representatives of the National Park Service, July 31, 1946, RG 200, Box 1, NARA Maryland. This document mentions trying to obtain the lead-lined tanks, Jumbo, and "any remains of the tower if still available (which is doubtful)," and a promise to build a temporary shelter to cover the "existing glazed sand."

19. Draft document, "'Establishing the Atomic Bomb National Monument' By the President of the U.S.A. A Proclamation," RG 79, Box 382, Folder L58, NARA Denver.

20. Rothman, *Preserving Different Pasts*, 212, cites Drury's tenure as 1940–52. I culled the other designations from signatures on memos and letters in miscellaneous NPS records.

21. Elizabeth M. Tucker, Management Services Office, memo summarizing actions at Trinity site, March 6, 1961, 15.006.228, WSMR archive.

22. Ben H. Thompson, Chief of the Division of Recreation Resource Planning, NPS, to a publisher, April 3, 1957, RG 79, Box 381, Folder L58, April 1953–57, New Mexico Trinity Site folder, NARA Denver.

23. Rothman, *Preserving Different Pasts*, 167.

24. As of October 15, 1966, all National Historic Sites and National Historical Parks were automatically listed on the National Register of Historic Places. For a full list of NPS parks and their designations, see "National Park System," National Park Service, last updated October 19, 2022, https://www.nps.gov/aboutus/national -park-system.htm.

25. W. L. Kindred, Col. G 5, Acting Chief, Facilities Branch, Service Division, to Chief of Ordnance, Pentagon, Washington DC, memo, "Proposed Trinity Atomic National Monument," n.d., 15.006.228, WSMR archive. Rieder and Lawson, *Trinity at Fifty*, 74, note that the U.S. Army and the New Mexico State Historic Preservation Division also came to be involved.

26. B. H. Ferdig, Chief, Facilities Management Division, Trinity Site National Historical Monument, memo, October 16, 1969, 15.006.232, WSMR archive. Szasz complicates the issue, too, saying that in December 1965 the Trinity site was entered into the National Register of Historic Places and that several years later it was declared a National Historic Landmark. Szasz Papers, Box 8, Folder 5.

27. Sprinkle, "'Of Exceptional Importance,'" 82.

28. Sources differ about dates: Mackintosh, *Historic Sites Survey*, 38. The National Historic Landmarks program was created in large part to help reduce the federal government's costs of historic site acquisition and preservation. Under the new program the federal government had only minimal expenses. In creating a National Historic Landmark it issued a formal certificate and placed an obelisk to denote a site. In addition to minimizing costs, the new program was also geared to reduce criticism that federal recognition of properties as nationally significant implied federal designs on them. Mackintosh, *Historic Sites Survey*, 26.

29. "Determining the Eligibility of a Property for National Historic Landmark Designation," National Historic Landmarks, National Park Service, last updated August 29, 2018, https://www.nps.gov/subjects/nationalhistoriclandmarks/eligibility.htm. Mackintosh, however, believes that one purpose of the NHL program was to save money. The federal government could issue a simple plaque to preserve historic properties but not assume further financial burdens.

30. Sprinkle, "'Of Exceptional Importance,'" 85–86.

31. Sprinkle, "'Of Exceptional Importance,'" 90.

32. Sprinkle, "'Of Exceptional Importance,'" 95. The others are the Experimental Breeder Reactor No. 1 in Arco, Idaho, and the Pupin Physics Lab at Columbia University. Some atomic energy sites did not make the grade. In 1967 the Advisory Board refused to include consideration of NHL status for the F Reactor at Hanford, arguing that atomic energy was adequately represented by existing NHLs. Inclusion of that reactor at Hanford continued to be an issue in debates about the Manhattan Project National Historical Park in the 2000s.

33. Eckles, *Trinity*, 78, and Merlan, *Life at Trinity Base Camp*, 76, list it as an NHL in 1967. Both state that the obelisk commemorates the Trinity site becoming a National Historic Landmark without noting that the obelisk has two different dates. Today a public Official Scenic Historic Marker sits on Highway 380 at State Road 525: "Trinity Site. The nuclear age began with the detonation of the world's first atomic bomb at the Trinity Site on July 16, 1945. J. Robert Oppenheimer, director of the Manhattan Project's Los Alamos Laboratory, stated that he suggested 'Trinity,' perhaps from the poetry of John Donne. After the blast, he was said to have recalled the line from the Bhagavad Gita, 'Now, I am Become Death, the destroyer of worlds.'" An earlier sign noted the date of "the world's first atomic explosion" and that the site, now part of the missile range, was closed to the public.

34. Merlan, *Life at Trinity Base Camp*, 76; Eckles, *Trinity*, 78.

35. Federal Register of Historic Places, vol. 37, no. 51, March 15, 1972.

36. Joseph Rumsberg to Superintendent of White Sands National Monument, memo, April 1974, RG 79, Box 382, NARA Denver. There is also a copy in the Szasz Papers, Box 8, Folder 5.

37. Rumsberg to Superintendent, memo, April 1974, NARA Denver.

38. My thanks to Bill Godby, archaeologist at the White Sands Missile Range, for sending me a copy of the preliminary working draft of "A Master Plan for Trinity NHS, NM," 3rd draft, September 1970. The copy of the 1970 master plan I had been working with, from the Szasz Papers, Box 8, Folder 5, did not include important material after page 15 such as drawings of maps, photos from the test site, and an appendix. Godby also included a June 1969 "advance copy" of the proposed Project Synopsis for the Trinity National Historic Site (with approval signatures from July and August 1969).

39. My thanks to David T. Kirkpatrick, at that time the associate director of Human Systems Research Inc., for sending me a 2001 copy of his firm's draft report about preserving the Trinity site. In an email, Deborah M. Dennis, executive director of Human Systems Research Inc., explained that, in her understanding, the original nomination was unacceptable because "it did not provide an enclosed space as required for a National Register nomination. The area in the original nomination was a tall, narrow triangle that was left open and ground zero was indicated in the center of the triangle." Bob Burton, the WSMR archaeologist at the time, "wanted the area to not only have definite boundaries (township and range) but also wanted to include ranches, commo lines, and test facilities as features to

indicate National Historic Site activities." Dennis notes that her firm produced many formal National Register nominations for areas of the wsмr, but none of them had gone farther than the wsмr Environmental Department files on the base. She added, "My guess is that the military wants to be able to manage their land as they see best without interference from any other agencies."

40. Proudfoot, Commanding Major General wsмr, to Director of nps, memo, March 21, 1975, Szasz Papers, Box 8, Folder 5.

41. The boundary confusion was not resolved in spite of the new cordiality between the nps and the wsмr. Bill Godby (see note 38 above), in discussion with the nps about the boundary problem, recalls that he was told "that because it involved a change in the boundary it would require congressional approval or something on that order." His other more pressing duties then prevented him from pursuing the nomination revision further.

42. On the process, see "Determining the Eligibility of a Property for National Historic Landmark Designation," National Park Service, last updated August 29, 2018, https://www.nps.gov/subjects/nationalhistoriclandmarks/eligibility.htm. There were 2,600 nhls in 2020.

43. Leslie P. Arnberger, sw Regional Director, to Chief of Park Planning, memo, April 11, 1980, Szasz Papers, Box 8, Folder 5.

44. A copy of the bill can be found in rg 368, Box 52, New Mexico Trinity Site folder, nara Denver.

45. Merlan, *Life at Trinity Base Camp*, 76.

46. Glenn O. Hendrix, Chief, Office of Environmental Planning and Design, Master Plan document, September 15, 1970, Szasz Papers, Box 8, Folder 5.

47. Carcie C. Clifford, Colonel, gs, Chief of Staff, to Commander, U.S. Army Material Command, memo, September 11, 1973, Szasz Papers, Box 8, Folder 5. Clifford stated that "this headquarters takes exception to Thompson's comments." The wsмr did not destroy bunkers as Thompson claimed: "The work was done in March 1967 under an aec sponsored project to reserve the explosives and radioactive waste left in the bunkers. The material was removed and the bunkers were covered up."

48. Leslie P. Arnberger to Chief Office of Park Planning and Environmental Quality, Washington Support Office of the National Park Service (waso), April 11, 1980, includes "Review of Proposals for Establishment of Trinity National Historic Site" (fifteen pages), Szasz Papers, Box 8, Folder 5. In 1980 Arnberger became the new director of the nps Southwest Region, and he created the historical account of preservation attempts at the Trinity site.

49. U.S. Senate, "Statements on Introduced Bills and Joint Resolutions." The bill authorized the nps, working with the secretary of energy and secretary of defense, to undertake a special resource study to assess designating various Manhattan Project sites and facilities as a National Historical Park.

50. References to Trinity were removed from the Senate Committee version (May 20, 2004) and from the version passed by the Senate (September 15, 2004) and

Congress (September 28, 2004). After 2004 the congressional records make no references to the Trinity site, and no information was provided about their removal.

51. Tom McCulloch of the Advisory Council on Historic Preservation and Skip Gosling, a federal preservation officer for the Department of Energy (DOE), responded to my inquiry in October 2019 by saying that they had worked on the project for many years and believed that the decision not to include the Trinity site lay with it being "behind the fence in an active military installation." Kamerick, "Passions Flare Over Memory of the Manhattan Project," took note of concerns that the NPS was under pressure to give a "positive spin to the Manhattan Project" and remarked on the omission of the bomb's effect on local communities.

52. National Park Service and U.S. Department of the Interior, *Manhattan Project Sites*, a 216-page document with eleven appendixes. The study stated that the NPS would find it unfeasible to operate the noncontiguous site. It explained that even though the DOE "has indicated it would continue to bear responsibility for safety, national security, historic preservation, and upkeep," the NPS had concerns about liability "and unforeseen costs in addressing visitor and employee safety, national security, cleanup, historic preservation, and maintenance of the facilities in the future." The document proposed several alternatives for the four sites including doing nothing, making them part of a national nonprofit consortium, formally designating them a National Heritage Area, designating each an affiliated area of an ongoing national park, and lastly, creating a Manhattan Project National Historical Park only at Los Alamos. The sites at Hanford, Oak Ridge, and Dayton, Ohio, would be associated with but not operationally part of the Los Alamos–based National Historical Park. Dismissing the alternatives, the DOE planning team eventually advanced the plan of a modified version of a national park at Oak Ridge, Hanford, and Los Alamos.

53. Oak Ridge capitalizes on its atomic history with bus tours of the former K-25 plant, where uranium was processed into fissionable material for the "Little Man" bomb dropped on Hiroshima. Tourists to Oak Ridge can also visit the Y-12 History Center in the Y-12 National Security site or take a CD-narrated car tour around the "secret city" of World War II.

54. Rick Hampson, "Voices: A Close Encounter with Nuclear Tourism," *USA Today*, May 20, 2014.

55. Freeman, "A Plutonium Tourism Ode."

56. Harris, "Museums and Controversy," 1102–10, notes that history museums, generally insulated from the kinds of controversies engulfing art museums, began to be challenged in ways not seen earlier. The volume also contains articles about American historical memories of Hiroshima, Nagasaki, World War II in the Pacific, and the *Enola Gay* exhibition controversy.

57. Solnit, *Savage Dreams*, part 1, is about protests at the Nevada Test Site.

58. U.S. Senate, "Statements on Introduced Bills and Joint Resolutions."

59. The Atomic Heritage Foundation now offers online virtual tours of Manhattan Project sites and includes information about African Americans, Native tribes at Hanford, and the environmental legacies at various sites.

60. National Park Service and U.S. Department of the Interior, *Foundation Document*, 2.

61. National Park Service and U.S. Department of the Interior, *Foundation Document*, 14.

62. National Park Service and U.S. Department of the Interior, *Foundation Document*, 31. See also Blum, "Public Need to Know."

63. Lawrence Bartell, interview by Cindy Kelly, 2003, "Voices of the Manhattan Project."

64. Szasz, *Day the Sun Rose Twice*, 160–61.

65. *Albuquerque Journal*, September 9, 1953, RG 79, Box 381, Folder L58, April 1953–57, NARA Denver.

66. B. H. Ferdig, memo for the record, January 16, 1973, 15.006.232, WSMR archive.

67. Ferdig, memo for the record, WSMR archive.

68. Wills, "Bomb Bursting in Air," viii. Visiting the site as research for her master's thesis, Wills interviewed some thirty visitors whom she regarded as "atomic tourists" enjoying the "kind of carnival" that, after a quarter-mile walk, led them "to the most exotic attraction of all: nothing" (p. 74).

69. Wills, "Bomb Bursting in Air," 74.

70. When the public is allowed into the Trinity site area they must come on buses from Albuquerque arranged by the Chamber of Commerce or by private cars through the Stallion Gate entrance 130 miles south of Albuquerque, between the small New Mexico towns of Socorro and Carrizozo.

71. For detailed explanations of Jumbo, see Eckles, *Trinity*, and Loring, *Birthplace of the Atomic Bomb*. Alan Carr notes insightfully that Jumbo was "a monument to doubt. . . . The steel behemoth must have remained to some a very tangible and unwelcome harbinger of potential catastrophe." Carr, "Thirty Minutes Before the Dawn," s6.

72. Engelhardt, *End of Victory Culture*.

73. To NPS Director from Ronald F. Lee, Chief Historian, memo, October 7, 1947, RG 79, Box 382, Folder L58 (2), NARA Denver.

74. Edgington, "Fragmented Histories," 189.

75. See preface.

# BIBLIOGRAPHY

ARCHIVES AND MANUSCRIPT MATERIALS

Birge, Raymond Thayer. Papers. Bancroft Library, University of California, Berkeley.

Center for Research Libraries (CRL). Chicago, Illinois. https://www.crl.edu.

Chancellor's Administrative Files. Archives, University of California, Los Angeles (UCLA).

Chemical and Biological Warfare Collection. National Security Archive, George Washington University, Washington DC.

Hamilton, Joseph Gilbert. Papers. Archives, University of California San Francisco Medical School.

Inventory of Records of President of UC. Special Problem Folders, 1899–1954. Bancroft Library, University of California, Berkeley.

Lamont, Lansing. Papers. Harry S. Truman Library.

Lawrence, Ernest O. General Files. Bancroft Library, University of California, Berkeley.

Lawrence, Ernest O. Papers. Microfilm. Bancroft Library, University of California, Berkeley.

Library Without Walls Project. Los Alamos National Lab Research Library.

Los Alamos Historical Document Retrieval and Assessment Study (LAHDRA) materials. Government Documents. University of New Mexico Library, Albuquerque.

National Archives and Records Administration, College Park, Maryland (NARA Maryland).

Advisory Committee on Human Radiation Experimentation (ACHRE) Collection.

RG 77. Office of the Commanding General, Manhattan Project. Office of the Chief of Engineers.

RG 200. Groves, Leslie. Papers.

RG 326. Records of the Atomic Energy Commission.

National Archives and Records Administration, Denver, Colorado (NARA Denver).

RG 79. National Park Service Records.

RG 368. Heritage Conservation and Recreation Service Records.

"Remembering Los Alamos: World War II." Interviews conducted in 1992 by the Los Alamos Historical Society. Los Alamos Historical Society Archives.

Sublette, Carey. Nuclear Weapon Archive: A Guide to Nuclear Weapons. Last updated June 12, 2020. https://nuclearweaponarchive.org/.

Szasz, Ferenc Morton. Papers. Collection 552. Southwest Research Center, Zimmerman Library, University of New Mexico, Albuquerque.

UCSF Human Radiation Committee Administrative Records 1993–19. University of California San Francisco Medical School.

U.S. Department of Energy. Nevada Site Office, Public Reading Room, Las Vegas.

U.S. Department of Energy. OpenNet database. https://www.osti.gov/opennet.

U.S. Federal Census Collection. Ancestry.com. https://www.ancestry.com/search /categories/usfedcen/.

"Voices of the Manhattan Project." National Museum of Nuclear Science and History. Joint project with the Atomic Heritage Foundation and the Los Alamos Historical Society. https://www.manhattanprojectvoices.org/.

Walker, Gregory. Trinity Atomic Web Site. https://www.abomb1.org/.

Warren, Stafford Leake. Administrative Files 1925–68. Series 300 Papers. Archives, UCLA.

Warren, Stafford Leake. Oral history. "An Exceptional Man for Exceptional Challenges." 1983. Special Collections, UCLA.

Warren, Stafford Leake. Papers. Collection 987. Special Collections, UCLA.

White Sands Missile Range, New Mexico. (WSMR archive; no readily available records; requires personal contact.)

PUBLISHED WORKS

Advisory Committee on Human Radiation Experimentation (ACHRE). Final Report. Washington DC: U.S. Government Printing Office, 1994.

Albright, Joseph, and Marcia Kunstel. Bombshell: The Secret Story of America's Unknown Atomic Spy Conspiracy. New York: Times Books, 1997.

Badish, Lawrence, ed. Reminiscences of Los Alamos, 1943–1945. Boston: D. Reidd, 1980.

Bainbridge, K. T. Trinity. Los Alamos NM: Los Alamos Scientific Laboratory, 1976.

Baker, Michael E. Redstone Arsenal Yesterday and Today. Redstone Arsenal AL: Secretary of the General Staff, U.S. Army Missile Command, 1993.

Ball, Howard. Justice Downwind: America's Atomic Testing Program in the 1950s. Oxford: Oxford University Press, 1986.

Balmer, Brian. Secrecy and Science: A Historical Sociology of Biological and Chemical Warfare. London: Routledge, 2012.

Bellamy, A. W., J. L. Leitch, K. H. Larson, and D. B. Dunn. "The 1948 Radiological and Biological Survey of Areas in New Mexico Affected by the First Atomic Bomb Detonation." Report no. UCLA-32, October 12, 1949, 12. Abstract available at U.S. Department of Energy Office of Scientific and Technical Information, https://www .osti.gov/biblio/4268288. Copy with page numbers obliterated in Szasz Papers, Box 8, Folder 40.

Belnap, Michael R. Review of The Court of Private Land Claims, by Richard Wells Bradfute. Southwestern Historical Quarterly 79, no. 4 (April 1976): 488–89.

Bernstein, Barton. "Doing Nuclear History: Treating Scholarship Fairly and Interpreting Pre-Hiroshima Thinking about 'Radioactive Poisoning.'" *SHAFR Newsletter*, September 1996.

Bernstein, Jeremy. *Oppenheimer: Portrait of an Enigma*. Chicago: Ivan R. Dee, 2004.

Bird, Kai, and Martin J. Sherwin. *American Prometheus: The Triumph and Tragedy of J. Robert Oppenheimer*. New York: Alfred A. Knopf, 2005.

Blum, Hilary. "The Public Need to Know: Public Relations, Public History, and Secrecy at the Hanford Nuclear Site." PhD diss., Claremont Graduate University, in progress, 2022.

Blume, Lesley M. M. *Fallout*. New York: Simon and Schuster, 2020.

Boehm, William B. *From Barren Desert to Thriving Community: A Social History of White Sands Missile Range, 1945–1954*. HSR Project no. 9531, WSMR Project no. 97-14. Tularosa NM: Human Systems Research, 1997.

Boice, John D., Jr. "The Likelihood of Adverse Pregnancy Outcomes and Genetic Disease (Transgenerational Effects) from Exposure to Radioactive Fallout from the 1945 Trinity Atomic Bomb Test." *Health Physics* 119, no. 4 (October 2020): 494–503.

Boyer, Paul. *By the Bomb's Early Light: American Thought and Culture at the Dawn of the Atomic Age*. Chapel Hill: University of North Carolina Press, 1994. Originally published 1985 by Pantheon.

Bradfute, Richard Wells. *The Court of Private Land Claims: The Adjudication of Spanish and Mexican Land Grant Titles, 1891–1904*. Albuquerque: University of New Mexico Press, 1975.

Brodie, Janet Farrell. "Contested Knowledge: The Trinity Test Radiation Studies." In *Inevitably Toxic: Historical Perspectives on Contamination, Exposure, and Expertise*, edited by Brinda Sarathy, Vivien Hamilton, and Janet Farrell Brodie. Pittsburgh: University of Pittsburgh Press, 2018.

———. "Learning Secrecy in the Early Cold War: the RAND Corporation." *Journal of Diplomatic History* 35, no. 1 (September 2011): 643–70.

———. "Radiation Secrecy and Censorship After Hiroshima and Nagasaki." *Journal of Social History* 48, no. 4 (2015): 842–64.

Brophy, Leo P., Wyndham D. Miles, and Rexmond C. Cochrane. *The U.S. Army in World War II: The Technical Services. The Chemical Warfare Service: From Laboratory to Field*. Washington DC: Center of Military History, U.S. Army, 1988. https://history.army.mil/html/books/010/10-2/CMH_Pub_10-2.pdf.

Brown, Kate. *Plutopia: Nuclear Families, Atomic Cities, and the Great Soviet and American Plutonium Disasters*. New York: Oxford University Press, 2013.

Caffey, David. *Chasing the Santa Fe Ring: Power and Privilege in Territorial New Mexico*. Albuquerque: University of New Mexico Press, 2014.

Canaday, John. *Critical Assembly: Poems of the Manhattan Project*. Albuquerque: University of New Mexico Press, 2017.

Carr, Alan B. "Thirty Minutes Before the Dawn: The Story of Trinity." *Nuclear Technology* 207, no. SUP1 (February 4, 2021): s6. https://doi.org/10.1080/00295450.2021.1927625.

Carroll, James. *House of War: The Pentagon and the Disastrous Rise of American Power.* Boston: Houghton, Mifflin, 2006.

Childers, Leisl Carr. *The Size of the Risk: Histories of Multiple Use in the Great Basin.* Norman: University of Oklahoma Press, 2015.

Christman, Albert B. *Sailors, Scientists, and Rockets: Origins of the Navy Rocket Program and of the Naval Ordnance Test Station, Inyokern.* Washington DC: Naval History Division, 1971.

Conant, Jennet. *109 East Palace: Robert Oppenheimer and Dorothy McKibben and the Secret City of Los Alamos.* New York: Simon and Schuster, 2006.

Congressional Research Service. *The Radiation Exposure Compensation Act (RECA): Compensation Related to Exposure to Radiation from Atomic Weapons Testing and Uranium Mining.* January 13, 2021. https://crsreports.congress.gov/product/pdf/R/R43956.

Crim, Brian E. *Our Germans: Project Paperclip and the National Security State.* Baltimore: Johns Hopkins University Press, 2018.

Crum, Steven J. "Harold L. Ickes and His Idea of a Chair in American Indian History." *History Teacher* 25, no. 1 (November 1991).

Defense Nuclear Agency. *Final Report.* Report no. DNA 6028F. December 15, 1982.

DeVorkin, David H. *Science with a Vengeance: How the Military Created the US Space Sciences after World War II.* New York: Springer-Verlag, 1992.

Dunbar-Ortiz, Roxanne. *Roots of Resistance: A History of Land Tenure in New Mexico.* Norman: University of Oklahoma Press, 2007.

Ebright, Malcolm. *Advocates for the Oppressed: Hispanos, Indians, Genizaros, and Their Land in New Mexico.* Albuquerque: University of New Mexico Press, 2014.

Eckles, Jim. *Pocketful of Rockets: History and Stories Behind White Sands Missile Range.* Las Cruces NM: Fiddlebike Partnership, 2013.

———. *Trinity: The History of an Atomic Bomb National Historic Landmark.* Las Cruces NM: privately printed, n.d.

Eden, Lynn. *Whole World on Fire: Organizations, Knowledge, and Nuclear Weapons Devastation.* Ithaca NY: Cornell University Press, 2004.

Edgington, Ryan H. "Fragmented Histories: Science, Environment and Monument Building at the Trinity Site, 1945–1995." In *Militarized Landscapes: From Gettysburg to Salisbury Plain*, edited by Chris Pearson, Peter Coates, and Tim Cole. London: Bloomsbury Publishing, 2010.

———. *Lines in the Sand: An Environmental History of Cold War New Mexico.* Philadelphia: Temple University Press, 2012.

———. *Range Wars: The Environmental Contest for White Sands Missile Range.* Lincoln: University of Nebraska Press, 2014.

Eidenbach, Peter L. *Star Throwers of the Tularosa: The Early Cold War Legacy of White Sands Missile Range.* Tularosa NM: Human Systems Research, 1996.

Eidenbach, Peter L., and Beth Morgan. *Homes on the Range: Oral Recollections of Early Ranch Life on the U.S. Army White Sands Missile Range, New Mexico.* Tularosa NM: Human Systems Research, 1994.

Eidenbach, Peter L., and Robert L. Hart. *A Number of Things: Baldy Russell, Estey City, the Ozanne Stage. Historic Ranching and Mining on the U.S. Army White Sands Missile Range, New Mexico.* Tularosa NM: Human Systems Research, 1995.

Eidenbach, Peter L., Richard L. Wessel, Lisa M. Meyer, and Gail Wimberly. *A Brief History of the White Sands Proving Ground 1941–1965.* Extracted from *Star Throwers of the Tularosa: The Early Cold War Legacy of White Sands Missile Range.* Tularosa NM: Human Systems Research, 1997.

Endicott, Stephen, and Edward Hagerman. *The U.S. and Biological Warfare: Secrets from the Early Cold War and Korea.* Bloomington: Indiana University Press, 1998.

Engelhardt, Tom. *The End of Victory Culture: Cold War America and the Disillusioning of a Generation.* New York: Basic Books, 1995.

———. "The Victors and the Vanquished." In *History Wars: The Enola Gay and Other Battles for the American Past*, edited by Edward T. Linenthal and Tom Engelhardt. New York: Holt, 1996.

Fehner, Terrence R., and F. G. Gosling. *Battlefield of the Cold War: The Nevada Test Site, 1951–1963.* Vol. 1. Washington DC: U.S. Department of Energy, 2006.

Fermi, Laura. *Atoms in the Family: My Life with Enrico Fermi.* Chicago: University of Chicago Press, 1961.

Fermi, Rachel, and Esther Samra. *Picturing the Bomb: Photographs from the Secret World of the Manhattan Project.* New York: Harry N. Abrams, 1995.

Fetter-Vorm, Jonathan. *Trinity: A Graphic History of the First Atomic Bomb.* New York: Hill and Wang, 2012.

Fine, Lenore, and Jesse A. Remington. *U.S. Army in World War II: The Technical Services. The Corps of Engineers: Construction in the United States.* Washington DC: U.S. Army, Center of Military History, 2003.

Ford, Daniel. *The Cult of the Atom: The Secret Papers of the Atomic Energy Commission.* New York: Simon and Schuster, 1984.

Fox, Sarah Alisabeth. *Downwind: A People's History of the Nuclear West.* Lincoln: University of Nebraska Press, 2014.

Fradkin, Philip L. *Fallout: An American Nuclear Tragedy.* Tucson: University of Arizona Press, 1989.

Freeman, Lindsey A. *Longing for the Bomb: Oak Ridge and Atomic Nostalgia.* Chapel Hill: University of North Carolina Press, 2015.

———. "A Plutonium Tourism Ode: The Rocky Flats Cold War Museum." In *Moral Encounters in Tourism*, edited by Kevin Hannam and Mary Mostafanezhad. Farnham, England: Ashgate Publishing, 2014.

Galison, Peter. "Removing Knowledge; the Logic of Modern Censorship." In *Agnatology: The Making and Unmaking of Ignorance*, edited by Robert N. Proctor and Londa Schiebinger. Stanford CA: Stanford University Press, 2008.

Gallagher, Carole. *American Ground Zero: The Secret Nuclear War.* Cambridge MA: MIT Press, 1993.

Gerrard-Gough, J. D., and Albert B. Christman. *The Grand Experiment at Inyokern: History of the Naval Weapons Center, China Lake, CA.* Vol. 2. Washington DC: U.S. Government Printing Office, Naval History Division, 1978.

Gibson, Toni Michnovicz, and Jon Michnovicz. *Images of America: Los Alamos 1944–1947.* Charleston SC: Arcadia Publishing, 2005.

Gimbel, John. "German Scientists, U.S. Denazification Policy and the 'Paperclip' Conspiracy." *International History Review* 12 (August 1990): 441–65.

Gomez, Laura E. *Manifest Destinies: The Making of the Mexican-American Race.* New York: New York University Press, 2018.

Gomez, Myrriah. "Nuclear Alienation: A Literary Analysis of Race, Space, and Resistance Surrounding the Nuclear Coloniality of Los Alamos, 1942–2012." PhD diss., University of Texas, 2015.

——. "Unknowing, Unwilling, and Uncompensated: The Effects of the Trinity Test on New Mexicans and the Potential Benefits of Radiation Exposure Compensation Act (RECA) Amendments." Tularosa Basin Downwinders Consortium. Revised January 2017. https://www.trinitydownwinders.com/health-impact-assessment.

Gordin, Michael D. *Five Days in August: How World War II Became a Nuclear War.* Princeton NJ: Princeton University Press, 2015.

Gosling, F. G. *The Manhattan Project: Making the Atomic Bomb.* Washington DC: U.S. Department of Energy, National Security History Series, 2010.

Graf, William L. *Wilderness Preservation and the Sagebrush Rebellions.* Savage MD: Rowman and Littlefield, 1990.

Greene, Gayle. *The Woman Who Knew Too Much: Alice Stewart and the Secrets of Radiation.* Ann Arbor: University of Michigan Press, 1999.

Grinnell, David R. "Eichleay and the Atomic Bomb." *Western Pennsylvania History* 94, no. 1 (Spring 2011): 8.

Groueff, Stephane. *Manhattan Project: The Untold Story of the Making of the Atomic Bomb.* Boston: Little, Brown, 1967.

Groves, Leslie R. *Now It Can Be Told: The Story of the Manhattan Project.* New York: Harper and Brothers, 1962.

——. "Some Recollections of July 16, 1945." In *Alamogordo Plus Twenty-Five Years,* edited by Richard S. Lewis and Jane Wilson, 47–61. New York: Viking Press, 1970.

Gusterson, Hugh. "Nuclear Tourism." *Journal for Cultural Research* 8, no. 1 (January 2004).

——. "Secrecy, Authorship and Nuclear Weapons Scientists." In *Secrecy and Knowledge Production,* edited by Judith Reppy. Occasional Paper no. 23. New York: Cornell University Peace Studies Program, October 1999.

Hacker, Barton C. *The Dragon's Tail: Radiation Safety in the Manhattan Project, 1942–1946.* Berkeley: University of California Press, 1987.

——. *Elements of Controversy: The Atomic Energy Commission and Radiation Safety in Nuclear Weapons Testing, 1947–1974.* Berkeley: University of California Press, 1994.

Hahn, Michelle. "Between the Devil and the Deep Blue Sea: An Analysis of the Consequences of 20th Century American Imperialism and Nuclear Testing Upon the Marshall Islands and Its Inhabitants." Master's thesis, Claremont Graduate University, 2020.

Hale, Peter Bacon. *Atomic Spaces: Living on the Manhattan Project*. Urbana: University of Illinois Press, 1997.

Hämäläinen, Pekka. *The Comanche Empire*. Princeton NJ: Yale University Press, 2008.

Hamblin, Jacob Darwin. *Poison in the Well: Radioactive Waste in the Oceans at the Dawn of the Nuclear Age*. New Brunswick NJ: Rutgers University Press, 2008.

Hamilton, John A. *Blazing Skies: Air Defense Artillery, Fort Bliss, Texas, 1940–2009*. Washington DC: Army Defense Department, 2009.

Hansen, Wayne R., and John C. Rodgers. *Radiological Survey and Evaluation of the Fallout Area from the Trinity Test: Chupadera Mesa and White Sands Missile Range, New Mexico*. Los Alamos 10256-MS. June 1985. http://lib-www.lanl.gov/cgi-bin /getfile?00318776.pdf.

Harris, Neil. "Museums and Controversy: Some Introductory Reflections." *Journal of American History* 82, no. 3 (December 1995): 1102–10.

Harris, Sheldon H. *Factories of Death: Japanese Biological Warfare 1932–45 and the American Cover-Up*. New York: Routledge, 1994.

Hawkins, David. *Project Y: The Los Alamos Story*, part 1, *Toward Trinity: The History of Modern Physics, 1800–1950*. Vol. 2 of *The History of Modern Physics, 1800–1950*. Los Angeles: Tomash, 1983.

Haynes, John Earl, and Harvey Klehr. "On the Trail of a Fourth Soviet Spy at Los Alamos." *Studies in Intelligence* 63, no. 3 (September 2019): 5.

Herken, Gregg. *Brotherhood of the Bomb: The Tangled Lives and Loyalties of Robert Oppenheimer, Ernest Lawrence, and Edward Teller*. New York: Henry Holt, 2002.

Hermes, Robert E., and William B. Strickfaden. "A New Look at Trinitite." *Nuclear Weapons Journal* 2 (2005).

Hersh, Seymour. *Chemical and Biological Warfare: America's Hidden Arsenal*. Indianapolis: Bobbs-Merrill, 1968.

Hershberg, James G. *James B. Conant: Harvard to Hiroshima and the Making of the Nuclear Age*. New York: Alfred A. Knopf, 1993.

Hevly, Bruce, and John M. Findlay, eds. *The Atomic West*. Seattle: University of Washington Press, 1998.

Hewlett, Richard G., and Francis Duncan. *Nuclear Navy, 1946–1962*. Chicago: University of Chicago Press, 1974. Also online at https://www.energy.gov/lm/downloads /hewlett-and-duncan-nuclear-navy-1946-1962.

Hoddeson, Lillian, et al. *Critical Assembly: A Technical History of Los Alamos During the Oppenheimer Years, 1943–1945*. Cambridge: Cambridge University Press, 1993.

Houk, Rose, and Michael Collier. *White Sands National Monument*. Tucson AZ: Southwestern Parks and Monuments Association, 1994.

Howes, Ruth H., and Caroline L. Herzenberg. *Their Day in the Sun: Women of the Manhattan Project*. Philadelphia PA: Temple University Press, 1994.

Hunner, Jon. *Inventing Los Alamos: The Growth of an Atomic Community*. Norman: University of Oklahoma Press, 2003.

Hunt, Linda. *Secret Agenda: The United States Government, Nazi Scientists, and Project Paperclip, 1945 to 1990.* New York: St. Martin's Press, 1991.

———. "The U.S. Coverup of Nazi Scientists." *Bulletin of the Atomic Scientists* 41, no. 4 (April 1985): 16–24.

Jacobsen, Annie M. *Operation Paperclip: The Secret Intelligence Program the Brought Nazi Scientists to America.* New York: Little, Brown, 2014.

Jessee, Emory Jerry. "Radiation Ecologies: Bombs, Bodies, and Environment During the Atmospheric Nuclear Weapons Testing Period, 1942–1965." PhD diss., Montana State University, 2013.

Johnson, Charles W., and Charles O. Jackson. *City Behind a Fence: Oak Ridge, Tennessee, 1942–46.* Knoxville: University of Tennessee Press, 1981.

Johnson, Robert R. *Romancing the Atom: Nuclear Infatuation from the Radium Girls to Fukushima.* Santa Barbara CA: Praeger, 2012.

Johnson, Susan Lee. *Writing Kit Carson: Fallen Heroes in a Changing West.* Chapel Hill: University of North Carolina Press, 2020.

Johnston, Barbara Rose. "Half-Lives, Half-Truths, and Other Radioactive Legacies of the Cold War." In *Half-Lives and Half-Truths: Confronting the Radioactive Legacies of the Cold War,* edited by Barbara Rose Johnston. Santa Fe NM: School for Advanced Research Press, 2007.

Jones, Vincent C. *Manhattan: The Army and the Atomic Bomb. U.S. Army in World War II, Special Studies.* Washington DC: Center of Military History, U.S. Army, 1985.

Kamerick, Megan. "Passions Flare Over Memory of the Manhattan Project." National Public Radio. January 14, 2017. https://www.npr.org/2017/01/14/508743747/passions-flare-over-memory-of-the-manhattan-project.

Keever, Beverly Deepe. *News Zero: The New York Times and the Bomb.* Monroe ME: Common Courage Press, 2004.

Kelly, Cynthia C., ed. *Remembering the Manhattan Project: Perspectives on the Atomic Bomb and Its Legacy.* Symposium Sponsored by the Atomic Heritage Foundation. April 2002, published 2004.

Kirk, Andrew G. *Doom Towns: The People and Landscapes of Atomic Testing, a Graphic History.* Illustrated by Kristian Purcell. Oxford University Press, 2016.

———. "Rereading the Nature of Atomic Doom Towns." *Environmental History* 17, no. 3 (July 2012): 635–47.

Kistiakowsky, George B. "Trinity—a Reminiscence." *Bulletin of the Atomic Scientists* 33, no. 6 (June 1980): 19–22.

Klein, Christine A. "Treaties of Conquest: Property Rights, Indian Treaties, and the Treaty of Guadalupe Hidalgo." *New Mexico Law Review* 26, no. 2 (Spring 1996).

Kosek, Jake. *Understories: The Political Life of Forests in Northern New Mexico.* Durham NC: Duke University Press, 2006.

Kuletz, Valerie L. "Invisible Spaces, Violent Places: Cold War Nuclear and Militarized Landscapes." In *Violent Environments,* edited by Nancy Lee Peluso and Michael Watts. Ithaca NY: Cornell University Press, 2001.

———. *The Tainted Desert: Environmental and Social Ruin in the American West*. New York: Routledge, 1998.

Kunetka, James W. *City of Fire: Los Alamos and the Atomic Age, 1943–1945*. Albuquerque: University of New Mexico Press, 1979.

LAHDRA. *Final Report of the Los Alamos Historical Document Retrieval and Assessment (LAHDRA) Project*. Prepared for the CDC. Thomas Widner, project director. November 2010. https://wwwn.cdc.gov/LAHDRA/Content/pubs/Final%20LAHDRA%20Report%202010.pdf.

Lahti, Janne. *Cultural Construction of Empire: The U.S. Army in Arizona and New Mexico*. Lincoln: University of Nebraska Press, 2012.

Lamont, Lansing. *Day of Trinity*. New York: Atheneum, 1965.

Laney, Monica. *German Rocketeers in the Heart of Dixie: Making Sense of the Nazi Past during the Civil Rights Era*. New Haven CT: Yale University Press, 2015.

Lapp, R. E. "Survey of Nucleonics Instrumentation Industry." *Nucleonics* 4, no. 5 (May 1949): 100–104. https://pubmed.ncbi.nlm.nih.gov/18126152/.

Larson, Kermit H. "Continental Close-In Fallout: Its History, Measurement and Characteristics." In *Radioecology: Proceedings of the First National Symposium on Radioecology, September 10–15, 1961*, edited by Vincent Schultz and Alfred W. Klement Jr., 19–25. New York: Reinhold, 1963.

Lasby, Clarence G. *Project Paperclip: German Scientists and the Cold War*. New York: Atheneum, 1971.

———. "Project Paperclip: German Scientists Come to America." *Virginia Quarterly Review* 42, no. 3 (Summer 1966).

Lees, Virginia S., ed. "Sleeping Beauty Awakens." *The Atom* 4, no. 5 (May 1967): 8–13. https://library.lanl.gov/cgi-bin/getfile?00847030.pdf.

Lenoir, Timothy, and Marguerite Hays. "The Manhattan Project for Biomedicine." In *Controlling Our Destinies: Historical, Philosophical, Ethical, and Theological Perspectives on the Human Genome Project*, edited by Phillip R. Sloan. Notre Dame IN: University of Notre Dame Press, 2000.

Lewis, Richard S., and Jane Wilson, eds. *Alamogordo Plus Twenty-Five Years*. New York: Viking Press, 1970.

Lifton, Robert Jay, and Greg Mitchell. *Hiroshima in America: A Half Century of Denial*. New York: Avon Books, 1995.

Limerick, Patricia Nelson. *Desert Passages: Encounters with the American Deserts*. Albuquerque: University of New Mexico, 1985.

———. *The Legacy of Conquest: The Unbroken Past of the American West*. New York: Norton, 1987.

———. *Something in the Soil: Legacies and Reckonings in the New West*. New York: W. W. Norton, 2000.

Linenthal, Edward T., and Tom Engelhardt. *History Wars: The Enola Gay and Other Battles for the American Past*. New York: Henry Holt, 1996.

Loring, William S. *Birthplace of the Atomic Bomb: A Complete History of the Trinity Test Site*. Jefferson NC: McFarland, 2019.

Los Alamos Historical Society. *Los Alamos 1943–1945, Beginning of an Era.* 2nd ed. Los Alamos NM, 2007.

Maag, Carl, and Steve Rohrer. *U.S. Project Trinity Report.* Defense Nuclear Agency Report 6028F. Project Gutenberg.

Mackintosh, Barry. *The Historic Sites Survey and National Historic Landmarks Program: A History.* History Division, National Park Service. Washington DC: Department of the Interior, 1985. http://npshistory.com/publications/historic-sites-survey-nhl.pdf.

Malina, Frank J. "America's First Long-Range Missile and Space Exploration Programme: The ORDCIT Project of the Jet Propulsion Laboratory, 1943–1946." *Spaceflight* 15 (December 1973): 442–56.

Malloy, Sean L. "'A Very Pleasant Way to Die': Radiation Effects and the Decision to Use the Bomb Against Japan." *Diplomatic History* 36, no. 3 (June 2012): 515–45.

Malmgren, Peter, and Kay Matthews. *Los Alamos Revisited: A Workers' History.* El Prado NM: Wink Books, 2017.

Masco, Joseph. *The Nuclear Borderlands: The Manhattan Project in Post-Cold War New Mexico.* New ed. Princeton NJ: Princeton University Press, 2006.

McMillan, Priscilla J. *The Ruin of J. Robert Oppenheimer and the Birth of the Modern Arms Race.* New York: Viking, 2005.

Melnick, aj [sic]. *They Changed the World: People of the Manhattan Project.* Santa Fe NM: Sunstone Press, 2006.

Merlan, Thomas W. *Life at Trinity Base Camp.* Tularosa NM: Human Systems Research, 2001.

Merrill, Karen R. *Public Lands and Political Meaning: Ranchers, the Government, and the Property Between Them.* Berkeley: University of California Press, 2002.

Miles, R. C. *The History of the Ordcit Project up to June 1946.* Historical Monograph no. 4. U.S. Department of the Army, April 1961.

Miller, Richard L. *Under the Cloud: The Decades of Nuclear Testing.* New York: Free Press, 1986.

Moynihan, Daniel Patrick. *Secrecy: The American Experience.* New Haven: Yale University Press, 1998.

Nagle, Darragh E. "A Memorial Colloquium Honoring Herbert L. Anderson." U.S. Department of Energy Office of Scientific and Technical Information. August 31, 1988. https://www.osti.gov/biblio/5688241 or https://doi.org/10.2172/5688241.

Nash, Linda. *Inescapable Ecologies: A History of Environment, Disease, and Knowledge.* Berkeley: University of California Press, 2006.

National Park Service. "National Park System." Last updated October 19, 2022. https://www.nps.gov/aboutus/national-park-system.htm.

National Park Service and U.S. Department of the Interior. *Foundation Document: Manhattan Project National Historical Park.* January 2017. https://www.nps.gov/mapr/upload/MAPR_FD_PRINT.pdf.

———. *Manhattan Project Sites: Draft Special Resource Study/Environmental Assessment.* November 2009. http://npshistory.com/publications/mapr/srs-draft.pdf.

National Research Council. "Assessment of the Scientific Information for the Radiation Exposure Screening and Educational Program." Washington DC: National Academies Press, April 28, 2005.

Nolan, James L., Jr. *Atomic Doctors: Conscience and Complicity at the Dawn of the Nuclear Age.* Cambridge MA: The Belknap Press, 2020.

Norris, Robert S. *Racing for the Bomb: General Leslie R. Groves, the Manhattan Project's Indispensable Man.* South Royalton VT: Steerforth Press, 2002.

Palevsky, Mary. *Atomic Fragments: A Daughter's Questions.* Berkeley: University of California Press, 2000.

Pasqualetti, Martin J. Review of *Doom Towns: The People and Landscapes of Atomic Testing, a Graphic History,* by Andrew Kirk. *Geographical Review* 108, no. 3 (July 2018): 476–80.

Pasternak, Judy. *Yellow Dirt: An American Story of a Poisoned Land and a People Betrayed.* New York: Free Press, 2010.

Peffer, E. Louise. *The Closing of the Public Domain: Disposal and Reservation Policies, 1900–1950.* Stanford CA: Stanford University Press, 1951.

Perry, Nancy. "Eminent Domain Destroys a Community: Leveling East Arlington to Make Way for the Pentagon." *Urban Geography* 37, no. 1 (2016): 141–61.

Pritikin, Trisha T. *The Hanford Plaintiffs: Voices from the Fight for Atomic Justice.* Lawrence: University Press of Kansas, 2020.

Regis, Edward. *The Biology of Doom: The History of America's Secret Germ Warfare Project.* New York: Henry Holt, 1999.

Rhodes, Richard. *Dark Sun: The Making of the Hydrogen Bomb.* New York: Simon and Schuster, 1995.

——. *The Making of the Atomic Bomb.* New York: Simon and Schuster, 1986.

Rieder, Morgan, and Michael Lawson. *Trinity at Fifty: The Archaeology of Trinity Site National Historic Landmark, White Sands Missile Range, Socorro County, New Mexico.* Report no. 9439, WSMR Archaeological Report no. 95-8. Tularosa NM: Human Systems Research, 1995.

Rominiecki, Amanda. "A Chemical and Biological History." January 5, 2017. Reprinted in the newsletter of the Aberdeen Proving Ground, *APG News,* October 24, 2020, https://apgnews.com/special-focus/apg-100/chemical-biological-history/.

Rothman, Hal K. *On Rims and Ridges: The Los Alamos Area Since 1880.* Lincoln: University of Nebraska Press, 1992.

——. *Preserving Different Pasts: The American National Monuments.* Urbana: University of Illinois Press, 1989.

Rothman, Hal K., and Char Miller. *Death Valley National Park: A History.* Reno: University of Nevada Press, 2013.

Russell, Edmund. *War and Nature: Fighting Humans and Insects with Chemicals From World War I to Silent Spring.* Cambridge: Cambridge University Press, 2001.

Sackman, Douglas Cazaux, ed. *A Companion to American Environmental History.* West Sussex, UK: John Wiley and Sons, 2014.

Sapolsky, Harvey M. *Science and the Navy: The History of the Office of Naval Research.* Princeton NJ: Princeton University Press, 2014.

Sarathy, Brinda, Vivien Hamilton, and Janet Farrell Brodie, eds. *Inevitably Toxic: Historical Perspectives on Contamination, Exposure, and Expertise.* Pittsburgh: University of Pittsburgh Press, 2018.

Savage, John, and Barbara Storms. *Reach to the Unknown: The Trinity Story.* Tucson: Arizona Historical Society, 1965.

Schneider-Hector, Dietmar. *White Sands: The History of a National Monument.* Albuquerque: University of New Mexico Press, 1993.

Schwartz, Stephen I., ed. *Atomic Audit: The Costs and Consequences of U.S. Nuclear Weapons Since 1940.* Washington DC: Brookings Institution Press, 1998.

Shawcross, John T. *The Complete Poetry of John Donne.* New York: Doubleday and Company, 1967.

Shonka, Joseph. "The First Dirty Bomb, Trinity." Lecture presented at the Health Physics Society annual meeting, Orlando FL, July 11, 2019.

Simon, Steven L., André Bouville, Harold L. Beck, and Dunstana R. Melo. "Estimated Radiation Doses Received by New Mexico Residents from the 1945 Trinity Nuclear Test." *Health Physics* 119, no. 4 (October 2020): 428–77.

Solnit, Rebecca. *Savage Dreams: A Journey into the Landscape Wars of the American West.* Berkeley: University of California Press, 1999.

Spence, Mark David. *Dispossessing the Wilderness: Indian Removal and the Making of the National Parks.* New York: Oxford University Press, 1999.

Sprinkle, John H., Jr. "'Of Exceptional Importance': The Origins of the 'Fifty-Year Rule' in Historic Preservation." *Public Historian* 29, no. 2 (Spring 2007): 81–103.

Stannard, J[ames] Newell. *Radioactivity and Health: A History.* Edited by Raymond W. Baalman Jr. Washington DC: U.S. Department of Energy, 1988.

Szasz, Ferenc Morton. *The Day the Sun Rose Twice: The Story of the Trinity Site Nuclear Explosion July 16, 1945.* Albuquerque: University of New Mexico Press, 1984.

———. "Downwind from the Bomb: A Review Essay." *Nevada Historical Society Quarterly* 30, no. 3 (1987): 182–87.

Tucker, Kathleen M., and Robert Alvarez. "Trinity: 'The Most Significant Hazard of the Entire Manhattan Project.'" *Bulletin of the Atomic Scientists*, July 15, 2019. https://thebulletin.org/2019/07/trinity-the-most-significant-hazard-of-the-entire -manhattan-project/.

U.S. Congress. Joint Committee on Atomic Energy. "The Nature of Radioactive Fallout and Its Effect on Man." 85th Congress, 1st session, May 27–29 and June 3, 1957.

U.S. Department of Justice. "History of the Federal Use of Eminent Domain." Updated January 24, 2022. https://www.justice.gov/enrd/history-federal-use-eminent -domain.

———. "Radiation Exposure Compensation Act." Updated September 1, 2022. http:// www.justice.gov/civil/common/reca.

U.S. House. "White Sands Fair Compensation Act of 1989." Hearing before the Subcommittee on Administrative Law and Governmental Relations of the Committee on the Judiciary. 101st Congress, 2nd session, June 13, 1990.

U.S. Senate. "Acquisition of Land and Acquisition and Termination of Grazing Permits or Licenses Issued by the Bureau of Land Management Pursuant to the Taylor Grazing Act at White Sands Missile Range, New Mexico." Hearing. 98th Congress, 1st session, November 15, 1983.

———. "America's Nuclear Past: Examining the Effects of Radiation in Indian Country." Field Hearing before Committee on Indian Affairs. 116th Congress, 1st session, October 7, 2019.

———. "Statements on Introduced Bills and Joint Resolutions." Congressional Record, September 30, 2003. sgp.fas.org/congress/2003/s1687.html.

———. "White Sands Missile Range, New Mexico." Hearings before the Subcommittee on Public Lands and Reserved Water of the Committee on Energy and Natural Resources. 98th Congress, 1st session, November 15, 1983.

Vanderbilt, Tom. *Survival City: Adventures Among the Ruins of Atomic America*. Chicago: University of Chicago Press, 2002.

Veracini, L. *Settler Colonialism: A Theoretical Overview*. London: Palgrave Macmillan, 2010.

Voigt, William J. *Public Grazing Lands*. New Brunswick NJ: Rutgers University Press, 1976.

Voyles, Traci Brynne. *The Settler Sea: California's Salton Sea and the Consequences of Colonialism*. Lincoln: University of Nebraska Press, 2021.

———. *Wastelanding: Legacies of Uranium Mining in Navajo Country*. Minneapolis: University of Minnesota Press, 2015.

Wallace, Chris. *Countdown 1945: The Extraordinary Story of the Atomic Bomb and the 116 Days That Changed the World*. New York: Simon and Schuster, 2020.

Ward, Bob. *Dr. Space: The Life of Wernher von Braun*. New York: Naval Institute Press, 2013.

Warren, Stafford L. "The Role of Radiology in Development of the Atomic Bomb." In *Radiology in World War II*, edited by Medical Department, U.S. Army. Washington DC: Office of the Surgeon General, Department of the Army, 1966.

Wellerstein, Alex. *Restricted Data: The History of Nuclear Secrecy in the USA*. Chicago: University of Chicago Press, 2021.

———. *Restricted Data: The Nuclear Secrecy Blog*. https://blog.nuclearsecrecy.com.

Welsh, Michael. *Dunes and Dreams: A History of White Sands National Monument*. Professional Paper no. 55. Santa Fe NM: National Park Service, Division of History Intermountain Cultural Resources Center, 1995.

———. *White Sands Administrative History*. Book published online. Last updated January 22, 2001. https://www.nps.gov/parkhistory/online_books/whsa/adhi/adhit.htm.

Welsome, Eileen. *The Plutonium Files: America's Secret Medical Experiments in the Cold War*. New York: Dial Press, Random House, 1999.

Westwick, Peter J. "Abraded from Several Corners: Medical Physics and Biophysics at Berkeley." *Historical Studies in the Physical Sciences* 27, no. 1 (1996): 131–61.

——. *The National Labs: Science in an American System, 1947–1974.* Cambridge MA: Harvard University Press, 2003.

Widner, Thomas E., and Susan M. Flack. "Characterization of the World's First Nuclear Explosion, the Trinity Test, as a Source of Public Radiation Exposure." *Health Physics* 98, no. 3 (March 2010): 480–97. http://doi.org/10.1097/HP.0b013e3181c18168.

Wills, Kristel. "A Bomb Bursting in Air: Atomic Tourism and the Trinity Site." Master's thesis, University of Wyoming, 1999.

Wilson, Jane S., and Charlotte Serber, eds. *Standing By and Making Do: Women of Wartime Los Alamos.* Los Alamos NM: Los Alamos Historical Society, 2008.

Wrobel, David M., and Patrick T. Long, eds. *Seeing and Being Seen: Tourism in the American West.* Lawrence: Kansas University Press, 2001.

Yoshida, Kayoko. "From Atomic Fragments to Memories of the Trinity Bomb: A Bridge of Oral History Over the Pacific." *Oral History Review* 30, no. 2 (Summer/ Fall 2003): 62.

Zappia, Natale A. *Traders and Raiders: The Indigenous World of the Colorado Basin, 1510–1859.* Chapel Hill: University of North Carolina Press, 2014.

Zaretsky, Natasha. *Radiation Nation: Three Mile Island and the Political Transformation of the 1970s.* New York: Columbia University Press, 2018.

# INDEX

AAF. *See* Army Air Force (AAF)

Abelson, Philip M., 8, 204n14

Aberdeen NJ, 128

Aberdeen Proving Ground, 135, 137–38

ACHRE. *See* Advisory Committee on Human Radiation Experimentation (ACHRE)

Ad Hoc Committee on Chemical, Biological, and Radiological Warfare, 226n78

Adobe NM, 54

Advisory Committee in Biology and Medicine, 118, 121

Advisory Committee on Human Radiation Experimentation (ACHRE), 4, 169

Advisory Council on Historic Preservation, 190, 245n51

Aeby, Jack, 95, 113–14

AEC. *See* Atomic Energy Commission (AEC)

AEP. *See* Atomic Energy Project (AEP)

African Americans as Manhattan Project workers, 93–96, 221n106

AFSWP. *See* Armed Forces Special Weapons Project (AFSWP)

Agnew, Beverly, 209n112

Agnew, Harold, 11–12, 209n112

Air Corps Jet Propulsion Research Project, 229n16

Air Force Special Weapons Project, 121

Ake, Jeff, 50

Alamogordo Army Air Field, 28, 36, 71–72, 124, 130, 138–39, 216n11, 228n3

Alamogordo Army Base, 41, 52, 83, 109, 124

Alamogordo Bombing and Gunnery Range: changing names of, 3, 72, 124; and land, 70–72, 128–29, 143–45, 216n11; and secrecy, 19, 97; and White Sands National Monument, 177, 183

Alamogordo NM: blast seen near, 19, 38; changing names of base at, 72, 124, 228n4; division of AEP, 120, 156; and electricity, 130; and population, 208n92; and radiation concerns, 159; and roads, 78; and tourism of Trinity site, 176, 198, 200

Albuquerque NM: and AEC, 108, 115–16, 142, 225n58; and day of Trinity test, 24, 30, 33; and evacuation plans, 28; and Hiroshima and Nagasaki bombs, 39; and planning, 80; and secret communication, 15, 28, 36, 97; and tourism of Trinity site, 246n70; and transportation of supplies and people, 73, 76–77, 79, 82

Allison, Samuel, 21–22

Alvarez, Luis, 34

Alvarez, Robert, 150
Ancho NM, 63
Anderson, Alfred, 26
Anderson, Clinton, 189
Anderson, David, 31
Anderson, Herbert L., 16–18, 153, 205n49, 206nn54–55, 208n86
Antos, Lawrence, 81
AOMC. *See* Army Ordnance Missile Command (AOMC)
Apaches, 2, 44, 46–47, 49, 62, 211n19. *See also* Mescalero Apaches
Apodaca, Melecio, 52, 212n40
Apodaca, Pablo, 52, 212n40
Apodoca, Sinfuriana G., 52, 212n40
Arco ID, 192, 194, 243n32
Argo, Harold, 93
Argo, Mary, 92–93
Argonne National Nuclear Laboratory, 226n73
Arlington VA, 59, 204n17
Armed Forces Special Weapons Project (AFSWP), 230n32
Armijo family, 45
Army Air Force (AAF), 27, 70, 124–28, 130, 134–35, 138, 216n11
Army Corps of Engineers: insignia of, 83; and land acquisition, 41, 55, 128, 140, 215n71; and Pentagon, 204n17; and planning the Trinity test, 11, 30, 128–29, 140, 200, 219n70, 221n122; and SEDs, 85; and uranium, 10
Army Launch Area, 130
Army Ordnance Department, 128, 229n14
Army Ordnance Missile Command (AOMC), 131
Army Signal Office, 129
Army Specialized Training Program (ASTP), 84
Arnberger, Leslie P., 244n48
Arnold, Henry Harley "Hap," 70, 125
Ascarate, Guadalupe, 51

Ascarate, Helen T., 51
Ashbridge, Whitney, 85–86, 90
Atomic Bomb National Monument, 178, 180
Atomic Energy Act, 161, 233n80
Atomic Energy Commission (AEC): and costs, 13–14; establishment of, 11, 142–43, 233n80; and historical preservation, 182–83, 198; and J. Robert Oppenheimer, 12; and land, 128; and nuclear research, 134; and opening Trinity site to public, 116; and radiation, 92, 105–8, 115, 120–21, 156–59, 167–72, 231n45, 244n47; and radiological warfare, 118–21; and trinitite, 114–16, 224n55, 225n58, 225n65; and use of Trinity test land, 104–5, 117, 143–45
Atomic Energy Project (AEP), 120–21, 156–57, 159, 163, 236n29
Atomic Heritage Foundation, 4, 221n106

Babcock and Wilcox Corporation, 109
Baca, Barbarita Chavez, 49–50, 57, 229n18
Baca, Geronimo S., 49–50
Baca ranch, 52, 54
Bachelder, Myrtle, 91
Bagley, Charles, 84
Bainbridge, Kenneth: and building the Trinity test site, 20, 78, 92, 97, 206n59; and day of Trinity test, 6, 21–22; and naming the Trinity test, 73–74; and 100-Ton test, 16; and plutonium, 109, 210n120; and post-test events, 103; and radiation, 153, 235n16; and Trinity site selection, 68–71
Banda, Norman R., 110
Bandelier National Monument, 112
Barberton OH, 109
Bareras family, 52

Barker, Paul, 197
Barnes ranch, 54
Barnett, Henry, 21, 23, 27, 207n83, 208nn86–87, 235n20
Barschall, Heinz, 21
Barstow CA, 229n17
Bartell, Lawrence, 197
Bayo Canyon, 165, 238n69
Beasley, George, 51
Beasley, Sarah, 51
Beasley family, 50–51, 54
Bederson, B., 223n22
Belen NM, 98, 208n92
Bellamy, Albert, 92
Benson, Edward William, 90
Bernacci, Julian, 26
Bernstein, Jeremy, 13, 74
Bethe, Hans, 13, 25, 99, 152
Bettis Airport, 134
Bikini Island, 192
Bingaman, Jeff, 195
Bingham NM, 25–27, 29–30, 54, 168, 235n20, 237n53
biological warfare, 118, 137, 146, 226nn77–78
biophysics, 227n85, 236n31
Bird, Kai, 74
Blackwell, Charles D., 107–8, 223n14
Blondin, Charles, 12
Board on Radiation Effects Research, 172
Boehm, William B., 130
Bohr, Neils, 9, 75
Boice, John D., Jr., 162
Bosque Redondo, 46–47
Boyer, Paul, 167, 179
Bradbury, Norris, 12, 107–8
Bradley, Willard, 241n6
Breslow, Arthur, 26–27, 208n87
Bretscher, Egon, 8
Brixner, Berlyn, 21, 23, 69–70
Brown, Kate, 94–95
Brown, Robert J. S., 87–88, 112

Brown, Theodore R., 84, 219n69
*Brown v. Board of Education*, 95
Bruton ranch, 54
Buchanan, James, 209n113
Bugher (of AEC), 224n55
Bureau of Land Management, 63–64, 140
Bureau of Ships, 134
Burrage, Pat, 112, 224n40
Burris, B. O., 41
Burris, Laura. *See* McKinley, Laura E. (Burris)
Burris ranch, 41, 54
Bursum, Holm Olaf, 52, 63, 100–101, 212n37
Bursum, Holm Olaf, III (grandson), 51
Bursum Bill, 52
Bursum ranch, 51–52, 54
Burton, Bob, 187, 243n39
Bush, Howard C., 82, 90, 181
Bush, Vannevar, 132–33, 207n66

Cachupin, Velez, 45
Caffey, David, 47, 211n27
Caldwell family, 229n18
California Institute of Technology (CIT), 126, 128, 131–33, 230n36, 231n40
Cambridge University, 8
Campania Hill, 24–25, 203n4
Campbell, Allen, 116
Campbell and Kay Construction Company, 116
Camp Irwin, 229n17
Canaday, John, 75
Cantwell, Maria, 195
Canyon de Chelly, 47
Capitan NM, 149
Carlson, R. W., 223n22
Carrizozo NM: avoiding potential fallout at, 164; and population, 208n92, 238n67; and proximity to Trinity site, 164, 246n70; and roads, 78; and

Carrizozo NM (*cont.*)
  Trinity test activities, 19–20, 26, 30, 98
Carroll, James, 11
Carson, Kit, 46–47
Carter, Annie, 62
Carthage NM, 19
CCC. *See* Civilian Conservation Corps (CCC)
Center for Disease Control, 53, 169
Centerline MI, 133
Chadwick, James, 24
Chaves family, 45, 50
Chavez, Carpio, 49
Chavez, Dimas, 96, 221n116
Chavez, Nep, 54
Chavez ranch, 54
Chemical Corps, 125, 226n77, 232n65
chemical warfare, 118, 146, 226n77, 232n65
Chemical Warfare Service (CWS), 138, 226n77
Chicago Metallurgical Laboratory, 87
Chicago Toxicity Lab, 121
China Lake CA, 132, 146
Chupadera Mesa, 157, 209n103
Chupadera Peak, 93
CIT. *See* California Institute of Technology (CIT)
Civilian Conservation Corps (CCC), 77, 79, 129, 133, 230n24
Clifford, Carcie C., 189–90, 244n47
Clinton Engineer Works, 59
Coconino Plateau, 68
Coker ranch, 54
Cole (colonel), 219n69
Collinsworth, Rebecca, 4
Columbia University, 8, 10, 16, 86, 99, 221n106, 243n32
Committee on Energy and Natural Resources, 214n56
Conant, James Bryant, 133, 203n4, 207n66, 216n25

Conant, Jennet, 216n25
Congressional Research Service, 172
Cooney, James, 121
Cornell, H. H., 241n6
Courant, Hans, 36
Court of Land Commissioners, 215n71
Court of Private Land Claims, 48, 211n27
Courtright, W. Clarence, 222n14
Critchfield, Charles, 25, 34
Critchfield, Jean, 34
Cuba NM, 69, 165–66
Curie, Irene, 8
Custer, George Armstrong, 82
CWS. *See* Chemical Warfare Service (CWS)

Dahlgren VA, 231n45
Daley, D., 26
Danley, Meldene Green, 57
Davalos (captain), 81, 218n44
Davis, John K., 141
Davis, Marvin R., 78, 82–83, 98, 218n62, 219n64
Dayton OH, 191, 245n52
Dean, R. H., 30
Dean ranch, 54
De Baca County NM, 83
DeBello, Angelo J., 218n60
Defense Nuclear Agency, 131, 156, 160, 230n32, 237n54
Delano CA, 21, 206n64
Del Curts ranch, 54
Demaray, Arthur E., 140, 182, 241n4
Dempsey, John J., 177
Denfeld, Louis, 126
Dennis, Deborah M., 243n39
Denton, Jack, 38
Denver CO and secret communication, 97
Department of Defense (DOD): and AEC, 143; branches of, 126, 237n54; and historical preservation, 115, 176, 183, 189–90, 225n55, 225n58; and

missiles, 131; and ranchers' land, 60, 63–64; and U.S. Air Force, 125
Department of Energy (DOE), 104, 169, 173, 195–96, 231n45, 245nn51–52
Department of Justice, 60, 213n51
Department of National Defense, 182
Department of the Army, 130–31, 143–44, 226n72
Department of the Interior, 57, 60, 176–77, 183, 189, 214n56, 225n55, 245n52
DePaula, Felix, 81, 98
deserts: challenges of, 51, 77, 79, 97–98, 156, 160; and military, 145–47, 203n2; preserving, 138; and Tularosa Basin, 42–43
de Silva, Peer, 68
Dickason, Donald P., 105–6
Dingell, John D., 136
Diven, Beckie, 33
Division of Biology and Medicine, AEC, 118, 121, 156, 167
Division of Recreation Resource Planning, NPS, 180, 183
DOD. See Department of Defense (DOD)
DOE. See Department of Energy (DOE)
Domenici, Pete, 56–57, 64, 214n56
Dona Ana Range, 228n6
Donne, John, 74–75, 216n19, 217n26
Donovan, Richard, 27
downwinders: of Nevada Test Site, 167, 169, 171–72, 240n86; of other sites, 171; of Trinity site, 2, 69, 161, 166, 168, 170–74, 240n87
Drury, Newton B., 177–78, 182, 242n20
Dunbar-Ortiz, Roxanne, 45
DuPont Company, 94–95

Eagan, Gerald D., 107, 223n14
Ebright, Malcolm, 45
Eckles, Jim, 110
Eddy, George G., 183
Edgewood Area of Aberdeen Proving Ground, 137–38

Edgewood Plant, 137–38
Edgington, Ryan H., 2, 201
Eichleay Corporation, 80, 218n53
Eidenbach, Peter L., 129–30
Einstein, Albert, 9, 136
Eisenhower, Dwight, 136
Ela, Tom, 141
Elephant Butte Dam, 130
eminent domain, 58–59, 123, 213n51
Emmerson, Harryette Hunter, 93
Enlisted Reserve Corps (ERC), 89
Enola Gay, 181, 194
Ent, Uzal G., 70–71
Environmental Protection Agency (EPA), 156, 160, 163, 231n45
ERC. See Enlisted Reserve Corps (ERC)
Experimental Physics Division, 11

Fair Employment Practices Commission, 94
Faris, Johnwell, 112, 128, 134, 139–41, 232n70
Farm and Ranch Heritage Museum, 213n44
Farrell, Edward C., 209n113
Farrell, Thomas F., 6, 21, 27–28, 33, 90
Feather, Norman, 8
Federal Grazing Act, 57, 213n54
Ferdig, Bill H., 198, 223n19
Fermi, Enrico, 8–9, 17, 32, 37, 86, 204n16, 206n55, 207n66
Fermi, Laura, 9, 32, 96, 205n49, 209n104
Fernandez, A. M., 183
Fey, Frederic L., Jr., 107, 223n14
Feynman, Richard, 24, 37
First Armored Division, 131
Fission Studies group, 17, 205n49
Fitch, Val, 22, 24, 88
Fite ranch, 54
Foley, Richard, 26
Fort Bliss, 125, 128–31, 136–37, 228n6
Fort Huachuca AZ, 62
Fort Marion FL, 211n19

Fort Riley, 219n64
Fort Stanton, 46, 211n19
Fort Sumner, 26, 83, 238n67
Foster, George H., 54
Foster ranch, 54, 57
Fox, Sarah Alisabeth, 173, 240n95
Freeman, Lindsey A., 193
Frisch, Otto, 152
Fuchs, Klaus, 35, 98–100, 210n118
Fuqua, John, 21

GALCIT. See Guggenheim Aeronautical
    Lab at California Institute of Tech-
    nology (GALCIT)
Gallagher ranch, 54
Gallegos, Lupita Rodriguez, 57
Gallegos ranch, 50, 54, 57
Garcia family, 50
Garton Well, 139
Gee, H. C., 104
Geiger counters, 26, 29, 93, 153, 199
General Land Office, 177
genizaros, 45–46
Gentry, Fes R., 107
Germany: chemical weapons from, 138;
    and rockets and missiles, 128, 135–36,
    230n22; scientists from, 8, 99, 130,
    135–37, 152, 230n22, 231n58, 232n59;
    and war, 8–9, 14
Gibson (sergeant), 81
Gise, L. P., 108, 223n19
Godby, Bill, 187, 244n41
Goddard Space Flight Center Tracking
    and Data Relay Satellite Systems
    Facility, 131
Gofman, John, 238n57
Gold, Harry, 100
Gomez, Laura E., 46
Gomez family, 52, 214n63
Gonsales family, 50
Gonzalez, Severo, 89
Goodrich, B. F., 152
Gosling, Skip, 245n51

Government Accountability Office,
    215n70
Grants NM, 68–70
Graves, Al, 26
Graves, Elizabeth "Diz," 26
Gray, Gordon, 170
Great Sand Dunes National Monument,
    68
Green, Cicero, 54, 215n74
Greene, Joel, 26
Greenglass, David, 98–99
Greisen, Kenneth, 207n66
Griggs, D. T., 228n90
Groves, Leslie R.: and AEC, 142–43; and
    building the Trinity test site, 76–77,
    81, 83–86, 88–90, 127, 219n70; as
    head of Manhattan Project, 10–12,
    133; and historical preservation,
    177, 180, 198, 241n4; and J. Robert
    Oppenheimer, 12–13; and naming
    the Trinity test, 73; and 100-Ton test,
    14–16, 18–19; and Pentagon, 204n17;
    and plutonium, 109; and radiation
    concerns, 151–55, 206n61, 234n7,
    234nn10–11, 235n14; and secrecy, 32,
    97; and Trinity site selection, 59, 69–
    72, 163–64; and Trinity test, 20–21,
    23, 27, 203n2, 207n66; and Urchin
    experiments, 104
Guggenheim Aeronautical Lab at Cali-
    fornia Institute of Technology (GAL-
    CIT), 229n10, 229n14, 229n16

Hahn, Otto, 8
Hall, Theodore "Ted," 98–99
Hämäläinen, Pekka, 44
Hamill, James P., 135–37
Hamilton, Joseph Gilbert, 119–20,
    227n80, 227n83, 236n30
Hammel, Clarence, 98
Hammel, Marcella, 98
Hammel Brewery Building, 98
Hampson, Rick, 192

Hanford WA, 10, 16, 19; and histori-
cal preservation, 190–92, 195–96,
243n32, 245n52; and nonwhite work-
ers, 94–95, 221n106; and number of
workers, 93; and radiation, 195; and
women workers, 91
Harriet ranch, 54
Hawkins, David, 205n49
Hayashi, Kyoko, xiii–xiv, 202, 203n2
Health Physics Society, 170
Helm, A. D., 53
Helm, H. B., 53–54
Hempelmann, Louis, 21, 29, 154,
208n98, 209n104, 236n30
Henderson, R. W., 223n22
Herman, Edward C., 209n113
Herrera, Henry, 149, 169, 234n2, 239n76
Hills Home ranch, 54
Hindu, 6, 216n21
Hinton, Joan, 34
Hiroshima bomb: effects of, xiv, 1; and
public fears, 167; and radiation mea-
surements, 26, 155; transportation
of, 39; and Trinity-area tourism, 176,
179, 181, 192, 196, 199–200; and Trin-
ity workers, 32–33, 38, 121
Hirsch, Harold, 209n113
Hirschfelder, Joseph, 17, 91, 152–53, 208n86
Hispanos, 45
historic markers: and obelisk at Trinity
site, xiii, 1, 175, 186, 188, 200, 242n28,
243n33; and Official Scenic Historic
Marker, 243n33; and plaques, 186–88,
242n29
Hoffman, Joseph G., 26, 29, 154, 159,
164, 168
Hofmann, J. A., 223n22
Holloman, George V., 125
Holloman Air Force Base, 105, 124–25,
130–31, 138, 170, 183, 225n58
Holloman Bombing Range, 144–45, 170
Holtzberg, Theodore Alvin. See Hall,
Theodore "Ted"

Homestead Act, 47, 49–51, 212n33
Hoogterp, Carlton, 20
Hornberger, Carl, 26, 207n83
Hornig, Donald, 21, 31–32, 209n105
Hornig, Lilli, 31
Hueco Range, 128
Human Systems Research Inc., 188,
243n39
Hunner, Jon, 95

Ickes, Harold L., 69, 112, 163–64, 178
Illinois Distributing Company, 98
infant mortality rates, 150, 234n4
Inyo County CA, 171
Inyokern CA, 132, 230n36, 231n40,
231n45
Isaacks, J. D., 50
Isaacks, Myrtle, 212n34
Isaacks, Robert L., 57, 212n34
Isaacks land, 50, 212nn33–34

Jackson, Andrew Red, 107
Jackson, Charles O., 59
Jacobsen, Annie M., 136
Jemez Mountains, 32–34, 209n103
Jemez Pueblo NM, 95
Jensen, James A., 92
Jet Propulsion Laboratory (JPL), 131–32,
229n10, 229n14, 229n16
Johnson, Charles W., 59
Joint Radiological Warfare Committee,
226n78
Joint Range Coordination Committee,
130
Jones, Vincent C., 205n37
Jopp (sergeant), 20
Jornada del Muerto, 5, 43, 70, 243n33
JPL. See Jet Propulsion Laboratory (JPL)
Jumbo: after Trinity test, 103–4, 110–11,
246n71; decision not to use, 109–10;
development of, 80, 108–9, 223n22;
effect of Trinity test on, 110; and his-
torical preservation, 110–11, 181, 189,

Jumbo (*cont.*)
200, 241n18; transportation of, 70,
109–10, 218n53

Kaiser Wilhelm Institute, 8
Keller, Rex Edward, 111, 113
Kennedy, Joseph W., 204n14
Kent, Barbara, 150
Kiloore ranch, 54
Kirk, Andrew G., 146
Kirkpatrick, David T., 243n39
Kirtland Air Force Base, 28, 39
Kistiakowsky, George B., 21, 88–89, 152
Kosek, Jake, 174
Kraker, George P., 225n66
Krikorian, Pat, 32

La Fonda Bar, 210n122
LAHDRA. *See* Los Alamos Historical
Document Retrieval and Assessment
(LAHDRA)
land conflicts: and government, 58–60,
64–65; history of, 42–52; with ranch-
ers, 41–42, 52–58, 60–64, 212n42,
214n65, 215n70, 229n18
land patents, 50–51, 212n33
Lanter, Robert J., 107, 222n14
Larkin, Richard A., 207n83
Larson, Kermit H., 159–60, 223n15
Las Cruces NM, 41, 51, 55, 130, 135, 140,
213n44
Lassiter, James, 140
Las Vegas Atomic Bomb Museum, 193
Las Vegas NM, 230n24
Las Vegas NV, 4, 160, 192
Laurence, William L., 207n79
Lauritsen, C. C., 133
Lawrence, Ernest O., 13, 24–25, 34,
227n80
Lawrence Radiation Lab, 156
Lawson, Michael, 2
Lee, Charlie T., 213n49
Lee, Ronald F., 201, 228n94

Lees, Virginia S., 107
Leftwich, J. D., 83
Lehman, Joe, 5, 23, 28, 207n71
Leonard, Robert R., 26, 29–30, 235n20
Levine, Philip, 26, 208n86
Lilienthal, David E., 11, 13, 128, 143, 170
Limerick, Patricia Nelson, 43, 146
Lin, Maya, 194
Lincoln County NM, 219n68
Livermore Nuclear Lab, 238n57
Livesay, Naomi, 92
Long, Bartlett, 210n122
Los Alamos County NM, 96
Los Alamos Health Division, 114, 121
Los Alamos Historical Document
Retrieval and Assessment (LAH-
DRA), 53–54, 169–70
Los Alamos Historical Society, 4, 68
Los Alamos National Laboratory: and
building the Trinity site, 20–21,
76–81; and day of Trinity test, 5–6,
21–22, 24–26, 28–36; and employees
for Trinity site, 81–83; and historical
preservation, 186, 190, 196, 245n52;
and Jumbo, 109–10, 223n22; leadership at, 11–13, 133; and nonwhite
workers, 95–96, 163; and number
of employees, 93; and 100-Ton test,
15, 17–18; and radiation, 152, 154–55,
158–59, 163–65, 167–68, 174, 181; and
radiological warfare, 121; and roads,
78; and secrecy, 15, 19, 30–37, 73, 97,
221n117; and SEDs and PEDs, 84–91;
and spies, 98–100; and trinitite,
111–14, 116–17, 225nn64–65, 226n70;
and Trinity site selection, 68–72; and
Urchin experiments, 104–8, 222n14,
223n17; and wives of employees, 32–
34; and women workers, 91–93
Los Alamos NM and land, 214n63
Lowry, Adrienne, 33, 96, 221n115
Lowry, Joe, 33
Lucero ranch, 50, 54

Ludwick, Bob, 73
Lujan, Ben, 96
Lujan, Manuel, 214n63

Mack, Julian, 21
MacMillan, Donald P., 107
Maestas, Tony J., 107
Maez, Felix E., 107
Magee, John, 17, 152–53, 208n86, 234n11
Maher, Dillard D., 218n60
Malina, Frank J., 126, 128–29, 229n10, 229n14, 229n16
Mancuso, Thomas, 238n57
Manhattan Engineer District (MED), 7, 9–10, 30, 70–71, 73, 86, 97, 142, 230n32, 233n80
Manhattan Project: costs of, 13–14; and historical preservation, 190–91, 195–96; leadership of, 10–13; naming of, 7; overview of, 7–10
Manhattan Project National Historical Park, 176, 190–91, 195, 243n32, 245n52
Manley, John, 21
Manley, Kay, 33
Martin, Ernest R., 209n113
Martin, G. M., 223n22
Martinez, Jesus, 51
Martinez, Juan, 95
Martinez, Lydia, 214n63
Martinez, Maria, 95
Martinez, Montoya, 96
Martinez, Popovi, 95
Martinez, Tony, 95, 221n112
Martinez Fiorillo, Rosario, 214n63
Masco, Joseph, 165
Matthias, Franklin, 94
Maya, Florencio, 52
May test. See 100-Ton test
McChesney, John G., 209n113
McCormack, James, Jr., 120
McCulloch, Tom, 245n51
McDonald, Carmine, 57

McDonald, Dave, 57, 63–64, 217n43
McDonald, Emma, 215n74
McDonald, George, 54, 62, 80, 175, 179, 186, 215n74
McDonald, James T., 57
McDonald, Mary, 63
McDonald, Michael, 62
McDonald, Ross, 63
McDonald, Rube, 217n43
McDonald, Tom, 55, 62–63
McDonald ranch, 54, 61–63, 78–79, 186, 189–90, 201, 210n120
McElwreath, William J., 26, 29–30, 208n84, 235n20
McGregor Missile Range, 125, 129, 228n6
McGregor Mountain, 60
McGregor Range, 56, 60, 213n49, 215n70
McKibben, Dorothy, 75, 216n25
McKibben, Joseph, 20–21, 206n59, 209n105
McKinley, Ira, 41
McKinley, Laura E. (Burris), 41–42, 54, 212n42, 229n18
McKinley ranch, 54
McMillan, Don P., 222n14
McMillan, Edwin M., 25, 34–35, 121, 204n14, 228n90
McMillan, Elsie, 34–35
Mechem, Edwin L., 183, 225n55
MED. See Manhattan Engineer District (MED)
Meitner, Lise, 8
Mench, John, 221n116
Merrill, Karen R., 64
Mescalero Apaches, 43, 46–47, 164, 211n19. See also Apaches
Metallurgical Lab (Met Lab): creation of, 118; renaming of, 226n73; research at, 118, 204n16, 226n75; scientists at, 8, 11, 87, 209n112, 227n80
Miera, Joe, 98, 221n122
Military Liaison Committee, 143

military police (MPS): after Trinity test, 83; and building the Trinity site, 77–78, 81–82, 97–98, 218n48, 218nn59–60; and day of Trinity test, 22–23, 28, 30, 33; insignia of, 219n64; and ranchers' land, 62. *See also* mounted military police

Miller, Harry, 26

Miller, Hugh M., 182

Mockingbird Gap, 62, 79

Mockingbird Ranch, 62

Mojave Desert, 68, 132, 146

Monsanto Company, 24, 86

Monte Prieto ranch, 237n53

Montoya, Adolfo, 214n63

Montoya, Gabriel, 30

Montoya, Joseph, 189

Moody, Henry, 50–51

Moody, T. J., 50–51

Moon, P. B., 223n22

Morrison, Philip, 92

mounted military police, 82–83, 122. *See also* military police (MPS)

Moynihan, Daniel Patrick, 31

MPS. *See* military police (MPS)

Muncy ranch, 54

Muraki, Yoshihiko, xiii–xiv, 203n2

Muroc Bombing Range, 127

Murray ranch, 215n74

Nagasaki bomb: effects of, xiii–xiv; and public fears, 167; and radiation measurements, 26, 155; transportation of, 39; and Trinity-area tourism, 176, 179, 192, 196, 199–200; and Trinity workers, 121

Nagle, Darragh E., 18, 206nn54–55

National Cancer Institute (NCI), 162–63, 169

National Defense Research Council (NDRC), 9, 203n4, 207n66

National Historical Park status, 184, 190–91, 242n24, 244n49, 245n52. *See also* Manhattan Project National Historical Park

National Historic Landmark (NHL) program: about, 184–85, 242nn28–29; and other atomic energy sites, 185–86, 243n32; and Trinity site, 1, 174–76, 183, 186–90, 242n26, 243n33

National Historic Site status, 183–90, 240n96, 242n24, 244n39

National Military Establishment, 118, 124, 126, 128, 135, 143, 145

National Park Service (NPS): and historical preservation, 61–62, 115–16, 174–90, 195–98, 201, 225n66, 241n1, 244n49, 245nn51–52; and land, 58, 64, 140; and records, 4; and relations with military, 134, 138–42, 244n41; and trinitite, 112

National Park System, 185, 190–91

National Reconnaissance Office (NRO), 131

National Register of Historic Places, 185–88, 242n24, 242n26, 243n39

National Research Council (NRC), 172–73

Native Americans: and land, 43–46, 49, 52, 196; as Manhattan Project workers, 93, 95–96, 163; not displaced for Trinity test, 64–65, 69; and radiation, 164–65, 171; and Trinity site selection, 163–65

Navajos, 44–47, 166

Naval Gun Factory, 133

Naval Ordnance Missile Test Facility, 132

Naval Ordnance Plant, 133

Naval Ordnance Test Station (NOTS), 132–34, 230n36, 231n40, 231n45

Naval Reactors Branch, AEC, 134

Naval Research Laboratory, 132–33, 230n38

NCI. *See* National Cancer Institute (NCI)

NDRC. *See* National Defense Research Council (NDRC)

Neddermeyer, Seth, 111, 224n39
Nelly, Charles, 26
Nevada Test Site: establishment of, 65,
   117; and later land use, 234n97; and
   radiation, 159, 161, 167, 169, 171–72,
   240nn86–87; and testing, 144, 146;
   and tourism, 192
New Mexico Joint Guided Missile Test
   Range, 3
New Mexico State Historic Preservation
   Division, 242n25
Newson, Henry W., 32, 104
Newson, Meta, 32
New War Department Building, 143
NHL. *See* National Historic Landmark
   (NHL) program
Nichols, Kenneth D., 142–43
Nogal NM, 26
Nolan, James, 152, 235n14
Nolda ranch, 54
Norris, Robert S., 7
North 10,000 bunker, 21–25, 27, 80
NOTS. *See* Naval Ordnance Test Station
   (NOTS)
NPS. *See* National Park Service (NPS)
NRC. *See* National Research Council
   (NRC)
NRO. *See* National Reconnaissance
   Office (NRO)
Nyer, Warren, 21–23

Oak Ridge TN: and historical preservation, 190–91, 196, 245nn52–53; and
   land, 59; and nonwhite workers,
   93–94, 221n106; and radiological
   warfare research, 121; and Special
   Engineer Detachment, 86–89; and
   spies, 99–100; and women workers,
   91; work at, 10, 19, 186
obelisk at Trinity site. *See* historic
   markers
Office of Naval Research, 134, 230n38
Office of Radiation Programs, 156, 160

Office of Scientific Research and Development (OSRD), 9, 132–33, 207n66
100-Ton test, 14–19, 83, 153, 205n37
Oppenheimer, Frank, 6, 21
Oppenheimer, J. Robert: about, 12–13;
   and building the Trinity test site,
   78; and day of Trinity test, 6, 21; as
   director at Los Alamos, 12–13; and
   Jumbo, 109; leaving position, 108;
   and Leslie Groves, 12; and naming
   the Trinity test, 73–75; and 100-
   Ton test, 14; personal life of, 74–75,
   216n19, 216nn25–26; and radiation
   concerns, 152, 198; and research and
   development, 133; and secrecy, 97;
   and Trinity site selection, 68–69
Oppenheimer, Kitty, 34, 216n24
Oppenheimer, Peter, 216n25
Ordnance–California Institute of Tech-
   nology (ORDCIT), 128–29, 139–40,
   212n34, 229n16, 229nn18–19
Ortega family, 50
Ortiz, Priscilla Baca, 49–50
Oscura Mountains, 72, 178
Oscura NM, 19
OSRD. *See* Office of Scientific Research
   and Development (OSRD)
Ostrander, Don R., 183
Otero County NM, 215n71
Otero family, 45
Otero Mesa, 125
Owl Bar and Café, 221n122

Padilla ranch, 54
Padre Island, 68
Palevsky, Mary, 203n2
Palmer, T. O., 28, 217n33
Parsons, W. S., 133
Pasadena CA, 126, 132
Pasco WA, 94
Patraw, P. P., 182–83
Patton, George S., 69
Pecos River, 46

PED. *See* Provisional Engineer Detachment (PED)
Peierls, Genia, 32
Peierls, Rudolf, 152
Pentagon, 11, 59, 185, 204n17, 239n72
Perea family, 45
Philip SD, 192
Pierce, Claude C., 19
Pierce, Elsie, 220n98
Pitcher (colonel), 140
Pittsburgh PA, 80, 134, 218n53, 238n57
plutonium: and development of bomb, 9–11; discovery of, 9, 186, 204n14; and historical preservation, 191–92; and Jumbo, 108–9; and radiation, 16, 18, 120–21, 154, 156–60, 163, 170, 238n56, 239n80; transportation of, 92, 210n120, 220n100; and trinitite, 111
Pojoaque Pueblo NM, 165
Pope NM, 109
Porton, Bob, 36–37, 90–91
Price Anderson Act, 239n77
Project Camel, 133, 231n40
Proudfoot, Robert J., 188
Provisional Engineer Detachment (PED), 28, 84, 90, 208n94, 219n70
pueblo communities, 43–45, 47, 52, 95–96, 163–65, 221n115
Pueblo de Cochiti NM, 95
Pueblo Indians, 44
Pueblo Uprising of 1680, 44
Puerco River, 166

Rabi, I. I., 11, 25, 203n4, 207n66
Radiation Exposure Compensation Act (RECA), 171–73, 240nn86–87
radioecology, 156, 227n85, 236n31
radiological warfare (RW), 18, 117–21, 151–52, 226nn77–78
RaLa experiments, 165, 238n69
RAND Corporation, 118
Rasmussen, Roger, 29, 36, 87

Ratliff family, 54, 167–68
RECA. *See* Radiation Exposure Compensation Act (RECA)
Redstone Arsenal, 131, 137, 232n62
Rehn, E., 26
Reinig, Phil, 223n14
Reynolds, Matthew Givens, 211n27
Rhodes, Richard, 75, 132–33, 147, 219n70
Richard, Jack R., 107, 223n14
Richland WA, 93–94
Rickers family, 51
Rickover, Hyman G., 134
Rieder, Morgan, 2
Rio Grande, 80, 82, 218n51
Robertson, Lupe Bernal, 229n18
Rocky Flats CO, 192
Roensch, Arno, 89
Rojas, Louis G., 96, 107
Romero, Lucero, 54
Romero ranch, 50, 54
Roosevelt, Franklin, 9, 124, 132–33
Rosenberg, Ethel, 99
Rosenberg, Julius, 99
Roswell NM, 26, 149, 165, 228n3
Royal City WA, 192
Roybal, Pat, 214n63
Rudolph, David P., 87
Ruidoso NM, 149, 164
Rumsberg, Joseph C., Jr., 187–88
RW. *See* radiological warfare (RW)
Rynd, Ed, 35, 95

Sachs, Alexander, 9
Salton Sea Navy Base, 231n45
San Antonio NM: ranches near, 50; and secret communication, 97; and Trinity test activities, 19–20, 36, 82
San Antonio TX, 97
Sandia Air Base, 82, 129, 142
Sandia Corporation, 231n45
Sandoval family, 45
San Ildefonso Pueblo NM, 95–96, 165, 214n63, 221n110

San Nicholas Island, 68–69
Santa Clara Pueblo NM, 95, 165, 221n110
Santa Fe NM, 26, 37, 223n24; and Jornada del Muerto, 43; and secret communication, 15; and spies, 100
Santa Fe Ring, 48
Sapolsky, Harvey M., 125–26
Savannah River, 192
Sawyer's Hill, 209n103
Schaffer, W. F., 223n22
Schmitt, Harrison, 63
Schreiber, Raemer, 105–6
Scoyen, E. T., 140, 181–82, 241n6
Seaborg, Glenn T., 204n14
Seborer, Oscar, 98, 100
Secret Intelligence Service, 99
SED. See Special Engineer Detachment (SED)
Segre, Emilio, 204n14
Sellers, Peter, 7
Selmanoff, Eugene, 209n113
Sena, Art, 107
Sena, Tomas, 209n113
Serber, Robert, 25
Sernas family, 214n63
Sherwin, Martin J., 74
Shipman, Thomas, 116, 225nn65–66, 236n30
Shjopp, Marjorie Powell, 220n98
Shonka, Joseph, 169
Sierra County NM, 215n71
Simon, Steven L., 162–63
Sissel, Otis, 107
site selection for Trinity test, 67–72
Skeen, Joe, 57–58, 63–64, 213n56
Smith, Cyril, 25, 207n66
Smith, Jack H., 209n113
Smith, Stuart, 100
Snapp, Roy B., 170
Socorro Chamber of Commerce, 110–11
Socorro County NM, 49–50, 215n71
Socorro NM: about, 98; and historical preservation, 110–11; and popula-

tion, 208n92, 238n67; and proximity to Trinity test site, 246n70; ranches near, 50, 52, 62–63; and roads, 78; and trinitite, 112; and Trinity site selection, 70; and Trinity test activities, 19, 26, 30, 80, 82, 93, 98, 101, 218n51
Soledad Canyon, 50–51, 54
South 10,000 bunker, 21–22, 80
Special Engineer Detachment (SED): about, 84–91, 95, 219n70, 219n75, 220n83, 221n116; and building the Trinity test site, 20, 77, 81, 98–100; and day of Trinity test, 5, 21–22, 24, 29, 36; and Jumbo, 109; and 100-Ton test, 15; and radiation measurements, 103; and trinitite, 112
spies, 35, 98–100
Spindel, William, 87
Stallion Gate, 199, 246n70
Stallion Site, 52
Stannard, James Newell, 120, 158
"Star-Spangled Banner," 21, 207n64
Stevens, W. A., 68, 76, 217n42
Stevenson, E. P., 226n78
Stevenson Committee, 226n78
Stewart, Alice, 238n57
Stimson, Henry, 10
Stone, Robert, 227n80
Story, Charles H., 54
Story ranch, 54, 57
Strassman, Fritz, 8
Sublette, Carey, 4
Swank, Margaret, 92
Szasz, Ferenc Morton, 4, 80, 101, 208n98, 240n96
Szilard, Leo, 8, 204n11

Tapman, Ken, 190
Tatlock, Jean, 74–75, 216n19, 217n26
Taylor Grazing Act, 64
TBDC. See Tularosa Basin Downwinders Consortium (TBDC)

Tearle, Oliver, 217n26
Teller, Edward, 13, 25, 92–93
Tennessee Valley Authority (TVA), 59
Thomas, Betty, 31
Thomas, Charles, 24
Thomas, Earl, 31
Thompson, Ben H., 180, 183
Thompson, Theodore E., 189, 244n47
Thorlin, J. Frederick, 1, 129, 186
Three Mile Island, 166
Thurman, F., 54
Tillotson, M. R., 112, 176–77, 182–83,
    241n6
Tinian Island, 38, 77, 192
Titterson, W. W., 20
Titterton, Ernest, 207n68
Tolman, Richard, 14–16, 207n66
Tolson, Hillory A., 140, 180, 182
Tonopah Bombing Range, 127
tourism: and Hanford, 195–96; nuclear,
    191–94, 202; and Oak Ridge, 245n53;
    and Trinity site, xiii–xiv, 61, 115, 174–
    79, 190–91, 196–202, 246n68
Townsend, Mertes May, 63
Trask, C. W., 222n14
Trask, Wes, 222n14
Treaty of Guadalupe Hidalgo, 46,
    211n24
trinitite: about, 111–12; and radiation,
    104, 112–17, 199, 225n55, 226n70;
    removal of, 105, 108, 111–17, 181,
    225n59, 225n65; as souvenir, 88, 92,
    112, 116, 197, 201; and tourism, 112,
    115, 198–99
Trinity Atomic National Monument,
    183, 185
Trinity Base Camp, 54, 61, 63, 79–83,
    189–90, 207n66, 230n24
Trinity test: day of, 19–38; naming of,
    73–75; and Project Trinity, 76–77, 83;
    and secrecy, 19, 30–38, 97–98
Truman, Harry S., 11, 32, 125–26, 134,
    136, 142–43, 180–81, 233n80

Tucker, Kathleen M., 150
Tularosa Basin: about, 42–43, 49; mil-
    itary land in, 124–25, 127–28, 140;
    ranches in, 41–42, 49–58, 62; and
    space program, 141
Tularosa Basin Downwinders Consor-
    tium (TBDC), 171, 173
Tularosa Grazing District No. 4, 72
Tularosa NM, 20, 51, 63, 149, 208n92,
    238n67
Tularosa Valley, 42, 64, 68
Turner, Harold, 72
Tybout, R., 26, 207n83
Tyler, Carroll L., 145, 183, 224n55
Tyler, Gerald R., 33, 86, 222n3

Udall, Stewart, 141
University of California, Berkeley, 8, 12,
    24, 186, 204n14, 227n80, 236n30
University of California, Los Angeles
    (UCLA), 4, 120–21, 156–60, 163
University of Chicago, 8, 17, 86, 118,
    204n16, 206n55, 221n106, 226n73,
    226n75
University of New Mexico, 4
uranium: and Church Rock disaster,
    165; and early research, 9, 204n11,
    204n16, 231n45; and historical pres-
    ervation, 186, 191; mining of, 165–67,
    171, 240n86; production of, 10–11,
    245n53
Uranium Committee, 9
Urchin experiments, 104–8, 116–17
Urey, Harold, 86
USS Indianapolis, 38–39
USS Nautilus, 134

Valencia, Harold, 214n63
Van Winkle, Thomas, 209n113
Vaughn NM, 208n92, 238n67
Venona Files program, 99
Victorio (Apache chief), 47
von Braun, Wernher, 136–37

WAAC. *See* Women's Army Auxiliary
    Corps (WAAC)
WAC. *See* Women's Army Corps (WAC)
WAC Corporal, 129
Wahl, Arthur C., 204n14
Walker, Robert, 21
Walker, Wesley L., 61
War Department, 116, 123–24, 127, 138,
    143, 177, 204n17, 213n51
Warner, Roger S., Jr., 104
Warren, Stafford Leake: and day of
    Trinity test, 207n66; and naming the
    Trinity test, 73; and radiation con-
    cerns, 120, 154–55, 167, 234n8, 234n11,
    235n23, 236n30, 239n74
water: and radiation, 149, 166, 168,
    170; and Trinity Base Camp, 79–
    80, 83, 98, 129, 139, 218n48, 218n51,
    232n70
Weapons Physics Division, 121
Wechsler, Jay, 73
Wellerstein, Alex, 4
Wells, Wayne, 107
Welsh, Michael, 138–39, 141
Wendover Bombing Range, 68, 70, 127
Western Shoshones, 65, 146
Westinghouse Electric Corporation, 134
West 10,000 bunker, 21, 25, 80
Whipple, Harry O., 114, 168, 207n83
White, R., 26
White Sands Fair Compensation Act of
    1991, 213n56
White Sands Missile Range (WSMR):
    changing names of, 3, 52–53, 131,
    228n4; and historical preservation,
    175–76, 185–91, 243n39, 244n47; and
    Jumbo, 110–11; and land, 49–50,
    56, 58, 62, 212n34, 212n42, 229n18;
    and missile testing, 129; and other
    tests, 131; and preservation of desert,
    146; and radiation concerns, 106–8;
    records at, 4; and tourism, 1, 197–
    200; and trinitite, 116; and Trinity

test site, 72, 79, 123; and White Sands
    National Monument, 141
White Sands National Monument
    (WSNM), 1, 36, 42, 112, 128, 134, 138–
    42, 176, 187
White Sands Proving Ground (WSPG):
    changing names of, 3, 123; establish-
    ment of, 123, 127–29; and historical
    preservation, 183, 225n58; and land,
    41, 52, 61, 72, 229n19; work at, 129–31,
    134–38, 140, 144, 229n14, 230n34
White Sands Test Facility, 131
White Store NM, 27, 54
Whiting, Mary J., 220n98
Wieneke, Barbara, 223n24
Wigner, Eugene, 8
Wilhite, Lester A., 217n39
Williams, H., 218n54
Williams, John, 21
Williams ranch, 54
Wills, Kristel, 199, 246n68
Wilson, Robert, 21
Wirth, Conrad L., 182–83
Withers ranch, 54
Women's Army Auxiliary Corps
    (WAAC), 91
Women's Army Corps (WAC), 32, 91–93
Wriston, Roscoe, 71
WSMR. *See* White Sands Missile Range
    (WSMR)
WSNM. *See* White Sands National Mon-
    ument (WSNM)
WSPG. *See* White Sands Proving Ground
    (WSPG)

Yavapais, 46

Zia Company, 96, 107

Printed in the USA
CPSIA information can be obtained
at www.ICGtesting.com
LVHW040834170823
755486LV00003B/13

9 781496 232977